AIRCRAFT CARRIERS

AIRCRAFT CARRIERS

• AN ILLUSTRATED HISTORY OF AIRCRAFT CARRIERS OF THE WORLD, FROM ZEPPELIN AND SEAPLANE CARRIERS TO V/STOL AND NUCLEAR-POWERED CARRIERS

• FEATURING OVER 170 AIRCRAFT CARRIERS WITH 500 IDENTIFICATION PHOTOGRAPHS

BERNARD IRELAND

southwater

This edition is published by Southwater, an imprint of Anness Publishing Ltd, Hermes House, 88–89 Blackfriars Road, London SE1 8HA
tel. 020 7401 2077
fax 020 7633 9499
www.southwaterbooks.com;
www.annesspublishing.com

UK agent: The Manning Partnership Ltd; tel. 01225 478444; fax 01225 478440; sales@manning-partnership.co.uk
UK distributor: Book Trade Services; tel. 0116 2759086; fax 0116 2759090; uksales@booktradeservices.com; exportsales@booktradeservices.com
North American agent/distributor: National Book Network; tel. 301 459 3366; fax 301 429 5746; www.nbnbooks.com
Australian agent/distributor: Pan Macmillan Australia; tel. 1300 135 113; fax 1300 135 103; customer.service@macmillan.com.au
New Zealand agent/distributor: David Bateman Ltd; tel. (09) 415 7664; fax (09) 415 8892

Publisher: Joanna Lorenz
Editorial Director: Judith Simons
Project Editor: Felicity Forster
Copy Editor and Indexer: Tim Ellerby
Cover Design: Michael Reynolds
Designer: Design Principals
Editorial Reader: Jeremy Nichols
Production Controller: Steve Lang

The nationality of each aircraft carrier or carrier class is identified in the relevant specification box by the national flag that was in use at the time of the vessel's commissioning and service.

PAGE 1: ***Saipan* (LHA-2).**
PAGE 2: **Invincible class.**
PAGE 3: ***Chakri Naruebet.***

Contents

6 Introduction

THE HISTORY OF AIRCRAFT CARRIERS

10 First flights from ships
12 Zeppelins
14 Seaplanes versus landplanes
16 The Dardanelles Campaign
18 Fighters aboard ships
20 Air-dropped torpedoes
22 The *Königsberg* operation
24 Naval aviation at Jutland
26 The first naval air strikes
28 British shipborne aircraft of World War I
30 Rigid airships after World War I
32 The Sempill mission and Japanese naval aviation
34 The Washington Treaties (1921–22)
36 Carrier operational philosophies
38 "Billy" Mitchell and the US Navy bombing trials
40 Catapults and arresters
42 Aircraft aboard submarines
44 Inter-war development in carrier aircraft
46 Armoured versus "open" construction
48 Taranto
50 The *Bismarck* operation
52 The Battle of Matapan
54 Pearl Harbor
56 The Doolittle Raid and the Battle of the Coral Sea
58 The Battle of Midway
60 Escort carriers
62 Carrier aircraft development during World War II
64 The Battle of Santa Cruz
66 Battle of the Philippine Sea
68 Leyte Gulf
70 Post-war aircraft carrier developments
72 Carriers in the Korean War

74 Carriers for sale
76 Suez
78 The impact of helicopters
80 Carrier jet aircraft developments
82 Naval air power in Vietnam
84 Carrier battle groups and tactics
86 The introduction of V/STOL
88 Argument – large or small carriers?
90 Assault carriers
92 Carriers in the Falklands War

DIRECTORY OF AIRCRAFT CARRIERS

United States
96 *North Carolina* (CA-12) and *Huntington* (CA-5)
97 *Langley* (CV-1)
98 Lexington (CV-2) class
100 *Ranger* (CV-4)
102 Yorktown class (CV-5, CV-6, CV-8)
104 *Wasp* (CV-7)
106 Hybrid carrier studies
107 *Long Island* (AVG-1), *Wolverine* (IX-64) and *Sable* (IX-81)
108 *Bogue*-class escort carriers
110 *Sangamon*-class escort carriers
112 *Casablanca*-class escort carriers
114 *Commencement Bay*-class escort carriers
116 Essex class
118 Independence class
120 Midway class
122 *United States* (CVA-58)
123 Forrestal class
124 Improved Forrestal class
126 Essex class modernized
128 *Enterprise* (CVAN-65)
130 *John F. Kennedy* (CVA-67)
132 Nimitz class
134 Improved Nimitz (CVN-71) class
136 Iwo Jima class (LPH)
137 Wasp class (LHD)

United Kingdom
138 Balloon ships and early seaplane carriers
140 *Ark Royal* (I)
142 *Ben-my-Chree*, *Vindex* and *Manxman*
143 *Nairana*, *Pegasus*, *Brocklesby* and *Killingholme*

144 *Campania* (I)
146 *Furious* (I) and (II)
148 *Vindictive*
150 *Argus* (I)
152 *Hermes* (II)
154 *Eagle* (I)
156 *Courageous*, *Glorious* and *Furious* (III)
158 *Ark Royal* (II)
160 Illustrious class
162 *Illustrious*-class derivatives
164 *Unicorn*
165 CAM ships
166 MAC ships
167 *Audacity*
168 British-built escort carriers
170 Archer class
170 Attacker class
171 Ameer class
172 Colossus class
173 Majestic class
174 *Ark Royal* (III) and *Eagle* (II)
176 Malta class
177 *Perseus* and *Pioneer*
178 Centaur class
180 *Victorious* modernized
181 Centaur class as Commando Carriers
182 CVA-01
183 *Argus* (II)
184 Invincible class
186 *Ocean*
187 Queen Elizabeth class

Japan
188 Early seaplane carriers
189 *Hosho*
190 *Akagi*
192 *Kaga*
194 *Ise* and *Hyuga*
195 *Ryujo*
196 *Soryu* and *Hiryu*
197 Zuiho class
198 *Ryuho*
199 *Hiyo* and *Junyo*
200 Shokaku class
202 *Taiho*
203 Chitose class
204 *Mizuho* and *Nisshin*
205 *Shinano*
206 Unryu class
207 *Ibuki*
208 Taiyo class
209 *Shinyo* and *Kaiyo*
210 *Yamashiro Maru* and *Shimane Maru*
211 Akitsu Maru class and *Kumano Maru*
212 *Akitsushima*

France
213 *Foudre*
214 *Béarn*
215 Joffre class
215 *Commandant Teste*
216 *Dixmude*
216 La Fayette class
217 *Arromanches*
218 *Jeanne d'Arc*
219 Clemenceau class
220 *Charles de Gaulle*

Romania
221 Balloon and seaplane carriers

USSR
222 Moskva class
224 Kiev class
226 *Admiral Kuznetsov*

Australia
228 *Albatross*
228 *Vengeance*
229 *Sydney*
230 *Melbourne*

Canada
231 *Warrior*
232 *Magnificent*
232 *Bonaventure*

Italy
233 *Giuseppe Miraglia*
233 *Bolzano*, proposed
234 *Aquila* and *Sparviero*
235 Andrea Doria (I) class
235 *Vittorio Veneto*
236 *Giuseppe Garibaldi*
236 *Andrea Doria* (II)

Germany
237 Seaplane carriers, mercantile
238 Seaplane carriers, warship
238 Auxiliary carriers (World War I), proposed
239 *Graf Zeppelin*
240 Auxiliary carriers (World War II), proposed

Argentina
241 *Independencia*
241 *Veinticinco de Mayo*

India
242 *Vikrant*
242 *Viraat*
243 Ex-*Admiral Gorshkov*

Netherlands
244 *Karel Doorman* (I)
244 *Karel Doorman* (II)

Brazil
245 *Minas Gerais*

Spain
246 *Dédalo* (I)
246 *Dédalo* (II)
247 *Principe de Asturias*

Sweden
248 Balloon ship
248 *Gotland*

Thailand
249 *Chakri Naruebet*

250 Glossary
252 Index
256 Acknowledgements
256 Key to flags

Introduction

At the time of writing, it is over 100 years since Orville Wright provided "the proof which actual flight alone can give ... [that] an engine-driven, man-carrying aerodrome [sic] had been constructed", at Kitty Hawk, North Carolina, USA. The flight inspired a rash of fabric and baling-wire contraptions that vied with lighter-than-air craft to establish mastery in the art of free flight.

Within five years, brave young men were demonstrating to their respective navies that these fragile machines could actually be flown to and from warships. Although deeply sceptical as to whether they could survive the rough and tumble of life at sea, and at the significant impact that their presence had on a ship, senior officers viewed aircraft with considerable interest. The promise of being able to loft a pair of keen eyes to several thousand feet to observe the movements of the opponent was the dream of every admiral, so it was a promise worth pursuing.

For the British Royal Navy, Admiral Fisher's dictum had been simply "Hit first, hit hard and keep hitting" which, in the days before radar and reliable fire control, was not easy to satisfy. If an airborne observer could report enemy movement, he could equally well report fall of shot to enable his admiral to get on target just that little bit more quickly.

From duelling with pistols, pilots quickly progressed to hand-dropped bombs but knew that the difference between this and toting a torpedo was only a matter of lift and engine power.

TOP: **A green-vested member of the catapult crew seems to be conducting the aircraft waiting to take off USS *Constellation* (CVA-64) in the South China Sea off Vietnam. Nearest is an F-4 Phantom while inboard and to the stern are RA-5C Vigilantes.** ABOVE: **The first of many, Britain's *Argus* (I), 1918, pioneered the functional combination of a "through flight deck" that was served by elevators connecting with the hangar below.**

Wartime development was rapid. In 1914, aircraft were still being set afloat to begin and end their flight. Four years later HMS *Argus* introduced the world to the through-deck aircraft carrier, a vessel of functional ugliness but of undoubted utility.

Before the peace, the Royal Navy lost the huge reserve of innovation and enthusiasm that had created the first-ever effective air arm, when it was transferred to the new, unified air force. During the inter-war years the Fleet Air Arm lapsed into near mediocrity compared with its major peers in the American and Japanese fleets. The Royal Navy deployed naval aviation in modest strength, its main objective being to injure and slow down a reluctant enemy enough to bring him within range of the fleet's heavy guns. Although, in this, it enjoyed some success, the other fleets were better appreciating the advantage of the big air wing, with its potential to deliver

ABOVE: **The Japanese carrier *Zuikaku*, together with her sister, *Shokaku*, spearheaded the task group that demonstrated, early in 1942, the potency of massed seaborne airstrikes.** RIGHT: **Although influential as the first "third generation" British carrier, *Ark Royal* (II) was a one-off. Her successors traded aircraft capacity for improved horizontal protection.**

overwhelming short-term force at a selected point. In this, they were far closer to adhering to Fisher's expressed aims.

World War II proved the concept of the deck-load air strike, confirming the carrier as the undisputed capital ship. However, many war-built vessels were soon rendered obsolescent as developments continued apace – jet propulsion, atomic weapons, angled decks and steam catapults, and finally nuclear propulsion.

Other fleets also deployed carriers and naval aviation, but for the most part discovered that the costs were not offset by the advantages. In the Royal Navy, naval aviation was only saved from oblivion because of the fortuitous introduction of Vertical or Short Take-Off and Land (V/STOL) aircraft. However, carriers that are configured to deploy V/STOL aircraft and helicopters are no substitute for "real" carriers.

The Americans, with their steadily diminishing number of carrier battle groups, are now virtually alone in being able to influence local events around the world by simply appearing in strength offshore. Such a latent threat, the contemporary equivalent of "gunboat diplomacy", is fully mobile, deployable at short notice anywhere that ships can float, and independent of costly, vulnerable and generally unpopular overseas bases.

From time to time, the large carrier, like the tank, has been written off as too vulnerable to survive in a missile-dominated battle environment. Like the tank, however, it continues to thrive and evolve, simply because there is nothing to replace it.

BELOW: **The embodiment of seapower, virtually unchallengeable by conventional means, American carrier groups have enjoyed a half-century of dominance at sea.** RIGHT: **Vast geopolitical changes near the end of the 20th century obliged major armed forces to redefine their missions. For the Royal Navy the big carrier made its comeback with the first of a new generation.**

The History of Aircraft Carriers

An aircraft first flew from a ship just four years before the outbreak of World War I. History has left us no reason as to why this was attempted, except that the marriage of aircraft and ship appeared to be a promising idea. Indeed, the possibilities of what came to be naval aviation have depended ever since on the steady evolution of the technologies that support it. Early ambitions thus went no further than observation and reconnaissance, and the low-powered and unreliable aero engine of the time was rivalled by a variety of lighter-than-air craft. Of these, the long-endurance Zeppelin had a profound influence on developments by obliging warships to take high-performance fighters to sea.

Within nine years of that first flight from a ship's deck, the first true aircraft carrier was at sea. Already its aircraft were designed to reconnoitre, to protect the fleet, and to torpedo the enemy.

From here, it was the aircraft carrier's rapidly assumed capacity to deliver a concentration of destructive force that was the secret of it finally displacing the big-gun battleship as the undisputed arbiter of sea power.

LEFT: **The USS *Intrepid* (CV-11) was an *Essex*-class carrier. These ships were the backbone of the US fleet in the Pacific war from 1943 to 1945.**

TOP: **The first aircraft purchased for the US Navy, the Triad (A-1) being tested at Hammondsport by its designer Glenn Curtiss and Lt Theodore G. Ellyson, who was to become naval aviator No. 1. Able to operate from both water and land with its floats and wheels, the Triad was the first successful amphibian.** ABOVE: **Eugene Ely gets airborne from the deck of the USS *Birmingham* at Hampton Roads, Virginia on November 14, 1910. The historic first flight from ship to shore was about 3.2km/2 miles.**

First flights from ships

Observing Glenn Curtiss demonstrating aircraft to the US Army in 1908, naval officers were moved to suggest putting one aboard a warship, as yet for no clear purpose. Enthusiasm for flying was general at this time and an American newspaper offered a substantial prize for the first pilot to fly from a ship to a point ashore. The German HAPAG line took up the challenge but, as it happened, its failed attempt in November 1910 was upstaged by the US Navy, which had quietly been preparing its own.

Two months later, Captain Washington Irving Chambers had been appointed to liaise and cooperate with the experimenters. With modest funding he was able to engage Eugene Ely, an associate of Curtiss, to undertake a flight from a warship.

A temporary ramp, sloping downward from bridge to stemhead, was built over the forecastle of the scout cruiser USS *Birmingham* and, on November 14, 1910, Ely opened the throttle and launched himself into history. In gusty conditions, his wheeled undercarriage brushed the surface, but he recovered to fly the 3.2km/2 miles to shore.

Witnessing the feat, the acting Secretary of the Navy deemed it good publicity, immediately supporting a proposal to undertake the more difficult exercise of landing-on.

A temporary wooden platform was laid over the quarterdeck of the armoured cruiser *Pennsylvania*. It was complete with refinements such as "round-down" and a score of transverse ropes, weighted with sandbags, to arrest the aircraft. On January 18, 1911, Ely duly landed-on, remaining aboard for an hour before "doing the double" by taking off again and flying ashore. Both *Birmingham* and *Pennsylvania* had been anchored.

In Europe, the British Admiralty, aware of activity on the part of both the French and Russian navies, had been training a first party of volunteer pilots through the good offices of the Royal Aero Club at Eastchurch, near Sheerness, and under the benevolent eye of the innovative then First Lord, Winston Churchill. The first two students gained their proficiency certification in April 1911. One of them, Charles Rumney Samson, not only taught Churchill himself to fly but went on to make the first flight from a British warship.

An inter-service committee had been considering the potential of aviation, the Royal Navy seeing its function as being to observe blockaded enemy harbours, "to ascend from a floating base" to scout for enemy forces at sea, to spot enemy submarines and minefields, and to direct naval gunfire.

Curtiss made a first flight in his "hydro-aeroplane" in February 1911 (the French had done it in 1910), the aircraft being symbolically hoisted by crane aboard the *Pennsylvania.* Two naval pilots, Schwann and Longmore, made the first British seaplane take-offs later in 1911.

During November 1911, Samson flew a Short S.27 off the forecastle ramp of the battleship *Africa* at a buoy off Sheerness. He used the same aircraft again in May 1912 for the next demonstration, staged during a Royal Fleet Review at Portland. Here, he made the first-ever take-off from a ship under weigh, flying from the battleship *Hibernia* to release a simulated 45kg/100lb bomb. Two months later, he made a similar flight from the battleship *London*, proceeding at 12 knots.

In the United States, the successes with Curtiss' wheeled aircraft had encouraged Chambers to talk in terms of "platform ships", i.e. with flight decks, but the growing potential of seaplanes sidetracked him from what would have been a promising direction of development.

TOP: **One of the great pioneers of manned flight, Glen H. Curtiss is seen here having just completed his record-making flight from Albany to New York in June 1910. He was to tell an interviewer, "Some day soon aeroplanes will have to start from the deck of battleships ..."** ABOVE: **A Short S.38 on the flying-off platform of HMS *Africa*. Reports, unconfirmed, state that Charles Rumney Samson made the first British flight from the *Africa* in December 1911.**
LEFT: **The first recorded flight by Samson from HMS *Africa*, on January 19, 1912.**

ABOVE: **Watched by crewmen crowding every vantage point, Eugene Ely makes the first ever touchdown on a warship's deck. The USS *Pennsylvania* was anchored off San Francisco on January 18, 1911.**

Zeppelins

The primary roles envisaged for early, low-powered heavier-than-air craft were based on observation and reconnaissance. In these, they were still inferior in many respects to lighter-than-air craft. Of these, the simplest were the tethered aerostats, of which the most common were kite balloons, deployed by many warships and auxiliaries.

Powered airships, capable of navigation, were properly termed "dirigibles". Those with an internal frame were termed "rigid", those without, "non-rigid". The latter, like balloons, were little more than inflated gas bags, and limited in size. As the British failed to master the technology of the rigid airship, they operated considerable numbers of non-rigids, popularly called "blimps". In naval service, their small size restricted them largely to coastal duties.

The most dominant airship was the large rigid, a category which, until after World War I, was virtually synonymous with "Zeppelin". These craft stemmed from the Friedrichshafen factory established by Graf Ferdinand von Zeppelin in 1898 to promote popular air travel as well as construct "air cruisers" for national defence.

Despite early setbacks and rivalry with the Schütte-Lanz company, Zeppelin's machines had been acquired for the German army by 1910 and, two years later, for the navy. Zeppelin had met the army's requirement for an operational endurance of 24 hours and it was this, together with its potential in long-range reconnaissance, which attracted naval interest. The placing of the naval order was, however, the

ABOVE: **Count von Zeppelin's main intention was to use his machines to popularize air travel. This pre-war impression emphasizes the more idyllic aspect of his enterprise.**

ABOVE: **An Italian non-rigid DE-type scouting airship communicating with an anti-submarine motor boat, or MAS. Of a total of 49 airships, the Italians lost seven in the course of the war, two of them as a result of accidents.**
LEFT: **With a volume of nearly 56,000m^3/2,000,000cu ft, the L.53 was one of the largest types of Zeppelin to see service. She was a victim of an RNAS Camel fighter, flown from a high-speed lighter on August 11, 1918.**

effective end of Zeppelin's personal direction of company affairs. He was not a trained engineer and, with the navy insisting on imposing its own constructors and naval architects to improve and enlarge his products, he lost interest. By the outbreak of war in 1914, the Zeppelin Company was virtually a state concern.

The Royal Navy's airship aspirations were effectively wrecked along with its prototype rigid in 1911. This failure was exacerbated by Admiral Sir John Jellicoe (soon to become C-in-C, Grand Fleet) and Captain Murray Sueter (Director, Admiralty Air Department) separately travelling as civilians in commercial flights by Zeppelins and returning enthused with the craft's potential.

Lacking a similar force, it is perhaps not surprising that the Royal Navy, during the course of its North Sea operations of World War I, developed a phobia known commonly as "Zeppelinitis". Symptoms were widespread and took the form of a conviction that the fleet's every move was being observed. The truth was quite different as Admiral Tirpitz, father of the Imperial Navy, distrusted new technologies and was little interested in anything but his battle fleet. Fortunately for the British, he had neglected both the submarine arm and the Naval Airship Division, both of which began their war seriously below the approved establishment.

In the Royal Navy, long-range, high-angle, anti-aircraft gunnery was still in its infancy. The only true antidote to the Zeppelin was therefore the high-performance fighter for, by dumping ballast, the airship had a rate of climb which left it immune to interception by anything else unless surprised or otherwise caught unawares.

As a result the Zeppelin was the primary catalyst in the protracted and innovative process by which the Royal Navy produced the world's first through-deck aircraft carrier.

In practice, too many Zeppelins were diverted to unprofitable and costly bombing raids on England, while those allocated to fleet operation proved to be hostage to weather conditions. Requiring enormous dimensions for a modest payload, the airship eventually proved to be an evolutionary dead-end, the aircraft proving to be much more efficient.

ABOVE: **A small, early example of a Zeppelin, L.9 had a volume of about 25,000m^3/880,000cu ft and a length of 161.2m/529.3ft comparable with that of the armoured cruiser *Blücher*.**

TOP: **During operations in the Baltic, a reconnaissance Zeppelin overflies a German battleship, probably the *Markgraf*.** BELOW: **Another of the largest Zeppelins, the L.45 is here seen above two of the three sheds at Tondern. She was lost through forced-landing in France in October 1917.**

Seaplanes versus landplanes

In February 1911, a month after Eugene Ely had shown that it was possible to land a landplane on a warship, Glenn Curtiss successfully took off in his "hydro-aeroplane", landed alongside the *Pennsylvania* and was briefly craned aboard. This then begged the question of which type of aircraft offered most for future progress. Superficially, the choice appeared simple. Take-off and landing platforms for landplanes were unwieldy and affected a warship's fighting power. On the other hand, a seaplane (as it came to be called) needed only to be transported, the water surface anywhere being its operating platform. This was attractive as an option but, perversely the sea is rarely calm and the aircraft was fragile. Further, its cumbersome float's and high undercarriage guaranteed that its performance would be inferior to that of an equivalent landplane.

From the outset, the Americans regarded the development of the catapult as a means to minimize the impact of aircraft on the launching ship. Their first successful launch of a seaplane from an improvised compressed air model occurred in November 1912, followed a month later by the launch of one of Curtiss' small flying boats. A practical catapult might be located more conveniently on a warship, but this still left unresolved the problem of alighting and recovery.

The British showed little initial enthusiasm for catapults and it was not until 1916 that they modified an Admiralty hopper, renamed *Slinger*, to conduct practical trials. For them, the simple, if ungainly, launching platform sufficed. As the average aircraft of the time could rise almost vertically from a standing position in as little as 45 knots relative wind speed, fast ships such as light cruisers needed no more than a platform. Capital ships began by locating platforms atop gun turrets, which could be trained to avoid having to steam into the wind.

TOP: **Seen at Mitylene during the Dardanelles campaign, the *Ark Royal* (I) has a Short 166 "on the hook". Although designed to carry a 356mm/14in torpedo, the aircraft was capable of only 105kph/65mph. Note the Union Flag marking that pre-dated the familiar roundel.** ABOVE: **Originally an engines-aft, steam-driven hopper, the *Slinger* was converted for trials with catapults. Trials were suspended in 1919 as aircraft of the time took off equally well from a simple platform.**

The seaplane, launched on an expendable trolley and recovered from the sea, gave way to a wheeled landplane of higher performance, which alighted on the surface with the aid of temporary flotation bags.

It was obvious to all, however, that the ideal lay in a ship configured to both launch and recover wheeled aircraft. Even as the Americans were making their first successful catapult launches, the Beardmore yard approached the British Admiralty with proposals for a 15,000-tonner with sided superstructures and a straight-through deck along its central axis. Capable of accommodating, launching and recovering aircraft, she might have been the first true carrier had the Admiralty been bolder.

Instead, the small cruiser HMS *Hermes* was modified early in 1913 with a take-off ramp and canvas "hangars" for two seaplanes, a French Caudron G. III and a British Short S.64, the latter already fitted with folding wings and a radio. During fleet manoeuvres of 1913 the *Hermes* staged over thirty successful flights, demonstrating that seaplanes, at least, could be deployed at sea on a sustained basis. This led directly to the Admiralty acquiring a hull capable of being remodelled into a specialist seaplane carrier. It was this ship that was completed in 1914 as *Ark Royal* (I).

Up to this point the French had, if anything been slightly ahead with their conversion of the *Foudre*, while the Japanese had modified the *Wakamiya* to operate a mix of British and French-built seaplanes.

ABOVE: **The Italian Navy constructed several big-gun monitors to bombard Austrian shore installations. Dating from mid-1917 the *Faà di Bruno*, shown here being directed by a flying boat, boasted two 381mm/15in guns on a displacement of only 2,854 tonnes/2,809 tons.** BELOW: **First of the Royal Navy's seaplane-carrier conversions, the cruiser *Hermes* was, in 1913, given a launch platform forward and a canvas hangar aft. She is seen sinking after having been torpedoed in October 1914, the remains of the seaplane on her quarterdeck clearly visible.**

ABOVE: **One of three Gotha WD 20s built for long-range reconnaissance flight for the German Navy. Developed from the WD 14 torpedo-bomber, the WD 20 swapped weapon load for additional fuel to give it up to 10 hours of endurance.** LEFT: **Glenn Curtiss, having successfully flown his first flying boat early in 1912, developed his designs through a series of early prototypes. The F-Type, seen here, typifies the flimsy nature of early models.**

The Dardanelles Campaign

Strategically brilliant but tactically inept, the Dardanelles campaign of 1915 quickly mired into static warfare. Considerable Allied military forces were confined to the Gallipoli peninsula, where they were totally dependent upon support by sea. During the ten-or-so months of the campaign, the fleets were based on nearby islands.

The newly-completed *Ark Royal* (I), with six seaplanes, was involved from the outset but, although lacking nothing in enthusiasm, the infant Royal Naval Air Squadron (RNAS), was as the service expression has it, “thrown in at the deep end”. During the initial naval bombardments, her aircraft were able to reconnoitre the many enemy fortifications but the boisterous February weather caused many flights to be aborted.

Hopes for the forts’ destruction rested much on the 381mm/15in guns of the new battleship *Queen Elizabeth*. This was to be achieved through indirect fire across the peninsula, with fall of shot being corrected from the air. However, no trained observers yet existed, (a midshipman was usually selected on the basis of being the lightest!) and communications proved unreliable as no time had been allowed for testing, training or rehearsal. When aloft, the under-powered aircraft had to fly so low that they were continually struck by rifle fire.

TOP: **HMS *Ark Royal* (I) is seen here soon after her arrival at Mudros in March 1915. The space abaft the cranes marks the hangar access hatch, while the long, unencumbered foredeck was intended for take-offs, although never used as such.** ABOVE: **Great things were expected from bombardment by HMS *Queen Elizabeth*'s 381mm/15in guns. Aerial spotting proved difficult, however, due to shortcomings in both aircraft and communications.**

In June 1915, the *Ark Royal* was relieved by the *Ben-my-Chree*, but for her the hot summer weather created its own problems. Seaplanes found it difficult to “unstick” from glassy water in the absence of wind, while the ever-present dust tormented already temperamental engines. Fortunately, enemy aircraft were few, however those that did appear were landplanes of higher performance and regularly reconnoitred the main fleet base at Mudros. “One of our lumbering seaplanes went up after it like an owl in sunlight” it was recorded, “but could rise no higher than the masts of the Fleet”.

By dint of the round-the-clock efforts from its artificers, the RNAS averaged ten to twelve sorties daily, usually eight devoted to bombing (a Short 184 could lift 236kg/520lb) or

ABOVE: **One of the *Ark Royal* (I)'s Short 166 seaplanes is seen here taxiing across the harbour at Mudros. Note that the roundel marking has been adopted. The harbour was always packed with merchant shipping carrying naval supplies.**

spotting for naval gunfire, and only two to reconnaissance, for which just one modern camera was available.

There was an obvious need for higher-performance landplanes. However, because there was no point on the peninsula secure from enemy artillery fire, these had to operate from Mudros, which allowed them little time over Gallipoli.

During the initial landings and any littoral operations, the kite balloon proved to be more reliable for observation. However, even with their ship anchored close inshore the useful range of observation was limited. Their telephonic links were reliable, and despite their crews suffering badly from motion sickness, they usefully directed naval gunfire. In addition to those deployed by warships, there were those from the balloon ship *Manica*, later relieved by the *Hector.*

Great hopes had been placed on spotting enemy minefields from aircraft but conditions made this impossible. Known fields could not be swept because they were covered by artillery and unknown, short-term fields wreaked considerable execution.

A "first" achieved by the *Ben-my-Chree*'s Short 184s during August 1915, was the torpedoing and destruction of two enemy merchantmen in the strait.

Overall, naval aviation at the Dardanelles was poorly rated by the Admiralty, but this was due in great measure to senior officers not appreciating the still-primitive nature of the technologies involved and thus failing either to husband their very limited resources or to employ them efficiently within their obvious limitations.

TOP: **Another view of Mudros, dominated by the elegant lines of a *Cressy*-class armoured cruiser, with an *Eclipse*-class protected cruiser beyond. The blimp overhead was more useful than heavier-than-air craft in spotting, but was more vulnerable to enemy ground fire.** ABOVE: **Wing Commander Charles Rumney Samson with a French-built Nieuport Two-seater of his No.3 Wing at the Dardanelles. Note the observer's upward-firing Lewis gun. The extra-warm jacket, pistol and last cigarette are also noteworthy.** LEFT: **Lightly-built and not very suitable for operations in the North Sea, the Sopwith Schneider proved effective in the eastern Mediterranean, both at the Dardanelles and in the Aegean, as seen here. The anchored brigantines evoke an age that was about to disappear.**

Fighters aboard ships

The first three channel packets converted to seaplane carriers (*Engadine*, *Empress* and *Riviera*) were equipped only with hangar space and cranes. Their aircraft were of low performance and intended for reconnaissance, spotting, and bomber/torpedo roles. Lacking any flying-off ramps, the ships were required to heave-to to both despatch and recover their seaplanes. Already slow for fleet operations, they thus incurred further delay.

Their primitive level of capability was demonstrated on Christmas Day, 1914, when the three transported a total of nine aircraft to bomb the Zeppelin base at Cuxhaven. Only seven machines took the air, one found the target but inflicted no damage, and just three aircraft returned to their ships. The raid had historical significance in that it was the first-ever seaborne air strike, attracting in return the first-ever bombing attack on a warship at sea. It also demonstrated the still-rudimentary nature of naval aviation.

Packets converted later were improved by the addition of forward flying-off ramps. Initially, these were intended for launching seaplanes with the aid of expendable trolleys. These ships were supplemented by the rebuilt ex-Cunard ship, *Campania*. Aged, and arthritic with machinery problems, she was, nonetheless, considerably larger. In place of 18–24m/60–80ft launching platforms, hers was 50m/165ft in length and, importantly, she could maintain her speed in a seaway.

Frustration with the limitations of seaplanes led Admiral Jellicoe, C-in-C Grand Fleet to demand that "aeroplanes", i.e. landplanes, be introduced. On November 3, 1915, the first, a Bristol Scout "C" fighter flew from the *Vindex*, starting a sequence that would evolve through the Scout "D", the Sopwith Pup, the 1½-Strutter and the Camel.

The short ramp of the *Vindex* was copied aboard half-a-dozen light cruisers, the first of which, HMS *Yarmouth*,

ABOVE: A Sopwith 2F.2 Camel lifts easily from the short launching platform of the Australian light cruiser *Sydney*. This picture dates from the latter part of World War I, the aircraft not being carried when the ship sank the celebrated German raider *Emden* in 1914. Note the 152mm/6in gun in an open mounting. BELOW: Another view of a light cruiser's launch platform. From HMS *Yarmouth*'s bridge its limited dimensions are very apparent. Note that the guard rails and jack staff support have been lowered. The aircraft is a Sopwith Pup, piloted by Squadron Commander Frederick J. Rutland.

ABOVE: **Fifty high-speed lighters were ordered in 1917 for the transport of flying boats. Equally able to launch fighters if towed above 25 knots, 12 were thus converted. Here Flight Sub-Lieutenant Stuart Culley, who would shoot down the L.53, lifts off in a Camel while in tow by the destroyer *Redoubt.*** LEFT: **Sideslipping around the superstructure, Squadron Commander Edwin Dunning lands on *Furious*' foredeck, August 2, 1917. The Pup is virtually hovering, and ship's officers are racing to haul it down to deck.**

successfully flew a Pup in June 1917 from a platform just 6m/20ft in length. This feat was quickly exploited for, on August 21, a Pup from the same ship intercepted Zeppelin L.23 near Terschelling, destroying it with "10 to15 shots".

Other launching platforms appeared atop the turrets of capital ships but, at this point, with recovery dependent upon flotation bags and the situation at the time, the aircraft was still very much an expendable item. Experience with the *Campania*, however, had led to a similar conversion on the new and fast "large light cruiser" *Furious*. She entered service in July 1917 and, on August 2, Squadron Commander Edwin Dunning used the Pup's excellent low-speed characteristics to make a risky side-slip and land on the *Furious*' forward flying-off deck. A repeat proved fatal but was instrumental in the ship being further modified with an after flying-on deck.

The Sopwith 2F.1 Camel was designed specifically as a shipboard fighter and on July 17, 1918, *Furious* launched seven of them against the Tondern Zeppelin base. Two airships were destroyed with bombs. A fortnight later, a Camel took off successfully from a specifically designed lighter, towed at high speed by a destroyer of the Harwich Force. Again, the stratagem was quickly exploited, the same pilot, the 18-year-old Lieutenant S.D. Culley, employing it on August 10 to bring down the L.53. The blazing, falling Zeppelin inspired Commodore Tyrwhitt to make the memorable signal, addressed to all ships, "See Hymns Ancient and Modern, Number 224, verse 7". Due consultation confirmed this to read:

"O happy band of pilgrims,
Look upward to the skies,
Where such a light affliction
Shall win so great a prize."

ABOVE: **In a scene that foreshadows the packed flight decks of later years, six of HMS *Furious*' Sopwith Camels are seen ranged forward in 1918. In the foreground is the hatch-like opening of the forward elevator. Note the palisade windbreaks, their paintwork continuing the ship's striped camouflage.**
BELOW: **Still wearing her wartime dazzle paintwork in this 1917 picture, the converted packet HMS *Pegasus* launches a Sopwith 1½-Strutter fighter. The crew members are standing on a portable platform section that permitted aircraft to be transferred from the hangar space below the goalpost mast.**

TOP: **Designed from the outset to carry the harder-hitting 457mm/18in torpedo, the Sopwith Cuckoo needed to be a robustly constructed landplane in order to carry the load. The torpedo's propellers are here covered by a protective cap.** ABOVE: **An interesting "nuts and bolts" view of a Cuckoo, taken from an instruction manual. Of immediate note are the sturdy undercarriage, the small volume of the engine and the obviously poor forward view enjoyed by the pilot when putting down on a carrier's deck.**

Air-dropped torpedoes

The idea of dropping torpedoes from seaplanes originated virtually with the seaplane itself, and can be attributed to no one person.

In the United States, the innovative Bradley Fiske, then a Rear Admiral, filed a patent for an air-dropped torpedo early in 1912. Although first favouring a weapon controlled by radio from an aircraft, he moved to the sounder idea of aiming the aircraft itself, increasing the probability of success through employing several simultaneously.

During the same year, Engineer Captain Alessandro Guidoni of the Italian Navy added floats to a French Henri Farman landplane to experiment with the dropping of deadloads to the limit of the aircraft's capacity. In 1913, he was given a more powerful, twin-engined seaplane, enabling him to demonstrate dropping a dummy 375kg/827lb torpedo on February 26, 1914.

Meanwhile at the Royal Naval Air Station at Eastchurch, Captain Murray Sueter enlisted the assistance of Thomas Sopwith to construct a rig for the evaluation of torpedo release gear at high speeds. This equipment Sopwith then incorporated into his Type "C" aircraft, with which he demonstrated that carrying a 363kg/800lb, 356mm/14in torpedo was feasible in 1913. Finally, on July 28, 1914, a first live drop was made by a Short Folder.

A 356mm/14in weapon had limited hitting power and, with his eye set on larger targets, Sueter set Sopwith the task of designing a landplane able to carry a 457mm/18in weapon. The existence of this project appears in minutes dated June 25, 1914, (and, therefore, pre-war) and was connected with the provision and location of coastal air stations. Inter alia, these stated that "the danger of raids would be greatly reduced by the prospect of torpedo-carrying aircraft stationed 80km/50 miles apart all along the coast ... The detection and attack of hostile craft would be rendered much more rapid by the introduction of this type of coast defence". In view of the German fleet's shortly-to-be-adopted tactics of hit-and-run bombardments of English east coast towns, this appraisal was prescient but, unfortunately, well ahead of the technology to support it, for it would be 1917 before Sopwith could introduce the required aircraft.

The then First Lord, Winston Churchill, informed Sueter and his colleagues as early as April 3, 1915, that a very large fleet of aircraft was required. In place of individual "dashing exploits", it was necessary to deal "a decisive blow ... at the enemy's capital ships ... either in a fleet action or in his harbours".

The first successful "dashing exploits" were themselves still several months in the future, being the August 14 attacks by the *Ben-my-Chree*'s aircraft in the Dardanelles theatre.

As the British moved toward their objective of a mass torpedo attack on the German and/or Austrian fleet, the Germans themselves were not idle. By November 1916, their twin-engined Gothas were torpedoing merchant shipping off the English east coast. To lift them from the water, these aircraft required two 119kW/160bhp engines. In contrast, Sopwith's landplane, lifting from the flight decks that Sueter envisaged, required only a singe, 149kW/200bhp unit.

The Sopwith T.1 (later named the "Cuckoo") first flew in June 1917 but was a further year entering service. On October 19, 1918, the first operational squadron embarked on the new, flush-deck carrier *Argus*. Within a month the plan for the mass torpedo attack was terminated by the Armistice. By then, its gifted but outspoken champion, Murray Sueter, had joined Churchill in the dark outer regions of official favour.

TOP: **A Blackburn-built Cuckoo here makes a perfect release. Flying straight and low at about 90 knots made the aircraft vulnerable to return gunfire, however.** ABOVE: **The pioneer carrier HMS *Argus* manoeuvres in the Grand Harbour, not a straightforward task for a high-sided ship in a crosswind. Note the smoke from the problematical exhaust ducting, and the rows of scuttles, a legacy of her passenger liner origins.** LEFT: **Not driven by the same degree of urgency, the US Navy did not develop torpedo aircraft until after World War I. Here, a Liberty-engined Curtiss R-6L releases a weapon in 1922. The Curtiss R-series aircraft with floats or wheeled undercarriage, were also used by the RNAS, but in non-combat roles.** BELOW: **In what turned out to be an evolutionary dead-end Curtiss designed his Model 24 with twin engines to solve the problem of the heavy load of a torpedo. The US Navy ordered nine of the aircraft, designated the CT-1, but only one, seen here, was fitted in 1922 to actually carry a torpedo.**

The *Königsberg* operation

At the outbreak of World War I, several German cruisers were at large as commerce raiders. Operating in the Indian Ocean was the *Königsberg*, which having destroyed two ships, went to ground. On October 30, 1914, she was located by HM cruiser *Chatham*, hiding several miles inside the maze of waterways that form the delta of the Rufiji River, in what was then German East Africa.

Too deep in draught to ascend the river themselves, the *Chatham* and consorts instituted a blockade. The *Königsberg* shifted berth from time to time and, pending arrival of the promised Royal Naval Air Service (RNAS) flight, the senior British officer kept track of her through the services of a civilian pilot. From giving public exhibitions in his Curtiss "hydroplane", this gentleman found himself a temporary commission, his aircraft purchased and, with it, shipped north to the British base on Mafia Island. The aircraft's life was short but a second one was located and brought in.

Meanwhile, following rapid preparation, RNAS Expeditionary Squadron No. 4 arrived in early February 1915, together with two seaplanes and a party that included a Sopwith mechanic and a propeller expert. Presumably, the outfit also included a supply of bombs of up to 23kg/50lb. The RNAS task, however, was primarily to cooperate with naval gunners to encompass the enemy's destruction.

The agency for this was two small river monitors, *Severn* and *Mersey*, which, while drawing only 1.68m/5ft 6in of water, mounted two 152mm/6in guns and two 119mm/4.7in howitzers apiece. Laying in Malta, they had to be prepared and towed to East Africa, not arriving until early June.

In the interim, the RNAS had found that in the humid heat their aircraft could get aloft with only the pilot aboard and no observer, bombs, and a minimum amount of fuel. Even then,

TOP: **Seen here at Dar-es-Salaam, the 3,455-tonne/3,400-ton light cruiser *Königsberg* was the pre-war station ship for German East Africa. With war, her orders were to use these territories as a base and to act against allied shipping in the Indian Ocean. Having achieved little, however, she inexplicably "went to ground" in the remote and inaccessible Rufiji delta.** ABOVE: **Blockaded by the British, the *Königsberg*'s commanding officer established observation posts and gun positions along the approaches. Colonial duties at the time demanded innovative personnel and *Königsberg* crew are here seen manning a strongpoint.**

ABOVE: The blockading forces made considerable use of aircraft for tracking the *Königsberg*'s movements and, finally, for spotting. They proved to be highly unreliable in the humid climate and here what appears to be a Short 827/830 is being towed by HMS *Severn*, one of the two small river monitors involved. ABOVE LEFT: One of the Short 827s of the expedition. Note the conspicuous top-mounted radiator and the forest of wire necessary to stiffen the large span of the wings.

they could only be coaxed to an altitude of 457m/1,500ft. Wooden propellers also warped and one aircraft was soon wrecked in a heavy landing. The other simply disintegrated as glue, rubber, and fabric failed in the conditions.

On April 23, three Short seaplanes were unloaded but these, too, were unable to climb sufficiently and all suffered damage from enemy fire; one being shot down.

Following the arrival of the monitors on June 3, four more aircraft were delivered, two Caudrons and two Henri Farmans. All were landplanes and had to be landed over the beach before being manhandled 2.4km/1.5 miles to an improvised air strip hacked out of the jungle by the now considerably enlarged RNAS party and native labour. The machines proved able to attain 1,219m/4,000ft but, again, two were soon lost.

On July 6 the monitors entered the river and, assisted by spotting aircraft, fired indirectly across the jungle. The enemy had long since established observation posts and a lively return fire ensued. Aircraft corrected about 80 of the 600-odd rounds fired by the British, who made three hits, suffering two in return.

Following repair, the monitors returned on July 11, and, after two hours and 200 more rounds, the Germans, low on ammunition, recognized the hopelessness of their situation, and scuttled their ship. Ironically, one of her final shots had brought down the sole remaining spotting aircraft, whose crew was rescued by the *Mersey.*

ABOVE LEFT: Before the *Königsberg* affair, the Germans drafted Bruno Buckner and his Pfalz-built Otto biplane into military service, shown here with Askari guard. ABOVE: Obsolete even by 1914 standards, this German floatplane could have operated under only ideal conditions. BELOW: With no prospect of escape and being systematically reduced by British indirect gunfire, the *Königsberg* was blown up by her own crew. The "petalling" of the shell plating around the two large nearer holes indicate that they were caused by internal explosions.

Arthur Balfour, Churchill's successor as First Lord, later felt able to announce (perhaps a trifle generously) to the War Committee that "the destruction of the *Königsberg* had been due almost entirely to the spotting of Naval aeroplanes".

Naval aviation at Jutland

The long-awaited trial of strength between the British Grand Fleet and the German High Seas Fleet finally came about off Jutland on May 31, 1916. For the former it proved to be a catalogue of disappointment and missed opportunity. On a day of fickle visibility, more and better aerial reconnaissance might well have made a significant difference to the outcome but, in truth, naval aviation was yet too fragile for such a major responsibility.

Admiral Jellicoe's Grand Fleet still had only the *Campania* and *Engadine* for air support and, farcically, the former failed to receive the signal to sail. Incorrectly assumed to be too slow to catch up, she and her ten seaplanes were ordered to remain at Scapa.

The action developed with the battle-cruiser squadrons of Beatty and Hipper heading for each other. Beatty had *Engadine* in company but, aware of the frailties of her aircraft, he refused to commit them to general reconnaissance. Only when the opposing cruiser screens had come into contact was the *Engadine* ordered to put up an aircraft. At 15:08 hours, therefore, "Seaplane No.8359" (a Short 184) took off to make history as the first aircraft to be involved in a naval battle. The pilot, Flight Lieutenant F.J. Rutland, was thereafter known widely as "Rutland of Jutland", and would go on to make a name in naval aviation.

With the cloudbase in places down to 274m/900ft and visibility of 1.6-6km/1-4 miles, Rutland had to get uncomfortably close to the enemy, attracting shrapnel bursts. His observer was able to radio one of the enemy cruisers' course changes before, at 15:45 hours, "a petrol pipe leading to the left carburretter [sic] broke". Forced to alight, Rutland "made good the defect with rubber tube" and reported that he could continue, only to be recalled by his ship.

TOP: What with ineffective anti-aircraft fire and hopelessly inadequate bombs, ships and aircraft of World War I posed little mutual threat. ABOVE: Converted from a cross-channel packet, the seaplane carrier HMS *Engadine* became the first warship to launch an aircraft in the course of a naval action. One of her Short 184s is here visible abaft the box-like hangar.

Already too slow to remain in contact with Beatty's hard-pressed squadron, the *Engadine* now completely lost touch with it and played no further active part in the action (although she would encounter the stricken armoured cruiser *Warrior* and, unable to prevent her foundering, took off her entire surviving crew).

Admiral Scheer, commanding the German High Seas Fleet, enjoyed little better support from the Naval Airship Division. His thrust into the North Sea was to have been preceded by a line of five Zeppelins, scouting in a bold arc from southern Norway

to a point off East Anglia. Poor visibility and crosswinds so delayed their departure, however, that none would observe any aspect of the daylight action of May 31.

Bent on returning to Wilhelmshaven, Scheer's fleet broke through the tail of Jellicoe's forces during the ensuing night. This triggered a series of desperately fought skirmishes, observed by at least two of a second group of five airships ordered out at dusk. Another, L.11, discovered Jellicoe's main body in the early light of June 1. For about 100 minutes, she held contact, coming under fire from all calibres of gun, at one stage from over 20 ships simultaneously. The bombardment by the frustrated British included main battery fire – "the line of ships could be made out from the muzzle flashes when the ships themselves were invisible". L.11 was not hit but "the passage of the big shells and the bursting of shrapnel nearby caused such heavy vibrations in the framework that it seemed advisable to increase the distance…"

Zeppelin L.11 was, therefore, the only aircraft to contribute significantly to the operation. It is a misfortune of history that, by then, the action was over.

ABOVE LEFT: **Beyond his epic flight at Jutland, Frederick Rutland was decorated for gallantry. His later career was clouded through his subversion by the Japanese and his eventual suicide.** TOP: **Short 184 No. 8359, "the aircraft that flew at Jutland", is here seen alongside her mother ship, HMS *Engadine*. Parts of the original aircraft survive to this day at the Fleet Air Arm Museum, Yeovilton.** ABOVE: **A German propaganda postcard purporting to show a British battle cruiser under fire at Jutland.**

LEFT: **Jutland was, for the British, a material defeat. Realizing, however, that they could never defeat the Grand Fleet in battle, the German High Command was forced to resort to submarine warfare. It was the brutality of this that brought the United States, following several warnings, into World War I. This, on top of privations resulting from the British naval blockade, reduced Germany to despair, revolution and, ultimately, defeat.**

The first naval air strikes

Probably because they themselves lacked experience of large rigids, the British overestimated the capabilities of German Zeppelins, both in reconnaissance and in their capacity to inflict targeted damage by bombing. The scale of the Zeppelin "bogey" is evident in the resources devoted by both the Royal Naval Air Service (RNAS) and the Royal Flying Corps (RFC) in dealing with it.

Thus, on October 25, 1914, not three months into the war, the Harwich Force crept deeply into the Heligoland Bight in order to cover its seaplane carriers, whose objective was the Zeppelin base at Nordholz, near Cuxhaven. A heavy rainstorm was sufficient to prevent their seaplanes rising from water, however and, disgusted at the outcome ("I am sick to death of everything connected with aviation…", wrote Commodore Tyrwhitt to his wife) the force was obliged to withdraw. Taking a broader view, Churchill, the First Lord, noted, "It is no use trying these enterprises with overloaded machines. Either aeroplanes or seaplanes with wheels instead of floats must be used." Probably in these few words lay the genesis of the true aircraft carrier.

As Tyrwhitt awaited a further opportunity, a flight of RNAS landplanes was moved to Belfort whence, on November 21, they flew the 193km/120 miles to the Zeppelin works at Friedrichshafen. Their 9kg/20lb bombs narrowly failed to destroy the new L.7.

On Christmas Day 1914, the Harwich Force was again in the Heligoland Bight where, in totally calm conditions, the three seaplane carriers (*Empress*, *Engadine* and *Riviera*) hoisted out nine aircraft, all Shorts, but of three types. Only seven were able to take off and these encountered fog and low cloud over the target area. Just one aircraft located the Nordholz site and its bombs caused no damage.

TOP: **Completed in July 1916, the Zeppelin L.31 had a life of just 12 weeks, being shot down by a British fighter. The latter's pilot reported her engulfed in flames, and just evading her "as she shot past me, roaring like a furnace".**
ABOVE: **Bomb damage inflicted upon innocent homes by Zeppelins, as here in Kings Lynn, aroused national anger.**

Nonetheless, the presence offshore of a powerful British force caused considerable German consternation. Tyrwhitt's waiting ships came under bombing and machine gun attack from two seaplanes and a Zeppelin. This, the first example of air attack on hostile warships at sea, caused some excitement but, again, no damage. Extended beyond their endurance, however, only two of the British raiders returned, although the missing crews were eventually recovered.

These disappointments set the tone for other attempts. As Churchill had observed, what was required was to operate landplanes directly from a ship's deck, implicitly with the necessary facilities for landing them on again. However, the development and provision of such would take time.

As an interim measure, the new "large light cruiser" *Furious* was converted in two stages. Between March 1917 and March 1918 she acquired a 69m/228ft flying-off deck forward and a 87m/284ft landing-on deck aft. With hangar space below for up to 16 landplanes, elevators and a rudimentary arrester system, she embodied the major features of a true aircraft carrier, although turbulence from the remaining superstructure left the landing deck too hazardous to use.

By 1918, ever-larger Zeppelins were able to carry 3.01 tonnes/3 tons of bombs, the largest of 300kg/661lb. Raids on England were becoming increasingly damaging and public indignation ran high. The Navy, under pressure to "do something", was now able to deploy the *Furious* against the more-distant Zeppelin facility at Tondern in Schleswig-Holstein.

On July 19, 1918, she duly despatched seven, bomb-armed Sopwith 2F.1 Camels in two flights, separated by ten minutes. The first arrived at 04:30 hours, achieving complete surprise. Two Zeppelins, L.54 and L.60, together with an aerostat, were destroyed by 23kg/50lb bombs. It was history's first successful naval air strike.

ABOVE: Zeppelins were the direct stimulus for the extraordinary efforts made by the Royal Navy to take high-performance fighter aircraft to sea. Here, ship's routine goes on beside three Sopwith Camels ranged on the foredeck of HMS *Furious.*
LEFT: HMS *Furious*' foredeck, looking aft, this time with Sopwith Pups. Note the two mercantile-style posts and derricks for hoisting aircraft from the hangar below. Elevators were fitted only in 1918.
BELOW LEFT: On November 21, 1914, four RNAS Avro 504s sortied from a French airfield at Belfort to bomb the Zeppelin factory at Friedrichshafen. One aircraft was lost and the small damage inflicted was outweighed by the consternation caused.
BELOW: The wreckage of L.54 and L.60, destroyed by *Furious*' aircraft. The airships burned without exploding and so, incredibly, their enormous shed at Tondern survived, blackened but intact.

British shipborne aircraft of World War I

As the British nation went to war in 1914 the Royal Naval Air Service (RNAS) operated an eclectic assortment of 78 aircraft types, including 20 of landplane, 12 of seaplane and 7 of non-rigid airship. Still largely experimental, it operated from shore bases, having only in the previous year sent aircraft to sea in HMS *Hermes* for evaluation in manoeuvres.

The functions of the service which had been defined by the Admiralty were observation, scouting and spotting. These duties could be undertaken by small, two-seater seaplanes, whose presence aboard a warship caused minimal impact and which, at least in theory, could use the sea for take-off and recovery, when conditions permitted.

However, the possibilities of using aircraft as torpedo carriers demanded a second category of larger seaplane for, with the low-powered engines available, the accommodation of such a load required far greater wing areas to provide the necessary lift.

From the outset, much of the RNAS' resources were mobilized to assist those of the Royal Flying Corps (RFC) in the defence of home soil against incursions by Zeppelin airships. Operations were, of course, land-based, using high-performance landplanes. Therefore, when the same Zeppelins began to dog the fleet in an observational role, the RNAS turned to solving the problems of operating landplanes from ships. A third category of aircraft had thus been added and modes of operation had been extended from neutral to both offensive and defensive. The problem, however, revolved not about launch but about recovery.

TOP: **Despite its diminutive size – its span was only 7.8m/25.8ft – and low power, the Sopwith Baby served until July 1917, when it was superseded by the Pup.** ABOVE: **Both British and German fleets explored the possibilities of aircraft working with submarines. Here, in May 1916, the E22 trims down to float off two ramp-mounted Sopwith Schneiders, instantly recognizable from their distinctive bull-nosed engine cowling.**

Radio communication between aircraft and ship had been demonstrated up to a range of 145km/90 miles, but the equipment remained fragile and unreliable.

The introduction of the folding wing by the Short brothers made for more compact stowage aboard ship. However, they were detrimental to a biplane's performance and easily removable wings were also tried.

Recreational flying was already popular before the war, with small seaplanes competing for the Schneider Trophy. Sopwith's design for a Schneider competitor provided the basis for his Tabloid. Even loaded, it weighed only 771kg/1,700lb and pioneered the evolution of launch and recovery routines, particularly in the use of flying-off ramps. Development of a more powerful engine saw the Tabloid evolve into the widely used Baby.

ABOVE: **In order to reduce the landing run of carrier aircraft, some had their wheels experimentally replaced by skids, as on this Pup. Note also the 1918 fore-and-aft arrester wires, raised by a portable wooden ramp.** LEFT: **A Sopwith 1½-Strutter suspended from *Furious*' starboard transfer derrick. As the ship had no usable landing deck, this spectacular damage was caused, presumably, by a drop.**

In contrast, the torpedo-carrying Short 184 appeared enormous, with over twice the wingspan and weighing in at over 3.01 tonnes/3 tons. Equipped with successively uprated engines, about 650 were built by a range of sub-contractors, and they saw service throughout the war.

Sopwith designs predominated for RNAS fighters, with Bristol and Parnall also of note. Introduced late in 1915, Sopwith's 1½-Strutter set a new standard, serving either as a two-seat fighter or as a single-seat bomber.

From early in 1916, the smaller Sopwith Pup complemented the 1½-Strutter. Agile, but with a low landing speed, the Pup served widely with the fleet. In turn, however, it was superseded by the 2F.1 Camel. Slightly larger and more powerful, the Camel had a greater useful payload and two forward-firing machine-guns.

By April 1918, when the RNAS and RFC were amalgamated into a single, unified Royal Air Force (RAF), over 100 aircraft were being carried by cruisers and capital ships, the Sopwith Cuckoo torpedo aircraft was in service and a new, anti-submarine role had been added.

ABOVE: **Out of her element; a Fairey Campania at a Royal Naval Air Station. As the name implies, the aircraft was designed specifically to operate from the ship of that name. Note the four-bladed propeller.**

Typical British shipborne aircraft of World War I

	Wing span	Speed	Power	Machine-guns	Payload
Sopwith Schneider	7.8m/25ft 8in	140kph/87mph	75kW/100hp	1	29.5kg/65lb
Sopwith Baby	7.8m/25ft 8in	161kph/100mph	97kW/130hp	1	59kg/130lb
Short 184	19.4m/63ft 6in	143kph/89mph	194kW/260hp	1	236kg/520lb
Fairey Campania	18.8m/61ft 8in	137kph/85mph	205kW/275hp	1	59kg/130lb
Sopwith 1½-Strutter	10.2m/33ft 6in	164kph/102mph	97kW/130hp	1	118kg/260lb
Sopwith Pup	8.1m/26ft 6in	180kph/112mph	60kW/80hp	1	29.5kg/65lb
Sopwith 2F.1 Camel	8.2m/26ft 11in	200kph/124mph	112kW/150hp	2	45kg/100lb
Sopwith Cuckoo	14.2m/46ft 9in	167kph/104mph	149kW/200hp	0	386kg/850lb

Rigid airships after World War I

For navies other than the German, the large rigid was very much a useful-looking invention that never found an application. Following the failure of its first effort in 1911, the Royal Navy did not begin again until 1914, its technology now well behind that of Germany. The first, R.9, went operational in April 1917 and, between then and 1919, when the Admiralty decided that no more would be built, a total of ten was produced, all considered experimental.

In 1918, R.23 was the first to carry its own defensive fighter aircraft. R.31 and R.32 were built to German Schütte-Lanz principles but the laminated wood frames were heavy and difficult to fabricate. R.33 onwards followed closely the design of the captured Zeppelin L.33, the R.34 making a celebrated first-ever double crossing of the Atlantic in July 1919.

Although a conference of December 1918 minuted that rigids were still considered to be valuable for fleet reconnaissance, the general lack of clarity over manning and responsibility following the establishment of the unified Royal Air Force in the previous April, led the Admiralty to cease further development. Some existing rigids soldiered on through the 1920s but never progressed beyond the experimental stage for military application. The R.101 disaster of October 1930 finished British involvement for good.

American naval aviation may be said to date from October 7, 1913, with the establishment by the Secretary of the Navy of a board to "prepare a comprehensive plan for the organization of a Naval Aeronautic Service". Although an unspecified "fleet dirigible" was listed as a requirement from the outset, resistance by many to "big bags" kept wartime dirigibles to non-rigids.

TOP: **The Armstrong Whitworth-built R.33 was a straight copy of the German L.33, which force-landed and was burned-out on the Essex coast. With the Admiralty losing interest in airships in 1919, the craft was transferred to the Air Ministry.** ABOVE: **The control car of the USS *Akron* was a beautiful example of American 1930s streamlined styling.**

A more specific requirement of November 1916 nonetheless specified one "experimental Zeppelin" for which the starting point would prove to be the acquisition of the German L.49,

LEFT: **Zeppelin technological know-how was used by Goodyear in the design and construction of the USS *Akron* (seen here) and *Macon*. Giant airship hangars became an architectural form in themselves.**

ABOVE: **To explore the possibilities of airship co-operation with the fleet, the US Navy fitted the oiler *Patoka* with basic facilities, including a mooring mast, as depicted on this modern postage stamp.**

BELOW: **Both to extend visual reconnaissance range and for a measure of protection, the *Akron* and *Macon* carried the compact Curtiss F9C/09C Sparrowhawk. Carried within the airship's envelope, the aircraft could be lowered on a trapeze for launch and eventual recovery.**

captured in October 1917. To gain experience a close copy, even down to its Maybach engines, was constructed by the US Navy. Completed as the ZR.1 in 1923, but named USS *Shenandoah*, the craft was something of a disappointment. This was due mainly to her being inflated with helium, a safe gas but not as buoyant as the hazardous hydrogen used by the Germans. Vulnerability to weather was, as ever, the greatest danger and the craft was destroyed in a storm in September 1925 due, it was concluded, to ruptured gas cells.

This was already the US Navy's second such disaster. The epic flight of the British R.34 had resulted in the purchase of R.38, designated ZR.2, in 1921. Still on trials with an Anglo-American crew, she crashed in British waters in August 1921 with the loss of most of those aboard.

Delivered in October 1924, the US Navy's third large rigid was built by the Zeppelin company as war reparation. Officially ZR.3, but named USS *Los Angeles*, she operated successfully until retired in 1932.

ZRS.4 and ZRS.5, USS *Akron* and *Macon* respectively, were built by Goodyear jointly with Zeppelin. Their lives, too, were short. *Akron* was completed in 1931 and lost in April 1933, the *Macon* commissioned in 1933 and was lost in February 1935, both being destroyed in storms at sea.

All three later American rigids could launch and recover their own defensive fighter aircraft but, by the 1930s, they no longer had any military application. With the demolition of the *Los Angeles* in 1939 the large rigid airship, at least as a vehicle of war, passed into history. Feared, misunderstood, over-evaluated, it had proved to be an evolutionary dead-end for naval aviation.

ABOVE: **Based on the late Zeppelin L.49 design, the ill-fated USS *Shenandoah*, here seen moored to the *Patoka*'s mast, was built in the United States. Her buoyancy depended upon helium, giving her an inferior performance.**

The Sempill mission and Japanese naval aviation

At the end of the 19th century, British and Russian interests in the Far East differed sharply. The Russians also had differences with Japan which, having defeated China over Korea in 1894–95, was an up-and-coming regional power. Russia and Japan would themselves go to war in 1904–5 but during 1901, they had begun serious negotiations aimed at rapprochement, a development that caused great concern to the British, who feared an alliance between them.

Despite the size of Britain's late-Victorian navy, its resources were not infinite and many of its ships were far from up to date. Its representation in the Far East could probably have matched that of the Russians but not in combination with the Japanese who, in defeating the Chinese at the Battle of the Yalu, had demonstrated their ability to successfully fight a "modern" naval action.

Thus, with the first signs of Russo-Japanese understanding in 1901, the British made discrete diplomatic moves to pre-empt any formal treaty. The result, signed on January 30, 1902, was an Anglo-Japanese agreement, valid initially for five years. The new alliance agreed, inter alia, that if either were to be attacked by a third power, the other would remain neutral. The other would assist if requested only if a fourth power was involved. Thus it was that Britain did not intervene during the Russo-Japanese War of 1904–5, but Japan assisted militarily during World War I.

TOP: Dating from the turn of the century, the *Idzumo* (seen here) and her sister *Iwate* were 9,906-tonne/9,750-ton armoured cruisers from the renowned Elswick yard of Armstrong Whitworth. Following long and useful careers they were destroyed together at Kure by US naval aircraft in July 1945. ABOVE: With the virtual annihilation of a Russian squadron at Tsushima in May 1905, Japan became the primary sea power of the western Pacific. In a classic Japanese rendering, a Russian capital ship is overwhelmed by gunfire.

To Japan's advantage, Britain built her capital ships and trained her personnel to the point where she could proceed independently. In return, the British were content to have a strong Far Eastern ally, allowing the Royal Navy to build up its

RIGHT: **Seen aboard an unidentified carrier, the Nakajima A2N2 of the early 1930s was the first Japanese naval fighter capable of holding its own against any foreign competition. Used extensively against China, it was already obsolescent.**

BELOW: **In order to establish its own naval air arm, the Japanese government sought British assistance. A team of 30 experts, headed by Sir William Forbes-Sempill, here seen second from left, accordingly arrived in Japan in 1921.**

strength in home waters, where the naval race with Germany was gathering momentum. In 1905, both partners were pleased to tighten the terms of the alliance and to renew it for ten years. By this date, however, the United States was viewing Japan as an increasingly unfriendly power, and the new agreement caused considerable disquiet.

In 1914 the Japanese Navy modified the *Wakamiya* similarly to the early Royal Navy seaplane conversions, later adding a flying-off deck forward, in connection with which it acquired Sopwith Pup fighters.

At the close of hostilities the Japanese made a formal request for British assistance in setting up a naval air arm. Well aware of American hostility, Britain agreed, but only on a "semi-official" basis. Consequently, in 1921, a party of 30 experienced officers travelled to Japan under the leadership of Sir William Forbes-Sempill, late Deputy Director of the new Air Ministry (later Baron Sempill).

Japan, although well behind Britain in naval air aviation technique, was at this time little behind the United States. Her first carrier, *Hosho*, was nearly ready to launch and the British quickly trained-up their charges, so that the first deck landing was made in February 1923.

By this time, strong American opposition to the Sempill mission had been largely instrumental in bringing about the abrogation of the Anglo-Japanese Alliance at the Washington Conference, to the deep offence of the Japanese.

ABOVE: **Consequent to the Sempill mission, Japan acquired the designs of several British aircraft. Here Japanese ratings are seen with a licence-built Sopwith Cuckoo, produced by Mitsubishi as the B1M1 (Type 13).**

The Americans, it transpired, had good reason to distrust the mission for, although it was also a commercial success, with British products and designs being acquired, several of its members, including the renowned "Rutland of Jutland", were successfully subverted by their hosts.

The verdict of history is that, while the Japanese would eventually have caught up with American expertise in the field, the British considerably expedited the process.

The Washington Treaties (1921–22)

The British wartime policy of containment resulted in the German battle fleet being neutralized rather than defeated. In the Mediterranean, much the same could be said of the Austro-Hungarian fleet.

Following Jutland, the Germans switched emphasis to the submarine war but although considerably slowed, their capital ship construction programme still proceeded. Yet to be finished were two *Bayern*-class battleships and four *Mackensen*-class battle-cruisers. Already formidable ships, the latter were even more exaggerated by the conflicting and sketchy intelligence reports. Unsurprisingly, therefore, both the British and Americans embarked on new classes of super-dreadnoughts to counter them.

ABOVE: **The limits of 10,160 tonnes/10,000 tons and 203mm/8in guns set for cruisers by the Washington Treaty unintentionally triggered a "cruiser race". The Japanese *Kumano* was one of a long series that cheated on limitations.**

ABOVE: **Built to implement remaining carrier tons, the USS *Wasp* (here seen commencing builder's trials in late 1939) proved to be too small, her operational capability limited by inadequate speed and flight deck dimensions.**

Determined to be the dominant western Pacific sea power, Japan was not to be outdone, commencing her ambitious "8/8" programme. In the Mediterranean, the French and Italians were building as much in competition with each other as in the necessity to counter the largely inactive Austro-Hungarians.

The wartime alliance of the five powers had appeared solid enough, but this solidarity disguised deep divisions, suspicions, and rivalries that surfaced again all too readily once the primary, mutual threat was overcome. Because of these, and for reasons of national pride, a new and ruinously expensive "naval race" was quickly developing. Sensing that public opinion was broadly hostile, the Americans pre-empted a developing British initiative by inviting all five powers to a Conference on Limitation of Armament. This duly opened in Washington on November 12, 1921, and, on their home ground, the Americans were at a distinct advantage, their code breakers eavesdropping on communications between the delegations and their governments.

The powers surprised even themselves with their readiness to consign their new construction programmes and many existing warships to oblivion. It was agreed that Great Britain, the United States, Japan, France and Italy should limit their

LEFT: **Special clauses had to be built into the agreement to allow the oversized *Lexington* and *Saratoga* to be converted to aircraft carriers. *Lexington*'s fine entry is shown well here.** ABOVE: **The treaties allowed carriers to carry guns of up to 203mm/8in in the mistaken belief that they could, and should, be able to fight off cruisers. The *Saratoga*, which survived the war, had these useless appendages removed in favour of a 127mm/5in dual-purpose armament.**

global capital ship tonnage to a fixed ratio of 5:5:3:1.75:1.75, the respective maxima being 533,425:533,425:320,055: 177,808:177,808 tonnes or 525,000:525,000:315,000: 175,000:175,000 tons.

Aircraft carriers were also specifically limited. Defined as vessels of at least 10,160 tonnes/10,000 tons displacement, designed for the *specific and exclusive* purpose of carrying aircraft, they were subject to the same ratio of construction. In this case, the overall tonnages should not exceed 137,166: 137,166:82,300:60,963:60,963 tonnes or 135,000:135,000: 81,000:60,000:60,000 tons. Carriers in existence, or building, on November 21, 1921, would be deemed "experimental" and not count against global totals.

No new carrier could exceed 27,433 tonnes/27,000 tons except that two, of up to 33,530 tonnes/33,000 tons, might be converted from hulls that would otherwise be scrapped. Like capital ships, carriers could be replaced only 20 years after their date of completion.

The Japanese came away resentful. They had pressed for a 10:10:7 ratio but had failed, and their valued Anglo-Japanese Alliance had been diluted to a face-saving but ineffective Four-Power Pact. The British had agreed to this only under considerable pressure from the United States, Australia and New Zealand.

"I am convinced that a war with Japan is about as likely as a war with Mars." Senator Thomas Walsh of Montana. Debate following President Coolidge's address to Congress, December 1923

Concerned that the Japanese had been given mandate of many ex-German, western Pacific island groups, the Americans negotiated a general non-fortification clause, but with specified exceptions.

By agreeing to the aforementioned ratios Great Britain had also agreed to the abandonment of her traditional naval superiority. Since 1915, the US Navy had been pursuing a "second to none" policy and the British now accepted its demands for parity.

Ratified in 1923 and not to be terminated until 1936, the limitations imposed by the Washington Treaties would have a profound effect on the development and design of aircraft carriers in particular.

ABOVE: **The first battleships ever to mount 406mm/16in guns, the two Japanese *Nagato*-class survived the severe culls imposed by the Washington Treaties. Surprisingly, neither was sunk by hostile action.**

ABOVE: **By concentrating the main battery, the designers of the British *Nelsons* were able to work in thicker armour over a limited area in order to comply with treaty limitations.**

Carrier operational philosophies

Argus was the 100-eyed messenger of mythology and the name was entirely appropriate for Britain's first true aircraft carrier whose primary roles had been seen as spotting and reconnaissance as well as flying anti-Zeppelin patrols. So fast was naval aviation developing, however, that by the time of the ship's completion in 1918, mass airborne torpedo attack had been added. The objective here was specifically to neutralize a reluctant enemy fleet in its own ports. The attack never materialized because the necessary numbers of flight decks or aircraft were never available.

As it was accepted that capital ships at sea could not be destroyed by the small warheads of air-dropped 457mm/18in torpedoes, the objective was to use the weapon to slow an enemy sufficiently to be finished by gunfire – as would be demonstrated at Matapan and in the sinking of the *Bismarck*.

Thus, throughout the 1920s, the British carrier remained firmly wedded to the battle fleet, providing long-range reconnaissance, fighter air-cover and limited torpedo-bomber capacity. Only in the 1930s, and probably influenced by the Americans, did the Royal Navy start to look at operating carriers as a group, and independently of the battle fleet.

At the close of the Washington Conference in 1922, the British were well ahead in expertise but their ships were eclectic and not of efficient design. Unlike the United States and Japan, Britain had none of her planned super-dreadnoughts under construction and, therefore, was unable to take advantage of the treaty clause that permitted the conversion of two large hulls.

TOP: Fairey III Fs aboard HMS *Courageous* in the 1930s. Arrester wires were not then in use and these aircraft were not fitted with hooks. Note the "planeguard" destroyer, positioned to assist in the event of a flying accident.
ABOVE: As, by far, the largest carriers in the world the USS *Lexington* (seen here) and *Saratoga* were able to establish and develop operational philosophies based on large air wings and high ship speeds.

Flanking the Pacific, the fleets of America and Japan surveyed each other with thinly disguised hostility. With respect to the vast distances involved, each thought in terms of long endurance, with operational time extended by replenishment at sea.

The American Plan Orange was based on a battle fleet with a strong amphibious element advancing steadily through the presumed fortified Japanese-mandated island groups in order to recover lost territories. Land-based aerial opposition could be expected but the principal threat emanated from the Japanese fleet, specifically its carriers.

LEFT: **Seen here in 1930, the *Saratoga* has much of her air wing ranged on deck. Her battle cruiser origins are evident in the fine stern configuration and the enormous casing that was four funnels in one.** BELOW LEFT: **One of the best-known Fleet Air Arm aircraft between the wars was the Fairey III F. Although its first flight was made in 1926 it was not finally phased out until 1940. It served also as a float-fitted seaplane.** BELOW: **Within days of Pearl Harbor, Japanese air power again proved its potency when the British capital ships, *Prince of Wales* (seen here leaving Singapore) and *Repulse* were caught without air cover, overwhelmed and sunk off the Malayan peninsula.** BOTTOM: **Seen here being catapulted, the Japanese Kawanishi E7K (Type 94) was widely used for reconnaissance flying from capital ships and cruisers. Known to the Allies as "Alf", it had a very distinctive engine note.**

The two big *Lexingtons* allowed the US Navy to examine the merits of large air wings and how they should be composed, not least to provide fighter cover for the fleet. Not impressed with the average pilot's ability to hit a freely-manoeuvring warship by either level bombing or torpedo, the Americans pioneered the later deadly technique of dive-bombing.

For the Japanese, the American fleet was the primary target. Much of the reconnaissance role was assumed by the float planes carried aboard all major warships, leaving the carriers the maximum capacity for offensive aircraft.

In order to strike first, the Japanese emphasized range as a paramount factor in aircraft specification. The major barrier to the destruction of an American fleet would then be its carriers, which therefore became the primary objective. Their neutralization meant that the Japanese carriers (fewer than the Americans because of the limitations imposed by the Washington Treaties) would be freed from the need to directly support the battle fleet and could operate either alone or in mutually supportive groups. The increased risk implicit in this mode of operation was understood and accepted.

Interestingly, it was generally accepted wisdom that a carrier's aircraft could not sink a battleship, the torpedo warheads being too small and dive-bombers achieving insufficient dive velocity. Yet, at the outset of the Pacific war, the British *Prince of Wales* and *Repulse* were destroyed primarily by air-dropped torpedoes, although this was achieved with land-based aircraft.

> **"[The Japanese aircraft carrier] must be prepared to be impaled as it impales the enemy."**
> **Japanese Staff College study of November, 1936**

"Billy" Mitchell and the US Navy bombing trials

Unlike the British, who amalgamated Army and Navy aviation into a single, unified service in 1918, the Americans kept theirs separate. To avoid overlapping responsibilities and wasteful duplication, a Joint Army and Navy Board on Aeronautics had been formed in June 1919, but this did not prevent much agitation and politicking from those who supported the formation of an independent air force. These were mainly army personnel and none was more vociferous than Brigadier General William "Billy" Mitchell, despite President Harding's ruling before Congress in April 1921, that aviation was "inseparable from either the Army or Navy".

In January 1921, the Secretary of the Navy had announced that various ex-German warships would be expended as targets to evaluate the effectiveness of aerial bombing. In this, the Army was invited to participate, but an immediate Army demand for ship targets to conduct its own trials was turned down by the Navy as superfluous and unnecessary.

For the Navy, the exercise was designed to establish three major points: the ability of aircraft to locate ships in coastal waters; the probability of hitting ships with bombs while under

TOP: Last of the "pre-Dreadnoughts", HMS *Agamemnon* was demilitarized post-war and converted into a radio-controlled target ship. In this role, she was employed in both bombing and gunnery trials. She was scrapped in 1926. ABOVE: William Mitchell's publicly avowed aim was to erase the US Navy's function of the nation's "first line of defence", arrogating the role to an air force independent of either army or navy. He is seen here (right) with fellow Army flier L.J. Maitland (left).

weigh; and ascertaining the damage that such hits might inflict. It was therefore imperative that observers board the target vessel after each stage in order to note the cumulative damage and to make recommendations for improvement in future designs.

Mitchell's forte was to use exaggeration and innuendo to gain press publicity. To the Navy's anger he had recently published the unsubstantiated claim that aircraft could

"destroy or sink any ship in existence today". With such an unscrupulous operator, the Navy should have been forewarned, but exercised no authority over him.

In June 1921, the bombing trials were staged off the Virginia Capes with the ex-German targets all anchored, stationary and unmanned. To warm up, Navy aircraft sank three U-boats without difficulty. The Army fliers then took some 20 minutes to dispose of a destroyer. On July 18, interest grew with the light cruiser *Frankfurt*, which took aircraft of both services six hours to sink, using 113–272kg/250–600lb bombs.

The "star turn" was the battleship *Ostfriesland*. To allow naval observers to assess progressive damage, it was specified that only two 113–136kg/250–300lb bombs could be dropped at a time and that only one 454kg/1,000lb bomb could be dropped between each inspection.

On the first day, the ship suffered superficial damage from only light bombs. With the second day, however, Mitchell played his trump. Ignoring the rules and all Navy attempts to call a halt, he sent in a continuous stream of aircraft. The ship was hit from low level with three out of five 454kg/1,000lb bombs and an unspecified number out of six 907kg/2,000lb bombs. It was the near misses that sank the ship, their concussive strength staving-in her hull plating.

As there had been no assessment, the *Ostfriesland* sinking proved nothing other than the obvious truth that stationary ships, with incomplete watertight integrity and no damage control parties, might easily be sunk. Any Navy attempt to point this out, however, was drowned by the blare of Mitchell trumpeting to the press and to the world in general that he had been right all along. Spectacular pictures, released to the press, easily misled an uninformed public.

Accepting that Mitchell had staged a coup, the Navy gritted its teeth and got down to the necessary task of improving horizontal and torpedo protection in its ships. Mitchell himself escaped official censure but, while strengthening the case for aircraft carriers, failed to prove that for an independent air force.

ABOVE LEFT: **As a Brigadier General, William "Billy" Mitchell, like Trenchard in Great Britain and Douhet in Italy, was firmly committed to the concept of the heavy bomber as arbiter of future wars. The means by which he pursued his aims were, however, less than scrupulous.** ABOVE: **Dating from 1893, the USS *Indiana* (BB.1) was sunk by the US Navy in explosives trials, simulating bombing, on November 1, 1920. Details were leaked to the international press by, it was believed, Mitchell for his own purposes.** BELOW: **Effectively hijacking the Navy's 1921 bombing trials, Mitchell demonstrated that a battleship (the ex-German *Ostfriesland*) could be destroyed by the concussive mining effect of near misses.** BOTTOM: **The ex-German light cruiser *Frankfurt* was expended in the same series of bombing trials as was the *Ostfriesland*. While the sinkings gained extensive publicity, they proved nothing.**

"Day of the battleship ended."
Newspaper headline after the *Ostfriesland* sinking

Catapults and arresters

Not as ready as the British to accept simple, but effective, flying-off platforms, the Americans worked on catapults from an early stage. From 1916, the British trials ship *Slinger* was evaluating two separate patterns while the US Navy had fixed quarterdeck units on several armoured cruisers. Both programmes were fraught with technical problems, although the USS *North Carolina* made a first under-weigh launch on July 12, 1916.

With the introduction of the through flight deck aircraft carrier there was adequate space for the light aircraft of the time to make rolling take-offs and catapults (or "accelerators") were not fitted to HMS *Argus*. Not completed until 1922, the USS *Langley* had a catapult from the outset. Other patterns were also evaluated but all were removed by 1928 as not being much used.

Arrester gear was a different matter. First tried as transverse wires with deadloads when Ely made his pioneer landing on the *Pennsylvania* on January 18, 1911, it reappeared in 1917 in HMS *Furious*' second rebuild. Although her after flying-on deck was to prove virtually unusable, it was fitted with fore-and-aft arrester wires. These, raised slightly from the deck, were designed to engage in hooks protruding from the skids that served her Sopwith Pups in place of wheeled undercarriages. A transverse wire system with deadloads was also tried out, but so few landings were attempted that meaningful comparisons could never have been made. As a crash barrier, the *Furious* had a transverse frame strung with vertical cables.

Initially with an arrester system, the *Argus* was quickly fitted with a fore-and-aft wire arrangement, mainly to avoid wind gusts sweeping a landing aircraft over the side. Experiments

ABOVE: A Curtiss Model F, AB-3, gets airborne from the fixed catapult installation on the afterdeck of the armoured cruiser USS *North Carolina* (CA-12) on July 12, 1916. BELOW: Catapulted from the British escort carrier HMS *Empress*, a Grumman Avenger torpedo-bomber releases the strop as it gets airborne.

RIGHT: **Before aircraft land-on, a crew member sets up the barrier aboard an escort carrier of World War II. The torpedo-like object is a paravane streamed to divert mine cables.**

ABOVE: **Despite the longitudinal arrester wires, this skid-fitted Sopwith Pup has still slewed. Note the barriers used for these trials, the one in the foreground to prevent overshooting, the other (together with the handling party) to prevent the aircraft toppling overboard.**

involved the use of paired ramps that served both to elevate the wires and to slow the aircraft. It was soon found necessary to alter the cables so that they could be lowered to the deck to allow aircraft to taxi freely. A further refinement was introduction of a Landing Signals Officer, to indicate to a pilot when he was engaged with the wires and, by extension, to give him alignment on his approach to touch-down.

Fore-and-aft wires were far from satisfactory, not least in tending to cause aircraft to pitch on their noses. From 1925 until 1931, the Royal Navy abandoned them altogether on carriers. After the close of hostilities in 1918, the Americans no longer enjoyed the result of British experience and, in going their own way, benefited by the early adoption of transverse wire systems, retarded with friction brake-drums.

With no brakes and in the absence of wires, a carrier aircraft relied mainly on headwind to come to a halt. Heavier aircraft demanded the reinstatement of arresters as well as the installation of catapults. In the Royal Navy the first carriers so fitted on a permanent basis were the *Courageous* and *Glorious* in 1934. These were able to launch a 3,175kg/7,000lb aircraft at 56 knots. The aircraft themselves were also by now strong enough to withstand the considerable forces involved.

American carriers placed considerable importance on astern speed so that, in an emergency, aircraft could be landed over the bows. This entailed a second set of arrester wires forward. Large air strikes meant "spotting" ready aircraft on deck, and the technique was to catapult aircraft away until such time as there was sufficient free space to allow the remainder to make the slightly faster rolling take-offs.

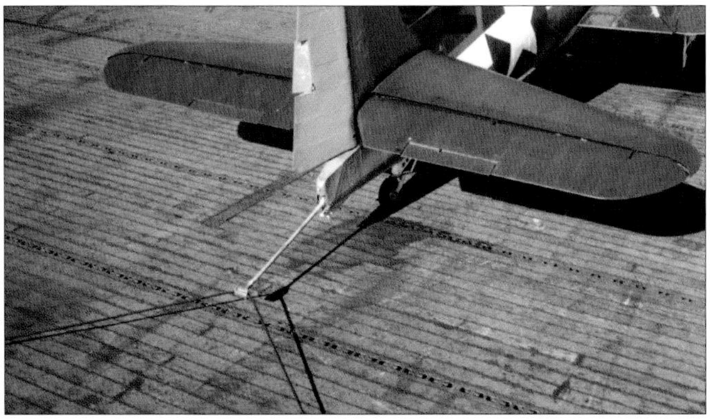

TOP: **An artificer conducts a pre-launch check on a catapult. Note how the Japanese dolly runs along a raised track, the wheels of the aircraft's undercarriage remaining on the deck.** ABOVE: **How it should be done. The hook of an F6F Hellcat has engaged with the transverse arrester wire which, damped by hydraulic cylinders, has decelerated the aircraft without damage. Note the light construction of the flight deck on wartime American carriers.**

LEFT: **The only British submarine designed to accommodate and operate an aircraft on a permanent basis was the *M2* of 1927. Note the haze of diesel smoke as she charges batteries while laying alongside in Haslar Creek.** ABOVE: **Despite the size of the *M2*, her aircraft, the two-seater Parnall Peto, was very small. It is recorded that its crew enjoyed both submarine *and* flying allowances!**

ABOVE: **Low forward freeboard made the *M2*'s aircraft arrangements vulnerable to damage. Terribly slow to dive, she was difficult to handle once submerged.**

Aircraft aboard submarines

Although by no means "aircraft carriers", submarines of most major fleets have carried aircraft, mainly with a view to extending their limited horizons.

No World War I U-boat appears to have been intended for such a function but, on January 6, 1915, the *U-12* of the Flanders flotilla carried a Friedrichshafen FF-29a floatplane on its casing to a point within range of the English coast. The boat was flooded down to float off the aircraft, which then made a symbolic flight over enemy territory. The risk to boat and crew was considerable, attracting official opprobrium.

This, however, was a time of considerable aviation innovation and several companies – Hansa-Brandenburg, LFG and Heinkel – were moved to build prototypes for use aboard submarines. None entered German service.

After the 1918 armistice, the US Navy acquired German U-boat technology. It was impressed by the big *U-142*-class cruiser submarines, apparently well-suited to Pacific operations. At some stage it appears that a small aircraft had been considered for these boats and the Americans conducted trials aboard their submarine *S-1*, using a Caspar-Heinkel U-1 floatplane. The results were not encouraging, so plans to incorporate a pressure-tight, topside hangar on the cruiser submarines *V-5* and *V-6* of 1926, were abandoned.

In 1927, the British converted the big minelaying submarine *M2* to carry a specially-built Parnall Peto floatplane. A cylindrical, pressure-tight hangar was built into the forward side of the superstructure, its door opening directly on to the catapult which ran the length of the forward casing. The arrangement was cumbersome, slow in operation and not judged a success. Its complexity and vulnerability probably caused the loss of the boat by foundering in 1932.

The *M2* experiment was quickly taken up by the French who, between 1927 and 1934, built their monster *Surcouf*, for a long time the world's largest submarine. She was large enough to incorporate two 203mm/8in guns into her forward superstructure and, at its after end, a cylindrical hangar for a knocked-down Besson MB.411 "observation seaplane". Although the submarine operated, and was lost, under the Free French flag during World War II, there is no evidence that either aircraft or guns had ever been of significant use.

Ever committed to the deployment of reconnaissance floatplanes from all conceivable platforms, it was the Japanese that most fully exploited the concept of aircraft aboard submarines. Experimentation with a small Heinkel aircraft began as early as 1923. Given folding wings, this design was developed as the Yokosuka E6Y1 and flew from the large minelaying submarine *No.48* in 1927.

When other fleets had dropped the practice, the Japanese persevered. In 1935 they produced the little Watanabe E9W1 ("Slim"), superseded in 1941 by the more capable E14Y1 ("Glen"). These were intended for reconnaissance but, as the war moved against the Japanese, a new, offensive role was explored. During 1944, the first of the I-400 class submarines was completed. These dwarfed even the French *Surcouf* and held the record as world largest until the advent of nuclear power. Their designed function was to attack high-value targets on American soil, using a new, high-performance floatplane, the Aichi M6A1 Seiran. Three of these, plus spares, were accommodated in an enormous cylindrical topside hangar which gave on to a foredeck catapult.

In the event, Japan's desperate straits by 1945 saw the craft used for cargo-carrying. Only two were completed as Seiran carriers, and both of these too late to be of any use.

ABOVE: **For a long time the world's largest submarine, the French *Surcouf* was designed around an observation aircraft and a pair of 203mm/8in guns.**

ABOVE AND BELOW: **During 1923 the US Navy also explored the possibilities of submarines carrying seaplanes. A knock-down Martin MS-1, derived from a wartime German design, was stowed in a pressure-tight canister abaft the conning tower. The facilities were not as elaborate as those of the *M2* but, like the British, the Americans saw little value in the venture and future development was abandoned.**

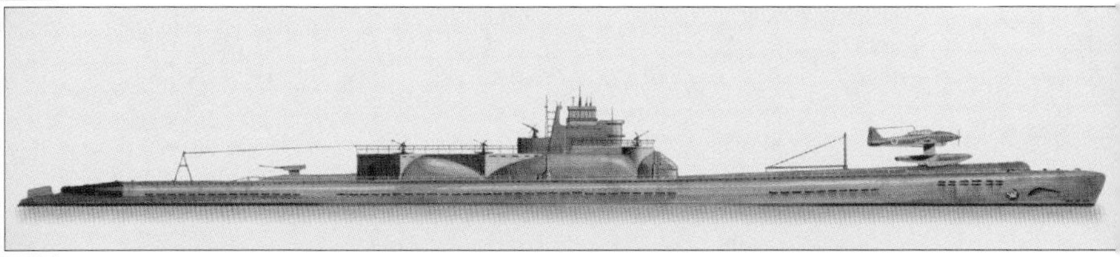

LEFT: **Probably the ultimate in aircraft-carrying submarines, the Japanese I-400 class of World War II copied the layout of the British *M2* in that the centrally located pressure-tight hangar gave directly on to a foredeck catapult. As three floatplanes could be accommodated, however, the scale was considerably greater.** ABOVE: **An I-400 type in profile with an Aichi M6A1 floatplane on the catapult. Note the crane, which could be folded down into the casing, and the 139.7mm/5.5in gun aft.**

Inter-war development in carrier aircraft

During 1918–39, the undisputed lead in naval aviation enjoyed by the Royal Navy was emphatically lost to the fleets of the Japanese and the United States. Operating philosophies and, later, ship design resulted in too few aircraft aboard each carrier, so each aircraft design was multi-purpose. For navigation purposes, each usually was at least a two-seater, and most had to be interchangeable between floats and wheeled undercarriage, all of which reduced performance. A cash-strapped Royal Air Force, now responsible for the provision of Fleet Air Arm (FAA) aircraft and personnel, could afford only the minimum of either. By 1939, the FAA was back under naval control but damage already done was sufficient to adversely affect the service's performance during World War II.

British carrier aircraft were defined as spotter/reconnaissance, fighter/reconnaissance and torpedo/bomber (later torpedo-dive-bomber). The run of Sopwith fighters was broken in 1923, when the Camel was superseded by the Fairey Flycatcher. The Fairey III F three-seater spotter/reconnaissance aircraft served until replaced by the Hawker Osprey (fighter/reconnaissance) and the Fairey Swordfish (torpedo/spotter/reconnaissance). Only in 1937 did the FAA receive an effective dive-bomber in its first monoplane, the Blackburn Skua. Its poor performance as a fighter, however, saw it replaced largely by the still-ineffective Fairey Fulmar, with eight guns but insufficient speed.

American naval aviation received a tremendous boost in 1926 when the Morrow Board recommended the acquisition of 1,000 aircraft. Unlike in Britain, naval aviation remained fully under naval control. Aircraft were thus not "navalized" land designs but robust machines designed for the hard life aboard a carrier.

The first fighter *was*, however, modified from an existing design but this, the Boeing FB-2, then progressed to be FB-5 before being replaced in 1928 by the F2B. The series continued until 1937 with the F3B and the well-remembered F4B. From

ABOVE: **Converted from a battleship hull and designed with a single hangar, HMS *Eagle* was beamy and moved comfortably, but could manage barely 21 knots on a continuous basis. The aircraft on the hook is a Fairey III F floatplane.**

1935, Grumman effectively took over the stubby F2F and F3F. In 1940 came the first monoplane fighter, the highly effective Grumman F4F (Wildcat), immediately ordered also by Britain and France.

The first torpedo-bomber, the Curtiss CS, was superseded in 1926 by the Martin T3M, then the T4M before the very similar 204kph/127mph Great Lakes TG.2. In 1937 came the first monoplane torpedo-bomber, the 332kph/206mph Douglas TBD Devastator. All of these could also act in the scouting role.

The first purpose-designed dive-bomber, the Great Lakes BG-1, entered service in 1934 and could carry a 454kg/1,000lb bomb. In 1938 came the monoplane Northrop BT, which was refined to the Douglas SBD Dauntless by 1941.

Starting with no experience, the Japanese acquired mainly British designs. The Nakajima A1N1 (Type 3) was thus a Gloster-designed fighter, but was improved by 1930 to the A2N1 (Type 90). Replacements passed successfully through

ABOVE: **Designed as a fighter/dive-bomber, the Blackburn Skua was hopeless in the former role but, in its limited existence in the latter, made history by sinking the German cruiser *Königsberg* in Bergen in April 1940, the first major warship to be destroyed by dive-bombing.**

ABOVE: **Introduced in 1936, the Fairey Swordfish has been dismissed by too many wartime writers as "antiquated". It was, however, an aircraft with very special qualities, proving lethal to surface ship and submarine alike. Particularly, Swordfish are associated with Taranto, Matapan and the *Bismarck* pursuit.**

LEFT: **Properly known as the Curtiss Falcon, a multi-purpose dive-bomber/fighter/observation aircraft, the F8C became firmly associated with the first role, adopting the popular name of Helldiver.** BELOW: **One of a trend to "tubby" fighters, the Grumman F2F entered carrier service in 1935, but in 1938 was superseded by the slightly enlarged and more powerful F3F. This had departed squadron service by the end of 1941.**

the 352kph/219mph A4N1 (Type 95) to the first monoplane fighter, the Mitsubishi A5M4 (Type 96) "Claude" to the legendary A6M (Type O) "Zeke" or "Zero".

The first dedicated attack bomber was the Mitsubishi B1M1 (Type 13) which could carry a 457mm/18in torpedo or 500kg/1,102lb of bombs at 209kph/130mph. Its 1930 replacement, the B2M1 (Type 89), also a Blackburn design, carried a heavier load but was unreliable. It was superseded in succession by the smaller Yokosuka B3Y1 (Type 92), its derivative, the B4Y1 (Type 96) "Jean" and, by the outbreak of war, the monoplane Nakajima B5N2 (Type 97) "Kate".

As a first dive-bomber, the Japanese licence-built the Heinkel He 66 from 1934 as the Aichi D1A1 (Type 94), refining it to the D1A2 (Type 96) "Susie". The Aichi D3A1 (Type 90) "Val" was the first monoplane dive-bomber, serving well into World War II, but proving vulnerable to American fighters.

ABOVE: **The Japanese became interested in dive-bombing in 1930 and, in 1933, acquired rights to the German Heinkel He 66. This was developed successively as the Aichi D1A1, then the improved D1A2 (seen here). Known to the Allies as "Susie", this rugged dive-bomber saw second line war service.** LEFT: **With echoes of a Fairey III D, the Mitsubishi B1M series was conceived by British designers in Japanese employ.**

Armoured versus "open" construction

With tight limitations on individual and global carrier displacement imposed by the 1921–22 Washington Treaties, hard decisions had to be made with respect to carrier design.

The British took the view that a carrier's aircraft comprised her only offensive asset and, therefore, required the maximum reasonable protection. All aircraft were thus to be accommodated internally, protected above from bombing and, to the side, from shellfire. In the early days, the bombing threat was comparatively slight but, with a carrier still expected to be engaged in opposed reconnaissance, that from cruiser gunfire was real. For purpose-designed ships (as opposed to conversions) this led to an arrangement where the flight deck constituted the main strength deck, the hull being continuously plated up to that level and creating an enclosed "box" hangar.

The Americans and, to a lesser extent, the Japanese were influenced by the sheer size of their initial carrier conversions and the obvious advantages that large air wings would confer in a long-range Pacific war. Deck parks were accepted at an early stage but, to maximize below-deck capacity, an "open" design predominated. In this, the hangar (or lower hangar) deck became the strength deck, the hangar walls and flight deck being a relatively light structure that added little to structural strength. Because of their greater depth, British-style hulls suffered lower stresses and could be made lighter. On the other hand, in order to ship an acceptable number of aircraft, British

ABOVE: The surprisingly elegant lines of HMS *Ark Royal* (II) are seen to advantage following her launch on April 13, 1937. Still in position is the poppet that supported the bows during launch. BELOW: The launch of the USS *Ranger* (CV-4) in February 1933. Her very fine lines are apparent, as are the light flight deck substructure and the apertures for three elevators and two groups of three folding funnels.

LEFT AND BELOW: **Views of *Illustrious* (left) and *Ark Royal* (below) show several points to advantage. Vertical protection of hangar walls was set inboard to allow for a large number of side apertures to accommodate boats, harbour handling arrangements, etc. The aerial view shows how the British arrangement of armament, although giving good all-round coverage, intrudes into the flight deck area.**

carriers required two hangars. The resulting high freeboard kept the flight deck drier but placed it at a height where its weight, hence thickness, became critical.

British operational doctrine between the wars was expressed in terms of small, six-aircraft formations, for which the carriers were adequate. Elsewhere, full deck-load strikes called for much pre-warming of aircraft engines. This had largely to be conducted below and only an open design could provide the necessary ventilation.

From the early 1930s, the dive-bomber emerged as a major threat to carriers. Level bombing from a considerable height could result in horizontal protection being penetrated by relatively small bombs, but accuracy was low. Dive-bombing was accurate and the lower-level release of the bomb was compensated by its far larger weight.

The need to protect against this weapon had a dramatic effect on British carrier design. The 1937 *Ark Royal* (II) had two hangars, a light splinter-proof flight deck, an armoured lower hangar deck and an air wing of 54 aircraft. The following 1940 *Illustrious* had a flight deck armoured over the extent of the hangar, but only one hangar and an air wing of 36. Their size and displacements were comparable. The lower flight deck of the "armoured" carrier made it wetter, while the heavier elevators made operations slower.

The contemporary American view was that the British approach was too "defensive" and that the price to be paid in aircraft numbers was unacceptable.

Wartime experience duly showed British ships' resistance to both dive-bombing and kamikaze strikes, where American and Japanese carriers succumbed or were disabled by comparatively few hits. Conversely, the latter's carriers, with their large air wings, consistently inflicted far more damage.

There is, of course, no simple answer and, as with most ship design, the answer lies in compromise. Sufficient to say that British fleet carriers designed following war experience (*Ark Royal* (III), *Malta*) did not change in philosophy whereas the American equivalents (*Coral Sea*) did, with a corresponding huge rise in displacement.

"[T]he British gave up almost 50 per cent of their aircraft capacity to obtain partial protection of the carrier."
US Navy liaison officer aboard HMS *Formidable*, June 12, 1941

ABOVE: **As an experiment in small fleet carrier design the USS *Ranger* (CV-4) was not a success and was not repeated. Note the funnel arrangements.**
BELOW: **The great hull of the USS *Midway* (CVB-41) takes shape at Norfolk, Virginia. Larger, and more, aircraft, together with a measure of protection demanded a leap in size compared with the preceding Essex class.**

LEFT AND BELOW: **An old postcard invites a visit to the great Italian naval base at Taranto, an invitation taken up by the British Mediterranean Fleet in November 1940. The reconnaissance photography shows clearly how the arsenal fringes the grid of the old town, how ships anchored in the shallow harbour are vulnerable to torpedo attack, and how smaller vessels moored in a row, "Mediterranean fashion", make an excellent target for a bombing pass.**

BELOW: **Completed in 1915, the *Conte di Cavour* was reconstructed to modern standards in 1933–37. Although salvaged following her sinking at Taranto, she required such extensive refurbishment that she saw no further action.**

Taranto

During 1917, the Royal Navy developed plans to hit the German High Seas Fleet in its base with 120 torpedo aircraft. The plan never materialized but the concept survived. In 1938, therefore, with the prospect of war becoming a probability, the British Mediterranean Fleet trained for a moonlight air strike against the Italian fleet in its base at Taranto. In November 1940, the raid took place but on a far more modest scale than envisaged, for the Royal Navy never had sufficient carriers, of which two had already been lost.

Late in the evening of November 11, the new "armoured" carrier *Illustrious* was positioned off the Greek coast, some 274km/170 miles from Taranto. She had a close escort, with distant cover being provided by the Alexandria-based Mediterranean Fleet. The carrier's air group had been reinforced by aircraft from the elderly *Eagle*, temporarily inoperative following a severe shaking by high-level bombing. Even so, the combined strike force comprised just 21 Swordfish biplanes, organized in two waves of 12 and 9 respectively.

> **"Manoeuvre well executed."**
> **Signal from C-in-C Mediterranean Fleet to HMS *Illustrious* on her rejoining the fleet the morning after the Taranto raid**

Taranto had been under almost hourly surveillance by Malta-based reconnaissance aircraft and, suspecting a reason, the Italians were on high alert. For the raiders, the primary targets were the five battleships reported anchored in the outer harbour, the Mar Grande, protected by anti-torpedo net defences and by barrage balloons. The night selected would silhouette the targets against a three-quarter moon but, in case of overcast weather, the torpedo aircraft would be accompanied by flare-droppers. Further aircraft would provide distraction by dive-bombing ships and facilities in the neighbouring inner harbour, the Mar Piccolo.

In what was known as Operation "Judgement", the *Illustrious* launched her two formations at 20:40 and 21:30 hours. The first achieved surprise but the defences were quickly in action – Italian guns claiming to have fired 13,500 rounds. The cables of the barrage balloons were a considerable hazard to the torpedo aircraft, which came in

LEFT: **Like moths to a flame, *Illustrious*'s Swordfish orbit as they prepare to land-on. Note how flight deck area is maximized by a pronounced overhang at either end.**

ABOVE: **Dating from 1915, the extensively modernized *Caio Duilio* lacked effective sub-division and was put on the bottom by a single 457mm/18in torpedo. She returned to service within a year. The extra elevation of her modernized 320mm/12.6in armament allowed it to outrange the 381mm/15in of equally venerable British battleships.**

> **"Twenty aircraft had inflicted more damage upon the Italian fleet than was inflicted upon the German High Sea Fleet in the daylight action at the Battle of Jutland."**
> **Admiral Cunningham, C-in-C Mediterranean Fleet, writing of the Taranto raid**

very low over the outer breakwater, but the open cockpits of the Swordfish and its superb low-speed performance allowed the pilots to see and avoid them in the confused illumination of flares, searchlights and exploding ordnance.

Only about one-third of the planned anti-torpedo netting was actually in place, but this hung to a depth of nearly 10m/33ft, sufficient to protect the battleships from torpedoes fitted with standard contact pistols. However, the British were using newly developed duplex pistols, which would also be actuated by a target's magnetic field if the torpedo were set to run deep, below the target's keel and, by definition, beneath the protective net.

Low speed allowed the well-trained Swordfish aircrews to take their time and to launch accurately. Of eleven torpedoes expended, three hit the battleship *Littorio*, one the *Conte di Cavour* and another the *Caio Duilio*. Surprisingly, considering the small warheads of 457mm/18in torpedoes, all three were put on the bottom. The anchorage was so shallow that none was submerged to much more than upper deck level. All were therefore salvaged, but this operation and subsequent refitting took six months and the *Cavour* saw no further service.

For the loss of just two aircraft, a most economical raid had totally changed the balance of naval power in the Mediterranean at a critical juncture where the French fleet, expected by the British to be a powerful ally, had been immobilized by the unexpected collapse of France and the resulting armistice with the Germans.

ABOVE: **Brand new, the 15-inch battleship *Littorio* succumbed to three 457mm/18in torpedoes. She re-entered service in August 1941. The Italians riposted brilliantly in December 1941, using "human torpedoes" to put the British battleships *Queen Elizabeth* and *Valiant* on the bottom of Alexandria harbour.**

The *Bismarck* operation

One of the earliest functions prescribed by the British Admiralty for the Fleet Air Arm was that of slowing an enemy ship or formation to permit a decision to be reached by a classic gun action. Two such successful examples are afforded by the *Bismarck* episode and the battle of Matapan.

On May 21, 1941, the new German battleship *Bismarck*, accompanied by the heavy cruiser *Prinz Eugen*, sailed from Norway to raid commerce in the North Atlantic. Correctly guessing their intentions, the Admiralty quickly made fleet dispositions to intercept them.

In thick weather, the pair passed north of Iceland but on entering the Denmark Strait (between Iceland and Greenland) late on May 23, they were located by the patrolling cruisers *Norfolk* and *Suffolk*. These tracked and reported their progress southward, enabling British heavy units to intercept them early on the 24th. These, the veteran battle cruiser *Hood* and the brand new battleship *Prince of Wales*, opened fire at 05:53 hours. At 06:00 hours, with the range down to about 12,802m/14,000 yards, the *Hood* was destroyed by a massive explosion. Not yet battleworthy, the *Prince of Wales* broke off the action.

Herself damaged, *Bismarck* signalled her intention to make for a French port. The British cruisers remained in touch, their tracking reports bringing the carrier *Victorious* (also brand new) into range late on the 24th. At 22:00 hours she launched nine partially-trained Swordfish, which attacked by radar just after midnight. They obtained one torpedo hit that caused little damage.

TOP: HMS *Ark Royal* (II) with one of her Swordfish squadrons. During the *Bismarck* operation, both *Ark Royal* and *Victorious* deployed two Swordfish squadrons. Their admirable low-speed characteristics enabled their carriers to operate them safely in borderline weather conditions. ABOVE: The destruction of the battle cruiser HMS *Hood*, unofficial flagship of the Royal Navy, triggered a massive hunt to avenge the loss.

The *Bismarck* then made radical changes of course to disguise the detachment of the *Prinz Eugen*. These also caused the cruisers to lose touch. It was now 03:00 hours on the 25th, when Admiral Tovey with the battleship *King George V* and the *Victorious* were barely 161km/100 miles distant.

LEFT: **World War I had adequately demonstrated that sending warships on commerce-raiding cruises was an uneconomic proposition. The loss of the *Bismarck*, not long after that of the *Graf Spee*, proves that some lessons are never learned.** ABOVE: **In the conditions, the *Bismarck* proved to be a difficult target for aerial torpedoes. A single hit at a critical point was, nonetheless, sufficient to slow her and see her brought to battle.** BELOW LEFT: **The pleasing profile of the *Bismarck* was so similar to that of her consort, the heavy cruiser *Prinz Eugen*, that British gunlayers were confused.** BELOW: **Admiral Somerville's Force H, formed around the battle-cruiser *Renown*, the carrier *Ark Royal* (II) and the cruiser *Sheffield* operated with success out of Gibraltar. As such it was able to intervene decisively in the apprehension of the fugitive *Bismarck*.**

Throughout the 25th the British searched blindly, and only at 10:30 hours on the following morning did a patrolling RAF Coastal Command PBY Catalina re-establish contact. The *Bismarck* was under 1,127km/700 miles from Brest and had to be slowed.

Fortunately, the Gibraltar-based Force H had been ordered north and found itself right on the German's projected track. With the group was the carrier *Ark Royal*, whose own aircraft made visual contact by 13:00 hours on the 26th. The cruiser *Sheffield* was detached to sight her and continue tracking.

In a full gale and low, thick overcast weather, *Ark Royal* despatched 14 Swordfish at 14:50 hours. An hour later these attacked blind by radar, only to discover that their target, mistakenly, was the *Sheffield*, then 32km/20 miles from the *Bismarck*. By dint of skilful manoeuvring, the cruiser survived.

It was not until 19:10 hours that a second strike, of 15 Swordfish, could be launched. In truly appalling weather conditions they commenced their attack at 20:47 hours, scoring two hits. One damaged *Bismarck*'s steering and a propeller shaft. Slowed and with her manoeuvrability impaired, she was now doomed.

Throughout the night of the 26th–27th British destroyers worried at her but were unable to inflict further torpedo damage. Before daybreak, however, Admiral Tovey arrived with the battleships *King George V* and *Rodney.* Waiting until full daylight, Tovey divided his ships and pounded the *Bismarck* to a wreck. Refusing to sink, she was despatched by a cruiser's torpedoes.

The *Hood* had been avenged but it had taken the combined efforts of seven battleships, two aircraft carriers and twelve cruisers to bring the *Bismarck* to book, and then only by virtue of a single aircraft torpedo.

The Battle of Matapan

During March 1941, the British intervention in Greece generated a succession of convoys from the south and, following sustained pressure from their German allies, the Italians despatched a battle group. Sailing on March 26, Admiral Iachino wore his flag in the battleship *Vittorio Veneto* that headed towards eastern Crete in a loose formation, which included 6 heavy cruisers, 2 light cruisers and 13 destroyers.

Aware of the enemy foray, the C-in-C Mediterranean Fleet, Admiral Cunningham, temporarily suspended all convoy movements and sailed late on the 27th with his three veteran battleships, the aircraft carrier *Formidable* and nine destroyers. Already at sea near Crete were his "light forces", four light cruisers and four destroyers. These were ordered to rendezvous with Cunningham late on the 28th but at 06:30 hours that day, they were sighted by the *Veneto*'s catapulted search aircraft. Assuming this to be an isolated group, Iachino decided to engage.

At about 08:00 hours a reconnaissance aircraft from the *Formidable* was reporting the scattered elements of the Italian force at about the same time as three of its heavy cruisers established visual contact with the British light forces. These, outranged, went about and headed south-eastward at maximum speed to draw the enemy on to Cunningham's main body.

Suspicious, the Italians broke off and headed off westward. The British light cruisers complied, only to find that they had been lured on to the *Veneto*.

TOP: **The *Vittorio Veneto*, Italian flagship at Matapan. Although badly damaged by a Swordfish torpedo, she was not sufficiently slowed to allow the veteran British battleships to make an interception.**
ABOVE: **A later British air strike missed the *Veneto*, the primary target, but hit and stopped the heavy cruiser *Pola*. This brought about the battle of Matapan.**

The Italian flagship opened fire at 10:56 hours and, now under 381mm/15in shellfire, the British made a contact report and again fell back. Fortuitously, at this point six *Formidable* Swordfish made a first attack on the *Veneto*. It was unsuccessful but persuaded the Italian admiral to abandon his operation. At 11:30 hours, therefore, he too ceased fire and turned westward for home.

The far slower British battle group, some 105km/65 miles astern but apparently unsuspected, appeared unlikely to be able to intercept Iachino. Then, at 15:20 hours, five more Swordfish from the *Formidable*, supported by high-level RAF bombers from Crete, put a torpedo into the *Veneto*'s port quarter. Still about 644km/400 miles from Taranto, the battleship slowed to 10, then 15 knots.

LEFT: **Sister ship to the *Illustrious*, the *Formidable* flew the critical air strikes that brought about the battle. Like the *Illustrious*, the *Formidable* also survived a later ordeal by dive-bombing that would have destroyed lesser ships.** BELOW: **The widely separated funnels of the Italian cruiser *Pola* show that her machinery spaces were likewise separated. However, a single 457mm/18in torpedo was sufficient to bring her to a halt.**

Further air attacks from Crete inflicted no further damage on the enemy but, by 19:00 hours, Cunningham had closed to about 72km/45 miles. To protect the flag the whole Italian force was now tightly grouped and steaming in five columns. Between them, they put up a concentrated barrage of fire when, between 19:35 and 19:45 hours, eight *Formidable* and two Crete-based Swordfish attacked out of the failing light. Only one torpedo found a target, bringing the heavy cruiser *Pola* to a complete halt.

Not appreciating Cunningham's proximity, Iachino pressed on but directed the *Pola*'s two divisional colleagues, *Zara* and *Fiume*, together with four destroyers, to stand by her.

Formidable's aircraft had wrongly claimed to have again hit the *Veneto* so when, at 20:30 hours, the light cruiser *Ajax* reported a radar contact on a stationary ship, Cunningham assumed that it was the Italian flagship which, in reality, was 80km/50 miles further on and making 19 knots.

At 22:30 hours, assisted by radar, the British battleships were just 2,743m/3,000 yards from the preoccupied Italians. Instantaneously, searchlights snapped on and heavy salvoes crashed into the *Zara* and *Fiume* which, with their guns still trained fore-and-aft, were converted in to blazing wrecks. Accompanying destroyers finished off the still-immobile *Pola* and two Italian destroyers.

Although Cunningham was unhappy at the *Veneto*'s escape, what came to be known as the Battle of Matapan established a moral ascendancy that the Italians were increasingly reluctant to challenge. Their fleet remained a powerful threat, but suffered from a deficiency in bold leadership.

ABOVE: **A training session aboard a British escort carrier. The warrant officer and pilot discuss the arming of the torpedo below the Swordfish while crew lie awaiting the order to remove chocks. Note the American-style decking and helmets.** BELOW: **Commander-in-Chief, Mediterranean Fleet at the time of Matapan, Sir Andrew Cunningham is seen here, as Admiral of the Fleet, inspecting the crew of a cruiser. Note the torpedo tubes on the left.**

TOP: **Destroyed by explosion, the wreck of the battleship *Arizona* burns at her berth in Pearl Harbor. Searing images such as this galvanized the United States from its isolationist detachment.** ABOVE: **Standard torpedo-bomber with the Japanese carrier force, a Nakajima B5N2,Type 97 "Kate" leaves the deck of the *Shokaku*. Its torpedo was specially adapted to function in the shallow waters of the American base.**

Pearl Harbor

Aware that any war with the United States would be decided principally on the question of sea control, the Japanese decided to make a pre-emptive strike on the US Pacific Fleet at its forward base of Pearl Harbor. Located on the small Hawaiian island of Oaho, the base was effectively immune to attack except from the air.

All six available Japanese fleet carriers were unobtrusively assembled at a remote anchorage before departing with their escort on November 26, 1941. Having crossed 5,633km/3,500 miles of the lonely north Pacific, the force commanded by Vice Admiral Nagumo Chuichi arrived at its launch point, 443km/ 275 miles north of its objective, at 06:00 hours on December 7. A first strike of 40 torpedo-bombers, 49 high-level bombers, 51 dive-bombers and 43 fighters was immediately despatched.

Oahu is irregular and mountainous, with Pearl Harbor on its south coast. The first wave approached down the western side, some of its number peeling away to suppress potential interference from the several military airfields.

> **"[A]n unwarranted feeling of immunity from attack... seems to have pervaded all ranks at Pearl Harbor, both Army and Navy."**
> **Admiral Ernest J. King, Chief of Naval Operations to Naval Court of Inquiry, November 6, 1944**

The island had been well reconnoitred, the plan well rehearsed. It being a Sunday morning, the bulk of the fleet was alongside for the weekend. To the approaching enemy the view was as had been expected, the anchorage dominated by the line of seven battleships, berthed in pairs. There had been no formal declaration of war and surprise was absolute. In the absence of opposition, the aircraft arrived at 07:55 hours and were able to select their targets with deadly precision.

Armour-piercing bombs, fashioned from heavy naval projectiles, drilled through the battleships' horizontal protection, all but one being hit. Specially developed, shallow-running torpedoes lanced the calm harbour waters to devastate all five capital ships on the outer berth. Only rudimentary anti-aircraft armaments were mounted at this time, and return fire was uncoordinated. At each of the airfields and naval air stations aircraft, parked neatly in rows, were wrecked by bombing and low-level strafing.

At shortly before 09:00 hours the first strike was pulling out as the second arrived, having skirted the island's eastern side. Comprising 54 high-level bombers, 81 dive-bombers and

ABOVE: **Dry dock No.1 at Pearl Harbor after the attack. The battleship *Pennsylvania* was only lightly damaged but, in the foreground, the destroyer *Downes* is sitting on the blocks, flooded, while the destroyer *Cassin* has toppled. The smoke is from a distant fire.**

ABOVE: **Smoke from burning ships forms a backdrop to the devastation at Naval Air Station, Ford Island. An undamaged PBY Catalina patrol amphibian is parked at left.** LEFT: **Architect of the attack was Admiral Yamamoto Isoroku. An intelligent and gifted leader, he undertook the task only with the gravest of misgivings. He knew that Japan could sustain only a short war.** BELOW: **"Battleship Row" under attack. From left to right: *Nevada*, *Vestal* outboard of *Arizona*, *West Virginia* outboard of *Tennessee*, *Maryland* outboard of *Oklahoma*, and *Neosho*.**

36 fighters, this force again hit the already stricken "Battleship Row" and the dockyard. The airfields took a further working-over and few American aircraft were able to get airborne.

By 09:45 hours the attack was over. With losses of only 29 of their number, Nagumo's jubilant pilots were returned, still unopposed, to their waiting carriers. They left behind 18 sunken ships, 4 of them battleships. The US Navy had lost 92 aircraft, the Army 96 and over 2,300 servicemen were dead.

The attack on Pearl Harbor was universally condemned as an act of treachery yet, whatever the ethics of the Japanese action, it is undeniable that as a military coup the attack was boldly conceived and efficiently executed. However, it was not a total success. The battleships were elderly yet still commanded too much respect at a point when it was apparent to many that the aircraft carrier had already assumed capital ship status. The enemy's concentration on the battleships resulted in most of the dockyard facilities and oil storage area being left unscathed. By the removal, albeit temporarily, of the battleships from the order of battle, the US Navy was obliged to accept its carriers as more relevant to its interests than the battle line.

Most significantly, Nagumo had struck on a day when no American carriers were in port. They survived through being at sea and would eventually prove to be his nemesis.

The Doolittle Raid and the Battle of the Coral Sea

TOP: **Army Air Force B-25s crowd the deck of the carrier USS *Hornet*. Their wingspan was too great to allow them to be struck below, so sixteen was the maximum that could be handled. Note the escorting cruiser *Nashville* in the background.** ABOVE: **In a 1992 re-enactment aboard the USS *Ranger*, a veteran B-25 lifts off without difficulty. It may be remembered, however, that where the *Ranger*'s flight deck measures 319 x 72.5m (1,047 x 238ft), that of the *Hornet* was 251.3 x 33.4m (824.8 x 109.5ft) and encumbered with other aircraft.**

Carriers had inflicted the pain on Pearl Harbor and it was by carriers that the United States responded. Sixteen Army B-25 Mitchell bombers, led by Lt Col James H. Doolittle, were transported across the Pacific on the *Hornet*'s flight deck and on April 18, 1942, were launched at long range. Hitting Tokyo and three other cities, they flew on to Chinese airfields. Immortalized as "Thirty Seconds over Tokyo", the raid caused only symbolic damage but huge embarrassment to the Japanese authorities. It also served notice that their home soil was no longer beyond reach.

The southward Japanese advance continued, meanwhile, with the despatch of an invasion convoy, bent on doubling the "tail" of New Guinea to take Port Moresby, thereby directly threatening Australia. Forewarned by code breakers, however, the Americans had despatched Rear Admiral Jack Fletcher with the carriers *Yorktown* and *Lexington*.

As a preliminary move, the Japanese made unopposed landings on Tulagi and Guadalcanal in the Solomons. Hitherto unsuspected, Fletcher broke his cover on May 3, 1942, by an ineffective air strike against Tulagi. Approaching to cover the invasion force were the two large Japanese carriers *Shokaku* and *Zuikaku* whose commander, Vice Admiral Takagi Takao, now knew of Fletcher's presence.

A belt of heavy frontal cloud lay over the area on May 6, beneath which three separate groups manoeuvred, searching. Early on May 7, Japanese search aircraft located the American oiler and her escorts. Wrongly reporting her as a carrier, they caused Takagi to waste a full and massive air strike in their destruction.

Fletcher, not far distant, had meanwhile located the Port Moresby invasion convoy. This, accompanied by the small carrier *Shoho*, was so over-reported that it was assumed to be Takagi's main force. A maximum air strike duly despatched the *Shoho*, the first carrier casualty of the Pacific war.

LEFT: **Heavy with maximum fuel and a token bomb load, a B-25 leaves the *Hornet's* deck. Special guidelines, painted well to the port side, ensure that the bombers' wingtips miss the island.**

ABOVE: **An escort's view as *Hornet* launches her B-25s. The operation brought together Halsey in the *Enterprise* and Mitscher in the *Hornet*, two men who were to dominate the American carrier operations.**

"From Shangri-La."
President Roosevelt's response to reporters demanding to know from where Doolittle's aircraft had flown to bomb Tokyo

Both admirals were now aware that neither had discovered his major opponent, both of whom had about 120 aircraft. Daylight on May 8, found Fletcher in clear weather, whereas Takagi was still under low cloud. Nevertheless, by 08:30 hours, each had located the other and, in short time, 90 Japanese and 84 American aircraft were airborne.

Yorktown's torpedo aircraft enjoyed no luck but her dive-bombers hit the *Shokaku* twice, leaving her unable to launch aircraft. Many of the *Lexington*'s aircraft failed to find their objective but one further bomb hit was made on the *Shokaku.*

In return, the Japanese torpedo aircraft attacked *Lexington* simultaneously from either bow. Unable to avoid all the torpedoes, she was hit by two of them. Two bomb strikes added to her problems but, within the hour, her damage control teams appeared to be winning just as the ship was wracked by an explosion caused by aviation fuel vapour. It was the first in a devastating series that finally caused her destruction. The *Yorktown* had also been hit by a single heavy bomb.

The Battle of the Coral Sea was significant in that it was the first fought by carrier groups seeking each other's destruction without ever coming within sight of each other (this action was fought at a range of about 322km/200 miles). In material terms, the Japanese came off better in having destroyed the much heavier US carrier, even though the damaged *Shokaku* had to withdraw for major repair. Strategically, however, the Americans won as, with the destruction of the *Shoho*, the invasion convoy turned back. Port Moresby was never to be taken and the mountainous tail of New Guinea would mark the southern limit of what had appeared to be an unstoppable Japanese advance.

TOP: **Dauntless SBD scout/dive-bombers ranged on the *Yorktown*. They were instrumental in the destruction of the Japanese carrier *Shoho* at the Coral Sea, the first carrier loss of the Pacific War.** ABOVE: **The major loss of the Coral Sea action was the American carrier *Lexington*. Severely hit by Japanese torpedo aircraft, she suffered further from dive-bombers. She was destroyed finally by massive internal explosions.**

The Battle of Midway

The Japanese wished to provoke a decisive battle with the US Pacific Fleet before it gained in strength. Their plan was to seize Midway Island, west of Pearl Harbor but close enough to be a threat. On coming to its defence the Americans would be ambushed by Admiral Yamamoto Isoroku and the main Japanese battle fleet. A brilliant leader, Yamamoto had a weakness for very complex plans, that for Midway dissipated his otherwise overwhelming strength.

American intelligence was, however, extraordinarily detailed, enabling the Pearl Harbor-based Admiral Chester Nimitz, C-in-C Pacific to make counter-dispositions in good time, deploying his smaller forces to the best advantage. Once again, carrier groups would be both spearhead and major target. Lacking the two damaged at the Coral Sea action, Vice Admiral Nagumo would use his remaining four carriers to soften-up the defences prior to the assault landing. For the Americans, the *Yorktown*, another Coral Sea casualty, was rapidly patched up and joined by the *Enterprise* and *Hornet*, commanded by Rear Admiral Raymond A. Spruance.

At first light on June 4, 1942, Midway radar detected an incoming strike of over 100 aircraft, half of Nagumo's strength. In a fierce air battle, defending fighters prevented major damage to installations, obliging Nagumo to prepare for an unscheduled second raid. His force had already been located by Midway reconnaissance and was subject to sporadic but ineffective attack by island-based aircraft.

The attack aircraft held back by Nagumo had been fully armed with torpedo and armour-piercing bombs to meet a hoped-for intervention by the American navy. Now there was a requirement for a second strike against Midway and the machines were being rearmed with light-explosive bombs.

ABOVE: **SBD Dauntless dive-bombers ranged aboard the *Enterprise* at Midway. Two squadrons of these were carried, together with one of F4F Wildcat fighters and one of TBD Devastator torpedo-bombers.**

At this juncture, Japanese reconnaissance reported American warships to the north of the island. They might, it indicated, include a carrier. There were, in fact, three and they were about to launch their own strike against Nagumo's force.

Following anxious deliberation, the Japanese admiral decided that the warships had to be the priority target. Once again, his armourers unloaded bombs to rearm the aircraft with torpedoes. Below, ordnance unavoidably littered the hangars while, topside, the flight decks were cleared for the imminent return of the Midway strike.

LEFT: **Working with strong intelligence regarding Japanese intentions, Pearl Harbor-based Admiral Nimitz was able to ignore enemy feint movements and concentrate his forces to maximum advantage.**

ABOVE: **Bombed, torpedoed and listing badly, the *Yorktown* was abandoned. A day later, however, she was still afloat (as seen here with the destroyer *Gwin* standing by). Taken in tow, she fell victim finally to submarine torpedoes.**

> **"I felt bitter. I felt like swearing."**
> **Admiral Nagumo's Chief of Staff on losing four carriers at Midway, June 1942**

At this vulnerable point the American air strike arrived, its formations somewhat scattered. The torpedo-bombers suffered severe loss but their attack, although without result, drew down Nagumo's top cover. This left the following dive-bombers virtually unopposed and, within minutes, three Japanese carriers were fatally damaged.

The fourth ship of Nagumo's force, the *Hiryu*, put up her own dive-bomber force that followed the bearing taken by the jubilant, returning American fliers. This led it directly to the *Yorktown* which, in turn, was totally disabled by three bomb hits. (Still immobile, she was later despatched by two submarine torpedoes). *Yorktown*'s search aircraft had, however, already located the *Hiryu*, which was then destroyed by a dive-bomber force from the *Enterprise.*

Spruance remained in the area, his aircraft sinking the heavy cruiser *Mikuma* of the invasion force on June 6. He wisely held back, however, as the dispirited Yamamoto decided to abandon his operation.

The Japanese had suffered a major defeat despite the near presence of a substantial battle fleet that was powerless to change the course of the action. With Nagumo's group had been lost over 100 carrier-trained aircrew, continuing the haemorrhage of experienced personnel which the Japanese were never able to correct and which, ultimately, was to prove decisive.

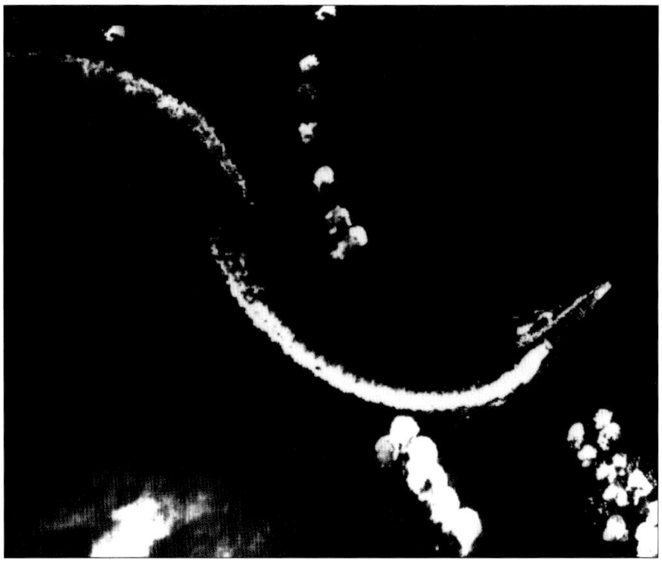

ABOVE: Nagumo's flagship *Akagi* is here seen manoeuvring violently to frustrate air attack. It availed her little for, in the words of her Flag Captain "we were unable to avoid the dive-bombers because we were so occupied in avoiding the torpedo attacks". BELOW: Disintegrating following a 127mm/5in hit from the *Yorktown*, a Nakajima B5N2 "Kate" sears a fiery trail to mark her passage. Note the torpedo falling away. BOTTOM: One of three Japanese bomb hits on the *Yorktown* exploded in the funnel, with the spectacular result shown here. It eventually made the island untenable and brought the ship to a standstill. Note the "not under control" balls.

ABOVE: The British escort carrier *Chaser*, seen from a catapulted Swordfish. Her mercantile origins are very evident in the hull and post-war, she was reconverted to a Dutch-flag general cargo ship. Note how the island is totally outboard of the flight deck edge. LEFT: Seen on her delivery voyage, the American CVE *Kwajalein* is carrying a deck-load of some seventy F4U Corsairs to Espiritu Santo in July 1944. All her short life was devoted to ferrying replacement aircraft. BOTTOM: An essential component to the US Navy's success in the Pacific was its adequate and highly efficient logistics service. Background to this scene of activity is the CVE *Casablanca*, name ship of a 50-strong class that was completed in under one year.

Escort carriers

Following the fall of continental Europe in 1940, Great Britain's very survival depended upon transatlantic convoys. By 1943, with Germany increasingly fighting on the back foot, the convoys were equally vital to the military build-up prior to the necessary invasion of Europe.

Throughout, the major threat to the convoys was the U-boat while, in the initial stages at least, British and Allied escorts were too few, their speed and endurance being too low. Fortunately, the workhorse of the German submarine service, the Type VII, although continuously improved, had a poor submerged performance, typically 1,287km/800 miles at four knots. It was sufficient, therefore, for an escort to keep a submarine submerged until her convoy had passed, for the submarine could not catch up again unless she hazarded herself by surfacing. The answer was a single patrol aircraft that could force down all U-boats in the convoy's vicinity.

Auxiliary to the U-boat was the Luftwaffe's long-range maritime aircraft, initially the Focke-Wulf Condor, which acquired a Zeppelin-like reputation for circling a convoy beyond gun range, transmitting its position, course, and speed to marauding submarines. As with the Zeppelin, the antidote was the high-performance fighter. History, having repeated itself, demanded a similar solution, aircraft carriers. Fleet carriers were too few and too valuable to be so employed except for specific operations, so the auxiliary carrier (officially "escort carriers" from August 1942) was reborn.

Both American and British navies had pre-war plans to convert specific large merchant vessels to auxiliary carriers (few of them were, in fact, so converted) but it was only when faced with the realities of convoy warfare in 1940 that both fleets produced prototype escort carriers based on freighter-type hulls of, typically, only 7,000 gross registered tons. Small though their flight decks were and meagre or non-existent their facilities, they could deploy Swordfish ASW and/or Martlet (F4F Wildcat) fighter aircraft. For suppression of U-boats or Condors they were immediately effective.

British yards concentrated on ship repair, so escort carriers (CVE) were series-built in dedicated American construction facilities. Successive classes grew in size and capability, the larger types being retained by the US Navy for the Pacific war. For convoy escort, those under the White Ensign increasingly deployed the F6F Hellcat and the TBF/TBM Avenger, the latter very effective in ASW, carrying bombs, depth charges and rocket projectiles.

Before the arrival of the CVE, U-boats in the so-called mid-Atlantic air gap were untroubled from the air except by the all-too-few specialist VLR (very long range) aircraft, typically Liberators of RAF Coastal Command. The escort carrier, however, could maintain near-continuous, radar-equipped air patrols, denying U-boats the freedom to work around a convoy on the surface, and effectively defeating their integrated "wolf-pack" tactics.

With increasing numbers, CVEs could be spared to form the core of dedicated hunter-killer groups. Armed with Ultra-based intelligence, these especially targeted the enemy's resupply submarines, used to extend the patrols of longer-range operational U-boats.

During the North African landings, at Salerno and, increasingly, in the Pacific, escort carriers took on the task of providing air cover during the assault, followed by close air support for those ashore. The main drawback to their effectiveness in these roles was their limited speed and, in windless conditions, particularly in the tropics, attrition in high-performance aircraft could be considerable. CVEs were also used widely in the endless task of ferrying replacement aircraft.

ABOVE: **Vast wartime programmes resulted in huge numbers of redundant warships post-war. Here, lines of nearly new escort carriers lay in Boston Naval Shipyard in April 1946 awaiting disposal. The nearest, CVE-67, was earmarked for transfer to the Royal Navy but, instead, entered service as the *Solomons.***

ABOVE: **Until early 1944, F4F Wildcats in Fleet Air Arm service were known as Martlets. Over 300 of these aircraft were acquired for the Royal Navy, giving its carriers a fighter at last equal to the enemy's shore-based machines.** LEFT: **By the close of the European war, the German fleet was largely neutralized. British fleet and escort carriers were thus increasingly able to target essential enemy seaborne supplies. Here, just days before the close of hostilities, aircraft from the CVEs *Queen*, *Searcher* and *Trumpeter* attack shipping near Narvik.**

LEFT: **Grumman Avengers on British service. Although designed to carry a 533mm/21in torpedo internally, the aircraft was more often employed by the Royal Navy in a bomber or anti-submarine role, carrying depth charges, bombs or rockets.**
BELOW AND BOTTOM: **Entering service in 1940, the Fairey Albacore was a logical refinement of the Swordfish, which it complemented rather than replaced. In flight, the Albacore showed a much less angular appearance than the Swordfish. Both could carry a 680kg/1,500lb bomb load, shown here as six 113kg/250lb bombs.**

Carrier aircraft development during World War II

British-designed Fleet Air Arm (FAA) aircraft continued to be hedged by requirements for multi-purpose capability, for at least two seats and for very low stall speeds. Fortunately, therefore, the existing and hopeless Blackburn Roc fighter was quickly superseded by the American-sourced Grumman F4F Wildcat. Serving as the Martlet it could, along with the shorter-ranged Seafire and Sea Hurricane, take on high performance enemy land-based fighters and bombers. The F4F, like its successor, the F6F Hellcat, was a dedicated fighter, not encumbered with a secondary function. From mid-1943, the magnificent Chance-Vought F4U Corsair was acquired to work in parallel as a fighter-bomber.

Contemporary two-seat fighter-reconnaissance aircraft were the Fairey Fulmar, then the Firefly. Attempts to utilize more powerful engines in a fighter/torpedo aircraft met failure in the Blackburn Firebrand.

Oft derided, but much respected, the Fairey Swordfish served throughout as a reconnaissance/torpedo aircraft and even, in the absence of fighters, as a dive-bomber. Its successor, the Albacore, was only ever regarded as a less-draughty alternative. From early 1943, the Fairey Barracuda was the FAA's choice dive/torpedo-bomber, serving alongside the excellent Grumman TBF/TBM Avenger, a combination ASW aircraft and torpedo-bomber.

For the US Navy, the single-role F4F and F6F were produced in what, by British standards, were prodigious numbers. With the large *Midway*-class carriers under construction, Grumman progressed to the twin-engined F7F Tigercat. Essentially a fighter-bomber, valuable in ground support, it entered service only in 1944 and would soon be displaced by jet aircraft.

Later than the Royal Navy, the Americans recognized the merits of the F4U Corsair, yet even these were surpassed by the remarkable Douglas AD-1 Skyraider, which entered service too late to make an impact on World War II.

Until 1943 the standard dive-bomber was the Douglas SBD Dauntless, it being superseded by the Curtiss SB2C Helldiver, capable of carrying a bomb load of up to 1,361kg/3,000lb.

The Japanese began the war with excellent aircraft of all three major categories. Although good performers, however, they had been designed close to their limits and were not

LEFT: **In Royal Naval service the Martlet/Wildcat was associated mainly with escort carriers where, despite the increasing availability of Hellcats after 1943, it served until the end of hostilities. Robust and reliable, it flew well and, in its six 12.7mm/0.5in machine-guns, packed an adequate punch. Note that deck crew were by now being colour-coded, flight decks being extremely noisy places.**

amenable to further improvement. Under war conditions their successors were too long in development and problem-prone in service, a situation exacerbated by the deteriorating quality of aircrew training.

Introduced in mid-1940, the standard naval fighter was the Mitsubishi A6M (Type O), known as the "Zeke", or "Zero". A light armament, no armour and a fragile airframe were here combined with good aerodynamics to produce a low-level fighter of superb manoeuvrability and exceptional range. It eventually met its match in the F6F, and its successor, the Mitsubishi J2M Raiden, came too late to be of use.

Also introduced in 1940, the Nakajima B5N2 (Type 97) "Kate" proved to be an excellent torpedo-bomber, directly derived from the B5N1. Again, however, its time in service saw it become ever more vulnerable to defences. Its eventual successor, the B6N Tenzan, proved to have only marginally better performance.

Last of the carrier trio, the Aichi D3A1 (Type 99) "Val" was a satisfactory dive-bomber which, in time, proved deficient in both speed and armament. Its intended replacement, the Yokosuka D4Y1 Suisei, proved to be the fastest carrier-based dive-bomber but was subject to continual technical problems and was difficult for poorly trained pilots to handle.

Ultimately, the Americans prevailed with greater numbers, better organization, and superior design. As importantly, they had plentiful and well-trained aircrew.

LEFT: **Introduced in 1943 as a replacement for the Douglas SBD Dauntless, the Curtiss SB2C Helldiver could deliver three 454kg/1,000lb bombs. Despite the amount of glazing, the crew comprised only pilot and observer/rear gunner.**
ABOVE: **Light and manoeuvrable, the Mitsubishi A6M "Zeke" was deadly in a one-on-one, low-level dogfight. It remained in service too long, however, and was defeated by American second-generation fighters employing manoeuvres and formations based on experience.**

The Battle of Santa Cruz

By October 1942, the island of Guadalcanal marked the southern limit of the Japanese advance. It was being bitterly contested, but the Americans held the initiative with their possession of the only airstrip, Henderson Field. The Japanese army was ordered to storm and take the airstrip on October 25, whereupon the Japanese fleet would close to facilitate the island's capture and, it was hoped, to engage the American carrier force that was providing deep cover.

Early on October 26, a shore-based PBY Catalina located and reported the waiting carrier *Zuikaku*, some 322km/200 miles north-west of the Santa Cruz islands. About the same distance to the south-east was Rear Admiral Thomas C. Kinkaid with the American carriers *Enterprise* and *Hornet*. At 05:00 hours these launched 16 dive-bombers on an armed reconnaissance and these, at 06:50 hours, found the smaller enemy carrier *Zuiho*. She, together with the *Shokaku* and *Zuikaku*, were operating in company, once again under the experienced Admiral Nagumo.

At 07:40 hours, two 227kg/500lb bombs wrecked the *Zuiho*'s flight deck, but she had already launched her contribution to Nagumo's opening strike of 65 aircraft. One of his reconnaissance aircraft had located Kinkaid at about 06:30 hours and the strike was away inside 40 minutes. A second strike, of 44 aircraft, was immediately prepared as back-up, using the two larger carriers.

TOP: The *Enterprise* with two of her SBDs. Although the dive-bombers badly damaged two enemy carriers at Santa Cruz, the ships survived. ABOVE: Under attack from dive-bombers and torpedo-bombers, simultaneously, the *Hornet* fights for her life.

Between 07:30 and 08:15 hours the *Enterprise* sent away 29 aircraft, the *Hornet* 44, which flew in three groups. En route, they encountered the Nagumo strike, both losing aircraft to the escorting fighters.

Awaiting the onslaught, both of Kinkaid's carriers had their escorts close in a tight, protective ring in order to concentrate defensive fire. Overhead were 38 F4Fs of the combat air patrol (CAP). This was poorly directed, and failed to intercept the first enemy wave at a safe range.

ABOVE: **The *Enterprise* (seen here) and the *Saratoga* were the only two pre-war American fleet carriers to survive hostilities.** LEFT: **Wreathed in the smoke from her own anti-aircraft weapons, the battleship *South Dakota* manoeuvres to avoid the attentions of enemy torpedo aircraft while covering the carrier *Enterprise*.** BELOW LEFT: **An American heavy cruiser, probably *Northampton*, threatened by a low-flying "Kate", whose torpedo is clearly visible.**

ABOVE: **Deck crews on the *Enterprise*, damaged by three bombs, work furiously to refuel, resupply and reposition her own aircraft and those from the stricken *Hornet*. Note the gun crew, closed-up in the foreground.**

At 09:00 hours the *Enterprise* was screened by a providential rain squall, so that the *Hornet* attracted the attack. First hit on the flight deck aft, she was then shaken by two near misses. A crippled aircraft clipped her funnel, crashed and penetrated her flight deck, then exploded. Two torpedoes from low-flying "Kates" hit her amidships. As the ship came to a halt, she took three further bombs and was crashed by another aircraft.

In return, the American dive-bombers caught up with the *Shokaku* in company with the already damaged *Zuiho*. Five 227kg/500lb bombs now put the larger carrier out of the action. Both, however, survived.

Nagumo's second blow, of 44 aircraft, concentrated on the yet undamaged *Enterprise.* Despite a doughty defence she took three bombs but succeeded in evading nine torpedoes.

Beyond Nagumo lurked a fourth Japanese carrier, the *Junyo*. Her own 29-plane strike hit the *Enterprise* group at 11:20 hours but succeeded only in damaging the escort. Unable to return to their carrier, *Hornet*'s aircraft landed either on the *Enterprise*, or flew to nearby Espiritu Santo.

Throughout the afternoon, crews battled to save the stricken *Hornet*, now under tow. Repeat small-scale formations from the *Zuikaku* and the *Junyo* hit her piecemeal with a further torpedo and two bombs. With the enemy fleet uncomfortably close, she could not be saved and was abandoned. Defying all efforts by her escort to sink her, her hulk had to be abandoned to the enemy, who sank her with torpedoes.

Although the Japanese lost other tonnage, all their carriers survived the Santa Cruz action. They had failed in their objective of seizing Guadalcanal, now of symbolic importance to both sides, but had claimed the valuable scalp of the *Hornet.* She had died hard, but her loss left the Americans desperately short of carriers.

Battle of the Philippine Sea

The year 1943 had transformed the situation in the Pacific, with a sequence of island-hopping Allied amphibious operations that gathered even more momentum in the following year. In June 1944, it was the turn of the Marianas, with the island of Saipan the objective.

By this time, too, the US Navy had established a powerful preponderance of aircraft carriers, nine *Essex*-class carriers (CVs) having been completed in parallel with nine *Independence*-class light carriers (CVLs).

Covering the amphibious fleet off Saipan was Admiral Raymond A. Spruance's Fifth Fleet, which included seven battleships, seven CVs and eight CVLs, deploying nearly 900 aircraft in total. With orders to destroy this armada "with one blow" was Vice-Admiral Ozawa Jisaburo's Mobile Fleet, whose five battleships were complemented by five fleet and four light carriers, with some 430 aircraft.

On June 18, Ozawa's fleet was crossing the Philippine Sea to attack Spruance from the west. Having aircraft of longer endurance, his plan was to stay beyond American range and to loose a series of air strikes that would hit the Fifth Fleet and fly on to Marianas airfields, there to refuel and rearm before raiding the Americans a second time in returning to their carriers.

Spruance's deputy, Vice Admiral Marc A. Mitscher had tactical control of the defence, his Fast Carrier Task Force (FT58) being divided into four task groups, typically of four carriers with a cruiser/destroyer escort.

Alerted to Ozawa's distant approach, Mitscher arranged his four groups in an "L" configuration with Vice Admiral Willis A. Lee's battleship task group TG.58.7 located in the angle.

TOP: **Riding at anchor at Majuro Atoll in the Marshalls, the Third/Fifth Fleet carriers are prominent. In the foreground is one of the distinctive *Independence*-class CVLs; in the distance is the veteran *Enterprise* and, beyond, *Essex*-class CVs.** ABOVE: **Desperately short of fuel, Fifth Fleet aviators are guided to their carriers by Admiral Mitscher famously burning their searchlights.**

All anti-aircraft guns were now supplied with proximity-fused ammunition and the carriers had, between them, 450 fighters. These were controlled by a fighter direction team experienced in meeting any combination of threat.

On June 19, between 10:00 and 15:00 hours, the Japanese hurled four waves of aircraft against this defence, which dissipated their efforts as a rock does a breaking sea. The first strike lost 42 aircraft from 69, the second 97 from 128. Those that went on to the island airfields found American intruder patrols overhead. The third wave became disorientated and, barely attacking, lost only 7 aircraft from 47, but the disastrous fourth lost 73 of 82. In the course of this massacre, Ozawa ran into an American submarine concentration, losing the carriers *Taiho* and *Shokaku*.

Having recovered about 100 aircraft Ozawa headed westward, followed by Spruance, less one carrier group. Finally sighting Ozawa at 15:40 hours on June 20, Mitscher launched 216 aircraft. These sank the carrier *Hiyo* and some tankers but, returning in darkness from maximum range, 80 aircraft ran out of fuel and ditched.

Ozawa had just 35 operational aircraft left but, mindful of his primary duty to protect the Saipan landings, Spruance did not press the pursuit to a conclusion, for which he attracted criticism.

Although the Japanese had lost three carriers, their greatest loss were the aircrew that manned the total of 426 aircraft destroyed. So overwhelming was Mitscher's success that his crews referred to it disparagingly as the "Marianas Turkey Shoot". In return, the Fifth Fleet suffered no losses in ships but 130 aircraft had been destroyed, together with a comparatively modest 76 aircrew.

The Americans were producing not only thousands of replacement aircraft but similar numbers of aircrew. The Japanese could nowhere near match this, and the situation was that their remaining carriers were effectively inoperable until more aircrew could be trained. This, the Americans had no intention of giving them time to do.

"Falling like plums."
Reference to Japanese aircraft in the action report of a picket destroyer at the Battle of the Philippine Sea, June 19, 1944

TOP: The *Essex*-class *Bunker Hill* suffers a near miss from an enemy aircraft (upper left) that has apparently had its tail shot off. A year later the carrier would be so damaged as to be beyond economical repair. ABOVE: An F6F Hellcat of the later, *Essex*-class *Yorktown* is readied for launch. Note that the pilot receives instructions by hand signal and by chalk board. BELOW LEFT: Having survived every major carrier battle to date the *Zuikaku* once again puts her faith in a smart use of the helm to come through. In the foreground, assisting in providing flak cover, is the rarely photographed cruiser *Oyodo.*

ABOVE: A distant view shows the *Shokaku* damaged and under concentrated attack. She survived this only to be destroyed by submarine torpedo.

Leyte Gulf

Just four months after the Battle of the Philippine Sea, the Americans landed on the island of Leyte in the Philippines themselves. The Japanese mustered their full available fleet in an all-out effort to dislodge them. As ever, their plan involved complex moves but in essence depended upon the invasion beaches being hit simultaneously by heavy surface warfare groups issuing from straits to the north and south.

Covering the American operation was the Third Fleet, which was the Fifth Fleet's title when under its alternative C-in-C, Admiral William F. Halsey. To prevent its intervention, Halsey was to be lured away by the irresistible bait of the remaining Japanese carriers which, in the near-absence of aircrew after the Philippine Sea debacle, were effectively useless. Vice Admiral Ozawa's mission, therefore, was to use his carrier group to trail its coat well to the north-east of the islands, attracting Halsey away to allow Vice Admirals Kurita and Nishimura to advance through the archipelago from the west.

Both the latter groups were detected early and, on October 24, 1944, subjected to prolonged air attack, Kurita by Mitscher's carriers, Nishimura by the lesser power of the Seventh Fleet, Vice Admiral Kinkaid's shore support force and land-based aircraft.

"It was like a puppy being smacked by a truck."
Officer of destroyer USS *Johnston* sunk by 356mm/14in salvo at the Battle of Samar, October 25, 1944

TOP: **The Battle of Samar. Taffy 3's escort carriers and their escort attempt concealment with funnel and chemical smoke as salvoes from Admiral Kurita's force fall among them. The carriers had been left uncovered once Admiral Halsey allowed himself to be enticed away by Ozawa's Northern Force.** ABOVE: **Alone on a wide sea; a pilot's view of his ship. A second aircraft, a Curtiss SB2C Helldiver, can be seen leaving the deck of this unnamed *Essex*-class ship.**

During the night of October 24–25, Nishimura's force was eliminated in a crushing gun and torpedo action in the Surigao Strait. However, the northern arm of the Japanese pincer advanced as planned.

The Japanese strategy had succeeded brilliantly, for Halsey, believing his pilots' reports that they had effectively destroyed Kurita's group, headed north after Ozawa, failing to leave behind even a precautionary covering force.

Ozawa could muster about a score of fighters, whereas Mitscher had about 500 aircraft of all types. Four carriers, *Zuikaku*, *Zuiho*, *Chiyoda* and *Chitose*, were easily destroyed during October 25, but annihilation of the whole group was prevented by urgent calls for Halsey's return.

LEFT: **Kamikazes continued their depredations following the main actions. On October 29, off Leyte, the CVL *Belleau Wood* suffered 92 fatalities and lost 12 aircraft in this spectacular incident.** BELOW: **Apparently armed with a 500kg/1,102lb bomb a kamikaze A6M "Zeke" readies for take-off in October 1944. As the aircraft made one-way trips, their range was effectively doubled.**

LEFT: **Admiral Halsey's legendary aggressive nature got the better of him at Leyte Gulf, only his national popularity saving him from censure. Admiral Fisher's dictum "Hit First, Hit Hard, Keep Hitting" has been paraphrased on this wartime poster.** BELOW: **Trailing defensive gun smoke, the *Zuikaku* and a *Terutsuki*-class destroyer are seen under attack at the Battle of Cape Engaño. Both the *Zuikaku* and the CVL *Chitose*, in the background, were sunk.**

Far to his south, the still-potent surface group of Kurita was, in the absence of the Third Fleet, heading southward down the coast of Samar. Between it and the vulnerable amphibious fleet lay only the unsuspecting escort carrier force of Rear Admiral Thomas L. Sprague. Attached to the Seventh Fleet, Sprague's 16 escort carriers (CVEs) were tasked mainly with close air support for forces ashore, but on the morning of October 25 they found themselves under fire from a force that included three battleships and six heavy cruisers.

One CVE is a useful unit but of limited potential. However, 16 CVEs together are much more formidable, deploying about 250 F4F Hellcats and 190 TBF/TBM Avengers. Organized in three groups, the force overcame its initial shock to hurl every available aircraft, armed or unarmed, against the apparently overwhelming force of Kurita. Their attacks gradually became more coordinated and were supported valiantly by Sprague's destroyer escort.

The scale and fury of Sprague's defence convinced Kurita that he was, after all, facing Mitscher's Third Fleet carriers and, after indecisive and largely ineffective action, he withdrew. During this, the Battle of Samar, the Americans lost two CVEs and three escorts, the Japanese three heavy cruisers. For the first time, the Americans were then subjected to organized kamikaze tactics by land-based enemy aircraft.

Halsey, having been recalled, arrived too late to intercept Kurita's retreat but the Leyte landings had been saved from interference by Sprague's action.

After Leyte Gulf, the Imperial Japanese Fleet ceased to be a factor that could influence the outcome of the Pacific War. It had been defeated, not in classic surface action but by the medium of carrier-based air power.

ABOVE: **Although a decade in development, the Douglas A3D Skywarrior did not enter service as a carrier-based, nuclear-capable bomber until 1956. Its size and weight was a convincing argument for larger carriers.** LEFT: **Considered cramped even by 1945 standards, the *Essex*-class carriers nonetheless continued to be valuable assets, and most were subjected to one or more modernizations. This is *Intrepid* (CV-11) in October 1968, having been fitted with a full angled deck.**

Post-war aircraft carrier developments

As World War II ended, the pressure to increase the size of carriers was as strong as ever. Bristling arrays of 40mm/1.57in and 20mm/0.79in anti-aircraft (AA) weapons had proved inadequate to stop the kamikaze which, often shredded and with the pilot dead, still had the momentum to follow a ballistic course to its target. The short-term solution was the adoption of the fast-firing 76.2mm/3in 70-calibre gun which could disintegrate the machine but this was only a stop-gap pending the introduction of the surface-to-air missile (SAM), with its associated bulky directors, launchers, storage and loading gear.

In 1945 the Cold War began and, during its earlier years, the prospects of nuclear war were very real. Before the introduction of the nuclear submarine (1952) and the nuclear-tipped Polaris intercontinental ballistic missile, or ICBM (1960), the most practical means of delivering a nuclear weapon into Soviet Russian heartland was the carrier-based bomber. Such aircraft were seriously large, the original being the 23,977kg/52,860lb North American AJ Savage, delivered from 1949. From 1956, this was superseded by the 37,195kg/82,000lb, jet-propelled Douglas A3D Skywarrior. Their spans, respectively, were 22.91m/75ft 2in and 22.1m/72ft 6in.

Even before the introduction of these monsters, with their increased demands on catapults and landing space, much thought was being devoted to the optimization of flight deck procedures, the importance of which had been demonstrated in the pre-1945 "deck-load" air strikes.

The revolutionary, but simple, answer was first proposed in August 1951. By angling the flight path from starboard quarter to port bow, aircraft would no longer be at risk in fouling the island. A large parking area was also created, starboard side

ABOVE: ***Ark Royal* (III)'s new steam catapult being proofed by a Westland Wyvern from a shore-based trials unit. The extra power of steam catapults enabled smaller carriers to launch heavier aircraft.**

forward, and any aircraft that jumped the arresters or crash barrier no longer ran on into the deck park. Indeed, the pilot could simply hit the throttle and go around again. This "angled deck" was also clear of the forward-mounted catapults, which could be used even while aircraft were landing-on.

First trials of the angled deck were conducted during 1951 by HMS *Triumph*, which had it simply painted on to her axial deck. Similar work with the *Midway* led the Americans in 1952 to make the first physical conversion, aboard the *Antietam*.

Existing hydro-pneumatic and cordite-powered catapults were also nearing their practical limits. The idea of using steam power had been proposed during the 1930s and this concept, allied to wartime German work on long, slotted cylinders, led to a prototype steam catapult being trialled aboard HMS *Perseus* in 1951. Again the US Navy quickly took up the idea, the USS *Hancock* being the first recipient of a steam catapult in 1954, this being capable of launching a 31,751kg/70,000lb aircraft at 200kph/124mph.

Introduced in 1954 was the third British innovation to be universally adopted. Faster approaches and the nose-up landing attitude of some aircraft made it difficult for pilots to see and act upon the signals of the Deck Landing Officer (DLO), or "Batman". The Mirror Landing Aid replaced the DLO with a stabilized assembly which reflected his own landing light back to a pilot in the approach path. Suitable mirror/lens arrangements made it possible to inform the pilot that his line was correct, not high or low, nor to one side.

The latter three innovations together revolutionized deck operations and in particular facilitated the emergence of the American "super carrier".

ABOVE: **The *Essex*-class *Lexington* (CV-16) seen in a late conversion to an attack carrier. With a full angled deck she could operate A-3 Skywarriors, A-4 Skyhawks and F-8 Crusaders. Prominent here are the Rotodomes of two early-warning E-2 Hawkeyes.**

LEFT: **A welcome sight to returning aviators, the Deck Landing Officer (DLO), otherwise the "Batman", used a standard range of signals (with personal variation depending upon the heat of the moment) to guide an aircraft to safe touchdown. Note the windbreak/sightscreen, the "steadier" and the communications number.** ABOVE: **The Mirror Landing Aid replaced the DLO. From the reflection of his landing lights a pilot could verify his altitude and height, while the two lateral rows of lights indicated his axial alignment.**

LEFT: For peacetime operation and under conditions of limited warfare the British Light Fleet Carrier proved to be flexible and economical. The Royal Navy could never maintain more than one off Korea. The *Ocean*, here seen with a deck-load of Sea Furies and Fireflies, arrived for her first tour in May 1951. BELOW: The Hawker Sea Fury was the last piston-engined fighter to be operated by the Fleet Air Arm. It also served in Korea aboard the Australian carrier *Sydney* and the example shown here is in Australian colours. BOTTOM: The *Boxer* (CV-21) was one of several *Essex*-class carriers to serve in Korea. Seen here largely as she was in 1945, before the days of angled decks, it is apparent how vulnerable the massed forward deck park was to any overshoot on the part of a landing aircraft.

Carriers in the Korean War

North Korea's invasion of the Republic of Korea (South Korea) on June 25, 1950, precipitated the first war to involve a coalition fighting under the United Nations (UN) flag. The war was primarily land-based and its course is not, therefore, relevant to this account. Korea, however, has an extensive coastline for its size, permitting warships to intervene effectively, particularly as the invaders possessed no reckonable navy.

Already in the theatre were the Japan-based US Seventh Fleet and the forces of the British C-in-C, Far East. Both services were now Cold War oriented and had run down their Far Eastern presence to token levels. Initially, the Americans there could muster little more than a carrier group, built around the solitary *Valley Forge* (CV-45). Even more thinly supported was the British "Light Fleet" carrier *Triumph*.

Greatly outnumbered, the forces ashore required close air support, with deeper incursions to hit strategic targets, particularly communications. Airfields for land-based aircraft were practically non-existent so that the US Air Force had to work from bases in Japan or Okinawa. Cross-service agreement made the Air Force responsible for strategic targeting, but post-war training had emphasized air combat, so that aircraft carriers assumed the tasking.

On July 3, 1950, the two carriers operated in concert for a first operation, although it was largely symbolic for the ships as aircraft and operating procedures differed markedly.

Post-war, the British Fleet Air Arm (FAA) had shifted back to mainly home-produced aircraft, the usual mix being Seafire fighters (later, Sea Fury) and Firefly strike aircraft. Larger and faster, the *Valley Forge* deployed the then standard American combination of Grumman F9F Panthers (the first navy jet-

Planeguard duty for British carriers off Korea was, for destroyers, a boring and repetitive chore. When so detailed, the Canadian destroyer *Athabaskan* signalled "St Luke, Chapter 22, Verse 42." This turned out to be "Father, if thou be willing, remove this cup from me; nevertheless, not my will, but thine be done."

LEFT: **Utilitarian in looks but a superlative performer, the Vought F4U Corsair was arguably the best-ever carrier-borne piston-engined fighter. Due to the propeller's enormous torque and the pilot's far-back location, the aircraft could provide anxious moments on landing.**

BELOW: **Winter off Korea is remembered without any great affection. Embalmed in a cheerless murk, the British "Light Fleet" *Theseus* has a non-flying day. Note the banded recognition markings and the rails for 27kg/60lb rocket projectiles on the nearest aircraft.**

propelled fighters to see combat), F4U Corsairs and AD Skyraiders. Both latter types were piston-engined but robust and versatile.

Despite experiences of World War II, the FAA still manifested relative matériel shortcomings. The Light Fleet could more economically deploy much the same air group as an armoured fleet carrier but proved to be too slow, cramped, and prone to weather damage and mechanical breakdown following extended tours on duty. Their aircraft, especially the Seafire, lacked the robustness of the Americans and, being of shorter range, were more limited in choice of targets. In contrast, the F4U and AD would stagger into the air hung about with bombs, rockets and napalm, yet still give four or more hours of close support.

Both navies operated helicopters for the first time in war. The Americans used the Sikorsky S-51 and S-55, the British only the former, known by them as the Dragonfly. Despite their limited performance, these early machines provided a new level of versatility, not least in their releasing an escort from the restricting duty of planeguard (i.e. to rescue pilots following overside flight deck accidents).

During the 37-odd months of the Korean War the Royal Navy was able to maintain just one Light Fleet on station at a time (and was pleased to accept Australia's offer of HMAS *Sydney* for one stint) for periods of up to seven months. Activity on-station was all-weather and unremitting, and the Light Fleets functioned so well because the enemy threat at sea was light to non-existent.

The US Navy's contribution was greater, building up to three, or even four, *Essex*-class carriers or light carriers (CVLs) on overlapping deployments, supported by escort carriers (CVEs) as available.

ABOVE: **Replenishment-at-sea (RAS) greatly extends the period that a warship can remain operational. Having simultaneously delivered to the carrier *Antietam* (CV-36) and the battleship *Wisconsin* (BB-64), the ammunition ship *Rainier* (AE-5) accelerates away.**

Carriers for sale

With the close of hostilities in 1945, the major powers all too quickly repolarized into East and West. The Cold War took grip, resulting by 1949 in the armed camps of the maritime-oriented North Atlantic Treaty Organization (NATO) and the predominantly military Warsaw Pact.

Greatly expanded during World War II, the navies of Britain and the United States were reluctant to dispose of their many, recently constructed capital ships, particularly the invaluable carriers, of which there had been too few to deter war.

Britain, impoverished by two major wars in thirty years, was in the grip of austerity yet still had obligations toward her remaining empire and NATO. The Naval Staff could justify two dozen and more "Light Fleet" or Intermediate carriers yet had not the funds to keep more than three or four in the active field. The large armoured fleet carriers, with their small aircraft capacity and large, expensive crews were thus phased out comparatively quickly. Surplus *Colossus*-class Light Fleets found their way into the Reserve Fleet trots, it being the intention of the Admiralty to complete the improved Majestics in slow time, releasing *Colossus*-class units for sale to offset the cost. With the rapid development of jet-propelled naval aircraft, however, the limitations of the Light Fleets in a shooting war became apparent and, with successive demands for fiscal cutbacks, ships of both classes were sold off, no Majestic ever serving in the Royal Navy.

TOP: The *Independence*-class carriers were, for the US Navy, a means of creating further flight decks with fleet speed. They were too limited for peacetime use, however, and all were discarded or transferred. The *Cabot* went to Spain as the *Dédalo*, seen here in later years with V/STOL fighters forward. ABOVE: With the British government failing to provide the maritime strength necessary to protect Far Eastern imperial interests during World War II, Australia strengthened her own fleet post-1945. Two British "Light Fleets" were acquired on a permanent basis, the *Melbourne* being seen here.

In accordance with the original plan, the *Colossus* herself went to France in 1946 as the *Arromanches*. In 1948 Australia took the *Terrible* (renamed *Sydney*) and Canada the *Magnificent*. Naval aviation appeared to have taken root when Australia then acquired the *Majestic* (renamed *Melbourne*) in

ABOVE: **The Indian carrier *Vikrant* (ex-HMS *Hercules*) enters Grand Harbour, Malta, her new ownership evident from a modified radar fit and the mix of British and French-sourced aircraft.** RIGHT: **Following a period on loan to the Australian Navy, the British *Colossus*-class *Vengeance* was sold to Brazil in 1956 as the *Minas Gerais*. Used primarily for ASW, she is shown carrying Grumman S-2G Trackers, Agusta-built SH-3A Sea Kings and two Aerospatiale UH-13 Ecureuils.**

1955 and Canada the *Powerful* (renamed *Bonaventure*) in 1957. Canada, however, abandoned carrier operation in 1970, and Australia in 1985. The French, having also acquired the light carriers (CVLs) *Lafayette* and *Bois Belleau* from the United States, went on to design and build their own carriers.

Having gained experience with Merchant Aircraft Carriers (MAC) and an escort carrier (CVE), the Dutch purchased the *Venerable* (renamed *Karel Doorman*) in 1948. However, she was sold-on to Argentina in 1969. Here she joined the ex-*Warrior*, which had gone south in 1958. Traditional rivalries had already seen Brazil acquire the *Vengeance* (renamed *Minas Gerais*) in 1960, although Chile never joined this "club".

A final Light Fleet transfer was that of the *Hercules* to India in 1961. Renamed *Vikrant*, she proved to be the foundation for a permanent air-arm as India developed into the regional naval power.

While smaller British carriers thus proved valuable to many other fleets worldwide, the equivalent American ships, the CVLs, were not, in general, sold out. Besides the aforementioned pair purchased by France only one more, the *Cabot*, went foreign, being acquired by Spain in 1967 and renamed *Dédalo.*

That so few fleets went on to develop permanent air arms demonstrates the high cost of conventional fixed-wing carrier operation, a situation hardly changed by the introduction of V/STOL and helicopters.

ABOVE: **Although the Korean War was fought in the jet age, the participating "Light Fleets" of the British and Australian navies were still limited to Fireflies and Sea Furies which, nevertheless, gave an excellent account of themselves. Here, a Firefly AS5 of 817 Squadron touches down on the *Sydney*.**

TOP: **Preliminary bombing of strategic targets, such as oil storage tanks in Port Said, sent a clear message to the Egyptians of the futility of prolonged resistance.** ABOVE: **Royal Marine Commandos wait on the flight deck of the *Theseus* as the ship's 11 Navy Whirlwinds operate a short shuttle service to shore.**

Suez

When, following years of nationalist agitation against foreign presence in Egypt, President Nasser nationalized the Suez Canal on July 26, 1956, it provoked strong Anglo-French reaction. A plan was concocted whereby Israel would attack Egypt, whereupon Britain and France would demand a ceasefire and a withdrawal of the warring forces to lines ten miles from either side of the canal. Anglo-French elements would then occupy key positions. Failing agreement on these points, Britain and France would intervene militarily.

During a long build-up period, Britain reinforced the Mediterranean Fleet and assembled her sadly run-down amphibious warfare vessels at Malta, the nearest "friendly" point with adequate facilities. The Royal Air Force was also reinforced on its Cypriot bases, although their distance from Egypt meant that fighter cover would be practicable only if carrier-based. To intimidate the Egyptians, there was little attempt at concealing concentrations and considerable international opposition to the plan resulted, notably in Britain and the United States.

The British assembled three jet-capable carriers (*Eagle*, *Albion* and *Bulwark*) with a mix of nearly 90 Sea Hawk ground attack fighters, Sea Venom all-weather strike fighters and turbo-prop Wyvern strike aircraft. The French carriers *Arromanches* and *Lafayette* added about 59 F4U Corsairs and TBF/TBM Avengers. None of these aircraft could match the performance of the Soviet-supplied MiG-15s of the Egyptian air force.

To the British force were added the Light Fleet carriers *Ocean* and *Theseus*. As training ships they were not equipped to operate aircraft, and their task would be to implement the strategy of "vertical envelopment", as being experimented with by the US Marine Corps. This involved the use of helicopters to

insert spearhead troops, in conjunction with parachute drops, ahead of a main amphibious assault. To transport and land men of 45 Commando, the *Ocean* embarked six Sycamores and six Whirlwinds of the joint army/navy experimental helicopter unit, and the *Theseus* eleven FAA Whirlwinds.

Israel duly attacked on the evening of October 29. Twenty-four hours later Nasser rejected the Anglo-French ultimatum and RAF bombing began, together with selective light naval bombardment. With Egyptian resistance continuing, the strike carriers hit airfields on November 1, wiping out all aircraft on the ground not already evacuated.

Stiffening resistance brought forward the amphibious landing and, in a change of plan, it was to be preceded by an Anglo-French parachute drop with the, as yet, untried helicopter landing down-graded to reserve. The carrier strikes continued, meanwhile, seeking out troop, supply, and vehicle concentrations. Their aircraft then switched to close support during and following the parachute assault of November 5. On the following morning, 40 and 42 Commando went ashore and, with some armoured assistance, moved into the outskirts of Port Said.

The beaches had too shallow a declivity to permit Tank Landing Ships (LSTs) to use them. Wharfage was essential, therefore, and the helicopter assault was thus directed at placing 45 Commando in a suitable position to secure the fishing harbour. Despite the total inadequacy of these early helicopters for the task in hand, over 400 men and 20 tons of equipment were put ashore in a continuous shuttle.

At midnight on the same day, international pressure enforced a ceasefire. The operation was wound down as United Nations forces assumed control, the canal remaining closed for the ensuing six months due to the necessity of salvaging the many Egyptian block-ships.

Militarily, the campaign was successful and the extemporized helicopter assault led directly to the conversion and building of "commando carriers".

ABOVE LEFT: **Seen from an inbound LST (Landing Ship, Tank) assault landing craft and the *Ocean*'s six Whirlwind helicopters ferry troops ashore at Port Said.**

ABOVE: **Alongside in Port Said the *Ocean*, with a French hospital ship beyond, is seen with the Whirlwind helicopters that successfully proved the principle of "vertical envelopment" in an opposed situation.**

RIGHT: **As three Whirlwinds head shorewards from the *Ocean*, a second wave awaits the signal to lift off. A Royal Marine officer can be seen sitting in the door, with his map case and cradling his submachine-gun.**

ABOVE: **Sea Hawk fighters provided very effective close support to ground forces during the Suez operation. Two 227kg/500lb bombs could be carried on underwing hardpoints and armourers are here seen "bombing up" on one of the British carriers.**

The impact of helicopters

TOP: **A string of *Bulwark*'s Westland Wessexes positions itself about its "spots" while a Type 82 frigate stands planeguard. Ships and helicopters have greatly influenced each other's design.** ABOVE: **Intended primarily for observation duties, the US Navy's Sikorsky HO3S-1 gave yeoman service during the Korean War and peacetime in the rapid rescue of ditched aviators, as of this F6F Hellcat.**

The advantages of aircraft supported by rotors rather than wings were apparent very early, the US Navy's first recorded interest being in 1916. At this stage, however, the concept was well ahead of practical reality and it would be the late 1930s before innovators such as Cierva, Focke-Achgelis and Sikorsky produced practical prototypes.

On May 13, 1940, the latter flew his VS-300 in free flight in a United States not yet involved in the European war. Circumstances, however, soon encouraged the helicopter's rapid development. By 1943, Sikorsky's VS-316 had become the world's first production model and, as the R-4, recorded a first under-weigh landing aboard the carrier *Bunker Hill* on May 7, 1943.

Still lacking power, early helicopters had little useful payload margin and, like early aircraft, were limited largely to observation. Extensive trials were conducted in flying from the deck of freighters to spot surfaced U-boats in the vicinity of convoys. Focke-Achgelis built wind-powered, man-carrying observation helicopters that could be assembled and towed behind surfaced U-boats.

Immediately post-war it was the R-4, as the Hoverfly I, which gave the British Fleet Air Arm (FAA) its first experience of rotor aircraft. Able both to hover and to cover large areas rapidly, there was obviously potential as an offensive anti-submarine warfare (ASW) platform. It needed little in the way of flight deck, as demonstrated in 1946 by a successful landing on a destroyer. With the emerging Cold War emphasizing ASW, a whole new line of development was instigated.

An early success was the Bell HTL/HUL of 1946, widely used as a utility aircraft, for casualty evacuation and for transfers between ships. In the following year, the British firm of Westland began to build Sikorsky designs under licence, its Dragonfly corresponding to the American S-51, which saw

considerable service in the Korean War. By now more reliable for use over water, helicopters appeared on aircraft carriers, their utility functions doubling with planeguard duty, thus releasing an escort ship for more appropriate employment.

Although the Sikorsky S-55 and S-58 (Westland's Whirlwind and Wessex) demonstrated considerable advances in capability during the 1950s and 1960s, they were too large to be considered for general ASW aboard flotilla ships.

For a frigate, the helicopter promised rapid, stand-off response to a submarine contact, but early machines such as the Westland Wasp were too small to carry the combined weight of sensors, weapons and data systems. The Americans sought to circumvent the problem by removing the crew, but the resulting Drone Anti-Submarine Helicopter (DASH) system was ahead of then-current technology, and proved unreliable.

The solution could lie only in either larger machines or in the operation of multiple smaller ones working as a team. This resulted in divergent development paths, with frigates being designed around ever-larger helicopters, ideally paired, and other aviation-capable ships such as the ASW helicopter carriers, commando carriers and amphibious warfare ships deploying them in numbers. The latter categories are also well able to fly ground attack helicopters such as the Apache, to compensate for their lack of the dedicated strike aircraft found aboard a conventional carrier. With their growing ability to operate V/STOL, and other novel forms of aircraft, such as the tilt-rotor V-22 Osprey, such ships are now blurring the once clear definition of what constitutes an "aircraft carrier".

TOP LEFT: **Carried for planeguard and utility duties, the Piasecki Vertol HUP-2 was also adapted for anti-submarine warfare. This picture, of Korean War vintage, shows an Essex class in near-original configuration and a McDonnell F2H Banshee.** ABOVE LEFT: **US naval interest in helicopters began late in 1943 with the acquisition (from the Army!) of 25 Sikorsky R-4Bs. Known in naval service as HNS-1s, they were used for pilot training.** ABOVE: **The latest British Iron Duke class of frigate is designed to carry a single anti-submarine Merlin in contrast to previous classes that had the advantage of carrying two of the smaller but less capable Westland Lynxes. The impact of the Merlin's size can be seen in the design of this frigate.** BELOW: **Carried typically aboard *Leander*-class frigates such as the *Aurora*, the Westland Wasp HAS.1 comprised the ship's major anti-submarine system. Note the two torpedoes carried by this machine, of 829 Squadron.**

Carrier jet aircraft developments

Although the first official all-jet landings were made soon after World War II (December 3, 1945, by a Sea Vampire on HMS *Ocean*, and July 21, 1946, by a McDonnell FH-1 Phantom I on USS *Franklin D. Roosevelt*) propeller-driven strike aircraft, at the peak of their development, remained in front-line service until after the Korean War (1950–53).

The first standard American jet carrier fighters were the McDonnell F2H Banshee and the F3H Demon. These would also have served alongside the big strategic bombers with augmented turboprop propulsion aboard the cancelled *United States* attack carrier (CVA-58).

The nuclear-capable attack bomber which actually entered service was the all-jet Douglas A3D (later A-3 Skywarrior), a 37,195kg/82,000lb aircraft which was introduced in 1957 and ended its time in reconnaissance and tanker roles. It operated from *Essex-* and *Midway*-class carriers as well as the giant Forrestal. Its supporting F3H Demons were superseded from 1962 by the outstanding F4H Phantom II, which acted both as fighter and as tactical strike aircraft.

The F4H (later F-4) served in tandem with the F8U (later F-8) Crusader, complementing an attack wing of "heavy" A-3s and "light" McDonnell Douglas A-4 Skyhawks. Already, the heavy investment required for developing new aircraft was forcing joint company projects, but the A-4 was particularly durable. By the late 1960s the offensive element was widened with a new medium attack aircraft, the Grumman A-6 Intruder, a 1,043kph/648mph twin-seat bomber that came also in tanker and electronic warfare variants.

TOP: **Dating from the early 1960s, the McDonnell Douglas F-4 Phantom was one of the best-ever carrier aircraft, being purchased also for the Royal Navy. This example has just been catapulted from the waist position aboard the American carrier *Independence* (CVA-62).** ABOVE: **In July 1950 the Grumman F9F Panther became the first Navy jet aircraft to see combat. Two Panthers are seen here on the catapults of the *Leyte* (CV-32). This *Essex*-class vessel is still in her original configuration: note the 127mm/5in gunhouses to the right.**

From 1973 the F-4 was gradually superseded by another superlative Grumman fighter, the twin-seat F-14 Tomcat, the first to feature variable wing geometry. Ten years later it was complemented by the small and lighter McDonnell Douglas F/A-18 Hornet, a multi-purpose machine.

During the Korean War, the smaller British carriers operated only piston-engined aircraft alongside their jet-equipped American allies. Nonetheless, there were by 1953 four Fleet Air Arm (FAA) squadrons flying the 950kph/590mph Supermarine Attacker, an interim jet fighter based on the RAF's Spiteful. It was quickly superseded by the successful but slower Hawker Sea Hawk, a single-seat ground attack fighter.

By the late 1950s, the Supermarine Scimitar had been introduced. Although multi-role and nuclear-capable, it represented a major improvement in performance and range, but at the cost of twice the weight. It flew alongside a new Blackburn design, the Buccaneer, a low-level nuclear-capable strike aircraft of exceptionally strong construction. It served until the Royal Navy's carrier force was controversially eliminated with the retirement of the *Ark Royal* (III) in 1978. For her final decade in service the *Ark Royal* had to operate American-sourced F-4 Phantoms, due to the cancellation of a new British fighter.

Where, owing to the limited numbers involved, the British government no longer considers domestically developed carrier aircraft a viable proposition and has purchased the American Joint Strike Fighter for its projected new carriers, the French have no such inhibitions. For their new carriers of the early 1960s they produced the durable Dassault Etendard fighter-bombers. More recently, for their confident new *Charles de Gaulle* carrier they have introduced the Dassault Rafale fighter, although production has been much delayed.

With the end of the Cold War, carrier-on-carrier actions have become only remote possibilities. The accent is now upon intervention and it may be assumed that future carrier aircraft will continue the priorities of air superiority and ground support, but with an increasing emphasis on stealth.

TOP: **On December 3, 1945 a converted deHavilland Vampire I made the first-ever landing by a pure jet aircraft aboard a carrier. Further strengthened, the aircraft went into limited production as the F.20 Sea Vampire. The carrier was the *Ocean*, a British "Light Fleet".** ABOVE: **Another Grumman success story was the F-14 Tomcat, the US Navy's first variable-geometry fighter. Designed to establish "air superiority", this example is carrying six Phoenix air-to-air missiles, long-range weapons capable of reaching beyond 180km/110 miles.**

ABOVE: **In various configurations, the Grumman A-6 Intruder has served in the US Navy long and well. Its primary role was as an attack bomber, in which service it could carry a 7,855kg/17,280lb bomb load.** LEFT: **Touchdown. The elegant McDonnell Douglas F/A-18 Hornet is a multi-role fighter flown by both Navy and Marine pilots. Capable of Mach 1.8 speed, it entered squadron service in 1983.**

Naval air power in Vietnam

TOP: **An LTV F-8 Crusader fighter awaits catapulting from the *Constellation* (CVA-64). Squadron deliveries for the aircraft were between 1957 and the late 1960s, with many earlier machines being successively modernized.**
ABOVE: **One result of the carrier operations off Vietnam was the life extension of the Douglas AD-1 Skyraider. By 1957 this highly versatile design was 12 years old. Universally known as the Spad, it is seen here in the A-1H single-seat low-level bombing version.**

During the early 1960s, Communist insurgents from North Vietnam were freely infiltrating neighbouring South Vietnam via the contiguous border with Laos. To buttress the South's democratic government, and to register overt disapproval, the United States maintained a naval presence offshore. Its frequent reconnaissance overflights and inshore incursions in pursuit of signal intelligence finally provoked North Vietnamese light forces to tangle with American destroyers in August 1964. A retaliatory two-carrier air strike opened what was to prove a ten-year, unwinnable conflict.

With widespread public approval, Congress authorized President Johnson "to take all necessary measures ... to prevent further aggression". Rapid reinforcement of two further carriers resulted in the immediate transfer of Chinese MiG jet fighters to bases around the North's capital, Hanoi.

As North Vietnamese activities continued unabated, the president, in December 1964, authorized a structured action plan. Air strikes against the Laotian infiltration routes would first warn Hanoi. If the hint were to be ignored, these would be extended to lines of communication inside North Vietnamese borders. A final escalation, if proved necessary, would target the North's airfields and fuel resources, while ports would be mined and blockaded. From the outset, however, for fear of Chinese or Soviet intervention, rules of engagement were suffocatingly constricting.

"Two SAMs, two o'clock low. Break right! Break right!"
One naval pilot warning another during a low-level incursion over North Vietnam

TOP: **As in Korea, air power in Vietnam was vested in the aircraft carrier. Here, the *Enterprise* (CVAN-65) is seen launching an air strike. The world's first nuclear-powered carrier, she is still in her original configuration.**
LEFT: **While it seemed improbable that the AD could ever be replaced by a jet-powered aircraft with similar versatility, McDonnell Douglas succeeded with the A-4 Skyhawk. It entered service in 1956 and, many variants later, was still giving a good account of itself in the 1982 Falklands War.** ABOVE: **The extensive mining of Haiphong and essential Vietnam waterways entailed, following cessation of hostilities, the massive Operation Endsweep. Aboard the *Inchon* (LPH-12) can be seen RH-53As, CH-53A Sea Stallions, re-equipped for mine clearing, June 1973.**

This was to be an aerial offensive, to be shared between the Seventh Air Force and carriers of Task Force 77 (TF77). To avoid overlap, North Vietnam and Laos were divided into target areas, or "route packages". Those "Up North" would be hit by carriers based on the so-called "Yankee Station", just south of Hainan Island, while those in Laos would receive attention from "Dixie Station" off the South Vietnamese coast.

The opening phases, "Barrel Roll" and "Steel Tiger", comprised armed reconnaissance missions over Laos. Their main result was that surface-to-air missile (SAM) sites began to appear. Because Soviet and Chinese technicians were likely to be involved, attacks during the vulnerable installation phase were banned.

SAMs, particularly the SA-2, became a major threat. They enforced high-speed, low-level flying, beneath radar coverage but within range of barrage fire from automatic weapons. This was far more deadly than enemy MiGs.

Yet having no effect, the American policy was extended to phase two in February 1965. This, code-named "Rolling Thunder", was a sustained bombing campaign of selected strategic targets, avoiding Hanoi and the principal port of Haiphong. For the first time, guided bombs were deployed against precision targets and cluster bombs on soft-skinned targets such as transport concentrations or dumps. On several occasions, the campaign was stood down to give the enemy an opportunity to negotiate. Each time, with no response, it was resumed with the "bomb line" extending ever nearer to the Chinese border and to ever more sensitive targets.

With the proliferation of SAM and associated flak sites, "Iron Hand", highly hazardous suppression strikes, had to be undertaken frequently.

In March 1972, the North Vietnamese army invaded the South in strength and now-President Nixon ordered Haiphong and strategic waterways to be mined. Over 11,000 were laid.

The ceasefire of January 1973 brought a generally unsatisfactory campaign to a close. TF77 carriers' contribution had been enormous, with 21 separate ships making a total of 86 deployments. A total of 859 aircraft were lost from all causes and some 620 aircrew were listed dead, missing or captured. Many more were saved by the crews of the Helicopter Combat Support Squadrons. In terms of operational experience, the campaign was invaluable.

Carrier battle groups and tactics

Even by the onset of World War II, it was realized, particularly by the Japanese and American navies, that the aircraft carrier was no longer just the handmaiden of the battle line but an offensive unit in her own right. Her independence was emphasized by her requirement even when equipped with catapults, to "chase the wind" to launch and recover her aircraft. Needing thus to leave the mutual security of the main group, she also needed her own dedicated escort.

As we have seen, the naval war in the Pacific became, increasingly, one of carriers seeking mutual destruction. Their mighty blows, each hoping to be the first to land, were aimed at each other, leaving the gun-armed fleet as bystander if not actively involved in the carrier's defence.

The carrier battle group became the choice tactical formation but, in the early days, when just two to four carriers were available, an admiral had to choose whether to concentrate them for maximum offensive effort or to disperse them for improved concealment and survivability. This could depend simply on the available number of escorts. The Japanese might place a small carrier group ahead in order to divert the initial strike from the major group following some distance behind.

A full deck-load strike was reckoned to stand a good chance of disabling an enemy through damaging her flight deck if not actually sinking her. This is reflected in the composition of air wings for, as the disparity in carrier strength grew ever more decisively in the American's favour, their proportion of fighters grew from 25 to 65 per cent.

With fifteen or more carriers at his disposal, Mitscher grouped them in threes and fours with common escort. Three of four Task Groups thus comprised a Task Force which was, effectively, the whole fleet less the fast battleships, to be used as a sort of mobile reserve.

TOP: **With no fixed-wing, conventional carriers remaining, the Royal Navy was reduced by the early 1980s to forming task groups around a V/STOL carrier. The *Invincible* is seen here in 1983, supported by a Type 12 frigate, two Leanders, a tanker and two multi-purpose store ships.** ABOVE: **Altogether a more formidable proposition, US Navy carrier battle groups, here centred on the *Kitty Hawk* (CVA-63), have the benefit of three-dimensional radar, airborne early warning and aircraft the equal of anything ashore. Trailing the group, unadvertised, will be a supporting nuclear submarine.**

At the time of the Battle of the Philippine Sea the sheer number of carriers, although deploying two-thirds fighters, could still muster an adequate offensive power while maintaining a defensive cover that simply overwhelmed the attackers.

ABOVE: **Despite post-World War II fleet rundown, Task Force 77, the US Navy's main presence off the Korean peninsula, was boosted with the arrival of new carriers. The *Philippine Sea* (CV-47) and another Essex class are visible over the deck park of the *Boxer* (CV-21).** LEFT: **Hard to believe, but 37 years separate the commissioning dates of the conventionally powered *Independence* (CV-62/1959) and the nuclear-powered *John C. Stennis* (CVN-74/1996). In terms of dimensions and aircraft capability, they differ little.** BELOW LEFT: **A lone Liberty ship stands silhouetted against the result of one of the post-war Bikini tests. The weight alone of the water in the column was sufficient to crush and swamp a conventional ship, and the possible use of tactical nuclear weapons required task groups to be more dispersed.** BELOW: **The atomic explosion to the left could easily encompass this 1955 task group. Here, the *Platte* (AO24) simultaneously refuels the *Essex*-class *Philippine Sea* (CV-47) and a *Fletcher*-class destroyer, the Watts DD-567.**

Radar now detected an incoming strike early enough for the escort, now often including a battleship, to close in a defensive ring. If the attackers escaped the Combat Air Patrol (CAP) at a distance, they then ran into a close-in barrage of proximity-fused ammunition.

The resulting attrition in Japanese aircrew led directly to the kamikaze. With a pilot no longer concerned for his survival, probability swung again in favour of the attacker. This strengthened arguments in favour of the larger carrier, supporting improved horizontal protection and a "beefed-up" armament, with greater inherent survivability.

By 1945, the big tactical groups of carriers and amphibious warfare craft dominated the Pacific war. A rethink was, however, in order with the advent of the Cold War and the very real possibility of nuclear weapon deployment. Even without particularly accurate delivery, its blast could sink or disable an entire group. Greater dispersion, although a solution, only increased the vulnerability to more likely conventional attack. This conundrum has a solution which must depend upon the nature of the threat at any specific time.

With the gradual diminishing of the number of available carriers, each becomes more significant. Her offensive capacity is eroded if her mission requires her also to deploy a credible anti-submarine component, in addition to airborne early warning, tankers, electronic warfare and utility aircraft. Accommodating all this, however, forces up the size of the carrier and, fortuitously, the larger the dimensions the greater the ability to absorb punishment while remaining operational.

The introduction of V/STOL

For a proven concept with obvious application, Vertical or Short Take-Off and Land (V/STOL) had a slow and difficult transition to naval use. It began with the Cold War assumption that the West's airfields and fixed aerial assets would be targeted and made unusable. Although some small supersonic aircraft could then still operate from suitable lengths of highway a V/STOL aircraft, using vectored thrust, could in theory require an area no larger than a tennis court. On this basis, the British Hawker company produced the prototype P.1127 (later "Kestrel") in 1960 and this, refined to the GR.1 version of the Harrier, entered RAF squadron service in October 1969.

In February 1966 an economy-driven Defence Review precipitated a run-down of British military presence "East of Suez", with the specious corollary that there would be no future role for aircraft carriers. The attack carrier CVA-01 was cancelled and no existing carrier would be replaced on its retirement. From the "mid-1970s" the Fleet Air Arm (FAA) would become all-helicopter.

Three years before, however, the prototype Kestrel had been demonstrated aboard the *Ark Royal* and, perhaps more significantly, had landed in 1966 aboard the commando carrier *Bulwark*, which could no longer handle conventional fixed-wing aircraft, deploying only helicopters.

Studies began for a ship combining the required facility for command and control with an area-defence SAM system and flight deck and accommodation for Sea King anti-submarine warfare (ASW) helicopters. The navy quietly extended the studies to complement the helicopters with V/STOL. Because the government could no longer consider a "carrier", the ship became a "command carrier", or "through-deck cruiser". Surprisingly, the project survived to the stage of the ordering, in 1973, of the ship that would become the *Invincible*.

It was fortunate that, in 1969, the less cash-strapped US Marine Corps had placed a substantial order for modified Harriers, maintaining the aircraft's high profile, but it was to be 1975 before studies were funded into what would become the Sea Harrier. The prototype made a first landing aboard the *Hermes* in November 1978 and entered FAA squadron service in good time to join the *Invincible*, completed in July 1980.

BOTTOM: In February 1963 the new Hawker P.1127, provisionally named the Kestrel, landed aboard the *Ark Royal* (III) and, four months later, operated from the commando carrier *Bulwark*. The long-term future of the Royal Navy's conventional carriers was already doubtful and the slow metamorphosis of the Kestrel to the Sea Harrier was one of great significance. BELOW: By its adoption of the aircraft, the United States Marine Corps rescued the Harrier from politically induced oblivion. This example gets airborne from the flight deck of the amphibious assault ship *Nassau* (LHA-4).

Britain's last fixed-wing carrier, *Ark Royal*, had paid off in 1978 but the *Invincible*, carrier-manqué, together with the *Hermes*, proved the continuing validity of fighter cover for the fleet during the Falklands War of 1982. Here, they operated RAF ground-attack Harriers alongside FAA fighter variants.

V/STOL (or, better, STOVL, for that is the preferred mode of operation) is no substitute for the high-performance, purpose-designed fighter. Its engine, designed to deliver sufficient vectored thrust to support the aircraft's weight, is over-large and uneconomical for long-duration cruising as, necessarily, is the aircraft's configuration.

Limited-performance fighters are, however, infinitely superior to no fighters at all, and the concept is therefore appealing to fleets that cannot afford the cost of developing and sustaining large conventional carriers. Importantly, as far as evolution is concerned, V/STOL has enabled a whole range of hybrid vessels, particularly in amphibious warfare, to deploy significant air defence and ground attack capability.

During the Falklands emergency of 1982 large roll-on, roll-off ships and container ships were also proven to be capable of carrying and, if necessary, deploying Harriers. The associated Arapaho project embraced the "containerization" of all related support services and the provision of sectioned, prefabricated take-off pads. Between them, V/STOL and rotor flight have effectively blurred the definition of what constitutes an "aircraft carrier", enabling specialist large assault ships to provide organic close air support for their operations.

ABOVE: **The need to justify the *Invincible* as a "through-deck cruiser" left her flight deck area significantly reduced by the Sea Dart area defence surface-to-air missile launcher and its guidance radars.** LEFT: **With the dissolution of the old Soviet Union, its armed forces suffered sudden reduction and a starvation of funding. The navy and its rapidly evolving conventional carrier capability were not spared and the future of such technologically advanced aircraft as the Yak-141 is far from certain.** BELOW LEFT: **The United Kingdom government is no longer willing to support an aviation industry capable of producing novel military aircraft. New aircraft are thus either the result of participation in international partnerships or are, like the F-35 Joint Strike Fighter, purchased directly.** BELOW: **The *Tarawa*-class amphibious assault ships are multi-purpose and, weighing-in at nearly 40,642 tonnes/40,000 tons full load, have a spacious flight deck capable easily of undertaking V/STOL operation. Here, a Marine Corps AV-8B leaves the *Belleau Wood* (LHA-3).**

Argument – large or small carriers?

Naval aviation, in the shape of Conventional Take-Off and Land (CTOL) carriers, is staggeringly expensive, yet it is abundantly clear that any fleet with pretensions to "blue water" capability cannot function without it. Once the decision is made to acquire carriers, however, battle is joined and argument rages – what represents the best value for money, one or two large vessels or several smaller? Here, the American experience is enlightening, for the US Navy has been building large carriers in an unbroken line of development for a half century. With almost each new acquisition, another but similar argument erupts and, again, the big ship has to be justified.

In studies, four sizes of carrier were considered: (1) a 91,444-tonne/90,000-ton or more carrier or nuclear carrier (CV/CVN); (2) a 40,642–60,963-tonne/40,000–60,000-ton carrier, vertical take-off and land (CVV), capable of operating conventional and vertical or short take-off and land (V/STOL) aircraft; (3) a 20,321–35,562-tonne/20,000–35,000-ton VSS capable of operating V/STOL in all modes; and (4) a less than 20,321-tonne/20,000-ton ship unclassified, capable of operating V/STOL only in the vertical mode.

Category (1) ships can include about nine types of aircraft in their inventory, and a reduction in size to category (2) would mean the loss of heavy long-range interceptors of the size of the F-14 Tomcat.

All else being equal, a 335m/1,099ft, 91,444-tonne/90,000-ton ship compared with a 275m/902ft, 50,802-tonne/50,000-ton vessel will have only 22 per cent greater dimensions yet 82 per cent more volume. Volume is the most critical parameter when designing to accommodate aircraft, magazine/fuel stowage and propulsion machinery.

Larger hulls are more easily driven. At 30 knots, a 91,444-tonne/90,000-ton vessel requires only one-third the horsepower per ton of a destroyer. A larger ship can continue to operate her aircraft in a higher sea state than a smaller one, while her overall accident rate is about half.

TOP: **Large carriers are more cost effective and more survivable, but are staggeringly expensive to acquire and maintain.** ABOVE: **Short take-off, vertical land (STOVL) is allied to small waterplane area, twin hull (SWATH) in this concept small carrier, designed to give a steady platform in poor weather.**

ABOVE: **This Thornycroft concept for a STOVL carrier dates from 1976, before ski-jumps were introduced. In comparison with a large carrier, her cost per ton would be significantly greater.** LEFT: **Concept drawings of STOVL fighter and airborne early warning AEW aircraft. The extra machinery weight, its complexity and its effects on aerodynamics will always mean that a STOVL aircraft will be an inferior performer compared with a conventional one.** BELOW: **An American concept for a small STOVL carrier. Note the landing spots aft and the angled take-off path which gives parking space forward of and abaft the island.** BOTTOM: **Resurrecting the old airship "skyhook" concept, this idea for a Harrier carrier entails the aircraft using excessive fuel in the hover mode. It also seems to be an awful lot of ship for very little aviation.**

In establishing sea superiority, the VSS compares badly with the CVV, its air wing being 30 against 50. Able to ship an anti-submarine warfare (ASW) component, the CVV could operate singly in all but a high-threat environment. In contrast, the VSS could operate singly in only low-threat situations and would require an ASW escort.

A 40,642-tonne/40,000-ton VSS could deploy about 30 aircraft, but a 20,321-tonne/20,000-ton ship only 8. Her capacity for self defence is low and she would require a capable, missile-armed escort. Ships of the smallest size would be able to operate V/STOL only in the uneconomical vertical take-off and land (VTOL) mode, reducing mission capability by nearly 50 per cent. The demands of a flight of, say, four aircraft would effectively squeeze out other roles for the ship.

Nuclear propulsion puts about 30 per cent more on the initial price of a ship but internal space thus saved enables her to stow four times as much aviation fuel and three times the ordnance. A nuclear ship can steam at high speed almost indefinitely and, while being free of tanker support herself, can offer limited fuel oil for her escorts. She has no smoke problem. Extra support costs appear to be of the order of three per cent.

In the face of enemy action, the larger carrier is the less vulnerable. Her extra size and compartmentalization enable her better to absorb penetration and shock. Her torpedo protection is more comprehensive and, if damaged, she has greater stability margins and more watertight subdivision. Not least, her extra aircraft make it less likely that she will be damaged in the first place. Initial cost per ton will be less but both air wing and through-life expenditure are considerable.

TOP: **Helicopters and V/STOL are complemented in the large assault ship, the one to give assault mobility, the other to provide limited ground support and fighter cover. This example is the *Nassau* (LHA-4).** ABOVE: **Even as the *Albion* and *Bulwark* proved the "commando carrier" concept for the Royal Navy, so did the *Essex*-class *Boxer* (CV-21) for the US Navy. Beyond landing most of her light anti-aircraft weapons, she appears little modified.**

Assault carriers

For amphibious warfare, the introduction of atomic weapons made speed of operation paramount, to clear the beach and to disperse shipping. The US Marine Corps (USMC) saw in the helicopter the means of, eventually, putting ashore a complete division but, in the early 1950s, the vision was ahead of the technology. Nonetheless, by 1956, Sikorsky had produced the HR25 helicopter, capable of lifting 20 equipped troops.

For the envisaged division, considerable sea transport would be required and the USMC requested the conversion of suitable reserve escort carriers (CVEs). Only one, however, was forthcoming, the *Thetis Bay* (CVE-90) emerging as the helicopter assault carrier CVHA-1 in July 1956 following limited modification for what was a temporary role.

In Britain these developments had been followed with interest and, in November 1956, the first such "vertical envelopment" operation was undertaken during the Suez intervention. Here, using an ad hoc collection of totally inadequate helicopters, two unconverted Light Fleet carriers took just 82 minutes to put ashore over 400 men and 23.4 tonnes/23 tons of stores at a selected point. This resulted in the conversion of the *Bulwark* and *Albion* to "commando carriers" in 1960 and 1962 respectively. In this role they could accommodate 750–900 troops and 16 helicopters.

The *Thetis Bay* could carry 22 helicopters but "spot" only five at a time. Exercises showed the unsuitability of CVEs for more elaborate conversion. Three *Essex*-class carriers (CVs) thus acted as interim assault carriers until a designed-to-task ship could be produced. This was the Amphibious Assault Helicopter Carrier (LPH) of which the *Iwo Jima* and six sisters were completed between August 1961 and June 1970. At 17,273 tonnes/17,000 tons they were smaller than the British pair yet could support a full marine battalion of 2,100 men together with 32 assorted helicopters. The Bulwarks did, however, carry four vehicle and personnel landing craft (LCVPs) under davits, allowing heavy material to be put ashore. Lacking these, the Iwo Jimas were limited to the 2,858kg/6,300lb that could be slung beneath a CH-46 helicopter.

The last of the class was fitted for a pair of LCVPs but the ships' general limitations for assault operations in poor weather resulted in a rethink. What emerged in 1976 to 1980 was the

ABOVE LEFT: **An unusual view of the after end of the *Nassau* (LHA-4's) flight deck, seen from flight control. It will be apparent that the superstructure, unlike the island of a conventional carrier, extends almost to the centreline.** ABOVE: **Sikorsky HUS-1/UH-34D Seahorses of US Marine Corps Squadron HMM-262 take off from an *Iwo Jima*-class LPH in the early 1960s during a training exercise.** LEFT: ***Nassau* participating in Desert Storm. Ships such as these, carrying 2,000 troops, their transport, helicopters and aircraft, are hugely versatile, yet represent an all-eggs-in-one-basket vulnerability.** BELOW: **LHAs are named after actions significant to US Marine Corps history. Here, the *Saipan* (LHA-2) has her communications antennas lowered for flight operations.**

25,401-tonne/25,000-ton *Tarawa*-class LHA (Amphibious Assault Ship), combining the floodable docking well and vehicle deck of an LPD (Landing Platform, Dock) with an LPH's hangar space and flight deck. These could accommodate four Landing Craft, Utility, (LCU) in the well, together with smaller landing craft under davits.

A Tarawa was soon involved in satisfactory operation of Marine Corps V/STOL Harriers, while under development at the time was the fast Landing Craft, Air Cushion (LCAC). Both were seen as having potential and the LHA was stretched to accommodate them.

The resulting Helicopter/Dock Landing Ship (LHD) of the Wasp class weighs in at over 28,449 tonnes/28,000 tons. Still designed around the transportation of a marine battalion, her well is dimensioned to accommodate three LCACs and her flight deck is strengthened for routine V/STOL operation. In addition, she was designed with an eye to conversion to anti-submarine warfare (ASW) duties.

With the demise of the commando carriers in the 1970s, Britain deployed only the *Hermes*, which doubled as an ASW carrier, and a pair of LPDs. However, with the catastrophic run-down of the British merchant fleet it is no longer possible to simply charter suitable ships in an emergency. Considerable investment has, therefore, been required to create a coherent assault squadron comprising the *Ocean,* the two Albions and four *Bay*-class auxiliaries, the latter fitted with wells.

Carriers in the Falklands War

When, in April 1982, the Royal Navy had urgently to form a task group to take an expeditionary force to reclaim the invaded Falkland Islands, only two carriers remained to it, neither capable of deploying high-performance, CTOL aircraft. These, the *Invincible* and *Hermes*, sailed on April 5 with a total of 20 Sea Harriers and 28 Sea King helicopters. Ahead lay the whole hostile Argentine air force with one carrier of its own.

Following regrouping of participating ships at Ascension Island the now-organized Carrier Task Group 317.8 (CTG 317.8) left for the 322km/200-mile Maritime Exclusion Zone declared about the islands. Further aircraft, including RAF ground-attack Harriers and troop-carrying Chinook helicopters, followed aboard roll-on, roll-off (ro-ro) merchantmen.

On April 25, with deceptive ease, a small Argentine garrison on South Georgia was persuaded to surrender, four ship's helicopters having sunk a submarine alongside their jetty.

On May 1, the task group entered the Argentine-declared exclusion zone and set about establishing sea superiority, opening with bombardments of selected targets. The carriers remained further to the north-east, their distance attracting endless ribaldry from those at the firing end. Nonetheless, the operation's success depended upon air cover and the loss of either carrier would have enforced its abandonment. This could not be risked.

"Every single Falklands casualty ... 778 is the official total – spent some part of his life in a helicopter."
Surgeon Cdr Rick Jolley, interview of October 24, 1989

TOP: **Despite furious fitting-out work at Wallsend, second-of-class *Illustrious* was completed just too late to participate in the Falklands War. She is seen here (nearest) taking over from the hard-worked *Invincible* in September 1982.**
ABOVE: **A Type 42's best defence against an Exocet was to deflect it by passive means. The *Sheffield* reacted too slowly to a clear warning of an approaching air-launched missile.**

The short-legged Sea Harriers had some local advantage as the enemy A-4 Skyhawks, Daggers and Mirages had to undertake a 1,127km/700-mile round trip, from the mainland, which left them no loiter time over the islands. The island-based Pucara ground-attack aircraft were no match for the British fighters.

One of three nuclear submarines in the area, HMS *Conqueror*, torpedoed and sank the Argentine cruiser *General Belgrano* on May 2. A controversial action, it was designed,

LEFT: **In 1982 the A-4 Skyhawk was already a 30-year-old design. Flown resolutely and boldly by Argentine pilots, however, it still caused the British considerable problems even though, in order to reach the islands, it had to fly with a reduced bomb load.** BELOW: **A Navy Sidewinder-armed Harrier rises from the *Hermes*' ski-jump.**

> **"You learn down here to weep silently in your cabin at man's folly." Rev Charles E. Stewart, Scottish Free Church chaplain to HMS *Hermes* at the Falklands**

successfully, to establish a clear moral ascendancy. The enemy fleet, including its carrier *25 de Mayo*, played no further part in the campaign.

The Argentine air force, on the other hand, redoubled its efforts. Ship after ship was hit by conventional low-level bombing. Many bombs fortunately failed to explode but ships were sunk and others severely damaged.

With a fair measure of sea control established, the army was put ashore on May 21 at San Carlos, nearly 97km/60 miles from its objective, the capital, Port Stanley.

Beyond the range of direct air attack, the enemy air force could reach the carriers only with their Super Etendard fighter-bombers flying to maximum range to release air-launched Exocet anti-ship missiles. In seeking to do this they failed, but succeeded in destroying the large ro-ro *Atlantic Conveyor*, together with her Chinook helicopters. The troops would now have to "yomp" to Port Stanley. This would take time, leaving the navy to hang on with minimal support, 12,875km/8,000 miles from home bases and in the depths of the Southern winter. It was with relief, therefore, that several brisk actions later, troops re-entered Port Stanley on June 14 enforcing the Argentine surrender.

A short but unpleasant war had cost about 1,000 lives, 75 per cent of them Argentine. From all causes, the British lost 10 V/STOL and 24 helicopters. About 100 Argentine aircraft are believed to have failed to return. Four Royal Navy ships, a fleet auxiliary, and a merchantman were sunk.

The Sea Harrier fighters were remarkably successful, as were their Sidewinder air-to-air missiles (AAMs). These aircraft flew over 1,400 defensive sorties, the RAF a further 150 in ground attack. Without the two aircraft carriers, however, they would not have been there.

ABOVE: **A view from *Hermes* of her "minder", the Sea Wolf-armed Type 22 frigate *Broadsword*. Type 22s were also paired with Sea Dart-armed Type 42s to form "missile traps".**

Directory of Aircraft Carriers

The overall total of true aircraft carriers, ships that conform to the treaty definition of being "designed for the specific and exclusive purpose of carrying aircraft … [and] so constructed that aircraft can be launched therefrom and landed thereon", is not large, not least because that same treaty limited their proliferation. Space here is, therefore, available to review the many other forms in which aviation has served the world's navies at sea. The following directory is comprehensive in including all conventional aircraft carriers and many of the peripheral vessels that appeared along the way – balloon and seaplane carriers, CAM and MAC ships, helicopter carriers and, latterly, helicopter/V/STOL-capable assault ships. All, in the widest sense, are aircraft carriers and form a rich variety. The directory explores the background to each design and the degree of its success in service. Comparison between ships or classes is facilitated by the addition of a standard data panel. Space considerations have required the grouping together of carriers with similar functions but varying characteristics. Data panels for such groupings logically refer to the most significant of the vessels treated.

LEFT: ***Invincible*. The V/STOL carrier now symbolizes the smaller navy. Fleets that can afford it will inevitably acquire large conventional carriers (CTOL), using V/STOL for special purposes.**

LEFT AND FAR LEFT: **Two views of the raised catapult installation aboard the *North Carolina* (CA-12) with a Curtiss pusher flying boat embarked and taking off. The boat-handling crane has been fitted with a lightweight extension to deal with the 1-ton aircraft. Designated AB-3, the "A" represented Curtiss, the "B" a flying boat and "3" the third in the series.**

BELOW LEFT: **Taken at Pensacola in 1917 this picture shows the *Huntington* (CA-5) putting aloft a rather under-inflated kite balloon. Note the long stabilizing tail on the balloon. Forward of the mainmast, to which a horizontal swinging derrick has been added, can be seen a Curtiss N-9H floatplane.**

North Carolina (CA-12)

Built: Newport News, Virginia
Commissioned: May 7, 1908
Displacement: 14,760 tonnes/14,500 tons (standard); 16,160 tonnes/15,870 tons (deep load)
Length: 152.9m/502ft (at waterline); 153.7m/504ft 5in (overall)
Beam: 22.2m/72ft 11in
Draught: 7.6m/25ft (mean)
Aircraft: Up to 5, no hangar
Armament: 4 x 254mm/10in, 16 x 152mm/6in and 22 x 76mm/3in guns
Machinery: 2 sets vertical triple expansion, 2 shafts
Power: 17,150kW/23,000ihp
Speed: 22 knots
Fuel: 2,000 tonnes/1,960 tons
Range: Not known
Armour: 76–127mm/3–5in (belt); 25–89mm/1–3.5in (deck)
Complement: 914 men

North Carolina (CA-12) and *Huntington* (CA-5)

US naval aviation effectively began in September 1910 with the nomination of Captain Washington Irving Chambers as contact for all bodies concerned with or interested in the exploitation of flying in a service context. Although his appointment initially lacked official status, Chamber's engineering expertise and enthusiasm quickly resulted in the Navy Department acting upon his recommendations. It was his cooperation with Glenn Curtiss that resulted in Eugene Ely's pioneering flights to and from ships in November 1910 and January 1911.

Chambers did not favour specialist "aviation ships", believing that an aircraft should be treated as just another piece of essential shipboard equipment. Consequently, he showed an early interest in catapults powered by the compressed air available in all ships equipped with torpedo tubes.

The first working catapult was demonstrated aboard a barge as early as November 1912, but considerable further work preceded the fitting of the first catapult aboard a warship in October 1915. This was to the armoured cruiser *North Carolina*, attached to the naval air station at Pensacola, Florida, USA.

Following a series of static firings, the first under-weigh launch, that of a Curtiss flying boat, was made in July 1916. The aircraft still had to be recovered from the water by crane. Although the structure was fixed, and impeded the ship's after turret, it was repeated in the cruisers *Seattle* (CA-1) and *Huntington* (CA-5). In June 1917, *Huntington* was also fitted for the deployment of a kite balloon, which by then was widely used in already combatant navies.

From the American declaration of war in April 1917 onwards, the ships operated in the North Atlantic, where weather conditions disappointingly dictated that the equipment had to be removed.

LEFT: Seen transitting the Panama Canal in about 1930 the *Langley* (CV-1) shows clearly her original hull with flight deck erected above. The aircraft appear to be a mix of Boeing F2B and F4B and, beyond them, can be made out the tips of the two fold-down funnels. ABOVE: Obsolete by the 1930s, the *Langley* was converted to a seaplane tender, and redesignated (AV-3). With her forward flight deck and structure removed she was able to ship large, knocked-down aircraft such as the Consolidated P2Y flying boats seen here.

Langley (CV-1)

When, in 1918, the British pioneer *Argus* demonstrated that wheeled aircraft could operate successfully from through-deck ships, the US Navy quickly acquired its own for experimental conversion. Although superficially an unlikely choice, the large (and slow) fleet collier *Jupiter* (AC.3) had favourable characteristics. Her bridge structure was located well forward, separated by six capacious cargo holds from the machinery spaces, which were sited aft. She was twin-screwed, and her boilers exhausted unusually through a pair of tall, sided funnels.

Renamed *Langley*, she retained her bridge structure, her near full-length wooden flight deck being carried over on a lofty steel framework. This was open beneath, permitting a pair of gantry cranes to serve any of the original holds. Of these, No.1 was dedicated to aviation fuel stowage and No.4 to the elevator that connected the former weather deck with the flight deck. In the remaining holds, aircraft were stowed in a knocked-down condition. The cranes would retrieve them for assembly, before their transfer by lift to the flight deck, which had two catapults.

The starboard-side uptakes were cross-connected to the port and exhausted through a single (later two) port-side funnel. This hinged downward during flight operations to leave an unobstructed flight deck.

Modified more than once, the *Langley*'s arrester system combined fore-and-aft with transverse wires. Known, from her odd appearance, as the "Covered Wagon", she entered service in 1922. The service learned much from her but, obsolete by 1936, she was converted to a seaplane tender. In February 1942 she was fatally damaged by Japanese aircraft off Java.

ABOVE: In her final configuration as a seaplane tender the *Langley* looked even more odd. Note the now-visible original bridge structure, the lack of structure below the flight deck and the fold-down funnels.

Langley (CV-1)

Built: Mare Island Dockyard, California
Commissioned (as carrier): March 22, 1920
Displacement: 11,250 tonnes/11,050 tons (standard); 14,970 tonnes 14,700 tons (deep load)
Length: 158.1m/519ft (at waterline); 165.2m/542ft 2in (overall)
Beam: 19.9m/65ft 4in
Draught: 5.0m/16ft 6in (standard); 6.7m/22ft (deep load)
Aircraft: About 33
Flight deck: 159.3 x 19.8m/523 x 65ft
Armament: 4 x 127mm/5in guns
Machinery: Turbo-electric, 3 boilers, 2 shafts
Power: 5,250kW/7,000shp
Speed: 14.5 knots
Fuel: 2,040 tonnes/2,000 tons
Range: 22,680km/12,250nm at 10 knots
Armour: None
Complement: 425 men

Lexington (CV-2) class

That the 11,177-tonne/11,000-ton, 14-knot *Langley* could be succeeded by the 36,578-tonne/36,000-ton, 33-knot *Lexington* in just five years was a dramatically ambitious step but, in proving successful, greatly facilitated the advance of naval aviation in the US Navy.

Stemming from the post-World War I naval race, the six 44,198-tonne/43,500-ton *Lexington*-class battle-cruisers were laid down in 1920–21. Sacrificed to the ensuing Washington Treaty, four were cancelled. Two hulls were retained, however, for conversion to aircraft carriers in accordance with treaty provisions. Their size greatly influenced the parameters written into treaty limitations.

Driven by consideration of speed the hull form was long and slender, with boiler spaces consuming a significant proportion. *Argus*-style ducted exhaust was out of the question, the necessary solution being a vast stack, some 24.4m/80ft in height and dwarfing the island proper.

For its day, the new hangar was large and capacious, supplemented by a deep hold for the storage of knocked-down aircraft. Reconstruction was slow, the ships not completing until 1927. Nonetheless, they anticipated later British practice in fully enclosing the hangar, the side plating extending right up to the flight deck, the main strength deck.

Cruisers were, at this time, considered a major threat to carriers, resulting in considerable vertical and horizontal protection as well as a substantial medium-calibre gun battery. At the Washington Conference the American delegation insisted on the 203mm/8in gun as the maximum allowable on a carrier. Only the *Lexington* (CV-2) and her sister, *Saratoga* (CV-3), were ever to carry such a battery. Its mass exacerbated the problems of asymmetric weight distribution while it was of doubtful value in being unable to fire across the flight deck. It was removed during 1940 in favour of the new dual-purpose 127mm/5in 38-calibre gun mounting (which only the *Saratoga* ever received).

ABOVE: The two Lexingtons were near-identical but, where both had their 203mm/8in turrets removed, only the *Saratoga* had 127mm/5in armament substituted. She is seen here in September 1942, listing at 9.5 degrees after a torpedo attack, while being repaired at Tongatapu in the Pacific.

BELOW: Because of the two ships' similarity, the *Saratoga* was marked by a broad vertical black stripe on the funnel until the loss of her sister. This image thus probably shows *Lexington* (CV-2) as completed, with 203mm/8in turrets and a narrow forward end to the flight deck.

Although widely criticized for consuming too great a proportion of the 137,166 tonnes/135,000 tons carrier tonnage permitted by treaty to the United States, the two ships convincingly demonstrated the superiority of the large carrier. Flight operations were facilitated by reduced ship motion and drier flight deck (notwithstanding higher transverse angular acceleration).

Above all, at a time when the exact role of the carrier was still being defined, the two proved the advantages of large air wings in the offensive strike role, an area also being explored by the Japanese.

During 1941, both ships were given widened flight decks forward but, as the *Lexington* was lost at the Coral Sea action in May 1942, only *Saratoga* received further modification. Her stability and survivability were enhanced by enlarged hull blisters and a lowering of the vast funnel casing. Larger blisters also increased the overall buoyancy to counteract the extra weight of years of additions and modifications, besides creating space for extra fuel oil. Asymmetry in the blisters also partially corrected the chronic problem of permanent list due to the island. The penalty was a quarter-knot loss in speed.

Worn out and obsolete, the ship was expended in 1946 at the Bikini atomic bomb trials.

LEFT: **The fine lines of the *Saratoga* (CV-3) are evident in this fine image. Note the unusual plan of the forward elevator and the line of palisades, or wind breaks, folded down. The 203mm/8in main battery is supported by twelve 127mm/5in weapons, disposed in groups of three in side pockets.** BELOW: **To the sorrow of many old "*Saras*", the *Saratoga*, shaken, patched and worn out by war, was expended as a "guinea pig" ship at the 1946 Bikini atom bomb tests.**

LEFT: **Considerable glamour was attached to naval aviation between the wars, a fact not lost on the recruitment service. The *Lexington*-class carrier is more obvious than the somewhat stylized aircraft, possibly Boeing F2Bs, flown from the *Saratoga* in the late 1920s.**

ABOVE: **The *Lexington* received a widened forward flight deck in her major 1936 refit. Note how the transition from the fine forward hull has resulted in distinctive knuckles. The stubby biplane fighter is a Grumman F2F, which flew from the ship until 1940.**

Lexington (CV-2) class

Built: *Lexington*, Bethlehem Steel, Fore River, commissioned December 14, 1927; *Saratoga*, New York Shipbuilding, Camden, commissioned November 16, 1927
Displacement: 39,450 tonnes/38,750 tons (standard); 48,500 tonnes/47,650 tons (deep load)
Length: 250m/822ft (bp); 270.5m/888ft (overall)
Beam: 32.1m/105ft 6in
Draught: 8.4m/27ft 6in (standard); 9.9m/32ft 6in (deep load)
Aircraft: About 80
Flight deck: 263.8 x 32.3m/866 x 106ft
Armament: 8 x 203mm/8in and 12 x 127mm/5in guns (as completed)
Machinery: Turbo-electric, 16 boilers, 4 shafts
Power: 134,300kW/180,000shp
Speed: 33 knots
Fuel: 2,700 tonnes/2,650 tons (original)
Range: 18,520km/10,000nm at 10 knots
Armour: 127–178mm/5–7in (vertical belt); 50mm/2in (deck)
Complement: 2,750 men

LEFT: **Despite the extreme fineness of her hull, the *Ranger* proved to be too slow. Note how far aft the flare is continued and the bulb, which can show maximum efficiency at only one speed.** ABOVE: ***Ranger* seen soon after her completion. Designed originally with no bridge structure, its late addition gave weight distribution problems. Note the sided sets of three fold-down funnels, an idea carried over from the *Langley*.**

Ranger (CV-4)

The first American carrier designed as such, the *Ranger* was considered unsuccessful, suffering from the limitations of both design inexperience and the restrictions imposed by the Washington Treaty.

Against the treaty global limit of 137,166 tonnes/135,000 tons carrier tonnage, the *Langley* was classed as "experimental" and did not count, but the giant Lexingtons consumed 33,530 tonnes/33,000 tons apiece. Only 70,107 tonnes/69,000 tons thus remained. American policy emphasized getting the maximum number of aircraft to sea and debate centred on whether this would be achieved best by building three ships, each of 23,369 tonnes/23,000 tons, four of 17,527 tonnes/17,250 tons or five of 14,021 tonnes/13,800 tons. Smaller vessels were considered ineffective.

The final choice of size needed to encompass the optimum number of existing and projected aircraft and how their accommodation and operation affected requirements for speed, protection, and armament, together with the dimensions and disposition of elevators.

Having experience only with the *Langley*, naval aviators insisted on a clear, obstruction-less flight deck. Current tactical doctrine also saw a carrier as an integral part of a force of scout cruisers but which, due to the speed and range of her aircraft, did not require to match their maximum speed. In terms of displacement tons per aircraft embarked, studies indicated that a flush-decked 14,021-tonne/13,800-ton ship of 29 knots offered the best compromise.

The ship that became the *Ranger* thus had her boiler spaces vulnerably concentrated and located well aft to minimize ducting and to allow exhaust via two groups of three small funnels, sided and capable of folding down during flight operations. The recently completed pair of British *Courageous*-class ships, however, resulted in a reassessment of the *Ranger* design that belatedly received a small island. This exacerbated a tight weight problem, which already demanded a very light construction. There was no armour built in and underwater protection was considered deficient. The hangar deck was the strength deck, the hangar being a light

LEFT: **The only American fleet carrier not to participate in the Pacific war, the *Ranger* nonetheless proved her worth during the North African landings in November 1942. She is seen here soon afterward in what appears to be Measure 12 camouflage and with enhanced anti-aircraft armament.** BELOW LEFT: **Seen here almost edge-on, the large antenna of the *Ranger*'s CXAM-1 long-range air search radar did nothing to solve her increasing topweight problems. With a "K-ship" blimp hovering above, three Grumman TBM/TBF Avengers are seen with bomb bay doors open.** BELOW: **A somewhat informal photograph shows SBD Dauntless dive-bombers aboard the *Ranger*, possibly during the North African operations. In company with just three escorts, *Ranger* contributed 496 of the 1,078 sorties flown over the American sector in four days.**

construction built on top and roofed by a wooden flight deck carried after the fashion of the *Langley*.

Recent exercises had highlighted the danger posed by the dive-bomber. This resulted in an armament biased to anti-aircraft warfare and an air wing that did not include torpedo aircraft, thus saving space on specialist facilities.

To achieve the required speed, the *Ranger* had fine lines but, in order to have a flight deck of useful width, had to adopt excessive flare. In poor conditions this made her wet, while her lack of length found her liable to pitch excessively in long-crested seas, a problem by no means unique.

Ranger's "open" hangar certainly pointed up advantages hitherto unsuspected but the design was too tight, necessitating that any catapult was fitted at hangar deck level, launching aircraft transversely through openings in the hangar walls, but eventually these were omitted as an economy measure.

Restricted to second-line duties during World War II, the ship went for disposal in 1947. She had been the only vessel of her size to be authorized and a rethink was obviously required for the definition of the ships that, similarly treaty-restricted, should succeed her.

Ranger (CV-4)

Built: Newport News, Virginia
Commissioned: June 4, 1934
Displacement: 14,021 tonns/13,800 tons (standard); 17,870 tonnes/17,550 tons (deep load)
Length: 222.4m/730ft (at waterline); 234.3m/769ft (overall)
Beam: 24.4m/80ft
Draught: 6m/19ft 8in (standard); 6.9m/22ft 6in (deep load)
Aircraft: About 76
Flight deck: 216 x 26.2m/709 x 86ft
Armament: 8 x 127mm/5in guns and 40 x 12.7mm/0.5in machine-guns (as completed)
Machinery: Geared steam turbines, 6 boilers, 2 shafts
Power: 39,900kW/53,500shp
Speed: 29 knots
Fuel: 1,595 tonnes/1,567 tons
Range: 18,520km/10,000nm at 15 knots
Armour: None
Complement: 2,140 men, including 760 aircrew

Yorktown class (CV-5, CV-6, CV-8)

All warship design is a compromise, and that of the Yorktowns shows the effects of both experience and the straitjacket of the Washington Treaty rules. By September 1931, when the small, one-off *Ranger* was laid down, the two Lexingtons had accumulated nearly eight ship-years of intensive fleet operations. Their speed margin over the battle fleet had enabled them to maintain station while flying had been continued in adverse conditions. This was largely a function of their great size, as were the large air wings that highlighted their offensive potential. It appeared that while a *Ranger*-sized carrier could satisfactorily augment a cruiser squadron in an opposed reconnaissance role, large carriers could enhance the striking power of the fleet itself. Even before the *Ranger* began to take shape it was therefore successfully argued that she should be followed by a pair of larger carriers.

Allowing for the *Ranger*'s planned displacement, the treaty permitted a further 55,883 tonnes/55,000 tons or so to the US Navy. This could conveniently be expended on a pair of 27,433-tonne/27,000-ton vessels, the largest ships permitted. Three ships were, however, more desirable.

The *Ranger* had been virtually unprotected but the new ships would be fitted with a horizontal armoured deck to counter the threat of dive-bombing, together with vertical protection to defeat cruiser gunfire. As the weight of the Lexingtons' 203mm/8in battery was prohibitive, the ubiquitous 127mm/5in was adopted, it having to be accepted that the carriers' defence would be vested in their escort and in their own aircraft (the latter concept not yet combat-proven).

TOP: The only survivor of the trio, the *Enterprise* (CV-6) came through despite participating in nearly every Pacific carrier battle. An interesting design point, visible here, is the widening of the flight deck towards the centre to compensate for the intrusion of the island structure. ABOVE: American carrier air wings were maximized by suspending knocked-down aircraft from the hangar deckhead. Here, an F4F is being assembled aboard the *Enterprise*, late in 1941.

Studies showed that this level of protection, together with improved anti-torpedo protection and a 32.5-knot speed could, in fact, be achieved within a 20,321-tonne/20,000-ton displacement. The resulting power requirement demanded a conventional funnel arrangement.

In the hope of circumventing flight deck damage, arrester wires were fitted at either end to permit aircraft recovery over the bow or stern. Two catapults permitted athwartships launch to either side from the hangar deck and three elevators were provided. Continuing the "open-hangar" concept, with deck park, an impressive total of 96 aircraft could be accommodated. An additional bonus was the ability to warm-up aircraft engines in the hangar before transfer to the flight deck.

Two ships, *Yorktown* (CV-5) and *Enterprise* (CV-6), were laid down in 1934. Their near-sister, *Hornet* (CV-8), followed only in late 1939, when war in Europe was a reality. Treaty restrictions now abandoned, she could be built quickly with existing drawings.

The trio saw intensive service in the Pacific, notably at the critical battle of Midway in June 1942, at which the *Yorktown* was lost. The *Hornet*, which had launched the famous "Doolittle Raid" on Tokyo, was sunk at Santa Cruz in October 1942. The *Enterprise* survived and was scrapped as late as 1958. She had two major upgrades in anti-aircraft armament which in combination with much other accumulated weight obliged her to be bulged (or "blistered") to increase displacement.

ABOVE: **With what appears to be an F4U Corsair flying directly above, this ship has to be the *Enterprise*, for the aircraft did not enter carrier service with the US Navy until 1944, by which time *Hornet* and *Yorktown* had been sunk.** RIGHT: **This picture shows well the "open" construction typical of American carriers. The hull is flared over its entire length in order to maximize flight deck width.**

ABOVE: ***Enterprise*, probably during running trials in 1937 or early 1938. The large stack was necessary to receive uptakes from three boiler rooms. Note the shutter doors enclosing side openings to the hangar.** RIGHT: **A group of Avengers warms up on deck as the deck crew await another coming up on the elevator. Note the depth of the deck beams, necessary to maintain stiffness in a large open structure.**

Yorktown class (CV-5, CV-6, CV-8)

Class: *Yorktown*, Newport News, Virginia, commissioned September 30, 1937; *Enterprise*, Newport News, Virginia, commissioned May 12, 1938; *Hornet*, Newport News, Virginia, commissioned October 20, 1941

Displacement: 20,240 tonnes/19,875 tons (standard); 25,960 tonnes/25,500 tons (deep load)

Length: 234.6m/770ft (at waterline); 246.6m/809ft 6in (overall)

Beam: 25.4m/83ft 3in

Draught: 6.5m/21ft 6in (standard); 7.9m/26ft (deep load)

Aircraft: About 96

Flight deck: 244.3 x 26.2m/802 x 86ft

Armament: 8 x 127mm/5in and 16 x 28mm/1.1in guns, 24 x 12.7mm/0.5in machine-guns (as completed)

Machinery: Geared steam turbines, 9 boilers, 4 shafts

Power: 89,500kW/120,000shp

Speed: 32.5 knots

Fuel: 4,380 tonnes/4,300 tons,

Range: 22,220km/12,000nm at 15 knots

Armour: 64–102mm/2.5–4in (vertical belt); 38mm/1.5in (deck)

Complement: 1,875 men

Wasp (CV-7)

As only about 15,241 tonnes/15,000 tons of treaty-permitted carrier tonnage remained to the Americans once the size of the Yorktowns had been decided, a second small carrier was inevitable. Although considerable design experience had been accumulated by this time, it was not yet operationally proven, as can be judged through the following summary of key dates:

	Laid down	Launched	Commissioned
Ranger **(CV-4)**	September 1931	February 1933	June 1934
Yorktown **(CV-5)**	May 1934	April 1936	September 1937
Enterprise **(CV-6)**	July 1934	October 1936	May 1938

The order for what became the *Wasp* (CV-7) was placed in September 1935. At this time, the Yorktowns were not even in the water and even though the *Ranger* had seen a year or more of service, the design process for the *Wasp* had preceded her completion. The *Ranger* had already pointed-up some of the deficiencies of small carriers, but further (albeit unproven) design work had highlighted desirable features possible in a larger hull. Inevitably, therefore, the *Wasp* would emerge as a small ship overburdened with large-ship features.

The policy of maximum-sized air wings resulted in hangar and aviation-related facilities dominating the ship above hangar deck level, leaving space below it at a premium. To keep to the mandatory displacement, major dimensions were tightly circumscribed, leaving little volume for machinery. Boiler rooms were thus vulnerably grouped, and sandwiched between two engine rooms.

TOP: **Superficially similar to the Yorktowns, the one-off *Wasp* was significantly smaller and can be identified easily through her far taller funnel casing. Above the attendant tug the hangar side door is half open.** ABOVE: **Initially restricted by her size to the Atlantic Fleet, the *Wasp* assisted during the siege of Malta in ferrying in two loads of British Spitfires. Although lacking folding wings, these fitted comfortably on to an elevator.**

ABOVE: **Like the preceding Yorktowns, the *Wasp*'s flight deck extended further on the port side in way of the island structure, a feature clearly visible in this overhead shot.**

ABOVE: **Personnel of an escorting British ship watch as the *Wasp* prepares to fly off a deck-load of Spitfires for Malta in April or May 1942. Shortly after, she sailed for the Pacific.** BELOW: **Struck by three submarine torpedoes as she was engaged in refuelling aircraft, the *Wasp* was rapidly engulfed in uncontrollable fire and explosion.**

With the *Ranger* already overweight and the *Yorktown* realistically expected to be so, there was immense pressure on the *Wasp's* designers to cut weight. The light scantlings of flight deck and supporting structure were again adopted. To increase deck area and to counteract the offset load imposed by the island without using weight-consuming permanent ballast, both flight deck and hull beneath were asymmetrically extended on the port side.

Although the hangar was generous in proportion to ship size, the air wing was boosted, as in the *Ranger*, by the omission of larger, torpedo-carrying aircraft. To optimize launch rates, upon which American operational doctrine placed a premium, and without the multiple flying-off decks then favoured by the British and Japanese, four catapults were fitted, two forward on the flight deck and two athwartships at hangar deck level. The third elevator was of a skeletal, weight-saving deck-edge design, the first of its type.

Further, unseen economy in weight resulted in a deficiency in anti-torpedo protection and a side belt that was more nominal than actual. Despite considerable pressure, however, the *Wasp*'s armament was kept in line with that of her larger contemporaries, but planned later upgrades of her ineffective pre-war automatic weapons were not carried out before her loss.

Considered too small and too slow, the *Wasp* joined the *Ranger* in the Atlantic early in the war. She rendered valuable assistance to the British in running two loads of fighters into Malta during the siege. Then sent to the Pacific, she was hit by three submarine torpedoes in September 1942. Like the *Lexington* before her, uncontrollable aviation fuel vapour explosions destroyed her.

Wasp (CV-7)

Built: Bethlehem, Quincy
Commissioned: April 25, 1940
Displacement: 14,970 tonnes/14,700 tons (standard); 19,100 tonnes/18,750 tons (deep load)
Length: 209.9m/689ft (at waterline); 225.8m/741ft 4in (overall)
Beam: 24.6m/80ft 8in
Draught: 6.1m/20ft (standard); 7.5m/24ft 6in (deep load)
Aircraft: About 74
Flight deck: 221.5 x 28.3m/727 x 93ft
Armament: 8 x 127mm/5in and 16 x 28mm/1.1in guns, 24 x 12.7mm/0.5in machine-guns
Machinery: Geared steam turbines, 6 boilers, 2 shafts
Power: 52,200kW/70,000shp
Speed: 29.5 knots
Fuel: 3,410 tonnes/3,350 tons,
Range: 22,220km/12,000nm at 15 knots
Armour: 16–19mm/0.63–0.75in (vertical belt); 32mm/1.25in (deck)
Complement: 2,165 men

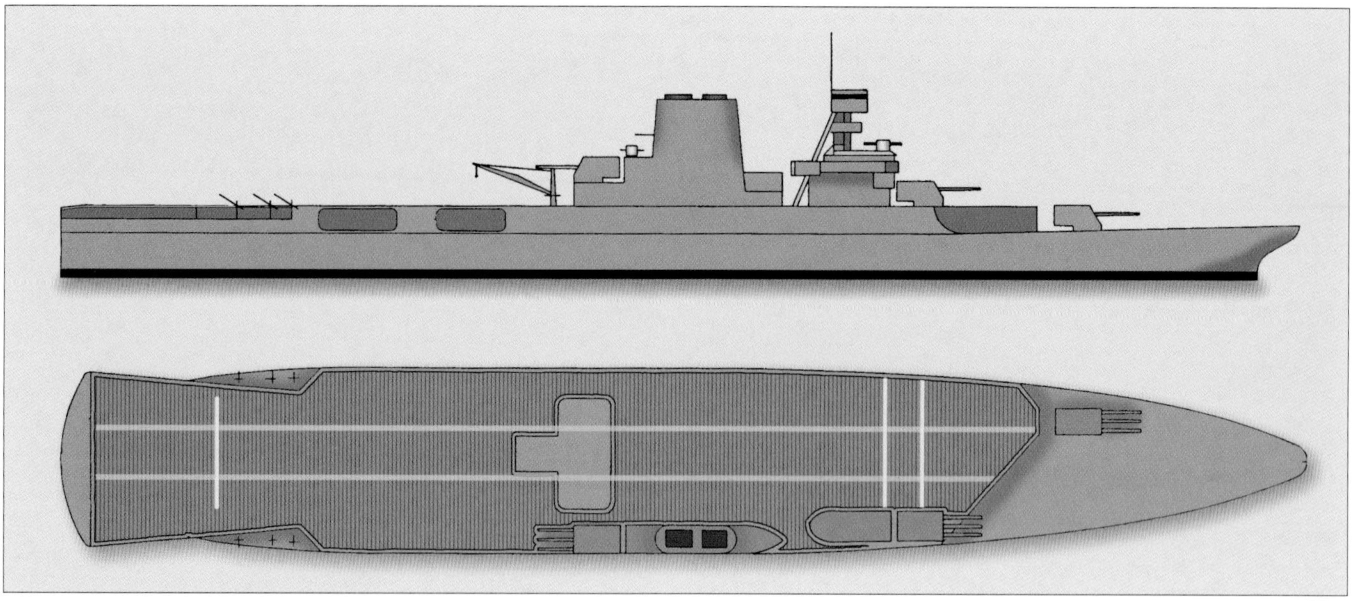

Hybrid carrier studies

The essential features of an aircraft carrier have now been consistent for so long that it requires an effort of mind to visualize the situation at the time of the Washington Conference.

Aviation at sea was still a new concept and although the Royal Navy was, by virtue of being at the "sharp-end", well ahead in the associated technologies, no immutable ground rules had been laid.

True the British had already produced the world's first flush-decked carrier in the *Argus*, mainly as a platform for the deployment of torpedo-carrying aircraft, but they remained hostage to the traditional "big gun" lobby, which viewed aviation in a supporting role for the battle fleet.

The idea of heavy gun armament was still firmly entrenched, and it was not yet established whether carriers should be large or small, heavily armed and protected, or "soft", depending upon their escorts and aircraft for protection, a role in which aircraft were not yet proven.

Arguments persisted in all major fleets with respect to a carrier's exact role and, therefore, form. It occupied the US Navy for a decade, resulting in a series of design studies for ships with a flight deck overlaying a hangar and also a cruiser's armament and (nearly) a cruiser speed.

The two requirements co-existed awkwardly. Eight or nine 203mm/8in guns required three or four large turrets. Satisfactory firing arcs for these demanded either a cruiser-style forward end with a truncated flight deck and hangar, or to site the armament at a sufficient height to safely over-fire the flight deck without causing blast damage.

The idea that a carrier could successfully fight off a "treaty" cruiser bent on destroying her persisted even to the point where such a ship was considered as an alternative contender to the design that became the *Yorktown*. The overriding argument, however, was that a carrier's principal weapon was her air wing. This could not operate with a damaged flight deck and therefore a carrier had no business engaging in a gun action with a heavy cruiser. A typical hypothetical design was proposed with the parameters that are shown in the specification box.

ABOVE: **In a single hull, the marriage of air operations and a heavy surface armament was doomed to incompatibility. Each of these major requirements interferes catastrophically with the other.**

BELOW: **Ideas abounded for adding aviation to cruisers to improve their efficiency in the particular roles of reconnaissance in force and in commerce raiding. This design would have experienced weight distribution problems.**

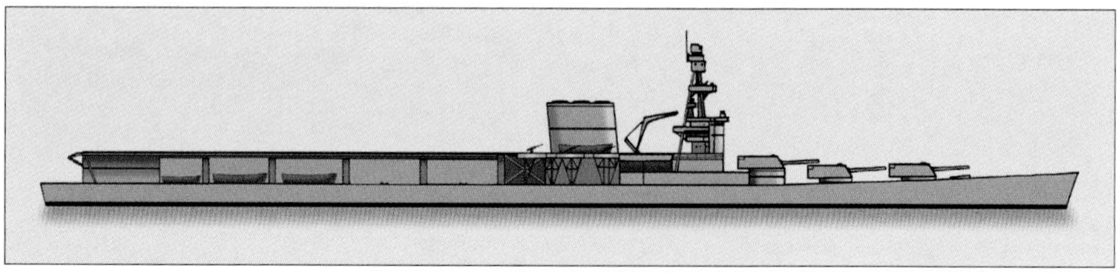

Hybrid carrier

Displacement: 27,490 tonnes/27,000 tons (standard)
Length: 233.4m/766ft (at waterline)
Beam: 27.4m/90ft
Draught: 8.3m/27ft 1in (mean)
Aircraft: About 75
Flight deck: Not known
Armament: 8 x 203mm/8in (4 double) and 12 x 127mm/5in (12 single) guns
Machinery: Turbo-electric, 4 shafts
Power: 104,450kW/140,000shp
Speed: 32.5 knots
Fuel: Not known
Range: 18,520km/10,000nm at 10 knots
Armour: 76mm/3in (vertical belt)
Complement: Not known

Long Island (AVG-1), *Wolverine* (IX-64) and *Sable* (IX-81)

Proposals for the conversion of smaller mercantile hulls to auxiliary carriers appear to have originated independently in the United States and Great Britain. Where the latter, however, saw their usefulness in convoy protection, the former viewed them as a general force multiplier, with specific roles in aircrew training and in aircraft transport.

The enormous American aircrew training programme proved to be critical to wartime success, and great credit is due to two unsung "heroines", *Sable* and *Wolverine*, which trained thousands in deck landings in the safe waters of the Great Lakes. Both had been converted from multi-decked paddle-propelled passenger vessels. They had few facilities beyond large flight decks, and aircraft flew from shore bases to exercise on them.

The first American escort carrier, *Long Island*, commissioned in June 1941, the same month as the pioneering British *Audacity*, and was converted from an existing C-3 merchant ship. She had much in common with the still-extant *Langley*, retaining her original superstructure block with the flight deck erected above it on a high, open-sided framework. Plated-in only abaft the late superstructure, the space encompassed a small hangar equipped with a single elevator. There was no island and, as originally built, the flight deck was only 110.3m/362ft in length, long enough to land observation aircraft on, which would need to be launched by the forward-mounted catapult.

Experience soon highlighted shortcomings and subsequent upgrades included lengthening the flight deck, relocating the catapult, and improving the sub-division and the protection for the magazines.

Although the *Long Island* design was quickly improved upon, she formed the basis of the first group of escort carriers to be supplied to the British.

Long Island (AVG-1)

Built: Sun Shipbuilding
Converted: Newport News
Commissioned: June 2, 1941
Gross tonnage: 7,880 tons
Displacement: 14,250 tonnes/14,000 tons (deep load)
Length: 141.7m/465ft (at waterline), 149.9.m/ 492ft (overall)
Beam: 21.2m/69ft 6in
Draught: 7.8m/25ft 6in (mean)
Aircraft: 16
Flight deck: 127.3 x 21.6m/418ft x 70ft 10in
Armament: 1 x 127mm/5in and 2 x 76mm/3in guns, 4 x 12.7mm/0.5in machine-guns
Machinery: Busch-Sulzer 7-cylinder diesel engine, 1 shaft
Power: 6,340kW/8,500bhp
Speed: 16 knots
Fuel: 1,415 tonnes/1,390 tons
Range: Not known
Armour: None
Complement: 410 men

BELOW: **Seen later in the war, when she operated as an aircraft transport, the *Long Island* still shows her early features, particularly the short hangar right aft, the open underdeck forward structure and the total lack of superstructure. The lightly loaded mercantile hull required large quantities of ballast to immerse the single propeller and to impart a stable ship movement.**

Bogue-class escort carriers

American experience with the *Long Island*, and British with the very similar *Archer*, quickly exposed shortcomings in the conversions having been too austere. The flight deck was shorter than it needed to be, and the volume below it under-utilized for hangar space. Although deliberately chosen for ease of rearrangement of exhaust ducting, the diesel propulsion proved to be unreliable.

A specific American complaint was that their ships were too slow. Merchant ships are built for long-haul service, requiring that their most economical speed be maintained. A C-3, typically, was thus designed to run at 16.5 knots at a deadweight of 12,193–13,209 tonnes/12,000–13,000 tons. As carriers, they displaced nothing like this figure and, unless comprehensively ballasted, required a large increase in propulsive power to achieve a very small increase in speed.

An unforeseen problem had also arisen in building the existing hangar over a deck which retained its original sheer and camber. The slope and curvature resulted in considerable difficulty with the movement of aircraft about the space. Later ships were therefore built with hangar decks both plane and horizontal.

Early remedial measures included the addition of considerable quantities of permanent ballast and increasing the scantlings of added top-hamper. This not only gave better immersion but also reduced an earlier tendency to excessive stiffness and consequent rapid movement.

A further improvement was to switch to steam propulsion, technology with which the Americans were more familiar. At the comparatively low powers involved, this was not expected to cause any great exhaust problem.

The last of the first batch, which would have become HMS *Charger*, was retained by the US Navy for evaluation and training purposes. She had a diminutive island, sponsoned out over the starboard side, because watch-keepers on earlier, flush-decked ships reported station-keeping and general ship control very difficult, with no points of reference.

BELOW: **On October 1, 1941 the Seattle-Tacoma Shipyard launched the freighter *Steel Advocate* for the Isthmian Steamship Company of New York. As can be seen from the temporary name, she had already been requisitioned for conversion to the escort carrier *Bogue* (CVE-9).**

BOTTOM: **The *Bogue*, as converted. The original forecastle and line of the upper deck can still be discerned and it is apparent that, to give adequate freeboard for the flight deck, the hull, in mercantile terms, is permanently in the ballast condition.**

TOP: **Although, of course, the flight deck has to be flat, without sheer or camber, the upper deck of the original hull had both. The small galleries projecting from the ship's side followed the original curve, only later ships having them in a horizontal line as indicated here.** ABOVE: **An anonymous ship in an anonymous yard. No carrier, either new or returning from repair or refit, was allowed to sail empty. This one is being loaded with TBF/TBM Avenger sections to meet the endless attritional demands of the Pacific fleet carriers.**

American requirements for large air wings had to be matched by adequate fuel stowage. To achieve this, it was accommodated in tanks integrated with the ship's structure. From the outset the British were heavily critical of this practice, preferring to accept a much lower factor in favour of accommodating fuel in cylindrical tanks, de-coupled from the structure and, where possible, immersed in water. The conflicting views of what the British viewed as safe working practice, and what the Americans saw as unacceptably high standards in time of emergency, was never satisfactorily resolved.

The eleven *Bogue*-class escort carriers addressed most of the above points, together with the luxury of a second elevator. Essentially identical with the British Attacker class, all stemmed from the same yard.

Continued refinement in escort carrier design soon left the Bogues looking relatively unsophisticated. They were used very effectively in the Atlantic and where supported by a division of destroyer escorts, they exploited high-grade Ultra information to become efficient U-boat killers.

ABOVE: ***Bogue*'s war service was in anti-submarine warfare in the Atlantic. Seen here from a patrol aircraft, she is in Measure 22 camouflage. Note how the small island is completely outboard of the flight deck edge, so that it appears deeper from starboard than it does from port.**

Bogue class

Class: *Altamaha* (CVE-18); *Barnes* (CVE-20); *Block Island* (CVE-21); *Bogue* (CVE-9); *Breton* (CVE-23); *Card* (CVE-11); *Copahee* (CVE-12); *Core* (CVE-13) *Croatan* (CVE-25); *Nassau* (CVE-16); *Prince William* (CVE-31)
Built: All by Seattle-Tacoma Shipbuilding
Commissioned: June 1942–April 1943
Gross tonnage: 8,400 tons
Displacement: 16,900 tonnes/16,600 tons (deep load)
Length: 141.8m/465ft (at waterline); 151.2m/495ft 8in (overall)
Beam: 21.2m/69ft 6in
Draught: 7.1m/23ft 3in (standard); 8.0m/26ft 3in (deep load)
Aircraft: About 24
Flight deck: 133.2 x 24.4m/436ft 8in x 80ft
Armament: 2 x 127mm/5in and 10 x 20mm/0.79in guns
Machinery: Geared steam turbine, 2 boilers, 1 shaft
Power: 6,340kW/8,500shp
Speed: 17 knots
Fuel: 3,260 tonnes/3,200 tons
Range: 48,710km/26,300nm at 15 knots
Armour: None
Complement: 900 men

Sangamon-class escort carriers

Once the American auxiliary aircraft carrier programme moved into top gear, early in 1942, every available C-3 hull, the preferred basis for conversion, was soon allocated. To overcome an immediate shortfall, four T-3 tanker hulls were substituted. This decision was not popular with the US Navy, for these were to be fast, twin-screw fleet oilers, urgently required for extended Pacific operations and always in short supply.

Except for their continuous sheerline, which had to be built over to provide a flat hangar deck, the ships made excellent carriers, the four being known as the Sangamon class. Being longer than the C-3-derived carriers, they incorporated a larger hangar and flight deck. Their twin screws enhanced manoeuvrability and provided a measure of redundancy, although machinery spaces were common to each. They were inherently well subdivided, while their size enabled them to retain some tanks for fuel which could be freighted or transferred to smaller and ever-thirsty escorts. Their own bunker spaces were 80 per cent larger than those of a C-3, giving them the theoretical ability to steam around the world at 15 knots without refuelling.

No other tankers were so converted but they were regarded as very successful, their design becoming the starting point for later classes. In appreciation, they looked long and lower, continuously plated up to flight deck level but with a characteristic line of rectangular openings below hangar deck level providing access for hose-handling facilities.

Like the preceding Bogues, the Sangamons had two elevators and a single catapult. Despite the need for maximum-sized flight decks, American practice was to terminate them short of bow and stern, to allow free arcs for the armament located there.

TOP: **The four Sangamons were modified from twin-screw, *Cimmaron*-class fleet oilers. Larger and more powerful, they were the best of the early escort carriers but further hulls were too scarce to be spared.** ABOVE: **The diminutive size of a Sangamon bridge structure is here well shown, with the blocks of the aircraft-handling derrick. Judging by the dress of the "goofers" watching the Avenger, the picture was taken on an open day.**

Although they saw considerable action, no Sangamons were lost, so that they received intermittent upgrades as opportunity offered. This included a second catapult, much improved electronics and considerable enhancement to the

LEFT: **A Sangamon was instantly recognizable by the row of rectangular recesses in the side shell plating, their lower edge following the line of the tankers' original upper decks. The class made its mark during the North African landings of November 1942, possibly the venue for this shot.**

ABOVE: **The distant mass of shipping suggests the North African landings. The aircraft to the left are Douglas SBD Dauntless dive-bombers. These were carried aboard only the *Sangamon* and *Santee*. The flight deck markings remain a mystery.** ABOVE RIGHT: **A deck crew races to release a hooked Avenger, fold wings and remove quickly from the landing area to free the deck for the next incomer.**

armament, which reflected the increased threat from air attack, particularly that of the kamikaze after October 1944.

As new ships, the four covered the American landings in North Africa in November 1942. At this point their armament comprised two 127mm/5in guns and two twin 40mm/1.57in mounts on the quarterdeck, with two further twin 40mm/1.57in and a dozen single 20mm/0.79in guns disposed in sided sponsons and on the forecastle. By the war's end the 40mm/1.57in weapons had increased to two quadruple and ten twin mountings. Only the close of hostilities prevented a further increase, with each of the 127mm/5in guns being traded for a further twin 40mm/1.57in, and all single 20mm/0.79in weapons being exchanged for twins. This enormous increase in top-weight was possible only because of their inherently stable tanker origins.

Compared with the C-3s, the Sangamons had greater survivability. Action damage included two kamikaze strikes, four bomb hits, one submarine torpedo and an internal explosion, yet all survived.

Sangamon class

Class: *Chenango*, converted Norfolk Navy Yard, commissioned September 19, 1942; *Sangamon*, converted Newport News, commissioned August 25, 1942; *Santee*, converted Puget Sound Navy Yard, commissioned August 24, 1942; *Suwannee,* converted Bethlehem Steel, Staten Island, commissioned September 24, 1942

Gross tonnage: 10,500 tons

Displacement: 24,500 tonnes/24,100 tons (deep load)

Length: 160.1m/525ft (at waterline); 168.7m/553ft (overall)

Beam: 22.9m/75ft

Draught: 9.3m/30ft 6in (deep load)

Aircraft: Up to 36

Flight deck: 153.1 x 25.9m/502 x 85ft

Armament (as designed): 2 x 127mm/5in, 8 x 40mm/1.57in (4 double) and 12 x 20mm/0.79in (12 single) guns

Machinery: Geared steam turbines, 4 boilers, 2 shafts

Power: 10,100kW/13,500shp

Speed: 18 knots

Fuel: 5,850 tonnes/5,750 tons

Range: 44,450km/24,000nm at 15 knots

Armour: None

Complement: 940 men

Casablanca-class escort carriers

In tropical conditions, escort carriers suffered from insufficient speed. A torpedo-laden Avenger required a relative wind speed of 30 knots to get airborne safely and, even when lightened by emptied tanks and ordnance racks, 25 knots to alight safely on a small carrier's crowded decks. Sometimes unable to raise 20 knots of relative wind in calm conditions, an escort carrier could be affected operationally, for to persevere with flying meant a high aircraft attrition rate.

Among the US Navy's enormous construction programmes, the President personally favoured those for escort carriers and destroyer escorts. When the industrialist Henry Kaiser proposed in mid-1942 to devote one of his yards to series production of escort carriers, he was quickly awarded a contract for 50. As good as his word, Kaiser produced these, the Casablanca class, in twenty months from the commencement of the first in November 1942 to the completion of the last in July 1944.

The Sangamons had been completed in August/September 1942 and were impressing people with their capability. It was decided to continue the less efficient Bogue type for British use, as they were adequate for anti-submarine warfare and convoy escort. Kaiser would build a new type for the US Navy, whose requirements differed.

To make a volume-critical hull of a given size go 3 knots faster requires a combination of greater power and improved lines, necessitating greater length. Time was saved by using the fore and after ends of an existing fast transport design and inserting a longer mid-body.

TOP: **Laid down as the *Alava Bay* (CVE-103), the *Roi* was completed in August 1944. Redesignated AVB-103 she spent her life ferrying aircraft and repatriating prisoners of war. Having seen just 20 months of service she was, like many others, discarded, and was scrapped in 1947.** ABOVE: **In contrast, those of her sisters commissioned early enough to provide ground support at Leyte Gulf saw more than enough action. Here, off Samar, a stricken Japanese aircraft dives at the *Kitkun Bay* (AVG-71).**

Heavy machinery manufacturers were booked to the extent that both the favoured steam turbine and the unloved diesel were unavailable in the required timescale. The choice of an

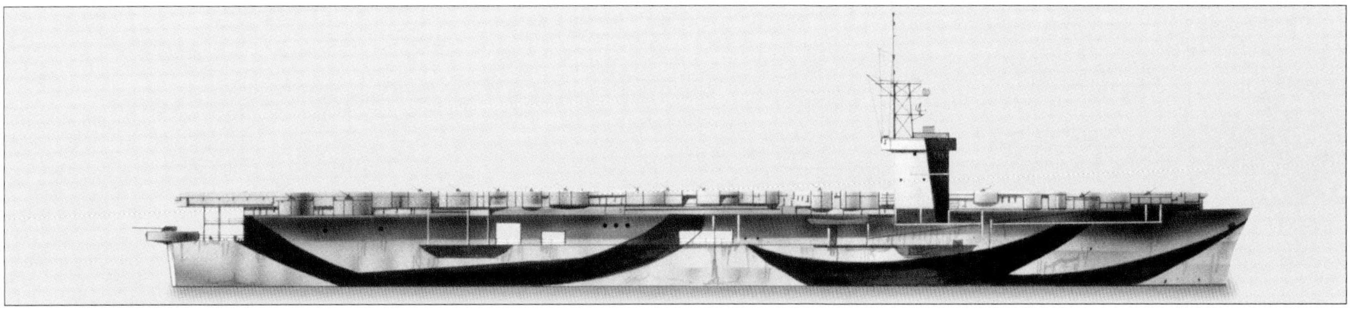

ABOVE: **This profile shows features unique to the *Casablanca*-class ships, the wide, flat transom stern and the "open" elevator serving the after end of the flight deck. The curves of the disruptive camouflage suggest a variant of Measure 32.**

ABOVE: **Another unit subjected to change of name is seen here as the *Tripoli* (AVG-64) but was laid down as the *Didrickson Bay*. The vertical bands of camouflage colour comprising Measure 32/4A are blended at their forward edges by spray painting.** BELOW: **During the Battle of Samar in October 1944 escort carriers of the US Seventh Fleet found themselves under fire from Japanese battleships and cruisers. This carrier has been nearly straddled by a salvo of heavy projectiles.**

alternative fell on the Skinner Uniflow reciprocating steam engine. This five-cylinder, multi-expansion unit was very compact and was also used in amphibious warfare ships.

Kaiser's ships were designed without the sheer that complicated early conversions, and their fine after run with twin screws resulted in a distinctive, broad transom stern. They were still too small to have adequate protection worked around magazines, a shortcoming that led directly to the violent explosion that destroyed the *Liscombe Bay* following a single torpedo hit.

Casablanca class

Class: *Admiralty Islands* (CVE-99); *Anzio* (CVE-57); *Attu* (CVE-102); *Bismarck Sea* (CVE-95); *Bougainville* (CVE-100); *Cape Esperance* (CVE-88); *Casablanca* (CVE-55); *Corregidor* (CVE-58); *Fanshaw Bay* (CVE-70); *Gambier Bay* (CVE-73); *Guadalcanal* (CVE-60); *Hoggatt Bay* (CVE-75); *Hollandia* (CVE-97); *Kadashan Bay* (CVE-76); *Kalinin Bay* (CVE-68); *Kasaan Bay* (CVE-69); *Kitkun Bay* (CVE-71); *Kwajalein* (CVE-98); *Liscombe Bay* (CVE-56); *Lunga Point* (CVE-94); *Makassar Strait* (CVE-91) *Makin Island* (CVE-93); *Manila Bay* (CVE-61); *Marcus Island* (CVE-77); *Matanikau* (CVE-101); *Mission Bay* (CVE-59); *Munda* (CVE-104); *Natoma Bay* (CVE-62); *Nehenta Bay* (CVE-74); *Ommancy Bay* (CVE-79); *Petrof Bay* (CVE-80); *Roi* (CVE-103); *Rudyerd Bay* (CVE-81); *Saginaw Bay* (CVE-82); *Salamaua* (CVE-96); *Sargent Bay* (CVE-83); *Savo Island* (CVE-78); *Shamrock Bay* (CVE-84); *Shipley Bay* (CVE-85); *Sitkoh Bay* (CVE-86); *Solomons* (CVE-67); *St. Lo* (CVE-63); *Steamer Bay* (CVE-87); *Takanis Bay* (CVE-89); *Thetis Bay* (CVE-90); *Tripoli* (CVE-64); *Tulagi* (CVE-72); *Wake Island* (CVE-65); *White Plains* (CVE-66); *Windham Bay* (CVE-92)
Built: All by Kaiser, Vancouver
Commissioned: July 1943–December 1944
Displacement: 8,350 tonnes/8,200 tons (standard); 10,750 tonnes/10,550 tons (deep load)
Length: 149.5m/490ft (at waterline); 152.2m/499ft (overall)
Beam: 19.8m/65ft
Draught: 6.3m/20ft 9in (mean)
Aircraft: About 27
Flight deck: 144.6 x 24.4m/474 x 80ft
Armament: 1 x 127mm/5in, 8 x 40mm/1.57in (4 double), and 12 x 20mm/0.79in (12 single) guns
Machinery: Steam reciprocating engines, 4 boilers, 2 shafts
Power: 6,700kW/9,000ihp
Speed: 20 knots
Fuel: 2,040 tonnes/2,000 tons
Range: 18,980km/10,250nm at 15 knots
Armour: None
Complement: 815 men

Commencement Bay-class escort carriers

During 1942, the President had declared that one hundred escort carriers would be built for the US Navy and, despite the already overwhelming Allied naval superiority by the autumn of 1944, this pledge would have been realized with the addition of 35 ships of the Commencement Bay type. This number, however, was simply not required and, with the hugely expanded service already experiencing personnel shortages, only 19 were actually completed. With hostilities ending, 4 more were dismantled in an incomplete state, while the other 12 were not laid down.

The very successful Kaiser production line for the Casablanca class saw the concept repeated by the award of 27 to the Todd organization. These, however, had to be spread between three yards and, with spare capacity emerging, Kaiser was given the other eight, only to have them cancelled.

It had been the size and adaptability of the Sangamons that had most impressed the navy but, with fleet oilers too few and too valuable for further conversions, it had to await a new design derived from the same characteristics.

The redundancy of twin shafts in the Sangamons was valued, but was offset somewhat by the grouping of the machinery spaces to mercantile standards, and vulnerability to a single torpedo. Redesigned, they were spread as far as the aviation facilities allowed.

With extreme urgency no longer a driving factor, the general specification could also be upgraded to accommodate larger and heavier aircraft. Larger and faster elevators were matched by a flight deck stressed to accept 7.7-tonne/17,000lb (as opposed to 6.35-tonne/14,000lb) aircraft. More generous flight deck dimensions permitted the use of a second catapult, although this partly overlapped the forward elevator. Modified from the model used in fleet carriers, this equipment could accelerate a 7.3-tonne/16,000lb aircraft to a speed of 145kph/90mph in a 30m/95ft run.

BELOW: **Purpose-designed and more sophisticated, the Commencement Bays came late in World War II, saw little action and, for the most part, were retained. The *Palau* (ACV-122) is seen here, probably about 1950, with an experimental Marine squadron of Piasecki HRP tandem-rotor helicopters.** BOTTOM: **The *Palau* again. Note the supports for the overhung weight of the bridge structure and the lofty mast, necessary to accommodate a comprehensive suite of electronics.**

ABOVE: ***Commencement Bay* (CVE-105) shows off shows off to advantage the sweeping curves of Measure 32/16A which used matt black with up to four shades of green or grey. Note the large stern galleries, each accommodating a quadruple 40mm/1.57in mounting.**

Externally, the Commencement Bays could be recognized by their more generously proportioned superstructure, with the lattice mast of earlier classes replaced by a solid lower mast, topped-off by a lighter, pole topmast. Pronounced tables supported the proliferating antennas of radar and communications.

The bulk of the class remained active after the end of the war for, being the only small carriers able to operate the latest aircraft types, they were assigned anti-submarine warfare (ASW) duties. As such, some were early recipients in the deployment of helicopters.

Some of the class were discarded in the large clear-out of reserve fleet escort carriers (CVEs) in 1959–61 but the majority of the survivors served on until the early 1970s.

LEFT: **The *Sicily* (ACV-118) saw service throughout the Korean War, flying F4U Corsairs in ground support. She is seen here a little later, probably 1953–54, still retaining her armament and deploying Sikorsky S-55s, probably in the HRS troop-transport version. The change of category from CVE to ACV also brought changes of name, the *Sicily* having originally been allocated the name *Sandy Bay*.**

Commencement Bay class

Class: *Badoeng Strait* (CVE-116); *Bairoko* (CVE-115); *Block Island* (CVE-106); *Cape Gloucester* (CVE-109); *Commencement Bay* (CVE-105); *Gilbert Islands* (CVE-107); *Kula Gulf* (CVE-108); *Mindoro* (CVE-120); *Palau* (CVE-122); *Point Cruz* (CVE-119); *Puget Sound* (CVE-113); *Rabaul* (CVE-121); *Rendova* (CVE-114); *Saidor* (CVE-117); *Salerno Bay* (CVE-110); *Siboney* (CVE-112); *Sicily* (CVE-118); *Tinian* (CVE-123); *Vella Gulf* (CVE-111)

Built: Todd (Tacoma, Portland, Willamette)

Displacement: 19,250 tonnes/18,900 tons (standard); 26,200 tonnes/24,000 tons (deep load)

Length: 160.1m/525ft (at waterline); 169.9m/557ft (overall)

Beam: 22.9m/75ft

Draught: 8.5m/28ft (deep load)

Aircraft: About 33

Flight deck: 152.8 x 24.4m/501 x 80ft

Armament: 2 x 127mm/5in, 36 x 40mm/1.57in (3 quadruple, 12 double), and 20 x 20mm/0.79in guns

Machinery: Geared steam turbines, 4 boilers, 2 shafts

Power: 11,950kW/16,000shp

Speed: 19 knots

Fuel: 3,300 tonnes/3,250 tons

Range: 15,740km/8,500nm at 15 knots

Armour: None

Complement: 1,050 men

ABOVE: **Names such as Kwajalein, Eniwetok and Majuro cement the connection between the Marshall Islands and the US Navy, hence this not over-accurate rendering of the *Essex*-class *Lexington* (CV-16).**

LEFT: **Sporting a full deck-load, this Essex is probably seen during the 1950s, but is much the same as her World War II configuration. The pronounced concave flare of the stern reflects the design requirement for an astern speed high enough to allow aircraft recovery over the bows, for which eventuality a second set of arrester wires was specified.**

Essex class

The Vinson-Trammell Act of 1934 provided for the US Navy to be expanded to the maximum tonnage allowed by treaty. Four years later, with international agreements collapsing, it was decided to increase American carrier tonnage from the treaty-limited 177,808 tonnes/175,000 tons to 218,450 tonnes/215,000 tons. This permitted construction of the *Hornet* (CV-8) and for another, CV-9, of about the same size, although limitation was, by now arbitrary.

Even before CV-9 was laid down, however, the war in Europe in April 1941 had triggered a new, emergency American naval expansion. In May 1940, CV-10 to CV-12 were added, followed by CV-13 to CV-19 in August. Rapid carrier production on this scale demanded that the design be tightly controlled. Desirable features included a high speed, an expanded air group, better protection and enhanced armament. No longer limited by treaty, this package demanded over 27,433 tonnes/27,000 tons displacement which, although considerably larger than the Yorktowns, was still greatly influenced by them.

The extra displacement allowed for greatly improved horizontal protection, the longer hull having space to arrange machinery compartments for maximum survivability. Longer hulls are also a factor in higher speed and, of course, in larger flight decks. The Americans were less tolerant than the British of armament, etc intruding into deck space, which was prioritized for aircraft manoeuvring and parking. Eight of the class's twelve 125mm/5in guns were thus grouped, *Lexington*-fashion, fore and aft of the island.

ABOVE: **In this apparently featureless view of an Essex after flight deck it is, nonetheless, possible to discern arrester wires, the after elevator and the reduction in flight deck width in way of the port quarter armament. Note the small screen sheltering the Deck Landing Officer. The carrier is proceeding slowly in a stiff chop that is causing her planeguard destroyer some discomfort.**

Named USS *Essex,* the first-of-class could accommodate an air group of 37 dive-bombers, 18 torpedo-bombers and 36 fighters (typically Helldivers, Avengers and Hellcats respectively). Three elevators were fitted, the first being a port-side deck-edge unit which folded into the ship's side when not in use. Two flush-mounted catapults were provided forward, but some early ships also received a transverse catapult located in the open-style hangar. Later ships had their bow section stretched by 4.88m/16ft to allow better arcs for the forecastle-mounted 49mm/1.93in battery.

ABOVE: **A picture-postcard Pacific day, but with sufficient cloud to make hostile aircraft difficult to spot. The ship is one of the earlier, short-hulled Essex class, a group which comprised CV-9–13, 16–18, 20 and 31. Later units were nearly 5m/16ft 5in longer with bow and stern gun positions extending from beneath the flight deck.**

BELOW: **Although it appears posed, this picture of *Yorktown* (CV-10) gives a good impression of a hangar space that seems vast – until aircraft are put in it. The F6Fs in the foreground enjoy about 1.37m/4ft 6in of clearance beneath the 5.33m/17ft 6in deckhead but the larger TBF/TBM had barely 0.3m/1ft.**

Although not beyond criticism, the Essex class proved effective, the class being enlarged by the ordering of CV-20 and CV-21 in December 1941, CV-31 to CV-40 in August 1942, CV-45 in June 1943 and, finally, CV-50 to CV-55 early in 1945. In all, 24 were completed by a total of five builders, forming the largest-ever series of fleet carriers.

From the Pacific war, the class went on to serve in Korea and Vietnam. Overcrowded even in 1945, the ships nonetheless proved amenable to modernization, notably with angled decks, for service in the jet age. This, fortunately, reduced crew numbers, which had grown from an initial estimate of 2,386 to 3,385 by 1945. Some of the class survived until the 1980s by which time there was a wide variation, no two ships being alike.

Essex class

Class: *Antietam* (CV-36); *Bennington* (CV-20); *Bon Homme Richard* (CV-31); *Boxer* (CV-21); *Bunker Hill* (CV-17); *Essex* (CV-9); *Franklin* (CV-13); *Hancock* (CV-19); *Hornet* (CV-12); *Intrepid* (CV-11); *Kearsarge* (CV-33); *Lake Champlain* (CV-39); *Lexington* (CV-16); *Leyte* (CV-32); *Oriskany* (CV-34); *Philippine Sea* (CV-47); *Princeton* (CV-37); *Randolph* (CV-15); *Shangri-La* (CV-38); *Tarawa* (CV-40); *Ticonderoga* (CV-14); *Valley Forge* (CV-45); *Wasp* (CV-18); *Yorktown* (CV-10)

Commissioned: December 1942–May 1946; *Oriskany* (CV-34), September 1950

Displacement: 28,000 tonnes/27,500 tons (standard); 37,050 tonnes/36,380 tons (deep load)

Length: 250.1m/820ft (at waterline); 266m/872ft (overall)

Length (later ships): 255m/836ft (at waterline); 270.8m/888ft (overall)

Beam: 28.4m/93ft

Draught: 7m/23ft (standard); 8.4m/27ft 6in (deep load)

Aircraft: 90–100

Flight deck: 262.9 x 32.9m/862 x 108ft

Armament: 12 x 127mm/5in (4 double, 4 single), 32 x 40mm/1.57in (8 quadruple), and 46 x 20mm/0.79in guns

Machinery: Geared steam turbines, 8 boilers, 4 shafts

Power: 111,900kW/150,000shp

Speed: 33 knots

Fuel: 6,450 tonnes/6,330 tons

Range: 37,040km/20,000nm at 15 knots

Armour: 64–100mm/2.5–4in (vertical belt); 38mm/1.5in (hangar deck); 38mm/1.5in (protective deck)

Complement: 2,630 men

Independence class

When contracts were signed for the early *Essex*-class fleet carriers, it was anticipated that deliveries would not begin before 1944. The President, as ever closely involved in naval affairs, was concerned. With war looming he considered that the fleet's few available carriers, CV-2 to CV-8, would, with losses, be insufficient to sustain operations until 1944. In the summer of 1941, he therefore proposed paralleling the escort carrier (CVE) programme with the rapid conversion of cruiser hulls into light carriers (CVL), fast enough to accompany the fleet in most weather conditions.

Having examined the proposal, the technical department responsible were united in their opposition to it. Besides disrupting the cruiser construction programme, hulls removed for the purpose would, they advised, be fundamentally unsuitable for the purpose, any carrier of this size being too lively and of inadequate freeboard to operate her aircraft in anything but favourable conditions.

A cruiser hull was of slender proportions so, built up with hangar and flight deck with necessary freeboard, it would present stability problems. To maintain speed in a seaway, cruiser hulls were given considerable sheer which, without major reconstruction, would result in the curved hangar deck that was already proving troublesome in early CVEs. The four widely spaced boilers would require separate uptakes, all of which would impinge on an already narrow hangar. The fine run at either end would limit the dimensions of elevators, forcing them well towards the fuller mid-body.

TOP: The high, narrow-gutted cross section of the CVL in the foreground makes the *Essex* astern look squat and beamy. Note the funnel casings, cranked out beyond the line of the island structure and the distance to which the gun tubs are sponsoned from the hull. ABOVE: While this aerial shot emphasizes the original cruiser hull beneath the narrow flight deck, closer inspection reveals the large, faired blister, which follows a curve while the line of the hangar wall is straight.

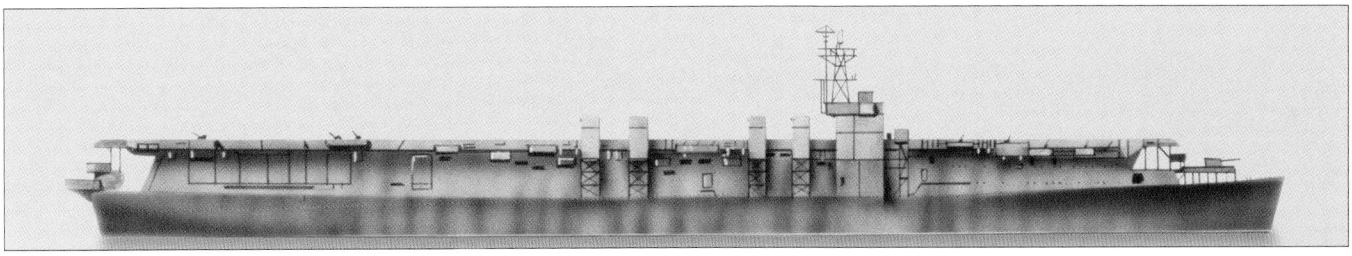

TOP: **The profile of the *Independence*-class CVLs was unique. In the initial design there would have been no island, navigation being conducted, Japanese-style, from below the forward edge of the flight deck.** ABOVE: **CVLs had narrow, cramped flight decks. Note here how the stern galleries appear to be "tacked-on", and the unusual supporting structure for the cranked funnel casings and the bridge.** RIGHT: **Working with the fleet, the CVLs required a full outfit of electronics, the main argument for including a bridge structure. The main input to the plan/position indicator shown here was from the standard SK air search radar, whose antenna was located on the stub mast between the two pairs of funnels.**

The President persisted. Speed was the overriding priority and there were to be no frills. Under direct pressure, the Board reconsidered, agreeing that a *Cleveland*-class light cruiser hull, suitably bulged (or "blistered"), might work. It did. Bulging adds considerably more buoyancy than weight, and in this case for the sacrifice of 1½ knots in speed not only effected the necessary improvement in stability but also provided for a considerable increase in bunker capacity. The boiler uptakes were led via four externally supported casings to a distinctive row of small funnels.

Known, from the lead ship, as the Independence class, the CVLs were always weight-sensitive. The diminutive island was only partly balanced by a port-side flight deck extension to enable aircraft to be wheeled around the forward elevator. The ships tended to trim by the stern. Ordnance capacity was small while overcrowding was unavoidable, the projected 1,200 cruiser crew being swollen by some 25 per cent. The provision of a second catapult demanded a reduction in armament.

Despite the inevitable problems, the CVLs arrived in good time to supplement the fleet's carrier strength at a critical juncture. As four of the seven fleet carriers were, in fact, lost during 1942, the President was vindicated. In practice, the ships *were* lively but crew and fliers learned to live with it. They were able to operate torpedo aircraft as well as dive-bombers and fighters but they were never intended to be more than a stopgap. Their inferior characteristics were acceptable in war but they subsequently had little application.

Independence class

Class: *Bataan* (CVL-29); *Belleau Wood* (CVL-24); *Cabot* (CVL-28); *Cowpens* (CVL-25); *Independence* (CVL-22); *Princeton* (CVL-23); *Langley* (CVL-27); *Monterey* (CVL-26); *San Jacinto* (CVL-30)

Built: All by New York Shipbuilding, Camden

Commissioned: January 1943–December 1943

Displacement: 11,050 tonnes/10,650 tons (standard); 15,170 tonnes/14,900 tons (deep load)

Length: 183m/600ft (at waterline); 189.9m/622ft 6in (overall)

Beam: 21.8m/71ft 6in

Draught: 6.4m/21ft (standard); 7.5m/24ft 6in (deep load)

Aircraft: 31

Flight deck: 168.4 x 22.3m/552 x 73ft

Armament: 24 x 40mm/1.57in (2 quadruple, 8 double) and 16 x 20mm/0.79in guns

Machinery: Geared steam turbines, 4 boilers, 4 shafts

Power: 74,600kW/100,000shp

Speed: 31.5 knots

Fuel: 2,650 tonnes/2,600 tons

Range: 23,150km/12,500nm at 15 knots

Armour: 83–127mm/3.75–5in (vertical belt – except in CVL-22 and-23); 50mm/2in (protective deck)

Complement: 1,500 men

Midway class

The *Midway* had a difficult gestation as the President disliked the idea of "big" carriers, agreeing with much naval opinion that more, and smaller (i.e. *Essex*- and *Independence*-class) ships, were needed, not least because they were required urgently.

By 1940, however, the *Essex* design work was complete and studies began to define her successor. Much influenced by the Yorktowns, the *Essex* echoed current thoughts that carriers should be protected primarily against gunfire from heavy cruisers. The anti-torpedo defence of the *Essex* was subsequently thought deficient.

With the European war in progress, American designers were more conscious of the threat from aerial bombing but, by now, having access to British carrier practice, were equally aware that heavy flight deck protection on a limited displacement meant greatly reduced aircraft capacity. Then, in 1941, the British *Illustrious* and *Formidable* suffered and survived savage dive-bombing and their repair in American yards afforded graphic first-hand evidence of the value of horizontal protection.

The mere provision of large areas of armour required considerable increase in dimensions and displacement to float it. To keep this within bounds, the Americans decided on a soft-sided "open" hangar structure, topped-off with a heavy flight deck. There being no definitive answer as to whether one very thick deck gives more protection than several thinner ones, the designers in this case backed-up the heavy flight deck with 50mm/2in hangar deck *and* main deck. Although this was beneficial in lowering the ship's centre of gravity, they still had a flight deck with a comparatively low freeboard, which decreased further with later accumulations of weight.

TOP: Dwarfed by the yard's hammerhead crane the *Roosevelt*'s already low hull appears even lower. Note the revised disposition of the 127mm/5in armament and the wide stern gallery for automatic weapons.
ABOVE: The main argument for the big carrier was the deployment of strategic nuclear-capable bombers such as the Douglas A-3 Skywarrior seen here. This 37.2-tonne/82,000lb monster had, in extremis, to be stopped by the nylon crash barrier being sorted out in the foreground.

Needing to be constructed in addition to the "production-line" Essex class, the big carriers, known as the Midways, did not receive presidential sanction until December 1942, resulting in their being completed too late to see combat.

The sheer size of the *Midway* resulted in an air group big enough to be considered unwieldy, a situation resolved by the rapidly increasing size and weight of aircraft.

ABOVE: **One of the world's three largest cruisers, the 17,273-tonne/17,000-ton *Des Moines* (CA-134), takes fuel from one of the world's three largest carriers. Note the side elevator lowered to hangar deck level.** BELOW: **Flanked by a row of McDonnell F2H Banshees, a Midway's crew of more than 2,100 assemble at divisions. The aircraft date the picture to the early 1950s.**

ABOVE: **Newly completed, the *Midway* (CVA-41) leaves her builders. Her huge, rectangular flight deck would be much modified in her later career.**
BELOW: **Fully modernized, with angled deck and enclosed "hurricane" bow, a Midway appears squat compared with the later, and larger, Forrestal type in the background.**

Only three of the planned six ships were ever built but post-war they proved to be good value for money. With the advent of the Cold War, the navy had the early responsibility for delivering strategic nuclear weaponry, and the Midways were the only carriers large enough to deploy the big "nuclear bombers" without extensive modification. They also trialled the launch of strategic missiles.

As naval aviation entered the jet age the class was much modified and modernized, gaining angled decks, up to four deck-edge elevators, steam catapults (including a third), and the plating-in of the bows up to flight deck level. Some compensation for the extra weight was achieved by the progressive elimination of the increasingly ineffective gun armament.

Impressive ships in their day, they were quickly made obsolescent by the new generation of "super carriers" and were paid off by 1992, after working lives that were comparatively short by American standards.

Midway class

Class: *Midway* (CVB-41), Newport News, commissioned September 10, 1945; *Franklin D. Roosevelt* (CVB-42), New York Naval Yard, commissioned October 27, 1945; *Coral Sea* (CVB-43), Newport News, commissioned October 1, 1947

Displacement: 48,250 tonnes/47,400 tons (standard); 61,000 tonnes/59,950 tons (deep load)

Length: 274.5m/900ft (at waterline); 295.2m/968ft (overall)

Beam: 34.5m/113ft

Draught: 9.9m/32ft 6in (standard); 10.6m/34ft 9in (deep load)

Aircraft: 136

Flight deck: 281.8 x 34.5m/924 x 113ft

Armament: 18 x 127mm/5in, and 84 x 40mm/1.57in (21 quadruple) guns

Machinery: Geared steam turbines, 12 boilers, 4 shafts

Power: 158,000kW/212,000shp

Speed: 33 knots

Fuel: 10,200 tonnes/10,000 tons

Range: 33,340km/18,000nm at 15 knots

Armour: 193mm/7.6in (vertical belt, port side), 178mm/7in (vertical belt, starboard side); 89mm/3.5in (flight deck); 50mm/2in (hangar deck); 44–50mm/1.75–2in (protective deck)

Complement: 3,550 men

LEFT: **The only official impression of the *United States* ever to be released. It shows four catapults, each served by its own elevator, but there is no indication of either electronics or funnel arrangement.** BELOW: **For giant hulls, building in a construction dock obviates the great stresses imposed by conventional launching from a slipway. The outer bottom plating of the *United States* (CVA-58) is here laid in the large graving dock of Newport News Shipbuilding.**

United States (CVA-58)

During that period following World War II it appeared axiomatic that not only would the new enemy be the Soviet Union but also that any hostilities would involve atomic weapons. The only means of delivery at that time was the bomber and, assuming that it flew from a carrier's deck, an aircraft with a 3,704km/2,000nm combat radius could strike at any worthwhile target there. Carrying a bomb load of about 5.1 tonnes/ 5 tons and a huge fuel load, at a required 500 knots, the resulting aircraft would have a wingspan of over 35m/ 115ft and weigh 45 tonnes/100,000lb at take-off.

No existing carrier could routinely deploy such an aircraft. As a completely flush deck would be essential, the draft design for a new ship showed conning positions at the forward deck edge and no masts, it being required that major electronics be carried aboard dedicated escort vessels. No hangar was at first deemed necessary, but the resulting shallow hull of considerable length would have experienced excess stresses. For the first time in American practice, therefore, a hangar was overlaid with an armoured flight deck that was also the strength deck.

Four catapults would be fitted, two forward and two angled outward in the waist. Each was served by a deck-edge elevator. Between 16 and 24 bombers were to be carried, together with about 50 fighters, probably McDonnell F2H Banshees.

That the first-of-class had been named *United States* indicated the importance that the US Navy attached to the project. However within days of her laying-down in April 1949, a successful putsch by the rival Air Force lobby saw her cancelled by a new Secretary of Defense.

LEFT: **For a vessel of such significance, the positioning of the first plate, the symbolic "keel-laying", appears remarkably low-key, the wider activity being lost to the solitary navy photographer. Today's initial laying of would be of a complete module.**

United States (CVA-58)

Built: Newport News, laid down April 18, 1949, then dismantled
Displacement: 68,250 tonnes/67,000 tons (standard); 80,500 tonnes/79,000 tons (deep load)
Length: 314.2m/1,030ft (at waterline); 331.8m/1,088ft (overall)
Beam: 39m/128ft
Draught: 10.5m/34ft 6in (deep load)
Aircraft: 70–80
Flight deck: 315.4 x 58m/1,034 x 190ft
Armament: 8 x 127mm/5in (2 double, 4 single), 16 x 76mm/3in (8 double) and 20 x 20mm/ 0.79in guns
Machinery: Geared steam turbines, 8 boilers, 4 shafts
Power: 209,000kW/280,000shp
Speed: 33 knots
Fuel: 11,200 tonnes/11,000 tons
Range: 22,220km/12,000nm at 20 knots
Armour: 38mm/1.5in (vertical belt); 19mm/0.75in (hangar walls); 50mm/2in (flight deck); 38mm/1.5in (hangar and protective decks)
Complement: 4,100 men

Forrestal class

Work expended on the aborted *United States* was not wasted. Firstly, the over-blown 45.4-tonne/100,000lb bomber actually entered service as the less ambitious 31.8-tonne/70,000lb Douglas A-3 Skywarrior, with only two-thirds the span but with a 6.94m/22ft 9in height that would demand a hangar of 7.62m/25ft headroom. Secondly, the navy's "floating" of more modest carrier studies coincided with the fortuitous outbreak of the Korean War in June 1950.

Within eight months a firm proposal was worked out, using the structure and layout of CVA-58 but with one less elevator. Psychologically, its design displacement was set at 102 tonnes/100 tons below 60,963 tonnes/60,000 tons. Scaled down, the flight deck remained flush but with a miniscule, retractable island. On either side amidships were four cranked "smoke pipes" that hinged after the fashion of those on the old *Langley*. In July 1952 the *Forrestal*, first of four, was laid down.

Major modifications were introduced during the construction process. British developments of steam catapults and angled decks were quickly exploited by the US Navy, in time for incorporation into the Forrestals. Adoption of the angled deck so altered the "ground plan" that it was possible to reinstate a conventional island, funnel and the customary masting and electronic arrays.

The four-ship programme spanned some seven years, during which time further developments resulted in significant variation between individual units. All experienced slamming problems in service from numerous sponsons and subsequent updates and service life extension programmes resulted in the exchange of conventional armament for missiles and close-in weapon systems. All four were decommissioned between 1993 and 1999, following about forty years' service.

ABOVE: **Only 39 months separate the laying down of the stillborn *United States* and the *Forrestal* (CVA-59) seen here, but a comparison of their deck plans shows considerable difference, the introduction of the angled deck allowing the reinstatement of the island structure. Note also that the bows have been enclosed.**

TOP RIGHT: **A planeguard helicopter keeps station on the *Saratoga* (CVA-60). In the foreground are parked an armed F/A-18 Hornet and an EA-6B Prowler electronics countermeasures (ECM) aircraft.** ABOVE: **Parked aircraft litter the vast deck of the *Saratoga* in an ordered confusion that leaves free only the port bow catapults. It can be appreciated from this view how the perennial design problem of weight distribution, caused by the island, has been largely solved by the adoption of the angled deck.**

Forrestal class

Class: *Forrestal* (CVA-59), Newport News, commissioned October 1, 1955; *Independence* (CVA-62), New York Navy Yard, commissioned January 10, 1959; *Ranger* (CVA-61), Newport News, commissioned August 10, 1957; *Saratoga* (CVA-60) New York Navy Yard, commissioned April 14, 1957

Displacement: 60,963 tonnes/60,000 tons (standard); 79,200 tonnes/77,800 tons (deep load)

Length: 302m/990ft (at waterline); 316.9m/1,039ft (overall)

Beam: 39.5m/129ft 5in

Draught: 11.4m/37ft 6in (deep load)

Aircraft (as designed): 32 A-3 Skywarrior bombers and 12 F3H Demon fighters

Flight deck: 310.5 x 72.3m/1,018 x 237ft

Armament (as designed): 8 x 127mm/5in (8 single) guns

Machinery: Geared steam turbines, 8 boilers, 4 shafts

Power: 194,000kW/260,000shp

Speed: 32.5 knots

Fuel: 7,940 tonnes/7,800 tons

Range: 18,520km/10,000nm at 20 knots

Armour: 38mm/1.5in (hangar walls); 50mm/2in (flight deck); 38mm/1.5in (hangar deck)

Complement: 4,500 men

Improved Forrestal class

During the time that it took to build the original Forrestals, technologies progressed to the point where each of the four exhibited significant variation. Their great size engendered new ideas in deck procedures. It also provoked hard criticisms on the grounds of cost. The question of successors was thus the subject of fierce debate.

Opponents argued that more, smaller and cheaper carriers were the sensible option. By the mid-1950s, however, the war-built Essex class were too limited to be considered viable attack carriers. Although still comparatively new, the Midways were having to undergo expensive and comprehensive updating. Large, capable carrier aircraft were a fact of life and the US Navy firmly believed that performance should never be compromised simply because they needed to operate from flight decks.

Attempts to design a replacement carrier of under 50,802 tonnes/50,000 tons displacement showed the impracticality of reconciling the likes of angled decks, high headroom hangar, and high speed within the limit. An updated, repeat Forrestal was obviously the best choice.

To encourage funding, it was advantageous not to increase displacement or, if possible, dimensions. This aim was assisted by a rapid decrease in the size of atomic weapons, arresting the explosive growth in that of the aircraft that carried them. A Forrestal hull remained adequate and, through being large, had better survivability than a smaller. A question mark remained over propulsion, however, for the prototype nuclear-powered carrier, *Enterprise*, then under construction, was years away from confirming that this was indeed the way forward.

Superficially similar, the second quartet incorporated improvements that placed it in a different class. The primary difference lay in flight deck layout, the wider centre section being lengthened to increase the area, the extra top-weight being compensated by the abandonment of gun armament.

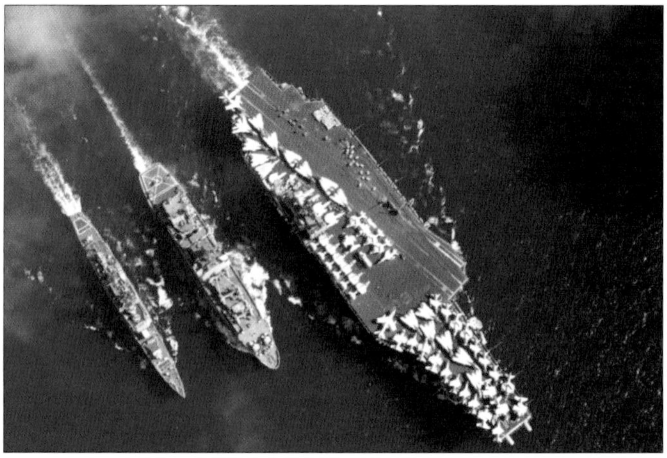

TOP: In the course of four decades of service and various Service Life Extension Programs (SLEPS) the Improved Forrestals have been altered considerably over the years with, for instance, conventional gun armament being replaced in turn by Terrier and Sea Sparrow missiles. ABOVE: Carrier and escort replenish simultaneously, from a multi-purpose supply ship. However large the ship, continuous operation is dependent upon regular top-ups.

Like the Forrestals, the new ships had three starboard-side, deck-edge elevators but, where the former had one forward of the island and two abaft it, the latter reversed this order, resulting in the island being located further aft. The port side elevator was also shifted to the after end of the flight deck sponson.

It was the intention to replace each former pair of 127mm/5in guns with a lighter twin Terrier SAM launcher, but individual fits varied. Able to be sited higher above the waterline, the missile systems reduced the wetness caused by the earlier gun sponsons impacting the sea. These early systems were, however, greatly dependent upon the ship for guidance, contributing greatly to the proliferation of masts and antennas.

Because of the danger of airborne nuclear attack, carrier task groups now observed considerable dispersion. With its escorts now necessarily more distant, a carrier needed a large, low-frequency sonar to meet the further threat posed by the fast enemy nuclear-propelled submarine.

With the nuclear-propelled *Enterprise* commissioning in 1961, the last of class, *John F. Kennedy*, was delayed but finally went ahead to a conventionally propelled, but further modified, design. *America* was decommissioned in 1996 and *Constellation* in 2003.

ABOVE: **The *Constellation* (CVA-64) shows off her forward detail. The two projecting horns project from the catapult ends and catch the aircraft launching bridles. Between them are five scuttles opening from the forward emergency conning position.**
BELOW: **Including aircrew, an Improved Forrestal carried about 5,000 personnel, or about 5 people for each 0.3m/1ft of the ship's length. As submariners live among their torpedoes so do carriermen live among their aircraft.**

ABOVE: **One convincing argument for large carriers is their longevity, the average hull seeing 40 years. Although the design pressure of the large strategic bomber has passed in favour of the missile, there is no saying what future development will be.**

Improved Forrestal class

Class: *America* (CVA-66), Newport News, commissioned January 23, 1965; *Constellation* (CVA-64), New York Navy Yard, commissioned October 27, 1961; *Kitty Hawk* (CVA-63), New York Shipbuilding, commissioned April 29, 1961

Displacement: 61,100 tonnes/60,000 tons (standard); 78,300 tonnes/76,900 tons (deep load)

Length: 302m/990ft (at waterline); 319.6m/1,048ft (overall)

Beam: 39.5m/129ft 5in

Draught: 11.2m/36ft 9in (deep load)

Aircraft: 8 x A-3 Skywarrior heavy bombers, 36 x A-4 Skyhawk light bombers, 44 x F-4 and F-8 (Phantom and Crusader) fighters, and 9 others (as designed)

Flight deck: 319.3 x 72.6m/1,047 x 238ft

Armament (as designed): Two twin Terrier SAM launchers

Machinery: Geared steam turbines, 8 boilers, 4 shafts

Power: 208,900kW/280,000shp

Speed: 33.5 knots

Fuel: 7,940 tonnes/7,800 tons

Range: 22,220km/12,000nm at 20 knots

Armour: 38mm/1.5in (hangar walls); 50mm/2in (flight deck); 38mm/1.5in (hangar deck)

Complement: 4,500 men

ABOVE: **Taking fuel on a sun-dappled sea, the *Kearsarge* (CV-33) clearly demonstrates the advantages of the angled deck, separating the functions of launch, recovery and parking.**
ABOVE LEFT: **With the plated-in "hurricane" bow and completely remodelled superstructure and armament, a modernized Essex bears little resemblance to an Essex of World War II.**

Essex class modernized

By the end of its building programme in 1946 there were 23 completed Essex class and the incomplete *Oriskany*. They represented a huge investment but faced an uncertain future, for it was yet to be determined how many would be retained for the peacetime navy. In addition, they already required expensive modification, for their pre-war design made few concessions to the new era of atomic weapons, jet aircraft and guided missiles.

Determined to retain as many as possible the US Navy conducted three major modernization programmes on the class, resulting in the upgrading of 15. Taking between 12 and 20 months to implement, the programmes were expensive at a time of greatly reduced budgets. Individual ships therefore tended to be completed with varying outfits. This was exacerbated by this being a period of great carrier innovation, with major developments occurring during the course of a programme.

In 1945, the piston-engined AD-1 Skyraider was the newly introduced state-of-the-art carrier strike aircraft. It was a magnificent machine but, within two years, Grumman was introducing the 933kph/580mph, jet-propelled F9F Panther. In the pipeline was the 24-tonne/53,000lb AJ-1 Savage, the designated carrier-based strategic nuclear bomber.

The incomplete *Oriskany* was selected for the pilot modernization, the need for which gained urgency with the June 1950 outbreak of the Korean War. Jet aircraft had little low-speed lift, resulting in higher launch and recovery speeds.

ABOVE: **Her landing area free, *Ticonderoga* (CVA-14) turns sharply into the wind to accept aircraft in May 1961. Note how she appears to be towing a decoy. The A-3 Skywarriors were so large that they invariably occupied the slot abaft the island.**

More powerful catapults were required as was a reorganized deck procedure. These problems were soon to be firmly addressed by adopting the British steam catapult and angled deck, improvements so fundamental that early Essex updates were given a second spell in dockyard hands to retro-fit them.

Jet aircraft required far more fuel but it proved possible to blend it, using the ship's own bunkers, but at a cost in endurance. Vertical armour and most gun armament was removed to save weight while bulges ("blisters") were skilfully blended into the hull to increase buoyancy, stability and bunker space, though at a small cost in speed. The island was rebuilt to improve smoke clearance and to allow the bulk of the

ABOVE: **The *Oriskany* (CV-34) was something of a prototype in the *Essex*-class modernization programme, receiving modified bows, angled deck and steam catapults.** RIGHT: **Name ship of the class, *Essex* (CV-9) shows off her new electronics suite to advantage. Limited space, and the avoidance of interaction, has obliged the antenna of the SPS 37A long-range, air search radar to be located well outboard while that of the smaller SPS 8 height finder set is opposite and inboard.**

proliferating electronic antennas to be grouped satisfactorily on a substantial pole mast. The flight deck, elevators and catapults were all upgraded to suit the anticipated weight of the AJ-1. Heavier bomb lifts and greater magazine space were also required. Not all modernized units received the full, angled-deck configuration but all those that did had their after centreline elevator shifted to the starboard deck edge.

The original, overhanging forward end of the flight deck had proved vulnerable to storm damage, so all had their bow fully plated up to flight deck level (the so-called "Hurricane Bow") with a secondary, emergency conning position set into its forward edge.

Full modernizations stretched the basic Essex hull to its absolute limit with added displacement and high structural stress levels. Those that did not receive angled decks served usefully in non-strike roles such as helicopter carriers and in anti-submarine warfare. As a training carrier, the *Lexington* survived until the 1980s.

ABOVE: **The *Shangri-La* (CV-38) was given a limited modernization but with enclosed bows, an angled deck and steam catapults, the latter evidenced by the forward-projecting horns. Note the after, deck-edge elevator in the lowered position.**

Essex class modernized

(Typical data for late, angled-deck conversions)
Displacement: 31,350 tonnes/30,800 tons (standard); 41,950 tonnes/41,200 tons (deep load)
Length: 251.5m/824ft 6in (at waterline); 271.5m/890ft (overall)
Beam: 30.8m/101ft
Draught: 9.2m/30ft 2in (full load)
Aircraft: About 80 (typically F2H Banshee or FJ-2 Fury fighters, AD Skyraider strike aircraft and, occasionally, AJ Savage bombers)
Flight deck: 262.6 x 43.3m/861 x 142ft
Armament: 11 x 127mm/5in and 16 x 76.2mm/3in (8 double) guns (typically less)
Machinery: Geared steam turbines, 8 boilers 4 shafts
Power: 111,900kW/150,000shp
Speed: 32 knots maximum
Fuel: 6,410 tonnes/6,300 tons
Range: 20,740km/11,200nm at 20 knots
Armour: 38mm/1.5in (hangar deck); 38mm/1.5in (protective deck)
Complement: 2,970 men

Enterprise (CVAN-65)

Although studies for nuclear-propelled warships began as early as 1950, the then primitive state of the technology and the very obvious costs saw the necessary shore-based experimental reactors not being given the go-ahead until 1954. In 1955, however, the pioneer nuclear submarine *Nautilus* gave the process a fillip with her record-breaking undersea passages, and apparently unlimited stamina.

The major argument for nuclear propulsion centred upon virtually unlimited endurance and higher speed. It applied best, however, to smaller, low-endurance vessels, for a carrier had been driven to such large dimensions by aviation requirements that she was able to carry adequate bunkers. For carriers, replenishment-at-sea was more often concerned with aviation fuel, ordnance and the necessary provisioning of 5,000-plus personnel, of whom one-third were aircrew.

A major advantage was that, having no requirement for uptakes and funnel, a nuclear carrier could be flush-decked, with no island. With the earlier requirement for large, strategic carrier-based bombers this factor alone would have justified the extra cost but, with already huge flight decks and aircraft pegged to under 36.3 tonnes/80,000lb, it was no longer relevant. An island was preferred even though the "command cruiser" had shown that necessary major electronics could be carried elsewhere, aboard a dedicated escort. It gave important visual command over navigation and flight deck activities.

TOP: **Although greatly changed from its original configuration, the bridge structure of the *Enterprise* retained its small, square footprint with the upper levels jettied outward.** ABOVE: **The *Enterprise* was completed with an all-missile armament, updated to Sea Sparrows, one of whose launchers and its associated director can be seen sponsoned out on the port quarter. The nearest aircraft is an anti-submarine S-3 Viking, by Lockheed.**

Ultimately, it was probably a mix of national prestige and the argument of "you'll never know until you've tried it" that moved the decision to build an experimental squadron of carrier, cruiser and escorts. Inter-service rivalry nonetheless caused the cost of the project to be endlessly reviewed, with naval concern that it would militate against future carriers, nuclear or conventional.

ABOVE: **The extreme flare necessary to support a large carrier's overhangs can lead to pounding in poor conditions and damage to projecting sponsons. Note the Vulcan/Phalanx CIWS located on the forward face of the bridge structure.** ABOVE RIGHT: **Arranging aircraft in tasteful displays occupies much of the peacetime carrierman's time, but can they be appreciated properly other than from the air?** RIGHT: **Manoeuvring a large carrier's bulk in restricted water is a task for tugs as the big ships lack side thrusters, a refinement common to merchantmen.**

Where later nuclear carriers would have only two reactors, the prototype *Enterprise* needed eight. To reduce the quantity of heavy shielding around them, they had to be grouped, vulnerably, together. Psychologically acceptable reductions were made where possible to reduce the ship's physical size but she was still to be 42.7m/140ft longer than an Improved Forrestal as laid down in 1958.

The island was made small and square at flight deck level. Above the height of aircraft tail fins, it was jettied-out to support the four great "billboards" of the experimental phased-array search radars. These, too, proved to be in advance of technology and, expensive to maintain, were eventually removed. Similarly, the unique conical structure supporting the 360-degree coverage of electronic support and counter-measures, gave way to a more conventional arrangement.

A considerable advantage of nuclear power was adequate steam for continuous operation of four catapults. Because it is incorporated in her anti-torpedo defence, *Enterprise* carries considerable quantities of fuel oil that can be used to top up escorts. Her aviation fuel capacity is 50 per cent greater than that of the preceding Improved Forrestals. She is scheduled to remain in service until 2013.

Enterprise (CVAN-65)

Built: Newport News
Commissioned: November 25, 1961
Displacement: 69,750 tonnes/68,500 tons (standard); 90,700 tonnes/89,100 tons (deep load)
Length: 317.2m/1,040ft (at waterline); 342.7m/1,123ft 6in (overall)
Beam: 40.6m/133ft
Draught: 11.3m/37ft
Aircraft: 99 (as designed)
Flight deck: 329.1 x 71.8m/1,079ft x 235ft 3in
Armament: 2 x octal Sea Sparrow SAM launchers and 3 x Vulcan/Phalanx CIWS (all fitted later)
Machinery: Geared steam turbines, 8 nuclear reactors, 4 shafts
Power: 209,000kW/280,000shp
Speed: 33 knots
Fuel: Nuclear
Range: Virtually unlimited between recoring
Armour: Not known
Complement: 5,500 men

John F. Kennedy (CVA-67)

In July 1960 the submerged submarine USS *George Washington* launched the Polaris intercontinental ballistic missile (ICBM) that effectively ended the career of the manned bomber as the chosen means of delivering strategic nuclear weaponry. It also had fundamental implications for the future form of the navy's carriers.

At this point in the carrier building programme, one Improved Forrestal (CVA-63) had been launched, a second (CVA-64) was soon to be, and a third (CVA-66) had been approved. The missing number in the series was borne by the prototype nuclear carrier *Enterprise* (CVAN-65) which was also about to be launched.

Fighting its own corner, the Air Force obliged the Navy to justify its continuing to build carriers of a size capable of deploying strategic bombers, as well as planning further hugely expensive nuclear-propelled carriers with a yet-unproven technology that might well be made redundant by the possibilities offered by a new generation of submarines. Once again, too, the air force resurrected the old and long-discredited argument that land-based air power, given the right aircraft, would offer a cheaper and equally effective alternative to carriers. The result of this agitation on a fiscally sensitive Congress was to delay the construction of the planned fourth Improved Forrestal (CVA-67) pending an exhaustive reappraisal of what form future carriers should take, an exercise useful also in delaying payments from over-stretched budgets.

TOP: **Although an intended bow sonar was never fitted to the *Kennedy*, it left its mark in the anchor located on the stemhead. Note how low the port side CIWS platform is situated.** ABOVE: **The *Kennedy*'s early air wing comprised the equivalent of 9 A-5 Vigilantes and 12 A-6 Intruders for heavy and medium attack, 24 A-4 Skyhawk light attack, 14 F-4 Phantom fighters, 6 E-2 Hawkeye electronic warfare and 3 RF-8 reconnaissance Crusaders.**

A starting point was the imminent entry into service of the A-5 Vigilante, an all-weather attack aircraft intended to replace the A-3 Skywarrior. Its take-off weight and dimensions were less than those of its predecessor. In particular, a folding tip to the tail fin reduced its stowage height by over one metre. As the 7.6m/25ft headroom of the hangars of current carriers was a dimension that very much influenced overall size, there was a possibility that it might be reduced to a money-saving 6.4m/21ft.

ABOVE: **Last of the conventionally propelled giant carriers, the *Kennedy* sports a uniquely canted funnel arrangement, reminiscent of late Japanese practice. Note the massive structure supporting the side elevator.** BELOW: **Designed for low-level attack, the long-lived Grumman A-6 Intruder can carry 7.85 tonnes/ 7.73 tons of external bombs and a centreline supplementary fuel tank.**

ABOVE: **Carrier superstructures have evolved an architecture of their own. The flood of data captured by the comprehensive electronics suite has to be presented in a form that can be rapidly understood while also being shared with other ships of a task group.**

Relieved of the responsibility of delivering strategic nuclear weaponry, the carrier force would assume tactical roles. This was reflected in other pending aircraft, such as the A-6 Intruder and the F6D air defence fighter, which were optimized as missile carriers rather than around high-speed performance. Take-off and landing speeds were actually being reduced.

It was argued, however, that, as far as CVA-67 was concerned, aircraft size and performance may have stabilized but, over the projected life of the ship, there was no guarantee that they would not, again, become demanding. The 7.6m/25ft hangar height was retained, for the smaller ship with a 6.4m/ 21ft hangar would be 2 knots slower, making her difficult to integrate with her sister carriers.

Short-term savings indicated long-term problems, so CVA-67, to be named *John F. Kennedy*, would be essentially a repeat Improved Forrestal, conventionally propelled, but with her design revised to take advantage of that of the *Enterprise*. She thus became a one-off, and the last boiler-powered "super carrier" of the US Navy. As if to underline the fact, her funnel was canted outboard, a distinctive recognition feature intended to improve smoke clearance. She is scheduled to be replaced (by CVN-22) in 2017.

John F. Kennedy (CVA-67)

Built: Newport News
Commissioned: September 7, 1968
Displacement: 61,850 tonnes/60,750 tons (standard); 84,200 tonnes/82,700 tons (deep load)
Length: 302m/990ft (at waterline); 320.6m/1051ft (overall)
Beam: 39.4m/129ft 4in
Draught: 11.2m/36ft 9in (deep load)
Aircraft: About 82
Flight deck: 313.5 x 72m/1,038 x 238ft 9in
Armament: 3 x octal Sea Sparrow SAM launchers, and 3 x Vulcan/Phalanx CIWS (all fitted later)
Machinery: Geared steam turbines, 8 boilers, 4 shafts
Power: 208,900kW/280,000shp
Speed: 33 knots
Fuel: Not known
Range: Not known
Armour: Not known
Complement: 5,400 men

Nimitz class

Having built a nuclear surface squadron of a carrier, cruiser and escorts, the US Navy had acquired experience and examples of three sizes of reactor. For the purpose of on-going studies aimed at the procurement of successors to the pioneer nuclear carrier *Enterprise*, this gave some flexibility in the design of the propulsion plant. Studies tended to favour proposals based on one overriding parameter, such as cost, size of air group etc, none of which could be enhanced except at the expense of the others. The most influential factors eventually proved to be the successful development of the A4W reactor (which avoided the complexity of the *Enterprise*) together with the length of catapults capable of launching the following generation of aircraft, and the sheer amount of space required by personnel, numbering over 5,600.

With the accelerating demise of the war-built Essex class, specialist anti-submarine warfare (ASW) carriers with fleet speed were no longer available. Fleet carriers thus had to shoulder a wider range of roles, their old CVA/CVAN designators being changed to CV/CVN. Their air group now had to include such as AS aircraft and helicopters, airborne early warning (AEW), tankers etc. These not only reduced the number of attack aircraft but also demanded a greater range of specialist maintenance facilities and personnel, all of which

ABOVE: **The *Nimitz* (CVAN-68) was the first of a long line of nuclear-propelled carriers. Her pristine trials condition emphasizes the considerable efforts that have been made to reduce hull protuberances.**
LEFT: **A contre-jour shot of a Nimitz engaged in replenishment. The mast and funnel of a supply ship are visible forward of the island while a UH-46 Sea Knight helicopter delivers at the carrier's after end.**

added to the pressures on space. It therefore came to be accepted that a Forrestal derivative represented the *minimum* size of hull that would meet realistic requirements.

Back in 1950, the sudden outbreak of war in Korea had consolidated the post-World War II case for carriers. In 1964, Vietnam performed the same service. This campaign, which made heavy demands on carriers, saw the required force level being raised to 15 with a total of 12 interchangeable air groups. Of the 15, only the *Enterprise*, 8 Forrestals and 3 modernized Midways actually existed. An integrated procurement programme was thus initiated to acquire three post-Forrestals at two-year intervals. These became the first of the Nimitz class.

Carrier beam had long since ceased being constrained by Panama Canal dimensions but a new limitation now arose in the 40.9m/134ft width of the construction facility at Newport News.

Improvements incorporated into the Nimitz class are far from obvious to the superficial glance. Flight deck layout has been optimized to create the smoothest air flow downstream, consistent with the most practical alignment of the angled deck with respect to elevators and catapults, which have their own requirement for rapid and efficient aircraft handling.

The external hull surfaces have been considerably "cleaned up", obviating the need for many of the earlier sponsons that had enforced speed reduction due to their slamming in a head sea. So few sponsons do, however, reflect a considerable reduction in armament and, as none of the class has yet been exposed to operations involving a high risk of heavy counter-attack, this could well change.

Extended operations off Vietnam emphasized the advantages of nuclear propulsion, which released internal volume that could be utilized in larger magazines and aviation fuel storage facilities.

ABOVE LEFT: **Higher associated costs pay off when it comes to mobility. For a conventionally powered carrier, continuous high speed is very demanding on fuel but the nuclear ship has no such problems.** ABOVE RIGHT: **Primary defence for the carrier is vested in her aircraft and the capability of her escorts. If the ring is breached, however, she can still deploy the short-range Sea Sparrow (on either quarter) or the last-ditch CIWS systems flanking the transom.**

Nimitz class

Class: *Carl Vinson* (CVN-70), Newport News, commissioned March 13, 1982; *Dwight D. Eisenhower* (CVN-69), Newport News, commissioned October 18, 1977; *Nimitz* (CVN-68), Newport News, commissioned May 3, 1975

Displacement: 82,500 tonnes/81,000 tons (standard); 93,150 tonnes/91,500 tons (deep load)

Length: 317.2m/1,040ft (at waterline); 332.5m/1,090ft (overall)

Beam: 40.9m/134ft

Draught: 11.2m/36ft 8in (deep load)

Aircraft: About 87

Flight deck: 333.1 x 76.5m/1,092 x 250ft 9in

Armament: 3 x octal Sea Sparrow SAM launchers and 3 or 4 Vulcan/Phalanx CIWS

Machinery: Geared steam turbines, 2 reactors, 4 shafts

Power: 194,000kW/260,000shp

Speed: 31.5 knots

Fuel: Nuclear

Range: Virtually unlimited between recoring

Armour: Not known

Complement: 5,950 men

Improved Nimitz (CVN-71) class

Commencing with the *Forrestal* (CV-59), a full half-century ago, the American super-carrier has changed surprisingly little and must be one of the most successful programmes in warship history. Oil-fired boilers have been superseded by nuclear-powered heat exchangers, but well-trusted steam turbines still drive each shaft, with individual get-you-home diesel engines for emergencies.

Dimensions have risen but little and flight deck configuration has settled to a standard layout with four deck-edge elevators, two forward of the island and two on opposite sides aft. On the currently building *George H.W. Bush* (CVN-77), last of the present series, the angle of the flight deck has been marginally increased to permit both catapults to be utilized while aircraft are landing. It is claimed that an aircraft can be launched every 20 seconds, although the rate of steam consumption would be enormous.

Impressions of CVN-77 indicate a very clean upper hull, with minimum projections to invite slamming. Unusually, it incorporates a bulb forward, not for the purposes of housing sonar, but for improved hydrodynamic efficiency.

Of hull protection, little detail is available, but it appears to be based on a system of parallel longitudinal anti-torpedo bulkheads, divided into compartments. Usually void, some may be filled with aviation fuel to supplement the 8,636 tonnes/8,500 tons already carried but which can be consumed within 16 days.

Kevlar composition armour has long since replaced steel, but is incorporated only in specific areas and up to a reported thickness of 63mm/2.5in.

CVN-77 and a retrospective refitting programme will see the now elderly NATO Sea Sparrow SAM and Vulcan/Phalanx CIWS replaced, probably by four Rolling Airframe Missile

ABOVE: **The enormous overhang is now almost symmetrical, i.e. on both sides of the hull, giving a flight deck so wide that the "angled deck" has, as in the very earliest experiments, evolved into no more than an angled painted flight path. This is the *Washington* (CVN-73).**

LEFT: **Compared with the giant carrier, *Forrestal* (CVA-59), the Improved Nimitzes have waterline length and beam increased by 15.3m/50ft and 1.4m/4.7ft respectively. The hull is finer but capacity (the most important parameter) has increased by about 9 per cent.**

LEFT: **Note how the *Roosevelt*'s superstructure is positioned to suit the three starboard-side elevators, and how the separate mast, bearing the antenna of the long-range air search radar, is enlarging to become a structure in its own right.**

(RAM) launchers. These will be integrated into the so-called Ship Self-Defense System (SSDS) that in the Mk2 version links all sensors, command and control systems, and weaponry for the fastest response against incoming and anti-ship missiles. The system can also link with other ships so fitted.

Following the *Bush* will be the so far unnamed CVN-78, first of a modified "CVN-21" class. At a projected 101,605 tonnes/100,000 tons displacement, the new ships are likely to change little in the hull but the island, once again, will be configured around a four-quadrant, three-dimensional, phased array radar.

Nuclear propulsion, once questioned, is now confirmed although it is no longer indispensable for steam generation to power four catapults at maximum utilization. The CVN-78 will have electromagnetically powered catapults, working like giant linear motors and demanding vast peaks of electrical energy. This may be associated with the dispersed electrical drive system to be used in the pending British carriers.

To address overcrowding and to reduce manpower costs it is forecast that the current 5,750 or so crew will be reduced by about 10 per cent through automation and simplifying procedures.

CVN-78 is scheduled to be laid down in 2007 for 2014 completion, with her CVN-79 follow-on being 2011 and 2019 respectively. The earlier construction tempo has slowed to one every five years, no longer sufficient to maintain a ten-carrier fleet or, probably, to sustain the Newport News building facility.

ABOVE: **An F/A-18 Hornet is readied on the inboard waist catapult. It sits on the blast deflector panel which will be raised when it moves forward. Note the low dome at left, permitting local deck control.**

ABOVE: **As in the days of explosive growth in battleships, the size of modern carriers limits the number of facilities that can accept them. They are also unable to transit the Panama Canal.**

Improved Nimitz (CVN-71) class

Class: *Theodore Roosevelt* (CVN-71), commissioned October 25, 1986; *Abraham Lincoln* (CVN-72), commissioned December 16, 1989; *George Washington* (CVN-73), commissioned July 4, 1992; *John C. Stennis* (CVN-74), commissioned December 9, 1995; *Harry S. Truman* (CVN-75), commissioned July 25, 1998; *Ronald Reagan* (CVN-76), commissioned July 12, 2003; *George H.W. Bush* (CVN-77), commissioned April 2008

Displacement: 82,500 tonnes/81,000 tons (standard); 93,150 tonnes/91,500 tons (deep load)

Length: 317.2m/1,040ft (at waterline); 332.5m/1090ft (overall)

Beam: 40.9m/134ft

Draught: 11.2m/36ft 8in (deep load)

Aircraft: About 87

Flight deck: 333.1 x 76.5m/1,092ft x 250ft 9in

Armament: 3 x Octal Sea Sparrow SAM launchers and 3 or 4 Vulcan/Phalanx CIWS (but see notes)

Machinery: Geared steam turbines, 2 reactors, 4 shafts

Power: 194,000kW/260,000shp

Speed: 31+ knots

Fuel: Nuclear

Range: Virtually unlimited between recoring

Armour: Not known

Complement: 5,750 men

LEFT: **The LPH design proved deficient in not including assault landing craft but effective in assumed roles of helicopter-centred minesweeping and anti-submarine operations.** ABOVE: **Derived from experiment with converted *Essex*-class carriers the Helicopter Carrier (LPH) was designed around the accommodation and transport of about 2,000 troops and the helicopters with which to put them ashore.**

Iwo Jima class (LPH)

The helicopter revolutionized the landing of spearhead troops ahead of a main amphibious landing. Early carrier conversions during the 1950s proved the principle, leading to the construction of seven *Iwo Jima*-class Amphibious Assault Helicopter Carriers (LPH) during the next decade. They had a flight deck, hangar and two deck-edge elevators but no facilities for the launch and recovery of conventional aircraft.

Accommodation was provided for a Marine battalion landing team of about 2,100 personnel, together with their equipment and light vehicles. For landing purposes they depended upon an embarked Marine helicopter squadron, which normally comprises 24 CH-46 Sea Knight assault helicopters, 4 CH-53 Sea Stallion heavy-lift helicopters and 4 UH-1 Iroquois utility observation helicopters. The last-named could be replaced in specific roles by AH-1 Sea Cobra attack machines.

The Americans also placed much faith in aerial minesweeping, covering large areas using specially equipped sleds towed behind helicopters. This has the advantage of speed; however, the benefit was, at best, superficial. For this role the LPH was temporarily equipped with the RH-53 and MH-53 variants of the Sea Stallion, fitted for aerial towage.

Later in their careers, the LPHs proved quite capable of operating Harrier V/STOL aircraft, which required no arrester gear, catapults or angled deck.

The LPH needed to be complemented by an LSD (Landing Ship, Dock) which had the facilities to transport and land associated heavy equipment such as armoured vehicles, artillery and bulldozers. Stowed forward on vehicle decks, these could be loaded into a variety of landing craft which were carried in a floodable after well, accessible through a wide, lowering stern gate. The well deck could be roofed with removable deck sections which, together, formed a clear area large enough to operate heavy-lift helicopters. No facilities, other than for refuelling, were incorporated for these machines, accommodated elsewhere.

All were decommissioned between 1993 and 2002.

Iwo Jima class (LPH)

Class: *Guadalcanal* (LPH-7), Philadelphia Navy Yard, commissioned July 20, 1963; *Guam* (LPH-9), Philadelphia Navy Yard, commissioned January 16, 1965; *Inchon* (LPH-12), Ingalls, Pascagoula, commissioned June 20, 1970; *Iwo Jima* (LPH-2), Puget-Sound Navy Yard, commissioned August 26, 1961; *New Orleans* (LPH-11), Philadelphia Navy Yard, commissioned November 16, 1968; *Okinawa* (LPH-3), Philadelphia Navy Yard, commissioned April 14, 1962; *Tripoli* (LPH-10), Ingalls, Pascagoula, commissioned August 6, 1966

Displacement: 17,300 tonnes/17,000 tons (standard); 18,680 tonnes/18,350 tons (deep load)

Length: 180.6m/592ft (at waterline); 183.6m/602ft (overall)

Beam: 25.6m/84ft

Draught: 7.9m/26ft (deep load)

Aircraft: 30–32 helicopters

Flight deck: 181.5 x 32m/595 x 105ft

Armament: 4 x 76.2mm/3in (2 double) guns, 2 x octal Sea Sparrow SAM launchers and 2 x Vulcan/Phalanx CIWS

Machinery: Geared steam turbines, 2 boilers, 1 shaft

Power: 17,150kW/23,000shp

Speed: 21.5 knots

Fuel: Not known

Range: Not known

Armour: None

Complement: 680 men

LEFT: **A Wasp has no angled flight deck but a wide island superstructure. Space has been gained by deleting former armament pockets on either side, right forward, where the CH-53 is here parked.**
ABOVE: **The *Wasp*-class LHD was designed to complement the *Whidbey Island*-class LSD and *San Antonio*-class LPD.**

Wasp class (LHD)

The reliance of the *Iwo Jima* LPH on a dock-type ship to transport its heavy equipment was obviously limiting. This quickly led to a new type of ship that sought to combine the characteristics of each. Built in 1971–80, these were the five *Tarawa*-class vessels, which were very expensive and, although undeniably flexible, were liable to be criticized for their "all eggs in one basket" approach.

Known as Amphibious Assault Ships (LHA) they also have accommodation for a Marine battalion, but differ fundamentally in incorporating a floodable docking well dimensioned to stow four Landing Craft, Utility. These can put 142 tonnes/140 tons of cargo directly on to the beach.

In exercises, the LHA has demonstrated that it can function efficiently and alternatively as a V/STOL carrier, deploying 20 AV-8A Harriers.

Although the final four Tarawas were cancelled, the concept was resurrected within five years with the laying-down in May 1985 of the *Wasp*, name ship of an improved class. These are termed Helicopter/Dock Landing Ships, or LHD. Again configured around the requirements of a Marine battalion, their docking well accommodates three LCACS, or Air Cushion Landing Craft. Each can transport about 61 tonnes/ 60 tons at over 40 knots.

The Tarawas carry 127mm/5in guns, primarily for gunfire support, but these weapons have been suppressed in the Wasps to maximize flight deck area. Interestingly assuming names borne previously by regular carriers, the LHDs can deploy up to 36 helicopters. Equipped to operate ground-attack AV-8s, they can alternatively operate in the old escort carrier (CVE) role in providing close air support. They will also be able to deploy the MV-22 Osprey tilt-rotor aircraft which can be configured for either assault or ASW roles. LHAs can also function as Sea Control Ships or AS carriers (albeit expensive ones). To emphasize their versatility they have strengthened flight decks and incorporate lightweight Kevlar protection to limit splinter damage.

Wasp class (LHD)

Class: *Bataan* (LHD-5), commissioned September 20, 1997; *Bonhomme Richard* (LHD-6), commissioned August 15, 1998; *Boxer* (LHD-4), commissioned February 11, 1995; *Essex* (LHD-2), commissioned October 17, 1992; *Iwo Jima* (LHD-7), commissioned June 30, 2001; *Kearsarge* (LHD-3), commissioned October 16, 1993; *Wasp* (LHD-1), commissioned July 29, 1989; (LHD-8), due August 2007

Built: All by Ingalls Pascagoula (now Northrop-Grumman Ship Systems)

Displacement: 28,750 tonnes/28,250 tons (standard)/41,250 tonnes/40,500 tons (deep load)

Length: 237.1m/777ft 6in (at waterline); 257.3m/843ft 8in (overall)

Beam: 32.3m/105ft 10in

Draught: 8.1m/26ft 8in (full load)

Aircraft: Up to 36 helicopters or 20 Harrier V/STOL equivalents

Flight deck: 245 x 42.7m/803ft 3in x 140ft

Armament: 2 x 16-cell launchers for Sea Sparrow and RAM surface-to-air missiles, and 3 x Vulcan/Phalanx CIWS

Machinery: Geared steam turbines, 2 boilers, 2 shafts

Power: 57,500kW/77,000shp

Speed: 24 knots

Fuel: 6,300 tonnes/6,200 tons

Range: 17,590km/9,500nm at 20 knots

Armour: Kevlar only

Complement: 1,080 men

Balloon ships and early seaplane carriers

Kite balloons, which were configured to remain stable observation platforms in a wind, were deployed extensively from many classes of Royal Navy ship, but it was only the British that converted merchantmen to auxiliaries specifically for this purpose. Five such were taken up for service – the *Manica* and the *City of Oxford* from the Ellerman group, the *Hector* and *Menelaus* from Blue Funnel, and the *Canning* of Lamport and Holt.

Fairly standard in form, the conversion began with removal of the foremast and associated cargo gear. Ship's structure dividing the forward holds was then cut away to link the spaces, forming a continuous, unobstructed well. Collapsible wind breaks could be secured to the original hatch coamings to enable balloons to be safely inflated in a breeze.

Specialist equipment comprised a hydrogen gas generator and a compressor. Due to the explosive inflammability of hydrogen, routines were strictly observed.

Used mainly in service with the Grand Fleet, and in conjunction with coastal operations such as Gallipoli and in Belgium, their usefulness diminished as the war progressed and most reverted to cargo-carrying.

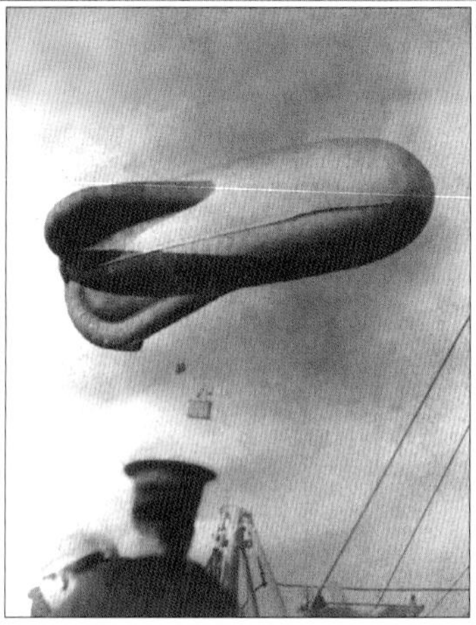

ABOVE: **Seen here aboard the light cruiser *Caradoc*, a kite balloon could extend the horizon for reconnaissance, but not at high speeds.**
RIGHT: **An unusually well-inflated specimen, this kite balloon has no observers in its basket, and may have just been transferred from a specialist balloon ship to a fleet unit with no facilities.**

Empress

During 1913 the second-class cruiser *Hermes* had demonstrated the possibilities of taking seaplanes to sea and operating them on a continuous basis. Most thought of the aircraft in terms of observation and reconnaissance; others, such as the offensively minded Murray Sueter, regarded them as potential torpedo-carriers.

As war broke out in August 1914, it was Sueter who was instrumental in the requisitioning of three cross-channel packets of the South-Eastern & Chatham Railway Company. Too small for use as troop ships they were, nonetheless, fast and handy.

LEFT: **Last of the three initial packet conversions, the *Empress* had the disadvantage of being four knots slower than her running mates. She can be identified by the short W/T (wireless telegraphy) spreaders aft.**

Like that of the *Hermes*, the initial "conversion" was primitive, involving little more than the clearance of afterdeck fittings and equipment, and the erection of a large, framed canvas "hangar" for three seaplanes, all of which were swung out and recovered by cargo derrick.

Completed in 1907, the *Empress* was the oldest of the three ships, all of which came from the specialist yard of Denny, at Dumbarton. Returned to commercial service in 1919, she was scrapped in 1933.

Engadine and *Riviera*

Together with the *Empress*, the Admiralty took up the slightly faster *Engadine* and *Riviera*. Once given the same initial, and very primitive, modifications, all three were attached to the Harwich Force. Their pioneer raid against the Zeppelin installations near Cuxhaven on Christmas Day, 1914 demonstrated both their potential and their limitations. It also highlighted the hazard of retaliatory enemy air attacks on the ships involved.

During 1915, therefore, all three ships were given a large, permanent, box hangar, together with cranes for aircraft handling. They also acquired a light anti-aircraft armament.

Once modified, however, they no longer operated as a coherent force but were attached to various commands to explore the possibilities of aerial cooperation. Serving with the Battle Cruiser Force, *Engadine* was thus able to make her modest, but historic, contribution to Jutland. *Riviera* was involved with army cooperation along the Belgian coast besides investigating the value of seaplane anti-submarine (AS) patrols. The slower *Empress* was employed, for the most part, in the Mediterranean. Proving small for the task, they were soon surpassed by larger ships, but all served throughout the war and were returned to commercial service during 1919.

Engadine survived until early 1941, being sunk by Japanese action in the Philippines, *Riviera* served the Royal Navy through a second war, not being scrapped until 1957.

ABOVE: **This early picture of the *Riviera* shows her in pre-war livery and equipped only with canvas protection for her embarked seaplanes.**

ABOVE: ***Engardine*'s permanent hangar extended well forward and involved demolition of the after end of the boat deck. No aircraft were carried on the foredeck.**

ABOVE: ***Engadine* following the installation of a permanent hangar and facilities in 1915. Except for landing most of her earlier lifeboats and receiving an enlarged bridge, her forward end remained unchanged. *Empress* was nearly identical.**

Engadine

Built: Denny, Dumbarton
Gross tonnage: 1,675 tons
Displacement: 2,600 tonnes/2,550 tons (normal)
Length: 95.4m/313ft (bp); 96.3m/316ft (overall)
Beam: 12.5m/41ft
Draught: 4.1m/13ft 6in (mean)
Aircraft: Hangar accommodation for 4 seaplanes
Machinery: Three sets direct-drive steam turbines, 6 boilers, 3 shafts
Power: 8,206kW/11,000shp
Speed: 20.5 knots
Fuel: 407 tonnes/400 tons (coal)
Range: 1,570km/850nm at 10 knots
Armour: None
Complement: 144 men plus 53 aircrew

Ark Royal (I)

The *Hermes* trials with seaplanes brought about two avenues of progress. As noted previously, cross-channel packets were converted to get aircraft to sea with minimum delay. In parallel with this, the Royal Navy acquired a larger vessel, the first one to be specifically designed to carry and maintain seaplanes at sea. As a new build would have taken too long, the Admiralty purchased a merchantman in a very early stage of construction. She was a typical workhorse of the time, a coal-fired, three-island single-decker with engine amidships. In her then-current state, it was not difficult to relocate engine, boilers, and bunkers aft. A resulting stern trim had to be countered by permanent ballast. In addition, capacious water ballast tanks were built in to adjust both freeboard and roll motion to facilitate the handling of the aircraft.

Occupying the central 40 per cent of the ship's length was a hold capable of stowing seven folded seaplanes. This was

ABOVE: **Seen entering Portsmouth Harbour during the 1930s, the *Ark Royal* has been fitted with a catapult for trials purposes. Her total lack of forward sheer is very evident.** LEFT: **Alongside at Portsmouth, the ship is seen with her jack half-masted. As she has already been renamed *Pegasus* the occasion could have been the death of King George V. The aircraft forward is a Fairey III F.**

accessed via a single large hatch served by two 3.01-tonne/3-ton cranes and a cargo derrick. Forward of the hold, and extending partly over it, were specialist workshops and store rooms.

The ship was built without sheer and, with all anchor gear relocated below, the foredeck was left clear and flat. The intention was that aircraft could be flown directly from the ship but, not least due to her very low speed, there is no evidence that this was ever done. With its low freeboard and lack of solid bulwarks, the forward end looked very prone to wetness.

Named *Ark Royal* (surely a peculiar use for an ancient name), she was a very simple vessel, entering service as early as December 1914. She was immediately sent to the Dardanelles where her seaplanes were among the earliest to support fleet activities in spotting and reconnaissance.

Losses consequent upon the eventual arrival of German U-boats caused a hasty re-evaluation of the manner in which the navy worked. The slow *Ark Royal* was considered too vulnerable and, replaced by later conversions, she was transferred to Salonika and the Aegean, where she spent the remainder of the war.

Between the wars, she gave useful service in a couple of low-level crises before being fitted with a catapult on the foredeck for use as a trials ship. Late in 1935 she was renamed *Pegasus*, her earlier name being passed on to the large new fleet carrier which had just been laid down.

At the outbreak of her second war, the *Pegasus* had been reduced to service as an aircraft transport. Naval-manned Fighter Catapult Ships were, however, being urgently created to supplement CAM ships in convoy escort. Despite her unsuitability for North Atlantic conditions, the *Pegasus* made several such trips before returning to a training role.

Sold out of service in 1946, she plied commercially until being scrapped in 1950. From humble beginnings she served the Royal Navy long and well.

TOP: **A trolley-mounted Sopwith Schneider ready for hoisting from the *Ark Royal*'s hangar deck. With a span of only 8.7m/28ft 8in the aircraft could pass through the hatch. Larger aircraft, such as the big Short seaplanes, had to have their wings attached topside.** ABOVE: **Captured intact, apparently after having force-landed due to an engine fire, a German seaplane is being put overside from the *Ark Royal*.** BELOW: **Seen in Malta's Grand Harbour, probably in the early 1930s, the *Ark Royal* passes an Aberdeen & Commonwealth liner of the class immortalized by the *Jervis Bay* in November 1940.**

Ark Royal (I)

Built: Blyth Shipbuilding, Blyth
Commissioned: October 12, 1914
Displacement: 7,210 tonnes/7,080 tons (standard); 7,580 tonnes/7,450 tons (deep load)
Length: 107.4m/352ft 6in (bp); 111.5m/366ft (overall)
Beam: 15.5m/50ft 10in
Draught: 5.5m/18ft (full load, mean)
Aircraft: Hangar accommodation for 7
Armament: 4 x 12pdr guns
Machinery: 1 set vertical triple expansion, 3 boilers, 1 shaft
Power: 2,240kW/3000ihp
Speed: 11 knots
Fuel: 509 tonnes/500 tons
Range: 5,560km/3,000nm at 10 knots
Armour: None
Complement: 120 men plus 60 aircrew

Ben-my-Chree, *Vindex* and *Manxman*

Rather larger than the earlier, Dover Strait vessels converted to aviation ships, the *Ben-my-Chree, Vindex* and *Manxman* were built for the Isle of Man Steam Packet Company. All three were converted with the addition of a seaplane hangar aft and a launch platform forward, intended mainly for wheeled landplanes.

Superficially, there was a strong resemblance, but they could be differentiated by the seaplane handling gear aft. The *Ben-my-Chree* had a simple post and cargo derrick, the *Vindex* had cranes which folded against the after superstructure when at sea, while the *Manxman* was fitted with a relatively heavy gantry crane which protruded beyond her counter.

Operating during the Dardanelles campaign, Short 184s from the *Ben-my-Chree* scored notable firsts with two successful torpedo attacks, one from the air, the other while taxiing.

Originally named *Viking*, the *Vindex* became the first Royal Navy ship to launch a landplane, a Bristol Scout, in November 1915. In August 1916, one attacked the Zeppelin L.17 with bombs, but without result.

The *Manxman* differed from her consorts in having a landplane added below her bridge structure. Serving with both the Grand Fleet and in the Mediterranean, she had the distinction of being the first Royal Navy ship to deploy the Sopwith Pup fighters.

Ben-my-Chree later had her forward launch ramp removed but while still operating as a seaplane carrier, she was hit by enemy artillery off the Turkish coast in January 1917. Aviation fuel caused an uncontrollable blaze that destroyed her.

Both of the other ships returned to commercial service in 1920 and went on to serve through World War II, the *Vindex* as a troopship (under her commercial name of *Viking*) and the *Manxman* as a radar training ship (renamed *Caduceus*).

LEFT: **The sided foremasts of the *Vindex* permitted a longer launch platform for landplanes to pass between while, aft, there was accommodation and cranage for five seaplanes.**

LEFT: **Although this profile shows the higher bridge and temporary forward launch platform, it is inaccurate in recording a derrick on the mainmast and a crows nest, neither of which were fitted. Funnels and masts should have a similar rake. Of all the packets similarly converted, the *Ben-my-Chree* was the only one lost to enemy action.**

ABOVE: ***Ben-my-Chree* could be instantly recognized by the tall derrick post right aft. Her mainmast would later be removed. The low bridge also indicates that the temporary forward launch platform has been landed.**

Ben-my-Chree

Built: Vickers, Sons and Maxim, Barrow
Completed: July 1908; commissioned as aviation ship January 2, 1915
Gross tonnage: 2,650 tons
Displacement: 3,970 tonnes/3,900 tons (standard)
Length: 114.4m/375ft (bp); 118.0m/387ft (overall)
Beam: 14.1m/46ft 2in
Draught: 4.6m/15ft (standard)
Aircraft: 4–6 depending upon type
Flight deck: Dimensions not known
Machinery: 3 sets direct-drive steam turbines, 4 boilers, 3 shafts
Power: 10,450kW/14,000shp
Speed: 24 knots
Fuel: 560 tonnes/550 tons (coal)
Range: Not known
Armour: None
Complement: 175 men

Nairana, Pegasus, Brocklesby and *Killingholme*

The *Nairana* and *Pegasus* brought to an end the line of development known to the Royal Navy as the "mixed carrier". Both ships were under construction when requisitioned in 1917, the *Nairana* for the Australian coastal service of Huddart, Parker and the *Pegasus* (as the *Stockholm*) for the Great Eastern Railway's North Sea route.

Modelled on the preceding *Manxman*, the two were very similar, except for the seaplane handling arrangements situated aft (gantry in *Nairana*, cranes in *Pegasus*). The forward launching ramp, extending from bridge front to stem head, had a removable section to allow cargo derricks to transfer fighter aircraft from forward hangar and hold.

ABOVE: **Resplendent in dazzle camouflage, the *Pegasus* also shows facilities for both landplanes and seaplanes. Note the "PS" recognition letters atop the hangar and the Fairey Campania on the afterdeck.**
BELOW: ***Pegasus* served briefly on the China station during the 1920s and is seen here in the usual buff and white livery. Note that the launch facility has been removed but the forecastle remains built up.**

By this point in the war, it was apparent that the future of naval aviation lay in larger, purpose-built vessels, as the smaller ships were seeing much activity but little action. The *Nairana* returned to commercial service in 1920 but the *Pegasus* was retained, serving as an aircraft transport until being scrapped in 1931.

Mention should be made of the *Brocklesby* and *Killingholme*, two of the Royal Navy's humblest aviation ships. These were specialist, shallow draught paddle steamers, built to operate the ferry service between Hull and New Holland on the wide, lower estuary of the Humber. Their upper decks were spacious and open, designed to accommodate vehicles or indeed cattle.

Enemy Zeppelins were nightly crossing the English east coast on bombing missions that caused little damage but considerable public disquiet. It was the Navy's task to establish an outer defence line to intercept them.

Converted during 1916 to carry two small floatplanes apiece, the pair worked in conjunction with modified trawlers. The measure enjoyed no success, however, and both ships were returned to commercial service during 1917.

Pegasus

Built: John Brown, Clydebank
Commissioned: August 28, 1917
Displacement: 3,360 tonnes/3,300 tons (standard)
Length: 100.5m/329ft 6in (bp); 101.3m/332ft (overall)
Beam: 13.5m/44ft 3in
Draught: 4.7m/15ft 4in (standard)
Aircraft: Up to 9 (5 fighters and 4 floatplanes)
Machinery: Two sets geared turbines, 6 boilers, 2 shafts
Power: 7,250kW/9,700shp
Speed: 20 knots
Fuel: 367 tonnes/360 tons
Range: Not known
Armour: None
Complement: 255 men

Campania (I)

Having lost the Blue Riband of the North Atlantic in 1889, Cunard ordered two new express liners for the purpose of its recovery. The *Campania* and *Lucania* were delivered in 1893 and fully came up to expectations. In order to achieve their 21-plus knots, however, each was fitted with two enormous and complex "three crank triple engines", five-cylinder triple-expansion machinery delivering 22,371kW/ 30,000ihp. At speed, these demanded 488 tonnes/480 tons of coal per day.

Twenty years and 250 round voyages later the ship was worn out and sold for scrap. As HMS *Hermes* had just demonstrated that seaplanes could be operated at sea the Admiralty purchased the old vessel for a knock-down price for conversion to a "seaplane-carrying ship". This work was in hand by September 1914.

In April 1915 the *Campania* joined the fleet with a 36.6m/ 120ft flying-off ramp extending from bridge front to stem head. She could now manage only 18 knots, barely sufficient to work with the fleet.

As an experimental ship, her first six months proved disappointing. Exercising with the fleet on seven occasions, she had been able to fly seaplanes on only three of them. On these, engine and radio problems "had the result that the seaplanes have not been of much value". Difficulties with the ramp already meant that seaplanes were being both launched and recovered from the sea. For this, however, larger aircraft were required.

ABOVE: **Following her second, and more comprehensive, rebuilding the *Campania*'s forefunnel has been divided to permit a longer forward platform. Her mainmast has been relocated forward of the after funnel to permit kite balloons to be deployed from a facility on the afterdeck.**

Her continued employment was, nonetheless, supported by the C-in-C, Admiral Jellicoe, who noted that "the value of the ship will be immensely increased when machines ... are supplied for the attack of enemy airships, and for scouting". The former role, he stressed, was "a most pressing necessity".

To correct her initial shortcomings, the *Campania* began a major remodelling in November 1915. Her bridge was removed and the forefunnel separated into two, sided casings. A new forward ramp, some 61m/200ft in length, passed between them. Beneath its after end was accommodation for "seven large seaplanes and three or four small fighting seaplanes suitable for attacking Zeppelins". On her afterdeck had been added facilities for operating a kite balloon.

Even before her recommissioning in April 1916, the navy's Director of Air Services noted that "the vulnerability and lack of speed of the *Campania* severely handicap her utility". Just two months later, the ship's great opportunity to prove that utility was squandered when she failed to receive sailing orders prior to Jutland. In February 1917, it was recommended the *Campania*'s Sopwith Baby seaplanes be changed for Pup landplane fighters and, soon afterward, a 1½-Strutter demonstrated a successful take-off.

By August 1917, new aviation vessels were being constructed and it was proposed to reduce the *Campania* to a training role with an "alighting deck" and a catapult. Probably in view of her condition, this was not put in hand.

Ever less than satisfactory, the *Campania*'s career was terminated just a week prior to the armistice. Dragging her anchors in a gale, she fouled other ships, was holed, and foundered quickly, due to poor subdivision.

TOP AND BELOW: **The poor subdivision of the *Campania* was always a source of anxiety to C-in-C, Grand Fleet. That his worries were well founded was confirmed by her rapid sinking following a collision in November 1918.**

ABOVE: **From 1917 the *Campania* deployed the Fairey F.17 (which also took the ship's name) an aircraft tailored in size to the ship's hatch. Here, one takes off with the assistance of a four-wheeled trolley.**

Campania (I)

Built: Fairfield, Govan
Commissioned: April 17, 1915 (into Royal Navy); originally completed April 8,1893
Displacement: 18,350 tonnes/18,000 tons (standard); 22,470 tonnes/20,600 tons (full load)
Length: 183.1m/601ft (bp); 189.5m/622ft (overall)
Beam: 19.8m/65ft
Draught: 7m/23ft (normal); 8.5m/28ft (full load)
Launching platform (in 1916): 74.7 x 13.4m/ 245 x 44ft) maximum
Aircraft: 10–12 plus 1 kite balloon
Armament: 6 x 119mm/4.7in (6 single) and 1 x 76.2mm/3in guns
Machinery: Two sets vertical triple expansion, 13 boilers, 2 shafts
Power: 22,380kW/30,000ihp
Speed: 23 knots/18 knots (sustained)
Fuel: 3,251 tonnes/3,200 tons (coal)
Range: 4,780km/2600nm at 21 knots
Armour: None
Complement: 443 men plus 157 aircrew

Furious (I) and (II)

The three extraordinary "large light cruisers" of the Courageous class were brainchildren of the controversial First Sea Lord, Sir John ("Jackie") Fisher. They fully embodied his theory that, if speed and firepower were adequate, protection could be greatly reduced since the ship could choose or decline action at will, while deciding her own range. This trio was conceived to be strong and fast enough to reconnoitre for the battle-cruiser force in any conditions.

Laid down in 1915, they were barely commenced when Fisher, their champion, resigned. Despite now being ceaselessly criticized, the two 381mm/15in armed ships, *Courageous* and *Glorious*, were completed in 1917 as designed. Their half-sister *Furious*, as yet unfinished, was due to be armed with a totally impractical single 457mm/18in gun forward and aft.

Sir John Jellicoe, C-in-C Grand Fleet, was keen to exploit the possibilities of aviation yet was continually frustrated by auxiliary carriers that were either too small and slow (*Engadine* etc) or unreliable (*Campania*). He had been demanding a carrier fast enough to maintain fleet speed and large enough to accommodate both high-performance fighters and seaplanes able to carry a torpedo. Jutland had largely discredited Fisher's ideas regarding battle-cruisers and the then unwanted *Furious* was selected for conversion by a committee headed by the new C-in-C, Sir David Beatty.

TOP: Following her second remodelling, the *Furious* had flight decks that completely surrounded her original funnel and superstructure. Note the palisade (wind-break) forward and the crash barrier aft, supported by a gallows structure. ABOVE: Extensive experiments were conducted with non-rigid airships ("blimps") in this case a "North Sea" type.

Still incomplete, she had her forward turret removed in March 1917. It was replaced by a large box hangar with a flat top. From its forward edge a flying-off ramp sloped down to the stem head, similar to that fitted on the *Campania*. Apparently designed around accommodating eight seaplanes, the ship entered service in July 1917 with three Short 184 seaplanes and five Sopwith Pup fighters.

On August 2, 1917, encouraged by the ship's high speed and the excellent low-speed characteristics of the Pup, Squadron Commander Edwin Dunning of the RNAS

ABOVE: As she first entered service in mid-1917, the *Furious* had lost her forward turret in favour of a flying-off deck and hangar. By the end of the year, her after turret was also removed.

side-slipped around the bridge structure to effect a first landing on the hangar top. Five days later, he repeated the feat but a third attempt was fatal, the aircraft toppling overboard.

Suitable landing decks had frequently been proposed to obviate the need for fighters to alight on the sea, where they had to rely on the precarious assistance of flotation bags. Possibly influenced by Dunning's example, the *Furious* re-entered dockyard hands in November 1917. Four months of work saw her after 457mm/18in turret replaced by a second hangar and a flat, 91.4m/300ft landing deck. This communicated with the forward flight deck by elevated tracks flanking the remaining superstructure. Both flight decks were now served from the hangars by electric elevators, while the afterdeck was fitted with an embryonic arrester system comprising weighted transverse wires with longitudinal wires laid ahead of them.

Although by then-current standards, the *Furious* could successfully deploy aircraft, she remained unable to recover them for the remaining superstructure created violent and unpredictable eddying, which caused aircraft to lose control. A necessary third remodelling was only a matter of time.

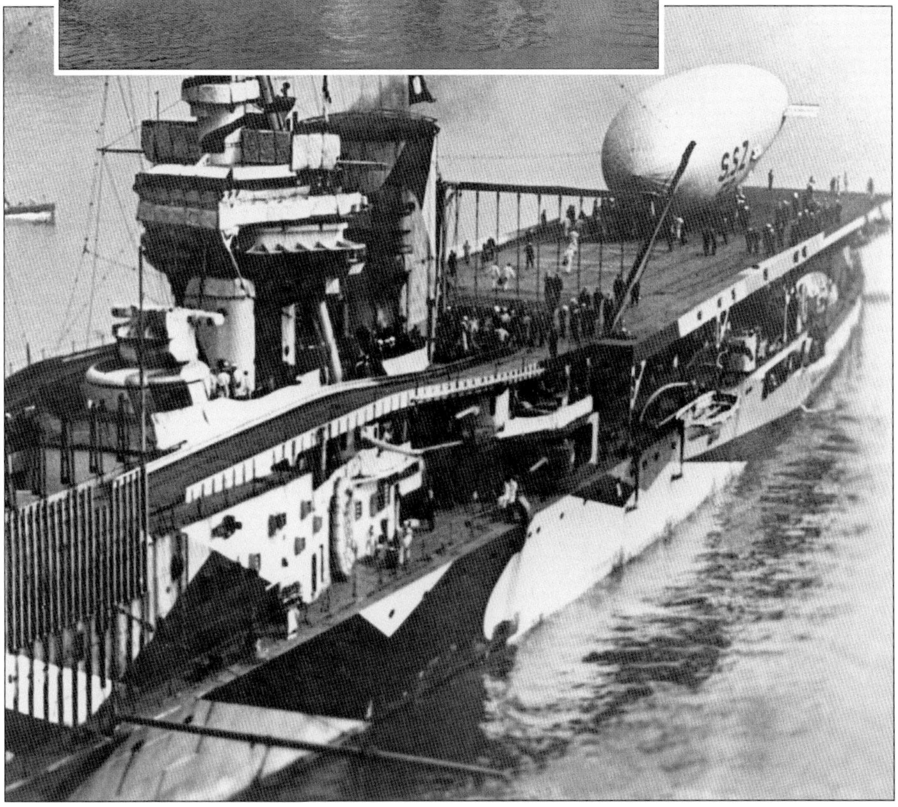

ABOVE: **Even in calm conditions it was only just possible to manoeuvre a fully assembled Sopwith Pup through the *Furious*' access hatch.**
LEFT: **This view of the *Furious* at the fitting-out quay shows her aft 457mm/18in gun, which was of no practical use as a single weapon.**
BELOW LEFT: **A Sea Scout Zero, or SSZ, blimp hauled down on to *Furious*' afterdeck. The view shows interesting detail including the tracks interconnecting the forward and after flight decks.**

Furious (II)

Built: Armstrong, Whitworth, Newcastle
Commissioned: June 26, 1917
Displacement: 19,450 tonnes/19,100 tons (standard); 22,800 tonnes/22,400 tons (full load)
Length: 228.5m/750ft (bp); 239.6m/786ft 6in (overall)
Beam: 26.8m/88ft
Draught: 6.0m/19ft 9in (normal); 7.3m/24ft (full load)
Flight decks: 48.7m/160ft long (forward-ramp); 91.4 x 15.2m/300 x 50ft (aft)
Aircraft: 16 various
Armament: 10 x 140mm/5.5in (10 single), 5 x 76.2mm/3in (5 single) and 4 x 3pdr guns
Machinery: Geared steam turbines, 18 boilers, 4 shafts
Power: 70,100kW/94,000shp
Speed: 31.5 knots
Fuel: 3,450 tonnes/3,400 tons
Range: 11,110 km/6,000nm at 20 knots
Armour: 50–75mm/2–3in (vertical); 20–45mm/0.75–1.5in (horizontal)
Complement: 930 men

TOP: **Very much a diminutive of the *Furious*, the *Vindictive* had only a short flying-off platform forward, enabling her to retain some of her main armament. The light mainmast was offset to the starboard side.**
ABOVE: ***Vindictive* in company with a Grand Fleet battle-cruiser, either *Indomitable* or *Inflexible*. Even by 1917, the use of disruptive colour schemes was far from universal.**

Vindictive

By mid-1917 the Royal Navy's need for purpose-built, through-deck carriers was fully established. The first two were in hand but the completion of the first was still a year away. Further conversions were therefore required to provide a stop-gap.

These needed to be reliable and fast enough to work with the battle fleet. The *Furious* had recently entered service following her first remodelling but, presumably because her utility was not yet proven, the choice for a second ship fell not upon one of her already operational sisters but on the last of the large, "Improved *Birmingham*"-class cruisers, HMS *Cavendish*, which would prove to be too small.

A wide-ranging aviation policy document of August 30, 1917, proposed that, because of the limited capacity of converted "carriers", each should deploy only one category of aircraft, i.e. reconnaissance, fighters, or torpedo/bombers. The addition of *Furious*' after landing deck must already have been anticipated, as she, the *Cavendish* and the just-ordered through-deck carrier *Hermes* were proposed to operate an aerial reconnaissance screen ahead of the fleet. A secondary role was to provide decks for the recovery of fighters from other ships, obviating the need for "ditching". The Admiralty's response to the paper was to direct that the *Furious* and *Cavendish* should be converted as seaplane and not standard aeroplane carriers.

Furious thus underwent her second remodelling, with the *Cavendish* very much her diminutive. Hangars were constructed forward and aft, connected by a single, port-side, elevated track. Atop the forward hangar was a 32.3m/106ft take-off platform, aircraft being brought up via a large hatch plumbed by a pair of derricks. The 58.8m/193ft after landing deck was served by an elevator. Depending upon type, six to eight seaplanes could be accommodated.

Renamed HMS *Vindictive*, in recognition of the old cruiser that had recently led the morale-boosting raid on Zeebrugge, the ship joined the Grand Fleet in October 1918, just a month before the close of hostilities. As with the larger *Furious*, the landing deck proved too hazardous to use, only one touch-down ever being made.

In the upper Baltic, hostilities continued beyond the armistice. Britain opposed the Bolshevik revolution and an active naval presence was maintained. Carrying a dozen assorted aircraft, in possibly the first use of a carrier in a ferrying role, the *Vindictive* arrived in support.

As the theatre was geographically small, the ship could more conveniently operate her aircraft from an inlet on the Finnish coast. In raiding the rather inactive Bolshevik fleet at Kronstadt, however, aircraft were flown from the ship, which also acted as "mother" to the Coastal Motor Boats (CMB) involved in penetrating the Russian base.

Following her return, the *Vindictive* had her ineffective after hangar arrangement removed but had a catapult fitted on the roof of the retained forward hangar. In this mode, she could deploy four floatplanes and proved ideal for the peculiarities of the then China station.

In 1928 the catapult was removed and, no longer in an aviation role, the ship served in various rear-echelon activities. She saw some combatant service during World War II and was scrapped in 1946.

TOP: **The substantial forward hangar is very obvious in this view, as is the port-side inter-connecting track between flight decks. Note that the forward platform has to be cantilevered in order to allow the forward 191mm/7.5in gun to retain its firing arc.** ABOVE: ***Vindictive* manoeuvring at Malta. Her after landing deck was a substantial structure which provided further hangar space. Only one landing is known ever to have been made on it.** BELOW: **Following her 1923 refit, *Vindictive* retained only her forward hangar, with a catapult on its roof and served by an offset crane.**

Vindictive

Built: Harland & Wolff, Belfast
Commissioned: October 1918
Displacement: 9,930 tonnes 9,750 tons (standard); 12,170 tonnes/11,950 tons (full load)
Length: 172.1m/565ft (bp); 184.3m/605ft (overall)
Beam: 19.8m/65ft 1in
Draught: 5.3m/17ft 6in (light); 6.2m/20ft 3in (full load)
Flight decks: 32.3 x 14.9m/106 x 49ft (forward); 58.8 x 17.4m/193 x 57ft (aft)
Aircraft: 6+
Armament: 4 x 191mm/7.5in (4 single), 4 x 76.2mm/3in (4 single), and 4 x 12pdr (4 single) guns
Machinery: Geared steam turbines, 12 boilers, 4 shafts
Power: 44,750kW/60,000shp
Speed: 29.5 knots
Fuel: 1,500 tonnes/1,480 tons
Range: 10,000km/5,400nm at 14 knots
Armour: 38–76mm/1.5–3in (vertical); 25–38mm/1–1.5in (horizontal)
Complement: 577 men plus 71 aircrew

Argus (I)

William Beardmore of Dalmuir had unsuccessfully proposed a dedicated aviation ship to the Admiralty back in 1912 and, by the time of Jutland, an exasperated Admiral Jellicoe was complaining of the low capability of the aviation ships serving with the Grand Fleet. The Admiralty therefore purchased the incomplete hull of the Italian passenger liner *Conte Rosso* for conversion, which was laying on the slip at Beardmore's yard, her construction suspended by the war.

Although the Admiralty's intention was to produce a more reliable version of the *Campania*'s seaplane carrier, proposals for alternative configurations were also being aired. Two comparatively junior officers, with considerable naval aviation experience, were convinced that the way ahead was to provide a full length, unobstructed flight deck, capable of both launching and recovering high-performance landplanes. One, Lt Gerard Homes, proposed little or no superstructure, with all funnel gases being channelled aft for exhaust, via sided horizontal ducts. The other, Flight Commander Hugh Williamson, had separately interested Captain Murray Sueter in an alternative, with a narrow island superstructure offset to the starboard deck edge.

The responsible Admiralty Chief Constructor, J.H. Narbeth, was already supervising construction to a design combining a through-deck, sloping downward at the forward end and fitted with a Beardmore-style superstructure, with sided blocks connected by a bridge. The design incorporated Holmes' ducted funnel concept.

ABOVE: **A Sopwith 1½-Strutter making an early landing, probably when the *Argus* was fitted with a dummy island structure. Note the longitudinal arrester wires, raised by a transverse ramp.** BELOW: **The flight deck of the *Argus* retained the earlier feature of narrowing and sloping downward at its forward end. Her passenger liner origins are betrayed by the rows of scuttles, following the ship's original sheerline.**

In November 1916 and rather late in the day, wind tunnel tests indicated that the arrangement (and, incidentally, that of the *Furious*) would create severe turbulence, making landing-on impossible. To keep the project moving, all superstructure was therefore deleted, the final configuration being kept under review and subject to practical experience.

As completed, the *Argus* incorporated what would become regular carrier features. The hangar extended over about 60 per cent of the ship's length, its walls separated from the ship's sides by a run of compartments on either side. The hangar roof was a strength deck, continuous with the side shell plating and forming a coherent deep girder. The flight deck itself was a light structure, supported by a lattice, the equivalent of two decks higher.

LEFT: **Navigation in restricted waters was from a retractable wheelhouse set on the centreline of the flight deck, forward. Lacking the side apertures of later carriers, the *Argus* carried her boats at a considerable height.** BELOW: **A hangar view looking aft through the open roller door to the quarterdeck. For the aircraft of the day, the hangar deck had generous headroom but it was obstructed by centreline pillars.**

Beneath the after flight deck overhang, cranes could lift seaplanes from the water and transfer them directly, through a large roller door, to the hangar. Two large elevators connected the hangar with the flight deck.

Like the *Vindictive*, the *Argus* completed a month before the armistice and too late to see action. Embarked were the first squadron of Sopwith Cuckoo torpedo-carrying landplanes intended to pursue Sueter's project of attacking the reluctant German fleet in its own anchorages.

A first task was for the ship to model temporary structures which would decide the topside arrangements for the two follow-on ships (*Hermes* (II) and *Eagle*). An offset island superstructure proved to be beneficial, giving landing pilots a point of reference and vindicating Williamson's ideas.

The *Argus* also trialled arrester systems and, with her forward flight deck levelled, developed operational procedures. Ultimately, however, she proved to be too small and too slow. Serving throughout World War II as training carrier, aircraft transport and, when required, as a combatant, she was finally scrapped in 1946–47.

ABOVE: ***Argus*' small retractable wheelhouse can be seen in the raised position. The configuration of the forward end of the flight deck is also more apparent.**

Argus (I)

Built: Beardmore, Dalmuir
Commissioned: September 16, 1918
Displacement: 14,760 tonnes/14,500 tons (standard); 17,560 tonnes/17,250 tons (full load)
Length: 163.1m/535ft 3in (bp); 172.1m/565ft (overall)
Beam: 20.8m/68ft 3in
Draught: 6.4m/21ft (light); 7.6m/24ft 9in (full load)
Flight deck: 167.6 x 20.7m/550 x 68ft
Aircraft: About 20
Armament: 6 x 102mm/4in guns
Machinery: Geared steam turbines, 12 boilers, 4 shafts
Power: 15,480kW/20,750shp
Speed: 20.2 knots
Fuel: 2,290 tonnes/2,250 tons
Range: 6,670km/3,600nm at 10 knots
Armour: None
Complement: 375 men plus 120 aircrew

Hermes (II)

As the world's first aircraft carrier, designed-to-task from the keel up, HMS *Hermes* was a significant ship, yet displaying ample evidence that the British Admiralty was still not certain of what it expected a carrier to *do*.

At the time of her laying-down, in January 1918, conversion work was also in hand on the *Eagle* (nearly 22,353 tonnes/22,000 tons) and the *Vindictive* (less than 10,160 tonnes/10,000 tons). The former, capable of only 24 knots, would need to work directly with the battle fleet, but the latter, of about 30 knots, could use her reconnaissance aircraft to extend the useful visual range of a scouting cruiser force. The *Hermes* followed the *Vindictive* in having the size, scantlings and armament of a large cruiser, yet barely the speed of the *Eagle*. These mixed characteristics drew criticism from the then Admiral Commanding Aircraft. The unified Royal Air Force had been created in April 1918 and, in a spirit of cooperation, the Admiralty solicited interested opinion regarding the future employment of "heavier-than-air craft". In response (in September 1918), this Admiral adopted a chicken-and-egg approach by stating that this would depend largely upon "Their Lordships' building policy as regards Large Carriers. At present nothing is known of this policy after *Hermes*, which will be only a 25-knots craft, obviously too slow for most operations. As far as can be judged at present, no Aeroplane Carrier should be slower than *Furious* or *Vindictive*..."

TOP: With her enormous island and tripod mast, the *Hermes* was totally unlike the *Argus*. Note the lower freeboard and the pointed forward end to the flight deck. Anchors are housed in pockets to reduce slamming. ABOVE: What appear to be Fairey III Fs are seen here on *Hermes*' flight deck. Note the line of the flight deck, the 140mm/5.5in gun in the pocket and the 102mm/4in high-angle anti-aircraft gun. BELOW: The *Hermes* was the first carrier to present what might be termed a "modern" profile.

LEFT: ***Hermes'* low freeboard quarterdeck was at the same level as the hangar deck. It communicated with the hangar via vertical roller doors and with the overhanging flight deck via the after elevator, seen here in the "down" position. Note the "round down" of the flight deck.**

With her machinery developing nearly twice the power of that installed in the *Argus*, it was thought impracticable to follow her system of horizontal exhaust ducting. Vertical uptakes and funnel casings were, therefore, accepted, apparently in a Beardmore-style double-island arrangement. As experiments in island configuration were still in progress, however, this was kept under review. *Hermes*' construction was well advanced when the failure of the *Furious*' layout convinced the Admiralty that a single, deck-edge island would be required. With no experience upon which to draw, designers created a massively proportioned superstructure block and failed, with the ship's slender underwater hull form, to compensate well for the asymmetry. Consequently, throughout her career, the ship was sensitive to any change in weight distribution.

The *Hermes* had a full-length flight deck, featuring a peculiar swell right aft, deemed aerodynamically beneficial. Like the *Argus*, her after flight deck overhung the quarterdeck, allowing cranes to hoist floatplanes from the water and transfer them on trolleys to the hangar via a door, or to the flight deck by means of the only elevator. A second, forward, elevator was later added, along with arrester gear and a catapult.

Again, hull strength was maximized by continuing the shell plating right up to the flight deck, which formed the upper flange of the hull girder. As she was to operate with cruisers, however, the flight deck scantlings were increased to take account of aerial bombing. This exacerbated the existing weight problem, and bulges had to be added.

Criticism attended the size of her hangar that, again, did not extend to the sides of the hull. *Hermes* proved, in fact, that fleet carriers of this size were too small to be efficient.

Having spent much of her life in the Far East she was finally sunk there, Japanese carrier aircraft destroying her off Ceylon on April 9, 1942. She had never been large enough to function effectively as a fleet carrier.

ABOVE: **Caught without air cover, the *Hermes* was overwhelmed and sunk by Japanese carrier-based dive-bombers within 20 minutes.**

Hermes (II)

Built: Armstrong Whitworth, Newcastle
Commissioned: February 18, 1924
Displacement: 11,050 tonnes/10,850 tons (standard); 13,695 tonnes/13,450 tons (full load)
Length: 166.9m/548ft (bp); 182.8m/600ft (overall)
Beam: 21.4m/70ft 3in
Draught: 5.7m/18ft 9in (light); 6.8m/22ft 3in (full load)
Flight deck: 173.6 x 29.2m/570 x 96ft
Aircraft: About 20
Armament: 6 x 140mm/5.5in and 3 x 102mm/4in guns
Machinery: Geared steam turbines, 6 boilers, 2 shafts
Power: 29,850kW/40,000shp
Speed: 25 knots
Fuel: 2,040 tonnes/2,000 tons
Range: 10,370km/5,600nm at 10 knots
Armour: 76mm/3in (side belt)
Complement: 610 men

Eagle (I)

At the outbreak of war in August 1914, work ceased on two battleships being built by Armstrong Whitworth to Chilean account. Having promised that they would be returned at close of hostilities, the British Admiralty commandeered both. One, the *Almirante Latorre*, was completed as designed and served the war as the battleship HMS *Canada.*

Work on the second, *Almirante Cochrane*, was not resumed as her designated armament had been diverted to other new construction. Thus, when the Grand Fleet's post-Jutland needs for larger and faster seaplane carriers were considered, this hull was selected for conversion in January 1918. She was duly purchased outright and the name of HMS *Eagle* allotted. As the company was also working on the *Hermes* at this time, *Eagle* had to compete for materials and labour, and progress was slow.

Deletion of much heavy battleship armour saved over 2,032 tonnes/2,000 tons on displacement. She retained the hybrid coal/oil firing then common. Coal bunkers were arranged to give a measure of protection to machinery spaces and fired the boilers in normal conditions. For higher speed running, oil was used exclusively.

With the overall policy on carrier superstructures still unsettled, the *Eagle* was intended to receive a variant on the Beardmore proposals. She would have two, sided islands, each incorporating two funnels and a tripod mast. Each island would be arranged differently and they would be staggered. The resulting bizarre effect would make it virtually impossible

TOP: ***Eagle* shared with *Hermes* the massive tripod mast and fire control top. Note the "battleship" features of bows and faceted hull. Note also the light, swinging platform for flight deck control.** ABOVE: **A World War II picture shows the *Eagle* little changed except for the addition of an aircraft housing beacon atop the fire control.**

for an enemy submarine commander to estimate the ship's heading. Even before installation had begun, this was changed, the ship receiving a single, starboard-side island with two funnels and a massively proportioned tripod and fire control top, as installed in the *Hermes.*

With the post-war drawdown, work on the *Eagle* slowed until it was decided suddenly that flying trials were urgently required. Early in 1920, therefore, with one funnel, half boiler capacity and incomplete superstructure, the ship was transferred to Portsmouth Dockyard. Here she was completed with an experimental fore-and-aft arrester system, her flight

ABOVE: **From this angle, the *Eagle*'s original battleship hull is emphasized. Note the armoured belt. Two funnels were required due to the spread of the boiler rooms.** LEFT: **A good view of *Eagle*'s flight deck configuration. The aircraft are Fairey III Fs and Fairey Flycatchers. Note the latter's experimental markings.** BELOW: ***Eagle* and the looming mass of Gibraltar. The carrier spent much of her time in the Mediterranean and was eventually sunk there.**

deck was extended right forward and her hull bulged. The latter feature was an anti-torpedo measure rather than one to improve stability, and it cost the ship half a knot in speed.

Exhaustive trials with various types of aircraft established that the fore-and-aft system worked tolerably well once its form and position had been determined and the engagement fittings on the aircraft undercarriage improved. Although the large island proved to cause little problem, it was discovered that it was imperative to steam the ship dead into wind for flying operations, otherwise eddying became severe. A round-down on the flight deck, right aft, proved essential.

Larger, heavier aircraft, with high landing speeds, soon proved the arrester system inadequate, and it was removed in 1926. For ten years the ship proved large enough to land aircraft without arrester wires, but their continued growth dictated the fitting of a later, transverse system in 1936.

The *Eagle* was sunk by submarine torpedo on August 11, 1942, while covering the famous "August Convoy" to Malta.

ABOVE: **Always a most imposing vessel, the *Eagle*'s weakness was her low speed, but she had been designed as an inherently stable gun platform.**

Eagle (I)

Built: Armstrong Whitworth, Newcastle
Commissioned: February 20, 1924
Displacement: 22,250 tonnes/21,850 tons (standard); 27,180 tonnes/26,700 tons (full load)
Length: 191m/627ft 1in (bp); 203.4m/667ft 6in (overall)
Beam: 32.1m/105ft 2in
Draught: 6.6m/21ft 9in (standard); 8.1m/26ft 7in (full load)
Flight deck: 198.6 x 28.9m/652 x 95ft
Aircraft: About 20
Armament: 9 x 152mm/6in, and 4 x 102mm/4in guns
Machinery: Geared steam turbines, 32 boilers, 4 shafts
Power: 37,300kW/50,000shp
Speed: 24 knots
Fuel: 2,900 tonnes/2,850 tons
Range: 12,130km/6,550nm at 10 knots
Armour: 114.3mm/4.5in (vertical belt); 25mm/1in (horizontal)
Complement: 810 men

Courageous, *Glorious* and *Furious* (III)

With rapid post-war reduction of the Royal Navy, careful consideration needed to be given to the characteristics of the aircraft carriers that could be afforded and, subsequent to the Washington Treaty, permitted.

A battle-cruiser squadron had been retained and new doctrine called for a fast carrier to operate with it and to extend its reconnaissance capabilities. The obvious candidate was the *Furious* that was useless in her then-current configuration but capable of 30-plus knots. With the benefit of nearly two years' operation of the *Argus*, work began in 1920 to redesign the ship in her final through-deck form.

Balanced air wings, as now understood, had not yet evolved and carriers were still allotted separate roles. Aboard *Furious*, large three-seater spotter aircraft would need to be accommodated alongside reconnaissance aircraft and a number of fighters.

No definite result had yet stemmed from experiments with island structures and the *Furious* was redesigned, *Argus*-style, with none. On either side of the forward end of the flight deck was a partly recessed control position, one for navigational purposes, the other for flying operations. A totally retractable small wheelhouse for harbour manoeuvre was installed on the centreline.

TOP: Seen in the mid-1930s, *Glorious* has had her quarterdeck raised by one level and the flight deck extended right aft. Note the bulge to the hull and the swung-out flight control platform. ABOVE: Note how the upper hangar is closed-off by roller doors. Opened, these allowed fighter aircraft to take off directly down the clear, sloping foredeck.

To provide the required accommodation, hangars were arranged on two levels, but necessarily of lower headroom than that on *Argus*. The 175.7m/576ft flight deck formed the roof of the upper hangar that opened via large doors on to the flat forecastle deck. This was to allow fighters to respond rapidly by taking off directly from the hangar. The lower hangar similarly gave on to the quarterdeck, whence two cranes could transfer floatplanes to and from the water.

LEFT: **The Blackburn Shark torpedo-spotter-reconnaissance plane served the Fleet Air Arm only briefly, between 1936 and 1938, being quickly superseded by the Fairey Swordfish. Note the planeguard destroyer.**

BELOW: **Painted in the dark grey then standard for Home Fleet ships, the *Courageous* here shows her flight deck arrangements to advantage. Note the small island structure compared with those of *Eagle* and *Hermes*.**

A longitudinal arrester system was included but proved unpopular and was removed in 1927. Forward of amidships the flight deck was given a pronounced ramp to encourage aircraft to get airborne.

The double hangar gave the *Furious* a greater freeboard than *Argus* resulting in a drier flight deck but one with higher levels of roll acceleration. To improve overall stability to the slender hull conspicuous bulges were added.

Like *Argus*, the *Furious* needed to have horizontal smoke ducting but, due to the far greater quantity of gases to be exhausted, this was not particularly successful. At high speeds, the after end of the upper hangar became extremely hot and some spaces were untenable.

Furious' final remodelling was successful enough to encourage a similar transformation of her erstwhile sisters, *Courageous* and *Glorious.* From the outset, both featured a starboard-edge island, essentially a large funnel casing, around which were arranged navigational and flying control facilities.

Reconstruction of the pair commenced in 1924–25. No arrester gear was initially provided, the retained feature of the deck ramp being sufficient to bring recalcitrant aircraft to rest. In the 1930s, however, increasing size and weight of aircraft saw a necessity to fit a transverse system. Two catapults were also added right forward.

All three proved to be efficient carriers. *Furious* served with distinction throughout World War II, but both her sisters were lost in controversial circumstances, *Courageous* to a submarine torpedo in September 1939, and *Glorious* to enemy gunfire in June 1940.

Courageous and *Glorious*

Class: *Courageous,* Armstrong Whitworth, Newcastle, commissioned (as carrier) May 5, 1928; *Glorious,* Harland & Wolff, Belfast, commissioned (as carrier) March 10, 1930
Displacement: 22,650 tonnes/22,250 tons (standard); 26,750 tonnes/26,250 tons (full load)
Length: 223.9m/735ft (bp); 239.9m/786ft 6in (overall)
Beam: 27.6m/90ft 6in
Draught: 7.4m/24ft 3in (standard); 8.5m/28ft (full load)
Flight deck: 175.7 x 31.6m/576 x 103ft 6in
Aircraft: About 48
Armament: 16 x 119mm/4.7in (16 single), and 24 x 2pdr pom-pom (3 octuple) guns
Machinery: Geared steam turbines, 18 boilers, 4 shafts
Power: 67,150kW/90,000shp
Speed: 30.5 knots
Fuel: 3,760 tonnes/3,700 tons
Range: 12,500km/6,750nm at 10 knots
Armour: 50–76mm/2–3in (vertical belt); 19–44mm/0.75–1.75in (horizontal)
Complement: 835 men

Ark Royal (II)

With the completion of the *Courageous*-class conversions in 1930, design studies began for the next large newbuild. The Washington Treaty had set the global limit for British aircraft carrier displacement at 137,160 tonnes/ 135,000 tons. Based on recent experience this was best devoted to half-a-dozen ships, each about 22,352 tonnes/ 22,000 tons. It was hoped that 60, even 72, aircraft and machinery for 30-plus knots might be accommodated.

To achieve the hoped-for aircraft strength, American-style deck parks would have to be adopted. These in turn would demand transverse arrester wire systems and a deployable safety barrier to prevent landing aircraft from bolting into the parking spaces. Accelerators/catapults would also be necessary to economize on take-off space. It was also agreed that, with assisted take-off and arrested landing, less wind-over-deck was required and so the carrier could be slower.

Overall dimensions were important for a volume-critical carrier tended to be larger than a weight-critical battleship of the same displacement. This reduced the number of docking facilities open to her.

The use of catapults, backed by an efficient deck organization could, it was reasoned, improve the launch rate of aircraft to the point where a second (forecastle) take-off deck was unnecessary. The bows could, therefore, be plated

TOP: Bound for Mediterranean service at the time of the Spanish Civil War, the newly completed *Ark Royal* displays red-white-blue neutrality markings on her quarter gun mountings. Note how high-speed trials have scoured the forward paintwork. ABOVE: Located in sponsons just below flight deck level, the *Ark Royal*'s dual-purpose, high-angle guns had far better firing arcs than equivalent weapons in earlier carriers. What appears to be a de-gaussing cable has been cleated to the hull, suggesting that the date is 1940.

continuously up to flight deck level. Supported by a smooth flare it was then possible to maintain a considerable width of flight deck to the forward extremity.

Floatplanes were, by now, diminishing in importance and, by handling them only by the amidships cranes, this allowed the quarterdeck to be enclosed, supporting a flight deck to a point right aft, its round-down cantilevered beyond.

Two hangars were again necessary. They were both enclosed, the upper having the unarmoured flight deck as its roof. Patches of protection were provided in way of magazines,

LEFT: **The carrier's loss to a single submarine torpedo came as a shock. It led to the tightening up of damage control procedures and to future designs being less vulnerable to sequential flooding.** BELOW LEFT: ***Ark Royal*'s commissioned life was just 36 months and she was thus little modified. By incorporating larger overhangs, the deck plan more nearly approached a rectangle.** BELOW: **Not the best-ever portrait of the *Ark Royal*, this portrayal nonetheless emphasizes the close ties between the ship and the Gibraltar-based Force H. She was sunk almost in sight of the Rock.**

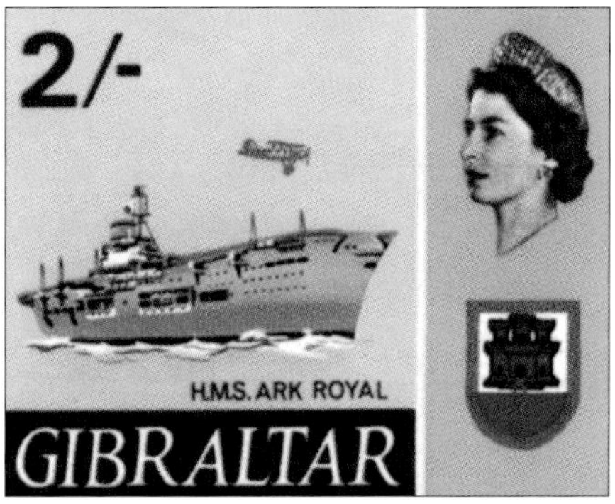

and a limited 114.3mm/4.5in side belt flanked machinery spaces. The hull was not bulged, and the internal torpedo protection arrangement was configured as an air-fuel-air sandwich.

As a carrier was now deemed to rely upon her aircraft and her escort for protection, gun armament could be confined to anti-aircraft weapons. Sixteen 114.3mm/4.5in dual-purpose guns were provided, located in twin mountings, two to each "corner". They were set a fraction below flight deck level to maximize firing arcs. Much was also expected of the new multi-barrelled 2pdr pom-pom mountings.

A prestigious name being required for this, the first third-generation British carrier, the veteran *Ark Royal* had to relinquish hers. On trials in May 1938, the new ship achieved her designed speed with barely three-quarters full power, suggesting that she could have been built with two, rather than three, shafts.

Ark Royal's World War II career was brief but eventful, providing no opportunity for a major refit before her loss in November 1941. Due to an insufficient understanding of damage control, she disappointingly succumbed to a single submarine torpedo.

ABOVE: **The conflicting demands of a relatively fine hull and a wide, straight-edged flight deck inevitably resulted in a strange and arresting geometry. Note the port side WT masts in the lowered position.**

Ark Royal (II)

Built: Cammell Laird, Birkenhead
Commissioned: November 16, 1938
Displacement: 22,352 tonnes/22,000 tons (standard); 28,210 tonnes/27,710 tons (full load)
Length: 208.9m/685ft (bp); 244m/800ft (overall)
Beam: 28.9m/94ft 9in
Draught: 6.9m/22ft 9in (standard); 8.5m/27ft 9in (full load)
Flight deck: 237.9 x 29.3m/780 x 96ft
Aircraft: About 60
Armament: 16 x 114.3mm/4.5in (8 double), and 48 x 2pdr pom-pom (6 octuple) guns
Machinery: Geared steam turbines, 6 boilers, 3 shafts
Power: 76,100kW/102,000shp
Speed: 31 knots
Fuel: 4,500 tonnes/4,420 tons
Range: 20,740km/11,200nm at 10 knots
Armour: 114.3mm/4.5in (vertical belt); (horizontal – patches only)
Complement: 1,740 men

LEFT: **The cost of a partly armoured deck was the acceptance of a single hangar, fewer aircraft and lower freeboard. Note the careful attention to streamlining on bridgefront and around the bow overhang to reduce eddies over the flight deck of the *Victorious*.** BELOW LEFT: **The British Pacific Fleet (BPF) in 1945 eventually included all six "armoured" carriers and the four surviving *King George V*-class battleships. The aircraft ranged in the foreground are F4U Corsairs.** BELOW: **BPF aircraft, such as this Grumman Avenger, had roundels without the red centre, to avoid any confusion with Japanese aircraft and "side tabs" to more nearly approximate American markings.**

Illustrious class

Even as the *Ark Royal* was laid down a European war was appearing likely. Neither of the dictatorships possessed carriers but, to operate offensively against their maritime interests, the Royal Navy would be opposed by powerful land-based air forces. In those pre-radar days it was unlikely that a handful of carrier search aircraft could detect every incursion by enemy bombers, nor give sufficient warning for her fighters to intercept them. Exercises had shown that naval anti-aircraft gunfire could dispose of only a low proportion of attacking aircraft while single-seat fighters, lacking navigators, were unable to operate safely beyond horizon range of their carrier. It was obvious that some enemy bombers must get through to threaten the huge expanse of the flight deck.

Bombers, too, were faster and carried far heavier weapons, and the dangers of level bombing had been joined by those from dive-bombing. It was a matter of concern that the horizontal protection of *Ark Royal* was designed mostly to resist 9.1kg/20lb bombs where 100kg/220lb, even 250kg/551lb, weapons were now under development. As fleet carriers were so few, and they were so valuable in both attack and defence, a new philosophy demanded that a carrier's main weapons system, i.e. her aircraft, be better protected. As a result, the concept of the armoured carrier emerged.

The 1936 programme funded the first two carriers designed to the new displacement limit of 23,369 tonnes/23,000 tons set by the recent London Treaty. These were to have flight decks capable of defeating a 226.7kg/500lb bomb dropped from 2,134m/7,000ft. This required 76mm/3in plate, weighing 586kg per m^2/120lb per sq ft. To resist cruiser gunfire beyond 6,401m/7,000yd, hangar side walls and transverse bulkheads required to be of 114.3mm/4.5in plate.

With an upper limit on displacement, this huge accumulation of weight had predictable consequences. Only one hangar was provided to minimize the area of vertical protection. This, in turn, reduced freeboard, compensating somewhat in stability terms for the heavy flight deck. It did, however, increase wetness on the flight deck and, of course, had a drastic effect on aircraft capacity, reduced from the *Ark Royal*'s 60-plus to only 33. Aviation fuel, the subject of elaborate precaution in the Royal Navy, was provided on this scale and when, later, American-

style deck parks increased the air wing to 54, this proved a severe limitation on operational endurance.

The three ships of what became known as the Illustrious class were laid down within the space of eight weeks in 1937, and their completion in 1940–41 was a matter of huge relief to an overstretched Royal Navy.

Power had been increased by about ten per cent over *Ark Royal*, and the triple shafts were now a necessity. As the war progressed, new equipment and more aircraft increased displacement, while the associated extra crew members made for increasingly cramped accommodation.

It was the class's good fortune that severe damage incurred during World War II was all from the air (which it was designed to resist) rather than from the more dangerous torpedo. *Illustrious* and *Formidable* were able to survive savage bombing attacks while all three were later able to resist Japanese kamikaze attacks that would have disabled more lightly constructed vessels. All survived the war.

ABOVE: **Bleak and inhospitable, the anchorage at Hvalfjord in Iceland was invaluable for the refuelling of escorts covering transatlantic convoys and for Anglo-American surface groups supporting Arctic convoys. *Victorious* is seen in company with British and American units.** ABOVE RIGHT: **A Home Fleet ship, *Victorious* came south on several occasions to support Malta operations. Note that the picture opposite was the inspiration for this impression.** BELOW: **This is a post-1943 picture, for the distinctive tub-like British homing beacon had been replaced by an American-type YE and the round-downs have been levelled to maximize deck space. The aircraft is a Fairey Barracuda dive-bomber.**

Illustrious class

Class: *Illustrious*, Vickers-Armstrong, Barrow, commissioned May 25, 1940; *Victorious*, Vickers-Armstrong, Newcastle, commissioned May 15, 1941; *Formidable*, Harland & Wolff, Belfast, commissioned November 24, 1940

Displacement: 23,369 tonnes/23,000 tons (standard); 28,400 tonnes/27,900 tons (full load)

Length: 205.3m/673ft (bp); 226.9m/743ft 10in (overall)

Beam: 29.2m/95ft 9in

Draught: 7.5m/24ft 6in (standard); 8.5m/27ft 9in (full load)

Flight deck: 189.1 x 24.6m/620 x 80ft

Aircraft: About 36 in hangar

Armament: 16 x 114mm/4.5in (8 double) guns, and 48 x 2pdr pom-pom (6 octuple) guns

Machinery: Geared steam turbines, 6 boilers, 3 shafts

Power: 82,800kW/111,000shp

Speed: 30.5 knots

Fuel: 4,940 tonnes/4,850 tons

Range: 19,816km/10,700nm at 10 knots

Armour: 114.3mm/4.5in (belt); 38mm/1.5in (hangar wall); 76mm/3in (flight deck); 38–50mm/1.5–2in (hangar deck)

Complement: 1,180 men

Illustrious-class derivatives

Large and expensive in relation to their aircraft capacity, the three Illustrious class were laid down only months before a modified version, HMS *Indomitable.* Lower hull and machinery remained identical but, by adding 1.8m/6ft to the total depth of hull, two hangars were included, the lower of half length. This increased underdeck aircraft capacity to 45, but at some cost. Where the lower hangar could be given the preferred 4.9m/16ft headroom, the upper had to be reduced to 4.3m/14ft, a factor that later constricted the range of aircraft embarked, barring, for instance, the F4U Corsair.

Much the same area of flight deck retained its 76mm/3in armour but the vertical protection of the hangar was cut severely from 114.3mm/4.5in to only 38mm/1.5in plate. As with her three predecessors, the *Indomitable* was fitted with just one catapult, with consequent effect on launch rate.

Carrier design was now firmly dictated by larger and heavier aircraft. The high location of the ship's dual-purpose armament improved arcs, but only at the cost of reducing flight deck area and making its shape irregular. Considerable extra space was gained by virtually abolishing the round-down and extending the flight deck as a straight, cantilevered overhang. Outriggers were also introduced, supporting the tails of aircraft outboard of the deck edge to save further space.

For the final pair of derivatives (*Implacable* and *Indefatigable*) it was desirable to increase the maximum speed by a knot or so. This may not sound much but, nonetheless, required a one-third increase in installed power. This necessitated four propellers which, in turn, demanded modified hull lines with an extra 6.1m/20ft on waterline length. Redesign took some time and meant that the pair were not laid down until 1939, entering service very late in the war.

TOP: The last two improved *Illustrious*-class ships were disposed of in 1955–56, but as training carriers still look pristine at the 1953 Coronation Review. Note the flag of Rear Admiral (Air). ABOVE: *Indefatigable* seen in her post-war training role. With peace, the lives of the big armoured carriers were short as the "Light Fleets" could be run far more economically while deploying as many aircraft. BELOW: By locating their main armament flush with the flight deck, British carriers had more effective firing arcs than did American. The cost was an indented flight deck plan that impinged on useful space.

Even at this late stage Britain endeavoured to respect treaty displacement. As four sets of machinery occupied a greater proportion of hull length, a greater area of armour was required. To reduce this area both upper and lower hangar were given only 4.3m/14ft headroom, with the aforementioned consequence. Vertical protection remained at 38mm/1.5in but

the vital horizontal protection was reduced to 64mm/2.5in. This was influenced by the acceptance that 500kg/1,102lb bombs would probably penetrate it in any case, leading to a proposal that future design should include thin flight deck protection to initiate the detonation of a bomb whose explosion would then be contained by a heavily armoured hangar deck.

Although the Royal Navy's armoured carriers became somewhat legendary in their ability to absorb punishment, the frequent battering took its toll. All spent considerable periods under repair, with the exception of *Implacable* that arrived in the Far East too late to be of much use.

Following hostilities these expensive ships, apart from the *Victorious*, all had very limited lives. For peacetime operations and in low-level conflict the "Light Fleets" could operate much the same air wing on half the complement. Except for the single modernization, which proved a very difficult task, all had been sold for scrapping by 1956.

ABOVE LEFT: **British Pacific Fleet carriers proved to be largely kamikaze-proof. This strike on the *Indefatigable* in April 1945 killed 14 and damaged the island, but disrupted flying operations for only half an hour.** ABOVE RIGHT: **A post-war picture of Sea Hornets and Sea Furies. The former type served afloat only between 1949 and 1951. The planeguard is a 1943-type *Battle*-class destroyer. Note that she has her seaboat ready swung-out for emergencies.**

BELOW: **A meeting of different worlds. The life of the average fellaheen and that of a fleet carrier crew member are about as far removed as can be imagined. *Indefatigable* transits the Suez Canal. The waterway was frequently mined by enemy aircraft.**

Illustrious-class derivatives

Class: *Indomitable*, Vickers-Armstrong, Barrow, commissioned October 10, 1941; *Implacable*, Fairfield, Govan, commissioned August 28, 1944; *Indefatigable*, John Brown, Clydebank, commissioned May 3, 1944

Details for *Implacable/Indefatigable*:

Displacement: 23,680 tonnes/23,250 tons (standard); 32,700 tonnes/32,100 tons (full load)

Length: 208m/682ft (bp); 233.8m/766ft 6in (overall)

Beam: 29.2m/95ft 9in

Draught: 7.8m/25ft 6in (standard); 8.5m/27ft 9in (full load)

Flight deck: 231.8 x 31.1m/760 x 102ft

Aircraft: About 55

Armament: 16 x 114.3mm/4.5in (8 double), 48 x 2pdr pom-pom (4 octuple, 4 quadruple) guns, and 53 x 20mm/0.79in (18 double, 17 single) guns

Machinery: Geared steam turbines, 8 boilers, 4 shafts

Power: 110,400kW/148,000shp

Speed: 32.5 knots

Fuel: 4,775 tonnes/4,690 tons

Range: 20,370km/11,000nm at 14 knots

Armour: 114.3mm/4.5in (belt); 38mm/1.5in (hangar wall); 76mm/3in (flight deck); 38–50mm/1.5–2in (hangar deck)

Complement: 1,375 men

LEFT: **With the Royal Navy already up to its treaty limit in carrier tonnage, the acquisition of an aircraft maintenance ship that looked like, and functioned as, a carrier was something of a bonus.**

BELOW: **Seen in the Far East during the Korean War, the *Unicorn* (left) with her double-hangar freeboard towers over the *Ocean* (right), a *Colossus*-class carrier.**

Unicorn

Putting the Mediterranean Fleet on a virtual war footing during the 1935–36 Abyssinian crisis was useful in exposing shortcomings. One such was the lack of heavy support for the existing, and planned, carrier force. This resulted in the one-off aircraft maintenance ship *Unicorn.*

To justify her cost, she would need to operate as a training carrier in peacetime. Topside, therefore, she would require carrier characteristics, much influenced by the completing *Ark Royal* (II). For her core business of storing, repairing and issuing aircraft (including floatplanes) she needed two, 4.9m/16ft headroom hangars. Her freeboard would be high but her draught was required to be limited, necessitating an unusually high power to ensure safe ship handling. An unlikely requirement to mount aerial patrols to safeguard her location also provided a justification for weapons stowage. As the ship would have considerable value, she was given a 51mm/2in flight deck and was armed with a twin 102mm/4in mounting at each "corner", each pair with its own director.

Putting these requirements together the Naval Staff created what was called a Fleet Air Arm Maintenance Ship. This was however, to all intents and purposes, a light fleet carrier built outside treaty limitations, but not completed until 1943.

A feature was the pronounced overhang aft. This increased the useful length of the flight deck while providing a gantry for transferring floatplanes and aircraft transport lighters directly from sea to hangar.

The *Unicorn* had a distinctive appearance, although viewed beam-on, her high freeboard gave the impression of a fleet carrier on a closing or receding heading. Delivered in 1943, she served as a regular carrier at Salerno before fulfilling a variety of roles in the Far East, including the Korean War.

ABOVE: **Complete with catapult, arresters, two hangars and two elevators, the *Unicorn* could, and did, function efficiently as a light carrier.**

Unicorn

Built: Harland & Wolff, Belfast
Commissioned: March 12, 1943
Displacement: 15,900 tonnes/15,600 tons (standard); 20,700 tonnes/20,300 tons (full load)
Length: 172m/564ft (bp); 196.1m/643ft (overall)
Beam: 27.5m/90ft
Draught: 6.3m/20ft 6in (standard); 7.4m/24ft 3in (full load)
Flight deck: 183 x 28.8m/600 x 94ft 6in
Aircraft: About 36
Armament: 8 x 102mm/4in (4 double), 16 x 2pdr pom-pom (4 quadruple) guns, and 13 x 20mm/0.79in (4 double, 5 single) guns
Machinery: Geared steam turbines, 4 boilers, 2 shafts
Power: 29,850kW/40,000shp
Speed: 24 knots
Fuel: 3,050 tonnes/3,000 tons
Range: 20,370km/11,000nm at 14 knots
Armour: 38mm/1.5in (vertical longitudinal bulkhead); 51mm/2in (flight deck); 51mm/2in (protective deck)
Complement: 1,100 men

LEFT: **By locating the catapult along the forecastle and offset to the port side of No.1 hatch, it was possible to retain a CAM ship's full cargo capacity.** BELOW: **The launch of a CAM ship's fighter often caused consternation in neighbouring ships. The blast of the rocket-assisted take-offs required the bridge front and the control officer's cubicle to be suitably protected.**

CAM ships

From airfields in western France and Norway, German long-range Fw200 Condors made forays deep into the Atlantic to locate convoys for U-boats to attack. From the German naval viewpoint there were always too few of the aircraft, they were unreliable and their use was greatly restricted by a dog-in-the-manger Luftwaffe. Their navigation on long flights was frequently inexact, so that positions reported were usually inaccurate to a significant degree.

To the convoy crews, however, the seemingly omnipresent "snooper" had much the same effect as had the hated Zeppelin on the Grand Fleet a quarter century earlier. Circling beyond gun range it was truly a harbinger of death.

In the Air Ministry were men with long memories who suggested reacting similarly, but launching fighters now from merchantmen fitted with catapults. In November 1940 several hundred such modifications were proposed, the ships concerned remaining under the Red Ensign and carrying normal cargoes. As in World War I, a fighter would be launched upon an enemy reconnaissance aircraft being sighted. Following an engagement, the fighter would "ditch" alongside a convoy vessel for the pilot (only) to be recovered from often freezing water.

Catapults proved to be not only in short supply but also difficult to obtain. Therefore only 35 Catapult Aircraft (or "Armed") Merchantmen, or CAM ships, ever entered service and most by April 1941. As the hoped-for cheap, expendable fighter never entered production, the ships embarked early marks of Hurricane or Fulmar.

The aircraft was hurled into the air, further assisted by sequentially fired rocket clusters, whose white-hot blast enveloped the asbestos-clad Launch Officer's cabin and ship's bridge front alike. This sight should have been cheering to more convoys but, due to perceived risk, only eight CAM launches were made in 170 sailings. These resulted in six "kills", two damaged and only one pilot lost.

Together with the similar, but naval-crewed Fighter Catapult Ships, the CAMs were only ever an expedient and disappeared quickly with the introduction of the Escort Carrier (CVE).

LEFT: **A quick comparison with Royal Navy conversions of World War I will show that there was nothing revolutionary about the CAM concept. Nor was it any more hazardous to the pilots involved.**

LEFT: **The dry-cargo MACs retained their original mercantile hull with its long, unbroken sheerline. Even by escort carrier standards the conversion was spartan. The "A"-bracket at the bows was for the suspension of an acoustic hammer.** BELOW: **The tanker-MAC also retained its original hull, the raised "islands" of forecastle, bridge and poop still being clearly discernable. All original pipework remained accessible, bridged by the flight deck.**

MAC ships

Large programmes of escort carrier construction were initiated during 1941 for the purpose of convoy protection. Austere as these conversions were, it still took time to effect results, and alternative interim measures were suggested. As any and all shipping capacity was precious, the possibility of building a flight deck over a functioning cargo ship appeared attractive. Thus was born the Merchant Aircraft Carrier, or MAC ship.

The flight deck overlaid all conventional cargo access and, of course, required the removal of the usual cargo handling gear. As a result, the ships could carry only those cargoes that could be handled by pumping notably grain and oil. A tanker's upper deck is a complex of piping, so only the dry cargo type could be equipped with a hangar and elevator. There was no catapult and, with a short flight deck and low speed, there was no question of operating fighters. All, therefore, were devoted to anti-submarine warfare (ASW), deploying up to four Fairey Swordfish to enhance the effectiveness of a regular convoy escort.

A first pair of conversions was ordered in June 1942. As building was at an early stage, it was possible to fit uprated machinery. Their flight decks were only 126.2m/414ft in length (later examples were longer) but equipped with arrester gear and safety barriers. The hangar occupied only that space over the aftermost hold. General encumbrance and extra topweight reduced earlier cargo deadweight capacity by nearly 30 per cent.

Anglo-Saxon, the Shell oil company's then shipping arm, operated considerable numbers of economical, standard-design tankers, known popularly as "Three Twelves", from their ability to shift 12,000 deadweight tons (12,193 tonnes) at 12 knots on 12 tons (12.2 tonnes) of fuel per day. Ideal for conversion, they compensated for a lack of hangar by having a longer, 140.2m/460ft flight deck. For safety's sake only high flashpoint cargoes could be carried and less than 10 per cent capacity was lost.

As the escort carrier programmes came on stream, the MAC conversions were reduced from a projected 30 to just 19, with two of them being Dutch-flagged.

LEFT: **Only the dry-cargo MAC was able to be equipped with a hangar. As can be seen, its rudimentary elevator was tailored to the folded-dimensions of the ubiquitous Swordfish.**

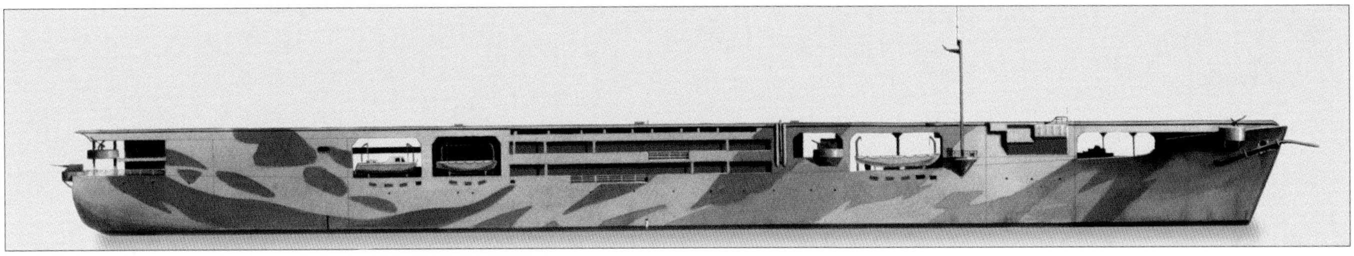

Audacity

While there was no lack of proposals for the conversion of merchant shipping to auxiliary carriers, HMS *Audacity* had the distinction of actually being the first so converted.

Built as the NDL cargo liner *Hannover*, she was captured by the Royal Navy in March 1940, but in a damaged state resulting from her crew's efforts to destroy her. Following the initial proposal for a bare-bones conversion, she was taken in hand in January 1941. By June, she had been cut down to her weather deck and fitted with a 138.2m/453ft flight deck. This was a light structure, mounted on pillars, but represented a considerable addition in topweight. To establish the required stability range and roll period it was necessary to add about 3,048 tonnes/3,000 tons of permanent ballast.

No hangar was provided, while the flight deck was graced with just two arrester wires and a safety barrier. Although she was intended to operate fighter aircraft, no catapult was fitted, thus necessitating considerable re-spotting of aircraft on deck.

There was no island superstructure, with navigation being conducted rather primitively from projecting platforms. As the vessel was a relatively low-powered motor ship, redirecting the exhaust through the starboard side posed no particular problem.

Audacity was converted specifically to counter the threat posed by the German Fw200 Condor aircraft, and primarily to the UK–Gibraltar convoys. She carried no Swordfish, therefore, but six of the newly available Grumman Wildcat, known to the British as the Martlet. These were permanently parked topside.

Commissioned in June 1941 (with a part-Merchant Navy crew) she proved remarkably successful. She undertook three round trips before being sunk by U-boat, her aircraft being credited with the destruction of seven Condors. Equally importantly, she had established the case for the conversion of many other mercantile hulls. By coincidence and (it is claimed) an independent evolutionary process, the US Navy commissioned its prototype escort carrier *Long Island* in the same month.

TOP AND ABOVE: **Although the flying arrangements of the *Audacity* were extremely basic, nobody complained about the accommodation for, as can be made out, both original amidships accommodation decks were retained. No hangar was provided although the space above the existing No.4 hold was plated-in.**

Audacity

Built: Bremer-Vulcan, Vegesack
Commissioned (as carrier): June 1941
Displacement: 8,350 tonnes/8,200 tons (standard); 10,450 tonnes/10,250 tons (full load)
Length: 132.6m/434ft 9in (bp); 146.1m/479ft (overall)
Beam: 17.1m/56ft
Draught: 6.6m/21ft 8in (full load)
Flight deck: 138.2 x 18.3m/453 x 60ft
Aircraft: 6
Armament: 1 x 102mm/4in, 4 x 2pdr pom-pom (4 single) guns, and 4 x 20mm/0.79in (4 single) guns
Machinery: One 7-cylinder diesel engine, 1 shaft
Power: 3,880kW/5,200bhp
Speed: 15.5 knots
Fuel: 680 tonnes/670 tons
Range: 22,220km/12,000nm at 15.5 knots
Armour: None
Complement: 210 men

British-built escort carriers

During the 1930s, one of the Royal Navy's major tasks remained the protection of trade, a requirement both facilitated and complicated by the growing maturity of aircraft. Aircraft-equipped "cruisers" could more easily apprehend surface raiders, thought to be a major threat to convoys, while the other menace, the U-boat, was already known to be considerably deterred by patrolling aircraft. Thought had also been given to the provision of defensive air cover to prevent air attack on convoys, but the effect of such an attack was as yet difficult to visualize.

Small "trade protection" carriers might well have been built but for the very tight global tonnage limitations imposed by the 1921–22 Washington Treaty. The alternative Admiralty strategy was, once again, to convert suitable mercantile hulls. Suitable ships should have been identified pre-war and the necessary design work instituted, but this was an era of fiscal constraint and staff shortage, so little was actually done.

British owners operated a wealth of shipping; however, this was built to a wide variety of trading requirements. As there was little standardization, the Admiralty drew up very broad specifications for three separate classes of carrier.

Their major characteristics were as follows:

	Flight deck larger than	Speed	Aircraft
Type A	167.6 x 22.9m/550 x 75ft	20 knots	25
Type B	152.4 x 21.3m/500 x 70ft	18 knots	15
Type C	137.2 x 18.3m/450 x 60ft	16.5 knots	10

Type A conversions would be based on diesel-powered passenger liners. These, however, proved to be so valuable in wartime as troop carriers that only one, *Pretoria Castle*, was ever converted. Although the rebuilding was a success the ship was not employed operationally, spending the war as a trials and training carrier.

TOP: **Swords into ploughshares. Little changed, the *Campania* lies in London docks in about 1950 promoting the Festival of Britain. Note her name, painted-up mercantile-style on her bows.** ABOVE: **Larger than the series-built American escort carriers, the *Campania* was a more comfortable ship to operate on the inhospitable Arctic convoy routes. In 1952 she acted as flagship for the British Monte Bello nuclear tests.**

With the recent experience of the massacre of merchant shipping during World War I it is surprising, in retrospect, that an auxiliary carrier conversion programme was not vigorously pursued from the opening of World War II. Even the substantial and increasing losses of 1940 appeared to make little difference. It took the rapid and effective conversion of the *Audacity* in January–June 1941 to demonstrate what could be done. By then, however, British hulls were in such short supply

LEFT: **Another escort carrier to repeat a World War I name was the *Nairana*. She, too, was employed mainly on Arctic convoy escort and in Atlantic anti-submarine operations.** BELOW: **Looks dramatic, feels uncomfortable but is quite safe. Any ship will pitch given the right combination of speed and wavelength. The remedy, if operations permit, is to adjust course and speed. This is *Nairana*.**

that the War Cabinet vetoed any large follow-on programme. Beyond the *Pretoria Castle*, only four others, all major cargo liners, were rebuilt as carriers. None entered service before 1943, by which time escort carriers (CVE) were being transferred from the large American construction programmes.

The four British examples, *Activity*, *Campania* (II), *Nairana* (II) and *Vindex* (II) were considered successful but, in view of the urgent situation at sea, were too few, too complex and too late. By adhering to tight, non-varying no-frills specifications, the Americans produced large numbers of simple, effective auxiliary carriers that combined a useful aircraft capacity on relatively small dimensions. This helped to permit British yards to concentrate on the enormous throughput of repairs to war-damaged ships.

LEFT: **Same ship, different paint scheme: the *Pretoria Castle* is seen in disruptive camouflage designed, not to conceal the ship, but to confuse her form and identity and, importantly, her heading.**

ABOVE: **Despite the pre-war plans, passenger liners were so valuable that only one, the *Pretoria Castle*, was ever converted to a carrier. Because of the ship's size she was employed almost exclusively for pilot training.**

Pretoria Castle

Built: Harland & Wolff, Belfast
Commissioned as carrier: April 9, 1943
Displacement: 20,000 tonnes/19,650 tons (standard); 23,880 tonnes/23,450 tons (full load)
Length: 170.1m/560ft (bp); 181.3m/594ft 6in (overall)
Beam: 23.3m/76ft 3in
Draught: 8.7m/28ft 6in (full load)
Flight deck: 170.1 x 23.2m/560 x 76ft
Aircraft: About 21
Armament: 4 x 102mm/4in (2 double), 8 x 2pdr pom-pom (2 quadruple) guns, and 20 x 20mm/0.79in (10 double) guns
Machinery: Two 8-cylinder diesel engines, 2 shafts
Power: 16,000kW/21,500bhp
Speed: 18 knots
Fuel: 2,500 tonnes/2,450 tons
Range: 29,630km/16,000nm at 16 knots
Armour: None
Complement: 665 men

ABOVE: **The first of the American conversions to be transferred to the Royal Navy, the *Archer* had no island superstructure. Except in way of the short hangar at the after end, the space below the flight deck was completely open.**

Archer class

Even before the entry of HMS *Audacity* into service, in July 1941, the Americans had begun work on six further auxiliary carriers to British account. Like so many that were to follow, they were based on the US Maritime Commission's standard C3 hull, the "C3" denoting a cargo vessel with waterline length of 137–152m/450–500ft.

First-of-class *Archer* differed from her near-sisters by having no island superstructure, but all were an advance on the *Audacity* in having a small hangar aft. Forward of this, the wood-on-steel flight deck was elevated on tall pillars. Although they also had a catapult, this was incompatible with British-built aircraft. All of this group were diesel-propelled and suffered from chronic machinery problems.

Built to commercial, two-compartment standards, they did not meet British stability requirements, necessitating the addition of about 1,016 tonnes/1,000 tons of permanent ballast. Following the loss of *Avenger* and *Dasher*, major modifications were ordered in the stowage of ordnance and aviation fuel.

The usual aircraft mix was nine Swordfish or Avengers, and six Martlet (Wildcat) fighters. The flight deck (later lengthened) was of thin steel plate overlaid with wood, designed to be easy to repair. It was served by a single elevator.

Archer class

Class: *Archer*, Sun Shipbuilding; *Avenger*, Bethlehem Steel; *Biter*, Atlantic Basin; *Dasher*, Tietjen & Lang
Commissioned: November 1941–July 1942
Displacement: 10,380 tonnes/10,200 tons (standard); 13,100 tonnes/12,850 tons (full load)
Length: 141.8m/465ft (bp); 150.1m/492ft (overall)
Beam: 21.2m/69ft 6in
Draught: 6.9m/22ft 6in (full load)
Flight deck: 125.1 x 23.8m/410 x 78ft
Aircraft: About 16
Armament: 3 x 102mm/4in, 16 x 20mm/0.79in guns
Machinery: 4 diesels, 1 shaft
Power: 6,340kW/8,500shp
Speed: 16.5 knots
Fuel: 1,425 tonnes/1,400 tons
Range: –
Armour: None
Complement: 540 men

LEFT: **Corresponding to the US Navy's Bogue class, the Attackers had a greatly extended hangar. This is *Ravager*, seen on an aircraft delivery trip. The tolerance of such small ships to large and varying topweight was remarkable.**

Attacker class

Sometimes referred to as the Tracker class, these 11 ships were a great advance on the Archers. Based on the American Bogue class they, too, were based on the C3 hull but were built from the keel up with a more comprehensive standard of subdivision. Sides were plated up to flight deck level, enclosing a hangar now large enough to accommodate a dozen Swordfish (or Avengers) and six Martlets. There was an elevator at either end of the hangar and a single catapult, port side forward.

With little experience of marine diesels the Americans also reverted to the tried and tested steam turbine. Offering no redundancy, the single shaft was a weakness in most escort carriers.

The Archers were transferred to the Royal Navy between November 1941 and July 1942, the Attackers following on between October 1942 and June 1943.

Attacker class

Class: *Attacker, Fencer, Stalker, Striker*, Western Pipe; *Battler, Hunter, Chaser, Pursuer*, Ingalls; *Searcher, Ravager*, Todd, Tacoma; *Tracker*, Willamette
Commissioned: October 1942–June 1943
Displacement: 10,380 tonnes/10,200 tons (standard); 14,650 tonnes/14,400 tons (full load)
Length: 141.8m/465ft (bp); 151.1m/495ft 6in (overall)
Beam: 21.2m/69ft 6in
Draught: 7.8m/25ft 6in (full load)
Flight deck: 134.2 x 25m/440 x 82ft
Aircraft: About 20
Armament: 2 x 102mm/4in,14 x 20mm/0.79in guns
Machinery: Geared turbine, 1 shaft
Power: 6,340kW/8,500shp
Speed: 18 knots
Fuel: 3,050 tonnes/3,000 tons
Range: –
Armour: None
Complement: 645 men

Ameer class

Modifications to earlier ships (improved subdivision, magazine protection and aviation fuel stowage), insisted upon by the British, created safer ships but at the cost of delays which Americans found unacceptable. Their rapid and efficient series production depended upon absolute conformation to a rigid specification. Unresolved differences probably influenced the decision not to transfer to the British any of the improved, but more complex, *Casablanca* (or "Kaiser") type. Further C3-based units therefore followed instead, these moving up to Vancouver for appropriate modifications to improving survivability, and taking six weeks per ship.

ABOVE: **Effectively follow-on Attackers, the extensive Ameer class were built as carriers from the keel up and fitted out for their differing primary roles of convoy escort, ASW operations or aircraft transport.** LEFT: **A Wildcat and two Avengers aboard a British escort carrier. Note the painted version of Flag "F" in the foreground, displayed prominently during flight operations.**

A further refinement of the basic type, the Ameers were transferred between July 1943 and February 1944 and featured a longer flight deck and hangar, as well as an all-American armament. The vexed question of aviation fuel safety was resolved only through shipping about one quarter of the ships' designed capacity, a severely limiting factor on extended operations.

All US-sourced escort carriers were returned at close of hostilities.

ABOVE: **Visible also at a distance in the picture above, the *Nabob* is seen after having survived a U-boat torpedo in August 1944. She was written off for further naval service but was converted to mercantile use postwar. Ironically, she was operated by the German Norddeutscher Lloyd company, retaining her RN name.**

Ameer class

Class: *Ameer; Arbiter; Atheling; Begum; Emperor; Empress; Khedive; Nabob; Patroller; Premier; Puncher; Queen Rajah; Ranee; Reaper; Ruler; Shah; Slinger; Smiter; Speaker; Thane; Trouncer; Trumpeter*

Built: Todd, Tacoma, with the exception of *Queen Rajah*, Willamette; *Trouncer*, Commercial Iron Works

Commissioned: July 1943–February 1944

Displacement: 11,600 tonnes/11,400 tons (standard); 15,700 tonnes/15,400 tons (full load)

Length: 141.8m/465ft (bp); 151m/495ft (overall)

Beam: 21.1m/69ft 6in

Draught: 7.8m/25ft 6in (full load)

Flight deck: 133.6 x 26.8m/438 x 88ft

Aircraft: About 20

Armament: 2 x 127mm/5in,16 x 40mm/1.57in guns

Machinery: Geared turbine, 1 shaft

Power: 6.340kW/8,500shp

Speed: 17.5 knots

Fuel: 3,150 tonnes/3,100 tons

Range: –

Armour: None

Complement: 640 men

LEFT: **A bankrupt British economy switched back to home-sourced aircraft post-war in order to save dollars. Fireflies and Sea Furies predominated.** BELOW: **Otherwise accurately depicted at sea, *Warrior*'s port anchor indicates that the ship is manoeuvring in restricted waters.**

Colossus class

Experience in Norway and the Mediterranean by mid-1941 had demonstrated to the Royal Navy that the fleet required better defensive air cover. Fleet carriers were too few and too valuable to solve what was a pressing problem. Conversion of warships would prove less than satisfactory, while passenger liners, favourites for re-building, were already indispensable as troop carriers. New construction was therefore the only option.

Discussion centred upon a vessel intermediate between the complexity and expense of a fleet carrier and the limited capabilities of the escort carriers soon to enter service. Above all, this "intermediate" carrier had to be capable of being built in 21 months.

Naval design staff and specialist naval builders were already fully stretched, so Vickers-Armstrong, well-versed in both naval and mercantile practice, was made lead authority.

Several rapid draught proposals were considered, finalizing in February 1942 in a ship built generally to mercantile standards. Subdivision would, however, be greatly enhanced and all void spaces would be fitted with buoyant sealed drums. Standard cruiser machinery would be installed, powering twin shafts for 25 knots.

As only one hangar was considered, it could be given a headroom of 5.3m/17ft 6in which, later, allowed the ships to deploy aircraft that the fleet carriers could not. Armament was restricted to two twin 102mm/4in mountings aft and a range of automatic weapons. An early alteration to the specification saw the flight deck enlarged, displacing the 102mm/4in guns. Urgency demanded that some important equipment had no back-up but, even so, the construction time had to be lengthened to 27 months.

Such was the strength of British shipbuilding that the orders for the first ten could be shared between eight yards. Two of the first three were completed within the target time but none could work-up and proceed to the Pacific in time to see action.

ABOVE: **As this late war picture shows, a Colossus' air wing was little inferior to that of a large British fleet carrier. The type's survivability was, however, never tested by kamikaze, bomb or torpedo.** BELOW LEFT: **Few of the Colossus class saw much in the way of modernization, soldiering on in their original form until their ultimate disposal, mostly in the early 1960s unless transferred.**

Majestic class

In all, contracts were issued for 16 of what became universally known as the "Light Fleets". However, as the programme and the war progressed, carrier aircraft developed rapidly. Physically larger, far heavier in loaded take-off, and with higher landing speeds, they demanded a general uprating of related equipment, in particular arresters, catapult and elevators, in addition to a strengthened flight deck.

At the same time, an improved Bofors and Oerlikon-based armament (the former with directors) was added, together with a new electronics outfit and fittings for replenishment-at-sea (RAS), so essential to extended Pacific operation. The final six differed sufficiently to form a subclass known as the Majestics.

Such modifications were facilitated by the lightness of construction but accommodation could not keep pace with the increase in crew numbers consequent upon the eventual introduction of deck parks and larger air groups.

Beyond 1945, the Light Fleets proved their worth during the Korean War. None, however, received battle damage to test the justification of their calculated constructional shortcomings. Surplus to requirements, several were transferred abroad, proving to be highly durable, two still being extant at over 60 years of age.

ABOVE: Completed as the Canadian *Bonaventure*, the *Powerful* differed considerably in detail, the new funnel and masting being visible here. She also operated McDonnell Banshees and Grumman Trackers. **BELOW: The name ship of the class, *Majestic* was completed in 1955 as the Australian *Melbourne*. Note that, even on a smaller carrier, an interim angled deck could be incorporated with advantage. The aircraft are A-4 Skyhawks, Trackers and Sea Kings.**

Colossus and Majestic class

Colossus class: *Colossus; Glory; Ocean; Theseus; Triumph; Venerable; Vengeance; Warrior*
Majestic class: *Hercules; Leviathan; Magnificent; Majestic; Powerful; Terrible*
Built: Various
Commissioned: December 1944–May 1948
Displacement: *Colossus* 13,440 tonnes/13,200 tons (standard); 18,350 tonnes/18,000 tons (full load)
Majestic 16,050 tonnes/15,750 tons (standard); 19,850 tonnes/19,500 tons (full load)
Length: 192.2m/630ft (bp); 212m/695ft (overall)
Beam: 24.4m/80ft
Draught: *Colossus* 5.6m/18ft 6in (standard); 7.1m/23ft 3in (full load)
Majestic 5.9m/19ft 6in (standard); 7.5m/24ft 9in (full load)
Flight deck: 210.4 x 24.4m/690 x 80ft
Aircraft: About 48
Armament: *Colossus* 31 x 40mm/1.57in (10 double, 11 single), and 24 x 2pdr pom-pom (6 quadruple) guns
Majestic 30 x 40mm/1.57in (6 double, 18 single) guns
Machinery: Geared steam turbine, 4 boilers, 2 shafts
Power: 29,850kW/40,000shp
Speed: 25 knots
Fuel: *Colossus* 3,260 tonnes/3,200 tons
Majestic 3,230 tonnes/3,175 tons
Range: 22,220km/12,000nm at 14 knots
Armour: None
Complement: 1,050 men

Ark Royal (III) and *Eagle* (II)

Although treaty restrictions no longer applied, the design process for the *Implacable*'s successor began in 1940 with the same underwater hull form. The emphasis was laid on more and larger aircraft, together with even better protection from bomb attack. Only a small increase in target displacement was initially allowed, and it proved insufficient to permit the thickening of the flight deck, although the beam could be increased sufficiently to accommodate folded aircraft four abreast. A required increase in hangar headroom could be achieved only by reducing the depth of the overhead beams, which supported the heavy flight deck.

This "Improved Implacable", presented early in 1941, was poorly received and no order was placed. Within months, the *Formidable* and *Illustrious* survived heavy bomb damage. This led to more detailed design analysis, complicated further by the loss of the recently completed *Ark Royal* (II) to a single torpedo, due largely to poor design features.

A new design target was set for a 27,433-tonne/27,000-ton (standard) vessel with a 102mm/4in flight deck and provision for 72 aircraft. The necessary calculations and experiment demonstrated that the best attainable with this level of protection was a 32,105-tonne/31,600-ton ship stowing 57–69 aircraft. It was, by now, 1942 and, as the ship would be at least four years in build, it is interesting to speculate upon how long the Director of Naval Construction (DNC) thought the war would last.

Because of the anticipated new Barracuda multi-role aircraft and the need also to operate American-sourced aircraft, it was then decided to adopt American standards of 5.3m/17ft 6in high hangars and elevators rated at 13.6-tonne/30,000lb capacity. The width of the hangars was further increased, requiring redeepening the deck beams and increasing the beam to 34.4m/112ft 9in. This, in turn, limited the number both of yards to build it and docks to stem it. The required 31.5 knots brought the overall length to about 243.8m/800ft and standard displacement to about 33,020 tonnes/32,500 tons.

ABOVE: **Seen near the end of her career, the *Ark Royal* (III) is operating Phantoms and Buccaneers. Note how, at full power, the relatively full hull form is pushing water over the flight deck. The ship now is unarmed.**
BELOW: **The *Eagle* (II) was instantly distinguishable from her sister, when, in the course of her 1959–64 modernization, she gained an enormous Type 984, three-dimensional radar.**

Approval was given for four of the class and, at last, in October 1942, the first-of-class was laid down, the second not until May 1943. With now no hope of any completions during hostilities, the scarcely begun third unit was eventually abandoned and the fourth cancelled. (If the Americans had pursued their Essex programme in this dilatory fashion, they would have lost the Pacific war.)

The *Audacious* assumed the name of *Eagle* (II) from the abandoned unit and was launched in 1946, mainly to clear the slip. Her remaining sister, *Ark Royal* (III), was not put in the water until 1950.

With post-war austerity and an uncertain future, further progress was slow. *Eagle* was completed in a classic configuration in 1952 but the less advanced *Ark Royal* received substantial modifications, not being completed until 1955, but featuring an "interim" angled flight deck, steam-powered catapults and a third elevator placed, American-fashion, on the deck edge, a location not greatly favoured by British designers.

ABOVE LEFT: **The siting of the dual-purpose main armament always encroached upon flight deck space in British carriers. Adoption of the angled deck enforced a partial suppression of conventional gun armament, compensated by the addition of the Sea Cat missile.**

ABOVE: **Notice how the angled deck and aircraft deck parks are safely separated. Also the *Ark Royal* (III)'s pronounced "horn" to catch the aircraft launch bridles.**

RIGHT: ***Ark Royal* (III) on a port visit in company with a *Leander*-class frigate and a *Ness*-class supply ship. Note the two double-mattress Type 965 radar antennas for high definition air search.**

ABOVE: ***Ark Royal* (III) in the mid-1950s being overflown by a flight of Fairey Gannets. Although some of these aircraft were converted for airborne early warning duties, these are all ASW versions.**

Ark Royal (III) and *Eagle* (II)

Class: *Eagle* (II), Harland & Wolff, Belfast, commissioned October 1, 1951; *Ark Royal* (III), Cammell Laird, Birkenhead, commissioned February 25, 1955

Particulars as built:

Displacement: 37,650 tonnes/36,970 tons (standard); 46,550 tonnes/45,720 tons (full load)

Length: 219.6m/720ft (bp); 245.1m/803ft 9in (overall)

Beam: 34.4m/112ft 9in

Draught: 10m/32ft 9in (full load)

Flight deck: 243.1 x 34.2m/797 x 112ft

Aircraft: 80

Armament: 16 x 114.3mm/4.5in (8 double), 64 x 40mm/1.57in (8 sextuple, 2 double. 12 single) guns

Machinery: Geared steam turbines, 8 boilers, 4 shafts

Power: 113,400kW/152,000shp

Speed: 30.5 knots

Fuel: 5,925 tonnes/5,820 tons

Range: 7,250km/3,915nm at 24 knots

Armour: 114.3mm/4.5in (vertical belt); 38mm/1.5in (hangar walls); 102mm/4in (flight deck)

Complement: 2,275 men

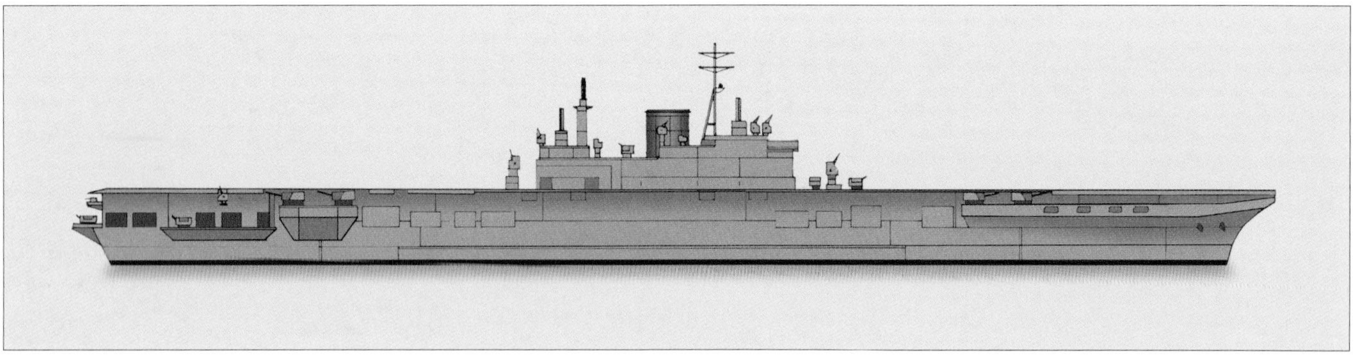

Malta class

Although never realized, the Malta design is of great interest in showing how far the experience of four years of war and close cooperation with the US Navy altered British philosophy with respect to carriers.

The strike role had emerged as paramount, so that not only were large numbers of aircraft required but also the means to launch them at a high rate to maximize strike potential. American-style "open" hangars permitted aircraft engines to be warmed-up below while further elevators would facilitate rapid transfer to flight deck level. The largest feasible flight decks allowed for efficient "spotting", mass take-offs and landings, but their greater area militated against their being heavily protected. British-style "closed" hangars and heavy flight deck made, paradoxically, for a lighter ship because of the greater depth of the continuously plated hull. Double hangars could also be provided, reducing the plan area (and, therefore, target area) for a given aircraft capacity.

A major argument against the "small area" ship, however, was the need for higher power, not only to maintain high speed when required but also to accelerate rapidly from cruising to launch speed.

With the design yet to be finalized, three (possibly four) Maltas were ordered in July 1943. Slightly larger than the American Midways then in build, the ships would have been of "open" design with two centreline and two deck-edge elevators. Over 149,140kW/200,000shp would have been dissipated over, probably, five propeller shafts, the centreline shaft being seen as less likely to incur torpedo damage. The number of rudders was not finally decided.

ABOVE: **The four projected *Malta*-class carriers were badly delayed by the Fleet Air Arm requesting that the design be recast along American, rather than British, principles.** BELOW LEFT: **In the words of the American official historian, kamikazes "crumpled like scrambled eggs" on the armoured flight decks of British carriers. This factor was hugely influential in later carrier design, both British and American.**

Even until their cancellation at the war's end, the Maltas were subject to continuous change, not least because the advent of the kamikaze and the heavy air-launched rocket challenged anew the acceptance of less well-protected ships.

Malta class

Projected class: *Africa*, Fairfield, Govan; *Gibraltar*, Vickers-Armstrong, Newcastle; *Malta*, John Brown, Clydebank; *New Zealand*, Harland & Wolff, Belfast
Commissioned: –
Displacement: 47,350 tonnes/46,500 tons (standard); 57,680 tonnes/56,650 tons (full load)
Length: 250m/820ft (bp); 273.6m/897ft (overall)
Beam: 35.3m/115ft 9in (bp)
Draught: 9m/29ft 6in (standard); 10.5m/34ft 6in (full load)
Flight deck: 273.6 x 41.5m/897 x 136ft
Aircraft: 80
Armament: 16 x 114.3mm/4.5in (8 double) and 42 x 40mm/1.57in (7 sextuple) guns
Machinery: Geared steam turbines, 8 boilers, 4 shafts
Power: 149,140kW/200,000shp
Speed: 32.5 knots
Fuel: 6,110 tonnes/6,000 tons
Range: Not known
Armour: 102mm/4in (hangar walls); 102mm/4in (protective deck)
Complement: 3,500 men

LEFT: **Aircraft maintenance support ships resulted from the high attrition rates suffered during intensive operations by the British Pacific Fleet. Here, the *Pioneer* has a Supermarine Sea Otter perched forward. In the Far East, these aircraft were usually shore-based and used for air-sea rescue.**
ABOVE: **Although a new ship in this 1945 picture, the *Pioneer*, lacking all her carrier impedimenta, gives the impression of being stripped for disposal.**

Perseus and *Pioneer*

Intensive pre-war carrier operation indicated the high levels of aircraft attrition that might be expected under wartime conditions. This resulted in the one-off expensive Maintenance Carrier HMS *Unicorn*. Even before her completion, however, the Admiralty was having to plan the reconstruction of a British Eastern Fleet. With an estimated 1,000 attached aircraft, it would obviously require further forward maintenance ships for, in so vast a theatre, the use of fixed, shore-based repair facilities was not a practical option. Conversion of American-supplied (and owned) escort carriers (CVE) could not be considered, so the choice fell upon two hulls from the "Light Fleet" programme, retaining two hulls that could also have been reconverted in an emergency.

Perseus and *Pioneer* were two standard *Colossus*-type ships but, as their new role would see aircraft transferred only by crane, flying control facilities, arrester systems and catapult were deleted and hangar space reorganized for fuselage repair, high-level maintenance and system testing. Engines and major component repair and maintenance was the task of other ships in the fleet train. Much of their already light armament was suppressed and strange erections, including a large Scotch derrick, appeared topside.

Along with unconverted Light Fleets, *Perseus* and *Pioneer* arrived in the Pacific just too late to be of operational use. Post-war, there was an abundance of carriers, so neither was reconverted, and they were re-rated Ferry Carriers, moving aircraft about the many extant British overseas bases and, on occasion, "topping-up" fleet carriers.

During 1951–52, the *Perseus* acted as floating test bed for the prototype steam catapult, under development since 1946. To generate sufficient speed for modern fleet aircraft without imposing dangerous acceleration forces, it was found that a 45.7m/150ft catapult was required. These could be fitted to fleet carriers but not to Light Fleets. Limited to a unit of only about 30.5m/100ft, the ships were thus always limited in their range of deployable aircraft.

The *Pioneer* was scrapped in 1954 and the *Perseus* in 1958, as the need for front-line aircraft heavy repair disappeared. For relevant data see under Colossus class.

RIGHT: **Looking rather more pristine, the *Pioneer* was fitted with only nominal armament and electronics. For her maintenance duties, she has been fitted with a Scotch derrick and an auxiliary accommodation block right aft.**

Centaur class

At the end of 1942, the requirements of future carrier aircraft were drastically reappraised. Maximum landing and take-off weight was nearly tripled, to 13.6 tonnes/30,000lb. Stall speed was increased to 75 knots, meaning that catapults had to accelerate them to this speed, and arresters had to stop them from it. Wingspan rose from 15.3m/50ft to 18.3m/60ft and take-off distance from 106.7m/350ft to 152.4m/500ft.

The planned 1943 building programme was to include eight "Improved Majestics", but it was clear that this design was simply too small to accept the new requirements. With an eye to the post-war fleet, it was also apparent that the six earlier armoured carriers would not be amenable to modernization. Assuming their enforced retirement, the planned Ark Royals would be the only modern fleet carriers. The new Majestic follow-ons would, therefore, need to work alongside them, necessitating a higher speed than that planned. A longer hull was, therefore, required on both counts and the installed power was doubled.

TOP: **Until 1958 the *Centaur* deployed Sea Furies and Avengers then, with full angled deck and steam catapults, Sea Hawks. There was insufficient space to incorporate any armament of larger calibre than 40mm/1.57in.**
LEFT: **Steaming on a pristine sea, the *Bulwark* (nearer ship) and *Albion* present a very uncluttered appearance, mainly due to having much of their armament landed.**

ABOVE: **Completed to a revised, post-war design the three *Centaurs* presented unusually "clean" hulls, free of the many common protuberances except the crane support three-quarters aft.** BELOW: **British and American carriers conducted frequent "crossdecking" exercises to prove commonality. Here, a Douglas AD Skyraider, probably from the *Forrestal*, lands on *Centaur*.**

The new specification called for a single hangar, meeting the later criterion of 5.3m/17ft 6in headroom. Accommodation, stores, and fuel were to be sufficient for an air group of 24 attack aircraft and 16 fighters. Beyond splinter protection and small patches over vital areas, no armour was to be incorporated. Because of the ships' greater value, they were to be given four twin 114.3mm/4.5in mountings.

As final approval was given only in March 1944, and the proposed build time was 33 months, it was never likely that they would participate in the war against Japan that was expected to be resolved by the end of 1946. With hostilities ending 16 months earlier than expected, contracts for four of the eight new *Centaurs* were therefore cancelled. Construction of the remainder slowed to a crawl, resulting in considerable design changes being introduced to accommodate new technologies and improved peacetime habitability standards.

Centaur class

Class: *Albion*, Swan Hunter, Wallsend, commissioned May 26, 1954; *Bulwark*, Harland & Wolff, Belfast, commissioned November 4, 1954; *Centaur*, Harland & Wolff, Belfast, commissioned September 1, 1953; *Hermes* (III), Vickers-Armstrong, Barrow, commissioned November 18, 1959

Displacement: 22,880 tonnes/22,470 tons (standard); 27,550 tonnes/27,050 tons (full load)

Length: 198.3m/650ft (bp); 224.5m/736ft (overall)

Beam: 27.5m/90ft

Draught: 7.1m/23ft 3in (standard); 8.3m/27ft 3in (full load)

Flight deck: 223.5 x 27.5m/732ft 9in x 90ft

Aircraft: 40–42

Armament: 32 x 40mm/1.57in (2 sextuple, 8 double, 4 single) guns

Machinery: Geared steam turbines, 4 boilers, 2 shafts

Power: 56,700kW/76,000shp

Speed: 28.5 knots

Fuel: 4,175 tonnes/4,100 tons

Range: 11,110km/6,000nm at 20 knots

Armour: None

Complement: 1,550 men

LEFT: **Looking most impressive, *Victorious* checks responses with a zig-zag manoeuvre. Right forward is a de Havilland Sea Vixen, a very capable all-weather interceptor or strike fighter.**

ABOVE: **Sea Vixens and Buccaneers predominate in this view of *Victorious* at anchor. The intention of locating the forward elevator on the port-side deck edge was thwarted by the ship's relatively low freeboard.**

Victorious modernized

There was a pressing post-war requirement to bring the six early armoured carriers up to a standard whereby they could operate modern aircraft. Designed with single hangars of 4.9m/16ft headroom, the three original (Illustrious) class were most suitable for a pilot reconstruction and, of these, *Victorious* was selected. It was estimated that the work, starting in October 1950, would take 43 weeks. The ship would be razed to hangar deck level and rebuilt with an increased beam and hangar height increased to 5.3m/17.5ft.

This, however, was a period of great innovation in carrier practice and the already considerable task was complicated by modifications and additions. Over 30 months into the job it was decided to install a full (8.5-degree) angled deck, although the ship's freeboard proved inadequate for the required deck-edge elevator.

Just two months later came the decision to add the huge new Type 984 three-dimensional radar. This would considerably uprate the ship's potential but greatly impacted on the layout of the superstructure and associated compartments below.

With much of the heavy horizontal structure replaced, it was belatedly forecast that the existing boilers (which now had also to provide steam for the two new catapults) could not last the extended life of the ship. Much work therefore had to be repeated in re-opening the hull for boiler replacement.

A final problem was that her planned British 76mm/3in 70-calibre armament was not ready, so that American-pattern 76mm/3in 50s had to be substituted.

The final result was judged successful but had been so difficult, so protracted (twice the estimated time) and so expensive (six times the first estimate) that the remaining five ships were phased out of service.

In her reconstruction, some of the *Victorious*' main statistics were changed. Length (overall) increased to 237.2m/778ft 4in, beam to 31.5m/103ft 4in. Standard displacement was now 30,886 tonnes/30,400 tons, full load 36,068 tonnes/35,500 tons. Main armament comprised six twin 76mm/3in guns. Up to 38 modern aircraft could be accommodated (which does not suggest very good value for money).

Victorious modernized

Built: Vickers-Armstrong, Newcastle
Commissioned: May 15, 1941
Displacement: 30,886 tonnes/30,400 tons (standard); 36,068 tonnes/35,500 tons (full load)
Length: 205.3m/673ft (bp); 237.2m/778ft 4in (overall)
Beam: 31.5m/103ft 4in
Draught: 7.5m/24ft 6in (standard); 8.5m/27ft 9in (full load)
Flight deck: 189.1 x 24.6m/620 x 80ft
Aircraft: Up to 38
Armament: 12 x 76mm/3in (6 double) guns
Machinery: Geared steam turbines, 6 boilers, 3 shafts
Power: 82,800kW/111,000shp
Speed: 30.5 knots
Fuel: 4,940 tonnes/4,850 tons
Range: 19,816 km/10,700nm at 10 knots
Armour: 114.3mm/4.5in (belt); 38mm/1.5in (hangar wall); 76mm/3in (flight deck); 38–50mm/1.5–2in (hangar deck)
Complement: 1,180 men

ABOVE LEFT: **Most thorough of the commando carrier conversions that of the *Hermes* (III) saw her ponderous Type 984 radar replaced by a less capable 965. Although she has been fitted with a ski-jump for V/STOL operation only helicopters, transport and stores are here ranged on deck.** TOP: **Amphibious group operation. As the carrier's Wessex helicopters wait to put their spearhead troops ashore, a flooded-down Fearless-type dock landing ship has her assault landing craft ready in support.** ABOVE: **As converted, the Centaurs carried variable numbers of Wessex and Sea King helicopters. The former were for lifting troops, the latter for anti-submarine operations.**

Centaur class as Commando Carriers

During the Suez campaign of November 1956 the *Colossus*-class *Ocean* and *Theseus* effectively demonstrated that special assault troops could be landed by helicopter to seize and hold key points ahead of a major amphibious landing.

It was decided to convert ships specifically for this role and between 1959 and 1962, the *Albion* and *Bulwark* were reconfigured as so-called Commando Carriers. In appearance they changed little but could now accommodate a full commando of about 750 men. In their new role, the ship's complement had been reduced by about 30 per cent and much hangar space had been freed so there was no problem with space.

The earlier air group was gone, in favour of 16 Whirlwind (later Wessex) helicopters. These required neither arrest gear nor catapults, which were removed. The interim angled-deck markings reverted to an axial configuration with nine widely spaced "spots" for helicopters.

To transport heavy gear, light transport and guns ashore, four assault landing craft were slung under substantial davits near the after end. All armament except four twin 40mm/1.57in guns was landed.

Between 1971 and 1973, with British fixed-wing carriers being phased out, the later and more capable *Hermes* (III) was converted to replace *Albion* which, with her never-converted sister, *Centaur*, went for scrap.

With extra experience, the *Hermes* (III) was given space for a second commando, although further troop-carrying helicopters were not provided. Fewer carriers, however, meant a diminished fleet anti-submarine warfare (ASW) capability. For this reason, *Hermes* (III) was reconfigured for ASW but acted also as a trials ship for V/STOL operation, with the Royal Navy seeking to acquire a marinized version of the Harrier. The wisdom of this was vindicated by the aircraft's versatile performance during the 1982 Falklands War.

Centaur class as Commando Carriers

Class: *Albion; Bulwark; Hermes* (III)
Displacement: 22,658 tonnes/22,300 tons (standard); 27,738 tonnes/27,300 tons (full load)
Length: 198.3m/650ft (bp); 224.5m/736ft (overall)
Beam: 27.5m/90ft
Draught: 7.1m/23ft 3in (standard); 8.3m/27ft 3in (full load)
Flight deck: 223.5 x 27.5m/732ft 9in x 90ft
Aircraft: 40–42
Armament: 8 x 40mm/1.57in (4 double) guns
Machinery: Geared steam turbines, 4 boilers, 2 shafts
Power: 56,700kW/76,000shp
Speed: 28.5 knots
Fuel: 4,175 tonnes/4,100 tons
Range: 11,110km/6,000nm at 20 knots
Armour: None
Complement: 1,550 men

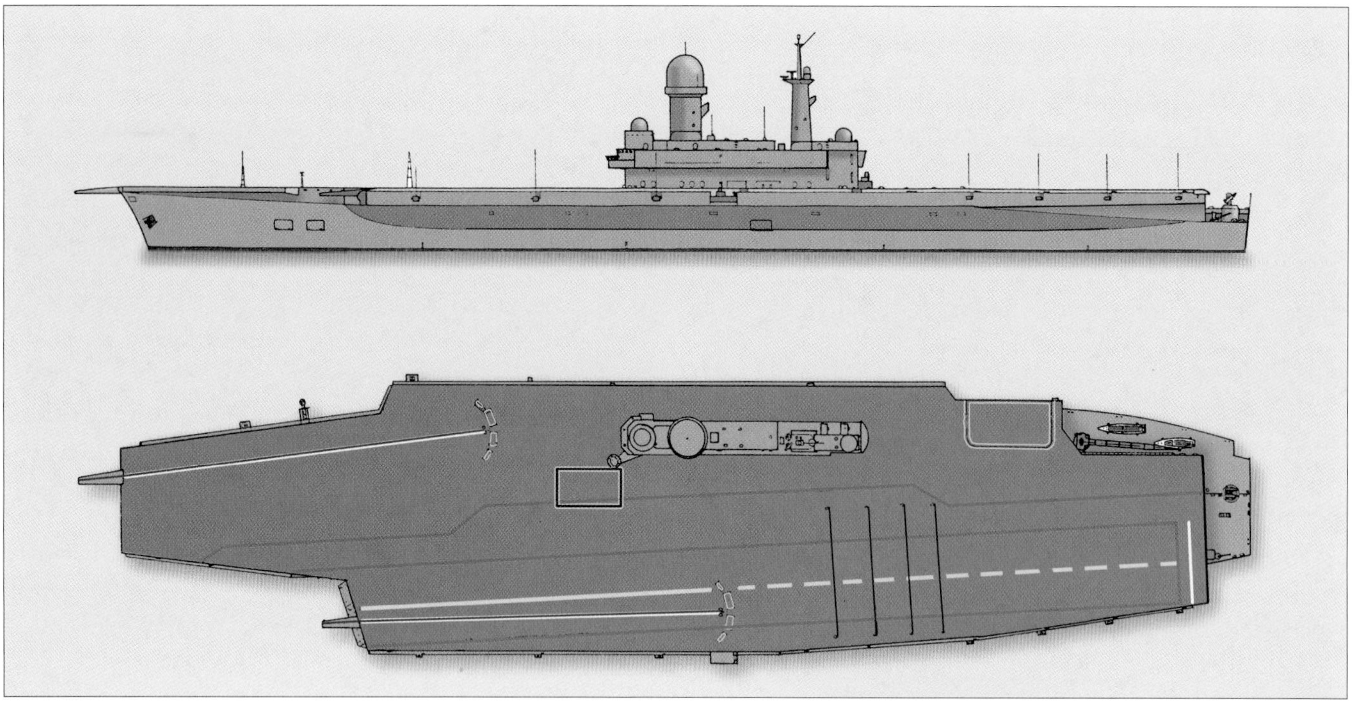

CVA-01

ABOVE: **Innovative deck layout was a feature of the planned CVA-01, with the after (starboard quarter) elevator feeding aircraft to the forward catapult via the "Alaskan Highway" outboard of the island. This would interfere neither with landing operations nor deck parks. Hangar space would be maximized by housing ASW helicopters aboard accompanying supply ships and replacing the CAP by missile defence.** ABOVE RIGHT: **Faced with the expensive prospect of building three CVA-01s, the British government preferred the RAF's proposal of cheaper, land-based air power. However, the proposed means, the variable geometry F-111K, was never acquired by the British, though variants continue to give good service to the USAF and RAAF 40 years after the F-111's first flight.**

By the mid-1960s it was becoming urgently necessary to lay down replacements for the Royal Navy's ageing carrier force. A design of a nominal 53,848 tonnes/53,000 tons was decided upon as being the maximum likely to receive Treasury approval, not least because of limitations in facilities at both builders and dockyards. It had also been conclusively demonstrated that a 10 per cent reduction in cost would result in 50 per cent reduction in capability. Dimensions were also driven by a demand for maximum commonality between naval and air force aircraft.

Coded CVA-01, the carrier would have been almost symmetrical in plan, the angled deck to port balanced by an access track outboard of the superstructure linking forward and after ends. The angled deck was offset at only 3.5 degrees, creating a three-zone working area. Two steam catapults and two elevators, one of them on the starboard-quarter deck edge, could handle aircraft of up to 34 tonnes/75,000lb weight.

Although essentially of closed design, the hangar opened out on to a quarterdeck to allow limited pre-warming of aircraft engines. The layout of the long, narrow superstructure was dominated by the requirement to efficiently separate the numerous and complex electronics systems.

The ship's strike capability would be maximized by operating in concert with a projected Strike Cruiser, which would incorporate all a task group's command facilities as well as deploying its force of ASW helicopters.

To guarantee the availability of one ship requires, ideally, three and the *Eagle*-sized CVA-01 was killed off by the 1966 Defence Review, which planned withdrawal from "East of Suez" and which capitulated to the RAF argument that the (stillborn) F-111 aircraft would be a cheaper and equally effective option. History, alas, proves invariably that the argument is specious.

CVA-01 (name never confirmed)

Built: Order never placed
Displacement: 50,900 tonnes/50,000 tons (standard); 55,650 tonnes/54,650 tons (full load)
Length: 271.5m/890ft (at waterline); 293.7m/963ft (overall)
Beam: 37.2m/122ft
Draught: 9.8m/32ft 3in (full load)
Flight deck: 283 x 58.3m/928 x 191ft
Aircraft: About 45
Armament: Twin Sea Dart SAM
Machinery: Geared steam turbines, 6 boilers, 3 shafts
Power: 100,700kW/135,000shp
Speed: 28+ knots
Fuel: 6,310 tonnes/6,200 tons
Range: 11,110km/6,000nm at 20 knots
Armour: Nominal
Complement: Not known

LEFT: **Maximization of underdeck hangar space resulted in an imposing accommodation block topside. The black scar of the main diesel generator exhaust must be the bane of the Chief Officer's existence.** ABOVE: ***Argus* (II) was designed as a commercial roll-on, roll-off/container ship. This required a wide transom for trailer access allowing, in conversion, for a rectangular flight deck without pronounced overhangs.**

Argus (II)

The naval force despatched to recover the Falklands in 1982 included many "ships taken up from trade" (STUFT). One was the roll-on, roll-off/container ship *Contender Bezant*, whose spacious vehicle decks made her ideal as an aircraft transport. Subsequent to the hostilities, she was purchased and converted to a helicopter training ship by Harland & Wolff. Renamed *Argus* (II), she is a Royal Fleet Auxiliary (RFA), civilian-manned but carrying a permanent naval party.

Prior to conversion she had excess stability in the unloaded condition, making for an unacceptably lively motion. To raise her centre of gravity she was given a heavy superstructure and a flight deck formed from the original deck, inverted and filled with reinforced concrete. The new hangar is divided into four by heavy doors and may be opened to allow engine warm-up. It is connected to the flight deck by two elevators. In peacetime the role of the *Argus* (II) is to train helicopter aircrew but, in hostilities, she can operate six to twelve ASW helicopters. She can also carry a dozen Harrier-sized V/STOL aircraft, although her configuration militates against their efficient use.

Argus (II) is a good example of how helicopters and V/STOL aircraft enable a variety of cargo vessels to act as auxiliary aircraft carriers.

Plans to similarly convert a sister ship were abandoned due to cost and, indeed, would be hard to justify in the long term.

Argus (II)

Built: Cantieri Riuniti "Breda", Venice, Italy
Commissioned: (as *Argus*): October 28, 1987
Displacement: 22,661 tonnes/22,256 tons (standard); 28,675 tonnes/28,163 tons (full load)
Length: 160m/525ft 3in (bp); 175.12m/574ft 10in (overall)
Beam: 30.4m/100ft
Draught: Not known
Flight deck: 113.52 x 28m/372ft 8in x 91ft 11in
Aircraft: A mix of up to 6 x Sea King helicopters and 12 x Harrier V/STOL
Armament: 4 x 30mm/1.18in (2 double) and 2 x 20mm/0.79in (2 single) guns
Machinery: Two diesels, 2 shafts
Power: 17,456kW/23,400bhp
Speed: 22 knots maximum
Fuel: 4,600 tonnes/4,527 tons (heavy oil); 1,590 tonnes/1,565 tons (diesel oil)
Range: 37,040km/20,000nm at 19 knots
Armour: 1.5m/4ft 11in reinforced concrete over flight deck
Complement: Not known

LEFT: **While the *Argus* (II) could, in theory, deploy V/STOL aircraft, her layout would limit operation to the expensive vertical take-off and land mode.** RIGHT: **Argus was a mythological character with 100 eyes. Following his death, his eyes were transferred to the tail of a peacock. The choice of name suggests that *Argus* (I) of 1918 was valued more for her reconnaissance than her strike potential.**

Invincible class

The aborted CVA-01 was planned to operate in concert with a Command Cruiser, which would have assumed command and control functions for a task group. This ship would also have housed a wing of helicopters and been responsible for the group's anti-submarine warfare (ASW) defence, numbers being more efficiently deployed and maintained by a single vessel.

The standard Sea King AS helicopter requires considerable headroom and design studies indicated that a carrier-style through-deck was the preferred configuration. Size was increased due to the need to incorporate the Sea Dart that would otherwise have been deployed by the similarly cancelled Type 82 escort.

Sea Dart, however, could not deal with the threat posed by Cold War-era Soviet fast bombers armed with stand-off air-to-surface missiles (ASM) whose optional nuclear warheads could lay waste a whole task group. Like the Zeppelin and the Fw200 before them, these needed to be countered by fast interceptors. The Admiralty was thus greatly interested in Hawker's P.1127 project, a V/STOL fighter able to operate from small decks.

The aircraft was demonstrated successfully aboard a carrier early in 1963 but, due greatly to the political decision to abandon "aircraft carriers", it was not acquired until 1975. Now in production as the Harrier, it had already been bought for the US Marine Corps and the Spanish Navy.

By the late 1960s, plans were already complete for a Helicopter/Command Cruiser of about 18,000 tonnes/ 17,716 tons, with hangar space for nine Sea Kings and three more on the through flight deck. Obviously, in confidence that the V/STOL argument would be won, the design was stretched to just below the psychologically important 20,000-tonne/ 19,684-ton mark in order to squeeze in a further five marinized Sea Harriers.

TOP: The *Invincible* satisfactorily operated RAF ground-attack Harriers (airborne, right) in the Falklands and, at the time of writing, the Royal Navy is due to phase out its Sea Harriers (on deck). ABOVE: Removal of the Sea Dart and extending the parallel flight deck has considerably increased the viability of the Invincibles. Note the new-design mainmast and Goalkeeper CIWS right forward.

RIGHT: **Carriers never operate unsupported. It therefore made more practical sense to maximize the aircraft capacity of what is quite a small carrier and put Sea Dart systems (as that being tested here) aboard a dedicated escort.**

ABOVE: **Note how V/STOL and helicopter operation have no requirement for an angled deck, the flight path being effectively parallel with the ship's but offset to port. The original forward Vulcan/Phalanx CIWS was poorly sited with bad coverage to the port side.** BELOW: **Still lacking some equipment, the new *Ark Royal* (IV) arrives at her Portsmouth home port for the first time. Note that she is still in builder's ownership and wearing a Red Ensign prior to commissioning.**

In April 1973, the resulting HMS *Invincible* was ordered "for but not with". For political purposes, the name was not a traditional carrier name, and the ship was termed a "through-deck cruiser". When common sense re-emerged her two sisters took the honoured names of *Illustrious* (II) and *Ark Royal* (IV).

Although the limited hybrid design has resulted in a hangar with a narrowed amidships section, the ships have proved flexible. Space has been saved by using scissors-type elevators, capable of being accessed from any side. The unobstructed flight deck permits fuel-saving rolling take-offs for the Harriers (RAF versions can also be deployed) and economy has been further enhanced by installing a "ski-jump" at the forward end.

Gas turbine propulsion has conferred great sprint potential and has reduced the size of machinery spaces, but has increased the silhouette and imposed the need for space-consuming removal paths for the regular replacement of gas turbines.

The V/STOL carrier cannot pretend to replace the conventional (CTOL) carrier in terms of potential but, having a scale not dictated by the likes of catapults and arresters, can be afforded by minor navies.

Invincible class

Class: *Invincible*, Vickers-Armstrong, Barrow-in-Furness, commissioned July 11, 1980; *Illustrious* (II), Swan Hunter, Wallsend, commissioned June 20, 1982; *Ark Royal* (IV), Swan Hunter, Wallsend, commissioned November 1, 1985

Displacement: 17,150 tonnes/16,850 tons (standard); 20,970 tonnes/20,600 tons (full load)

Length: 192.5m/632ft (bp); 206.2m/677ft (overall)

Beam: 27.4m/90ft

Draught: 8.8m/28ft 10in maximum

Flight deck: 183 x 35m/600 x 114ft 9in

Aircraft: 8 x Sea Harriers, 9 x ASW and 3 x AEW Sea King helicopters

Armament: 1 x Sea Dart SAM system and 2 x Goalkeeper CIWS

Machinery: 4 Olympus gas turbines, 2 shafts

Power: 83,500kW/112,000hp

Speed: 28 knots

Fuel: Not known

Range: 11,110km/6,000nm at 18 knots

Armour: None

Complement: 1,000 men plus 320 aircrew

LEFT: **A fine view of the *Ocean* at the 2005 Review clearly shows her stern vehicular ramp extended on to a Mexeflote floating causeway unit. All three of her Vulcan/Phalanx CIWS are visible, right forward, and on either quarter.** ABOVE: **The marriage of a boxy, volume-critical topside to a relatively fine underwater form results in a sharply sculpted appearance. Many merchantmen, e.g. pure car carriers, are similarly affected.**

Ocean

Although not true aircraft carriers in the sense that their function is not primarily that of operating aircraft, modern large amphibious-warfare ships have, with the development of helicopters and V/STOL, become potent aviation-capable ships in their own right. In the helicopter carrier HMS *Ocean* (L12), supporting the assault ships *Albion* (L14) and *Bulwark* (L15), the Royal Navy has a capable group, able to transport and land up to three military battalions and their equipment.

The *Ocean* has a through flight deck and starboard-side island but, being intended to operate helicopters only, she has no angled deck, arrester gear, catapult or ski-jump. Six helicopter spots are provided but, although her elevators are dimensioned to accept V/STOL aircraft, there are currently no plans to deploy them.

A military battalion, with light vehicles and equipment, can be accommodated and landed by the ship's four LCVPs (Landing Craft, Vehicle, Personnel) carried under davits in deep pockets in the hull. Normally also carrying Sea King helicopters, the flight deck can support Chinooks. In the future, these will be joined or superseded by Merlins or even a marinized version of the army's Apache ground attack helicopter.

Diesel-propelled, the *Ocean* is good for only 20 knots and, although fitted with comprehensive electronics to fit her as a headquarters ship, has a very light defensive armament, making her very escort-dependent.

The two *Albions* can also each accommodate a battalion at a pinch. However, they have extensive superstructure forward and a flight pad aft with only two helicopter spots. They complement the *Ocean* in having a large, floodable well, closed by a stern gate and are able to accommodate four LCU (Landing Craft, Utility) or two American-pattern LCAC (Landing Craft, Air Cushion). They also carry four LCVPs under davits. Like the *Ocean*, they are diesel-propelled and equipped only with light defensive armament.

Ocean

Built: Kvaerner, Govan
Commissioned: September 30, 1998
Displacement: 22,150 tonnes/21,750 tons (full load)
Length: 198.8m/651ft 10in (bp); 6.6m/21ft 8in (overall)
Aircraft: 12 x Sea King or 4 x Merlin plus 6 x Lynx/Apache helicopters
Flight deck: 170 x 31.7m/229ft 6in x 103ft 11in
Armament: 3 x Vulcan/Phalanx CIWS
Machinery: Two 12-cylinder diesel engines, 2 shafts
Power: 13,500kW/18,100bhp
Speed: 20 knots
Fuel: Not known
Range: 14,820km/8,000nm at 15 knots
Armour: Not known
Complement: 490 men, including aircrew

LEFT AND BELOW: **Current interventional policy demands that seaborne expeditionary forces have organic air power. The sheer cost of naval air, however, frightens successive governments into endless prevarication. Computer-generated images of what is a continuously evolving design are a poor substitute for the actual cutting of steel but, in lieu of action, may be expected for a while yet.**

Queen Elizabeth class

Long-planned, these carriers will be the largest warships ever to be operated by the Royal Navy. Because of the much-diminished condition of the British shipbuilding industry, and the politics inseparable from the allocation of naval orders, sections will be constructed at Govan, Portsmouth and Wallsend, and transported to Rosyth for final assembly.

Their strike component will comprise Lockheed Merlin F-35 Joint Strike Fighters (JSF) in their STOVL (Short Take-off, Vertical Land) variant. Although constructed with the requisite overhang for angled deck operations, the flight deck will not be so marked. No catapults, associated steam plant or arrester gear is fitted, although space for their possible later addition has been allocated.

For STOVL operations, the forward ski-jump is approached either axially from the after marshalling area or at an angle from the starboard side. This point, between the two islands (a new and unique arrangement) is served by one of the two deck-edge elevators. These are large enough to accept the non-folding wings of the F-35, the Merlin ASW helicopter and the as-yet unspecified airborne early warning (AEW) aircraft.

Propulsion is electric, both quiet and flexible. Generators, driven by gas turbines and/or diesel engines may be located where convenient, providing power for the motors that drive the shafts. Podded propulsion, much used in cruise ships, was considered but apparently rejected. The large electrical capacity may influence a later choice of catapult.

As currently planned, the forward island will be dedicated to navigation, the after one to flying control. Armament has not yet been finalized and all statistics are subject to change. Those for complement and speed appear, for instance, to be unrealistically low.

If the timetable suffers any further politically inspired delays, the existing Invincibles will be hopelessly inadequate by the time of their replacement.

Queen Elizabeth class

Class: *Queen Elizabeth*, laid down 2006, launched 2009, commissioned 2012; *Prince of Wales*, laid down 2009, launched 2012, commissioned 2015

Displacement: 59,000 tonnes/58,000 tons (full load)

Length: 284m/931ft 2in (overall)

Beam: Not known

Draught: Not known

Aircraft: About 35

Flight deck: Maximum width 75m/245ft 10in

Armament: Not known

Machinery: Gas turbines and/or diesel engines; electric drive

Power: Not known

Speed: 25+ knots

Fuel: Not known

Range: Not known

Armour: Not known

Complement: About 600 men plus aircrew

LEFT: **Converted to a seaplane carrier, the *Wakamiya* was little changed externally. Note the more complex rigging of the derricks and the after section of the forward flying-off platform.**

ABOVE: **Commencing in 1932, the *Kamoi* underwent a bewildering number of modifications to best equip her for her dual role of seaplane carrier and fleet tanker. The experience contributed to the design of purpose-built ships.**

Early seaplane carriers

During World War I, the vast island groups of the western Pacific were German territory and hostile to Japan which, following the peace, assumed a mandate. Given the scale of the area, it is not surprising that the Japanese Navy showed a lively interest in naval reconnaissance from its very inception. Floatplanes appeared on all major warships, but humbler ships were also converted to specialist seaplane carriers. Deploying floatplanes or flying boats, these could quickly establish a forward reconnaissance base from any suitable anchorage.

The first such ship was the *Wakamiya*, a 4,400 gross registered tons British-built cargo ship modified roughly in 1914 by the addition of steel-and-canvas hangars for four seaplanes. These were handled by the ship's cargo gear. In the Japanese Navy's first-ever seaborne air strike, the *Wakamiya*'s aircraft attacked the German bases at Tsingtao in 1914. After the war she was fitted with a flying-off platform over the forecastle, from which acquired Sopwith Pup fighters were flown. The ship was discarded in 1931.

Encouraged by the success of the *Wakamiya*, the Japanese modified two fleet tankers, *Notoro* and *Tsurumi*, in 1924. Covered accommodation was added for up to ten aircraft apiece before and abaft the central bridge structure, and conspicuous cranes were included for their handling. Retaining their full tanker capacity, the pair acted simultaneously as aircraft transports, but were capable of independent operation such as during the campaign against China. Both reverted to tankers during World War II, in the course of which the *Tsurumi* was lost.

Before the Japanese began to design and build specialist seaplane carriers in the 1930s a third and larger tanker, the *Kamoi*, underwent similar, but more elaborate conversion for the deployment of up to a dozen aircraft. She, too, reverted to tanker duties from 1943 and became a war loss. Targeted specifically by American submarines, tankers had become more valuable than seaplane carriers.

LEFT AND BELOW: **Superimposition of seaplane facilities on the fleet oiler *Notoro* resulted in a complex and unlovely structure, as the ship was required to retain her designed functions. A light spar deck was constructed over the topside pipework for the seaplanes. A second light deck at bridge level served both as a handling area and a support for the canvas sides to the "hangars".**

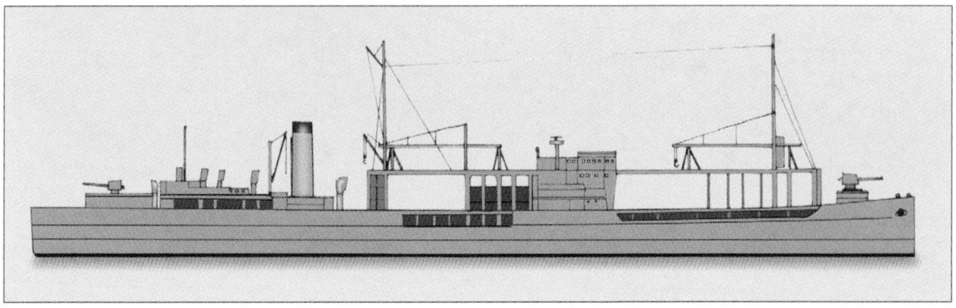

Kamoi, as modified

Built: New York Shipbuilding, Camden, NJ; commissioned as carrier in 1933
Displacement: 17,300 tonnes/17,000 tons (standard); 19,960 tonnes/19,600 tons (full load)
Length: 151.3m/496ft (at waterline)
Beam: 20.4m/67ft
Draught: 8.4m/27ft 8in (full load)
Aircraft: 12 floatplanes
Flight deck: None
Armament: 2 x 140mm/5.5in, and 2 x 76mm/3in guns
Machinery: Turbo-electric, 2 boilers, 2 shafts
Power: 6,700kW/9,000shp
Speed: 15 knots
Fuel: 2,540 tonnes/2,500 tons (coal)
Range: Not known
Armour: None
Complement: Not known

Hosho

Assertions that the *Hosho*, Japan's first through-deck carrier, began life as a tanker seem unlikely to be correct. Her waterline length-to-beam ratio was a fine 9.15:1 and she was powered for a most unmercantile 25 knots. In addition, her upper deck (also the hangar and strength deck) dipped by a full half-deck towards the after end, a typical Japanese warship design feature. Whatever her origins, she was completed in a very creditable three years, the process facilitated somewhat by the very experienced British mission then present to transfer hard-won technological detail under the auspices of the 1902 Anglo-Japanese Alliance.

For smoke discharge, the *Hosho* followed the American *Langley*-style fold-down funnels rather than the *Argus*' ducted arrangement. A diminutive island bridge, the first such, was located on the starboard deck edge but, being just forward of the funnels, created severe smoke eddying and was soon removed.

Hosho had a half-length hangar with an elevator at either end. Forward and aft, the flight deck was supported on an open structure, initially with a pronounced run-down at either end but later flattened forward and extended aft, overlapping the stern. Only over its after third was the hull plating continued upward to flight deck level and, over this length, the flight deck was of increased width.

Following the removal of the island, navigation and flight deck operations were conducted from sided open platforms, an unsatisfactory arrangement. A folding mast had also to be added.

ABOVE: **Probably a 1922 trials picture of *Hosho* which had its small island structure removed in the following year. Note that the hangar is only part length and of "open" construction, erected atop the hull proper.**

Although small, the *Hosho* (a planned sister was cancelled) taught the Japanese much. Classed as "experimental" she had an uneventful, if busy, career, even surviving the general massacre of the Japanese fleet during World War II. Following service in repatriating military personnel, she was scrapped in 1947.

Hosho

Built: Asano Shipbuilding, Tsurumi
Commissioned: December 27, 1922
Displacement: 7,585 tonnes/7,450 tons (standard); 9,930 tonnes/9,750 tons (full load)
Length: 155.5m/509ft 10in (bp); 168m/550ft 10in (overall)
Beam: 18m/59ft
Draught: 6.2m/20ft 3in (full load)
Aircraft: About 25
Flight deck: 158.3 x 22.7m/519 x 74ft 6in
Armament: 4 x 140mm/5.5in, and 2 x 76mm/3in guns
Machinery: Geared steam turbines, 8 boilers, 2 shafts
Power: 22,400kW/30,000shp
Speed: 25 knots
Fuel: 2,750 tonnes/2,700 tons (oil); 960 tonnes/940 tons (coal)
Range: 14,820km/8,000nm at 15 knots
Armour: Not known
Complement: 550 men

ABOVE: **The extreme narrowness of the forward flight deck caused the removal of the island, while the effective area was increased by levelling the pronounced slopes at either end.** LEFT: **Interesting detail here includes the funnels and WT mast lowered for flying, and the series of ramps and bridges associated with the longitudinal arrester system.**

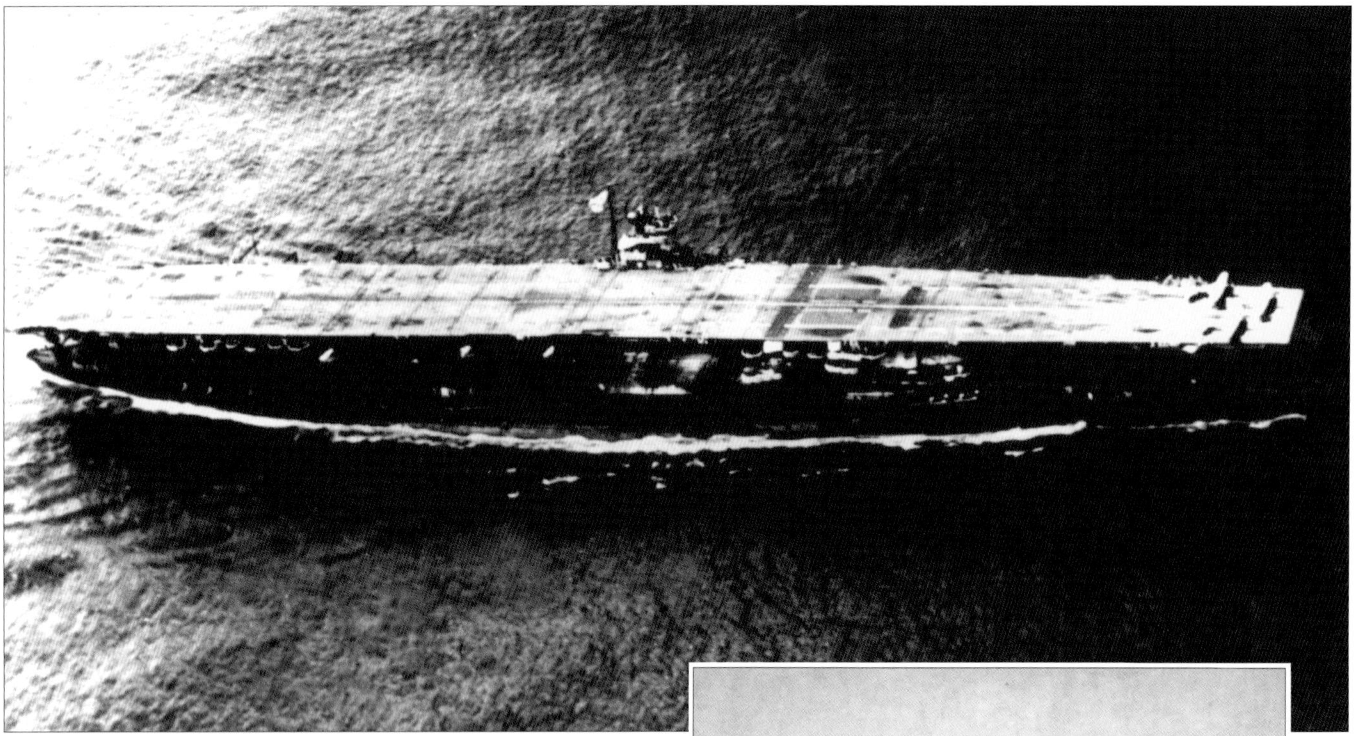

TOP: **The *Akagi* as she was post-1938. Note that the extended flight deck slopes continuously in either direction from the centre and that the new island is located on the port side.** ABOVE: **As completed, the *Akagi* retained some elegance of line. The starboard-side funnel was divided curiously into two distinct sections.**

Akagi

As with other signatories to the Washington Treaty of 1921–22, Japan had to abandon her ambitious capital shipbuilding programme. Two incomplete hulls could, however, be converted to aircraft carriers. Compared to the 137,160 tonnes/135,000 tons carrier tonnage allowed to Great Britain and the United States, Japan was permitted only 82,296 tonnes/81,000 tons. The two rebuilds might displace up to 33,528 tonnes/33,000 tons but subsequent ships were limited to 27,432 tonnes/27,000 tons apiece.

At the time of the agreement there were under construction two *Kaga*-class battleships and four *Amagi*-class battle-cruisers. Longer and faster, two battle-cruisers, *Amagi* and *Akagi*, were selected for conversion. The former, however, was damaged on the slip by earthquake, and a battleship hull, that of the *Kaga*, had to be substituted as the only one sufficiently advanced to undergo what could be called "conversion".

Reconstruction was a major task. The required air wing of 60 aircraft demanded a double hangar arrangement, imposing an unacceptable topweight on a slender hull. In order to reduce weight and to lower the centre of gravity, the main armoured deck was thinned from 96mm/3.8in to 80mm/3.15in and lowered by one level. As it linked with the upper edge of the side belt this, too, had to be lowered, simultaneously being reduced from 250mm/9.8in to 152mm/6in in thickness. This,

LEFT: **Although indistinct, this profile demonstrates the *Akagi*'s slightly hogged appearance, due to the sloping flight deck, also the considerable bulge and the substructure transferring the weight of the island to the hull.**

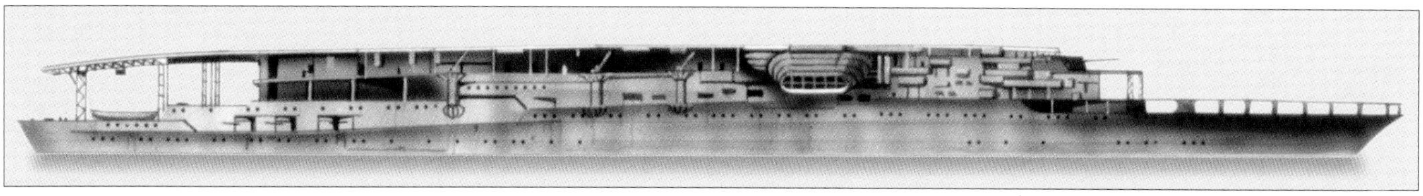

in turn, meant refashioning the bulge, earlier an anti-torpedo feature but now also enhancing stability.

Taking the design of the British *Courageous* a stage further, aircraft from either hangar could take off directly over the bows, the penalty for which was the flight deck being terminated over 61m/200ft from the forward end. Aft, the flight deck was supported on lofty pillars, beneath which a gantry crane could transfer floatplanes over the quarterdeck and into the lower hangar.

Article X of the treaty permitted carriers to be armed with up to ten guns not exceeding 203mm/8in in calibre. Armed to the limit, the *Akagi* had two twin cruiser-style turrets firing forward from upper hangar deck level and six armoured casemates well aft, but sited too low to be of any practical use. There was no restriction on the number of guns of less than 127mm/5in calibre, and 12 of 120mm/4.7in were installed.

There was no island superstructure, the many boilers exhausting through a curious, starboard-side casing, partly vertical, partly curved downward and outboard. A distinctive clipper stem set off a profile that was not inelegant. This did not persist, however, for operational shortcomings and the requirements of more and larger aircraft brought about further remodelling during 1936–38. This added a square, port-side island structure while the flight deck, which sloped downward in both directions from amidships, was continued right forward, supported on pillars and gaining two catapults. The forward 203mm/8in gun mountings were landed as the hangars were extended some distance forward. The complex funnel casing was simplified but enlarged. All improvements added further topweight and the bulges needed to be widened, costing about a half-knot in speed.

A Pearl Harbor veteran, the *Akagi* was sunk at Midway.

TOP: **This "as built" profile shows both the oddly configured funnel and the forecastle deck over which fighters could take off directly from the lower hangar. With the later forward extension of the flight deck, two forward-firing twin 203mm/8in turrets had to be sacrificed.** ABOVE: **An uncommon view of *Akagi*'s island from ahead. A most unusual feature is the wood-planked flight deck, with individual timbers correctly notched into the margin plank. The caulking, however, is none too tidy!**

ABOVE: **The *Akagi* is here seen lying off the Japanese Naval Academy at Yetajima, near Kure.**

Akagi

Built: Kure Naval Dockyard
Commissioned: March 25, 1927
Displacement (in 1938): 37,150 tonnes/36,500 tons (standard); 43,500 tonnes/42,750 tons (full load)
Length: 235m/770ft 6in (bp); 261.2m/856ft 5in (overall)
Beam: 31.4m/102ft 10in
Draught: 8.7m/28ft 6in full load
Aircraft: 72
Flight deck: 190.3 x 30.5m/624 x 100ft
Armament: 6 x 203mm/8in, and 12 x 119mm/4.7in guns
Machinery: Geared steam turbines, 19 boilers, 4 shafts
Power: 98,500kW/132,000shp
Speed: 31.5 knots
Fuel: 5,850 tonnes/5,750 tons
Range: 15,190km/8,200nm at 16 knots
Armour: 152mm/6in (vertical belt); 80mm/3.15in (armoured deck)
Complement: 1,570 men

LEFT: **A full deck-load in a pre-war picture of the *Kaga*. The nearer aircraft are Nakajima AZ2N1 Type 90 fighters, the first of indigenous design to be the equal of foreign peers. Behind are larger Aichi D1A2 Type 96 two-seat bombers. This type still serving in second-line units in 1942, was known to the allies as "Susie".**

Kaga

The necessity to select the *Kaga* as a running mate to the *Akagi* caused considerable operational problems due to the speed difference, as designed, of 6 knots (26.5 against 32.5). Being a battleship, the *Kaga* had a waterline length-to-beam ratio of a relatively bluff 7.77:1 compared with the battle-cruiser *Akagi*'s 8.59:1. The latter was also nearly 20m/65ft 8in longer. Within the restrictions of available space, any uprating of *Kaga*'s machinery could have only small effect on speed. A first improvement, however, was the conversion to full oil-firing from an earlier mix of eight oil-fired boilers, and four boilers that burned coal under oil spray.

Externally, the conversion closely followed that of the *Akagi*. The truncated flight deck was repeated, with two lower flying-off levels forward. The upper of these, i.e. that serving the upper hangar, was very constricted, flanked as it was by twin 203mm/8in gun turrets and also accommodating the navigation position, there being no island structure.

Possibly because of difficulties experienced with the *Akagi*, or possibly to evaluate alternative arrangements, the *Kaga* was fitted with long ducts, running outside the hull, just below the level of the flight deck that exhausted either side, just short of the quarterdeck. The flight deck itself was built without the *Akagi*'s "hump" and with two elevators and no catapults.

With her inherently better stability, *Kaga* experienced fewer problems with armour distribution. The main protective deck was thinned from 102mm/4in to 40mm/1.57in but, as it did not require to be lowered, the position and configuration of the side belt and bulges were unaffected. The belt, nonetheless, was reduced in thickness from 280mm/11in to 152mm/6in.

RIGHT: **The *Kaga* as completed, showing the forward flying-off decks and the ducting that originally carried exhaust gases well aft before discharge.**

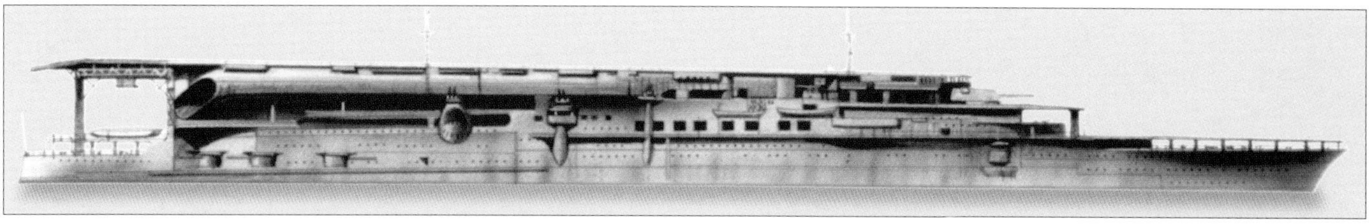

TOP: **Although *Kaga* was not a sister of *Akagi*, she shared a rakish elegance as completed. Note the 203mm/8in guns forward at upper hangar deck level and aft, located in very low casemates.** ABOVE: **As rebuilt in 1934–35, the *Kaga* gained a starboard-side island while the boilers now exhausted through a prominent funnel on the starboard side only.**

Exhibiting the same in-service limitations as the *Akagi*, the *Kaga* underwent extensive modification during 1934–35. The confined nature of the navigational arrangements had already resulted in the addition of a diminutive pilot house on the starboard edge of the flight deck. This was now superseded by a modest island structure which, unlike the *Akagi*'s, was located on the starboard side.

New and more powerful machinery and boilers (only eight in number) were installed. Being also lighter, they exacerbated the effect of the extra weight of the extensive topside improvements. Larger bulges had to be added, with the major result that the stern section had to be rebuilt and extended by over 10m/32ft 10in to regain an acceptable after run.

With her lengthened stern, the *Kaga*'s new, full-length flight deck was of almost identical length to that of her running mate. In being extended forward it gained a third elevator and two (later three) catapults. The exhaust ducts were replaced by a single, starboard-side, *Akagi*-style funnel casing.

The four 203mm/8in guns displaced by the forward extension of the hangars were relocated in two further casemates aft, as useless as the remainder. Sixteen 127mm/5in guns were located in sponsoned twin-mountings just below flight deck level.

Created together, the *Akagi* and *Kaga* operated together and, together, they were destroyed at Midway, where the loss of four carriers turned the course of the Pacific war.

ABOVE: **If this is truly a pilot's briefing, rather than a publicity picture, the practice compares poorly with those in Western carriers for over half the personnel can neither hear nor see what they are being told.**

Kaga

Built: Kawasaki, Kobe
Commissioned: March 31, 1928
Displacement (in 1935): 38,900 tonnes/38,200 tons (standard); 43,270 tonnes/42,500 tons (full load)
Length: 225.2m/738ft 3in (bp); 247.7m/812ft 2in (overall)
Beam: 32.5m/106ft 7in
Draught: 9.3m/30ft 6in (full load)
Aircraft: 72
Flight deck: 246.8 x 30.5m/809ft 2in x 100ft
Armament: 10 x 203mm/8in, and 16 x 127mm/5in guns
Machinery: Geared steam turbines, 8 boilers, 4 shafts
Power: 94,750kW/127,000shp
Speed: 28 knots
Fuel: 8,350 tonnes/8,200 tons
Range: 18,520km/10,000nm at 16 knots
Armour: 152mm/6in (vertical belt); 40mm/1.57in (armoured deck)
Complement: 1,460 men

Ise and *Hyuga*

Enlarged versions of the American Wyomings, the *Ise* and *Hyuga* also improved on the preceding Japanese Fuso class. They were completed in 1917–18 as 31,700-tonne/31,200-ton battleships carrying twelve 356mm/14in guns in six twin turrets of which one pair was superimposed in the waist. Originally two-funnelled, they lost the forward funnel in a 1934–37 modernization. In the course of this they acquired new machinery, extra horizontal armour and their distinctive "pagoda" bridge structure. Extra top-weight was compensated by enlarged bulges that, while improving resistance to torpedoes, required the stern to be rebuilt and extended by about 7.6m/25ft to comply with hydrodynamic requirements.

The loss of four front-line carriers at Midway shocked the Japanese Navy into emergency measures including the conversion of the *Ise* and *Hyuga* to hybrid battleship/carriers. Therefore, during 1943–44, their after two turrets were removed and a new deck erected over the after end. This had 11 aircraft "spots", connected by rail to two waist catapults. Beneath the deck was hangar space for 11 more aircraft, to be transferred by elevator.

The arrangement was designed around the Aichi D4Y3 ("Judy") dive-bomber, with an intended launch rate of one aircraft every two minutes. At this stage of the war, however, the aircraft could not be supplied in sufficient numbers and, as the catapults obstructed the waist turrets, they were removed. The ships were thus reduced to deploying a few floatplanes, handled by crane, the handling deck occupied largely by light anti-aircraft weapons.

Having never been operated in their intended role, both ships narrowly escaped destruction as part of the decoy force at the battle of Leyte Gulf, only to be sunk in shallow water at Kure by American carrier aircraft during the final weeks of the war.

TOP: **Following their 1934–37 rebuildings the two Hyugas emerged with a single funnel and an imposing "pagoda" foremast structure. Note the quarterdeck catapult and handling crane for three floatplanes.** ABOVE: **Six centreline turrets were very ambitious, their weight resulting in massive stresses on a hull with relatively fine ends.**

ABOVE: **After 1943–44, the ships carried an enormous box hangar, whose 22 aircraft were transferred for launch by two elevated waist catapults. The two central turrets were retained, but their firing arcs were greatly restricted by the catapults.**

Ise and *Hyuga*

Class: *Ise*, Kawasaki, Kobe, commissioned December 15, 1917; *Hyuga*, Mitsubishi, Nagasaki, commissioned April 30, 1918
Displacement (in 1944): 36,000 tonnes/35,350 tons (standard); 39,400 tonnes/38,700 tons (full load)
Length: 195.8m/642ft (bp); 219.6m/720ft (overall)
Beam: 33.8m/110ft 10in
Draught: 9.3m/30ft 6in (full load)
Aircraft: 22
Flight deck: None
Armament: 8 x 356mm/14in, and 16 x 127mm/5in guns
Machinery: Geared steam turbines, 8 boilers, 4 shafts
Power: 60,500kW/81,000shp
Speed: 25.5 knots
Fuel: 4,330 tonnes/4,250 tons
Range: 17,590km/9,500nm at 16 knots
Armour: 127–305mm/5–12in (vertical belt); 119mm/4.7in (armoured deck)
Complement: 1,460 men

ABOVE: **The conflicting requirements of maximum aircraft and minimum displacement resulted in the unsatisfactory *Ryujo*. Her very low forward freeboard was offset by considerable flare to prevent the bow plunging.** LEFT: **The port-bow view, looking aft, emphasizes the sheer complexity of Japanese ship design. Despite its massive appearance, the double-hangar top structure was of light scantlings and superimposed on a very low hull. Note the discontinuity in the latter's sheerline.**

Ryujo

Buried deeply in the Washington Treaty was a paragraph defining an aircraft carrier as having, *inter alia*, a standard displacement in excess of 10,160 tonnes/10,000 tons. Concerned that only 17,272 tonnes/17,000 tons of carrier tonnage were left to them, the Japanese decided to evaluate a sub-10,160-tonne/10,000-ton ship, which would not be reckonable. Laid down in 1929, the *Ryujo* would have worked satisfactorily with a modest air group but the 48 aircraft demanded required a double-hangared design that was over-ambitious on the displacement.

With weight restriction so tight, there was no margin for armour and the cruiser-style hull was built with low freeboard. To save weight, the upper deck sheerline undulated to follow the stress distribution in the lightly constructed hull. There was no island structure, the navigation bridge being located below the forward transverse edge of the flight deck, which terminated some 20m/65ft 7in short of the bows. Smoke was exhausted through two downward-curved casings on the starboard side while sponsoned below the deck edges were six twin 127mm/5in gun mountings.

Weak in structure, tender in motion, the *Ryujo* returned to dockyard hands within a year of her completion. During 1934–36 she was bulged to increase her beam. Her hull was stiffened, ballast added and two of the 127mm/5in mountings suppressed to reduce weight at that height.

These improvements inevitably increased her standard displacement to a reckonable figure, but they also increased her immersion. Her freeboard forward was now inadequate and a further modification was required to raise the forecastle by one deck level.

Ever a problem, the *Ryujo* was restricted to lesser wartime operations. Still useful, she had a short career, being overwhelmed by American carrier aircraft at the Battle of the Eastern Solomons in August 1942.

Ryujo

Built: Yokohama Dockyard Company
Commissioned: May 9, 1933
Displacement (in 1936): 11,000 tonnes/10,800 tons (standard); 13,850 tonnes/13,600 tons (full load)
Length: 167.9m/550ft 4in (bp); 180.1m/590ft 6in (overall)
Beam: 20.8m/68ft 3in
Draught: 6.8m/22ft 6in
Aircraft: 48
Flight deck: 156.8 x 23.2m/514 x 76ft
Armament: 8 x 127mm/5in guns
Machinery: Geared steam turbines, 6 boilers, 2 shafts
Power: 48,500kW/65,000shp
Speed: 29 knots
Fuel: 2,550 tonnes/2,500 tons
Range: 18,520km/10,000nm at 14 knots
Armour: None
Complement: 660 men

ABOVE LEFT: **This picture of the *Soryu* fitting out shows the very light construction of the forward flight deck extension. The athwartships gallery below its leading edge accommodated three twin 25mm/1in mountings.** ABOVE: **The imperial chrysanthemum is carried at the stemhead of every major Japanese war vessel. Note how riveted ships were so much better faired than their modern welded counterparts.**

Soryu and *Hiryu*

The Japanese Navy required further large carriers, but was limited by treaty to only 17,272 tonnes/17,000 tons more carrier-tons. Again, however, there was a possible means of circumvention in the treaty definition of an aircraft carrier which, while displacing at least 10,160 tonnes/10,000 tons, had to be "designed for the specific and exclusive purpose of carrying aircraft". Like the Americans and British, the Japanese were tempted into producing studies for hybrid cruiser/carriers with a limited air wing but a powerful main armament. All, however, proved to be unsatisfactory compromises.

Laid down in 1934, the *Soryu* was of conventional design therefore, and calculated to consume all the remaining tonnage allowance. Her cruiser-style hull was high-powered and capable of exceptionally high speed, but she was well designed in that the lower of her double hangars was recessed into the hull, keeping her overall profile low and avoiding the chronic problems being experienced by the still-new *Ryujo*. The main penalty for the high speed and large air wing was weak protection. A starboard-side island was fitted from the outset, with smoke exhausting through the preferred horizontal funnels on the same side.

During 1934, the Japanese had announced their proposed "Second Replenishment Programme" for their fleet, a programme which included a pair of *Soryu*-sized carriers. They hoped that the second of these could be built with Great Britain and the United States extending the Japanese allocation. However, the Japanese were to be disappointed at the Second London Naval Conference, from which their delegates walked out in January 1936. In the following July, and now in breach of treaty agreement, the second ship, *Hiryu*, was laid down. Feeling themselves no longer bound by tonnage restrictions, her designers increased her beam by one metre. In addition to improving her stability, this permitted a thickening of the belt armour and greater fuel capacity. Her island was on the port side.

Both ships were lost at Midway, early victims of dive-bombing.

ABOVE: ***Hiryu*'s bridge structure was located on the port side and almost exactly amidships. *Soryu*'s starboard-side island was set further forward because of the two funnels.**

Soryu and *Hiryu*

Class: *Soryu*, Kure Naval Dockyard, commissioned January 29, 1937; *Hiryu*, Yokosuka Naval Dockyard, commissioned July 5, 1939
Displacement: 17,600 tonnes/17,300 tons (full load); 22,350 tonnes/21,950 tons (standard)
Length: 209.9m/688ft 2in (bp); 230m/745ft 6in (overall)
Beam: 22.3m/73ft 3in
Draught: 7.9m/25ft 9in (full load)
Aircraft: 73
Flight deck: 217 x 27m/711ft 6in x 88ft 6in
Armament: 12 x 127mm/5in guns
Machinery: Geared steam turbines, 8 boilers, 4 shafts
Power: 113,400kW/152,000shp
Speed: 34.5 knots
Fuel: 4,430 tonnes/4,350 tons
Range: 19,080km/10,300nm at 18 knots
Armour (over machinery and magazine spaces only): 89–150mm/3.5-5.9in (vertical belt); 25–55mm/0.9–2.1in (protective deck)
Complement: 1,250 men

Zuiho class

A further means by which the Japanese could circumvent their treaty-agreed limits was through the construction of auxiliaries designed for rapid conversion to aircraft carriers in an emergency. Several such vessels were provided for by the 1934 "Second Replenishment Programme", with two of them being the submarine depot ships *Tsurugisaki* and *Takasaki*. The usual bulk associated with such ships was increased by a topside hangar, capable of accommodating three floatplanes, for which two catapults were provided.

Only the *Tsurugisaki* was ever completed in this configuration for, during 1941, the pair were transformed into the light carriers *Shoho* and *Zuiho*. In both size and aircraft capacity they matched the US Navy's *Independence*-class CVLs, though lacking their speed. Initially equipped with eight diesel engines, coupled four to a shaft, (the same arrangement, incidentally, as in the German so-called "pocket battleships") they acquired steam turbines during their conversion. There was no island superstructure, and the boilers exhausted through a horizontal, starboard-side funnel. Exceptionally slender ships, they nonetheless had the stability required for a single-hangar configuration and for four twin 127mm/5in gun mountings located in sponsons just below the deck edge. It was a feature of all Japanese carriers with horizontal funnels that only those gun mountings immediately abaft the casing were given enclosures to protect the crews.

The *Shoho* had the melancholy record of being the first Japanese carrier to be lost, being a casualty at the Coral Sea action in May 1942. *Zuiho* went on to give good service, having her flight deck extended almost to the bows. She, too, did not survive the war, being destroyed in the Leyte Gulf battles of October 1944.

TOP AND ABOVE: **Two views of the ships show them as originally converted, with the flight deck terminating well short of the bows. *Shoho* was sunk in this condition, only *Zuiho* surviving to undergo further modification.**

ABOVE: **Under overwhelming air attack in October 1944 the *Zuiho*, devoid of aircraft, manoeuvres at high speed. The thick, dark smoke is issuing from her downswept funnel while the light smoke from her forward end is from her defensive armament.**

Zuiho class

Class: *Zuiho*, Yokosuka Naval Dockyard, commissioned December 27, 1940; *Shoho*, Yokosuka Naval Dockyard, commissioned January 26, 1942

Displacement: 11,450 tonnes/11,250 tons (standard); 14,350 tonnes/14,100 tons (full load)

Length: 185m/606ft 7in (bp); 205.6m/674ft 2in (overall)

Beam: 18.2m/59ft 8in

Draught: 6.6m/21ft 6in (full load)

Aircraft: 30

Flight deck: 180 x 23m/590ft 2in x 75ft 5in

Armament: 8 x 127mm/5in guns

Machinery: Geared steam turbines, 4 boilers, 2 shafts

Power: 38,800kW/52,000shp

Speed: 28 knots

Fuel: 2,550 tonnes/2,500 tons

Range: 14,450km/7,800nm at 18 knots

Armour: None

Complement: 800 men

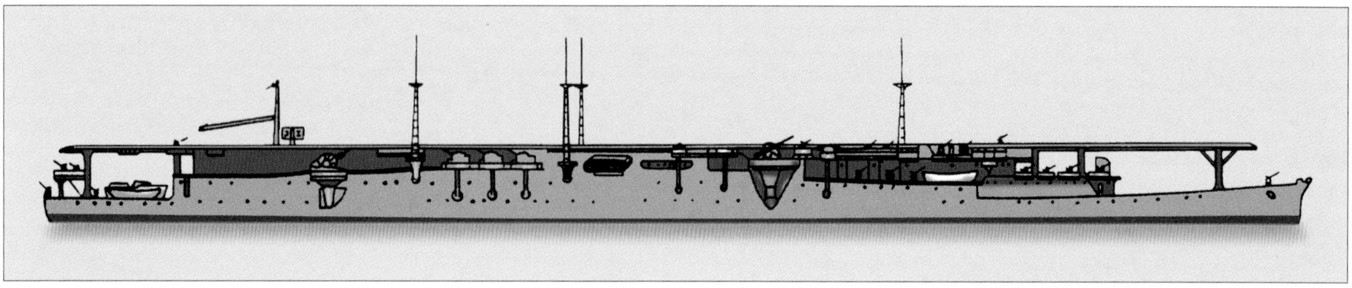

Ryuho

TOP: **Converted from a submarine depot ship, the *Ryuho* gave the impression of immense length. The reconstruction was not a success, the ship proving structurally weak and, for the greater part of her career, demoted to the training of aircrew.**
ABOVE: **High freeboard contributes to an easy motion.**

As with the two *Zuihos*, the *Ryuho* was converted from a submarine depot ship. In her case, it was the *Taigei*, a slightly larger predecessor of the two Tsurugisakis. Like them, she was exceptionally slender in her proportions (12.3:1 at the waterline) but proved to be structurally weak. In 1936, just two years after her completion, she was back in dockyard hands for stiffening and the addition of bulges to improve her stability. She was initially powered for only a 20-knot speed, which suggests that, unlike her follow-ons she really was intended to service submarines. She also carried three floatplanes, but in a more complex arrangement accessed by elevator.

Despite her less-than-satisfactory history the *Taigei* was taken in hand during 1941, along with the later pair, for conversion to a carrier, in this case the *Ryuho*. Not surprisingly, the end result looked very similar although, completed later, in November 1942, she was equipped with larger elevators.

Still suspect, the *Ryuho* spent most of her career in the still-valuable role of training carrier aircrews who, despite their specialist calling, were used in a variety of roles, many shore-based. Such profligacy eventually proved disastrous.

During June 1944, the major part of the remaining Japanese fleet was mobilized to counter the American invasion of Saipan. Among the carriers was the *Ryuho*, on her first combat assignment. She emerged virtually unscathed, but her aircrews, along with those of sister carriers, had been slaughtered in what the Americans came to call the "Marianas Turkey Shoot". Reverting to her previous unexciting existence the ship managed to escape retribution, despite being caught at Kure by the massive American carrier-based air strikes of July 1945. She was scrapped in 1946.

Ryuho

Built: Yokosuka Naval Dockyard
Commissioned: March 31, 1934
Displacement: 13,600 tonnes/13,350 tons (standard); 16,450 tonnes/16,150 tons (full load)
Length: 197.4m/647ft 4in (bp); 215.8m/707ft 6in (overall)
Beam: 19.6m/64ft 3in
Draught: 6.6m/21ft 9in (full load)
Aircraft: 30
Flight deck: 185.1 x 23m/607 x 75ft 6in
Armament: 8 x 127mm/5in guns
Machinery: Geared steam turbines, 4 boilers, 2 shafts
Power: 38,800kW/52,000shp
Speed: 26.5 knots
Fuel: 2.950 tonnes/2,900 tons
Range: 14,820km/8,000nm at 18 knots
Armour: None
Complement: 875 men

Hiyo and *Junyo*

Of a size with the Italian *Aquila*, the *Hiyo* and *Junyo* were among the largest of carrier conversions, but where the *Aquila* had served as a liner but never as a carrier, the reverse was true of the Japanese pair. They were laid down in 1939 as the *Idzumo Maru* (*Hiyo*) and *Kashiwara Maru* (*Junyo*) for the Japan–United States service of Nippon Yusen Kaisha (NYK). Listed at the time as 28,000 gross registered tons (grt) motor liners, they were taken over before launch by the Japanese Navy. Doubts have been expressed that the ships were ever intended to be completed as liners, but their relatively poor subdivision and the necessity to change from diesel propulsion to steam suggests otherwise. Like many ships designed to mercantile standards, however, they probably incorporated design features intended to facilitate conversion.

Completed in good time to replace some of the carrier tonnage lost at Midway, the pair was unusual in incorporating islands of considerable size, built around uptakes that terminated in a funnel that was canted outboard. The whole structure was sponsoned beyond the edge of the flight deck, facilitating the path of boiler exhaust but creating a mass that needed to be offset by asymmetric bulging. Their double hangar arrangement was possible only by restricting the headroom of each to 3.2m/10ft 6in. This proved acceptable only because the Japanese introduced few innovations in carrier aircraft during the war.

Operated as front-line units, they deployed air groups of 50-plus comprising the full range of dive-bombers, torpedo-bombers and fighters. Both were present at the disastrous Philippine Sea action of June 1944, during which the *Hiyo* was lost to American torpedo aircraft. Her sister survived being torpedoed by an American submarine in December of the following year.

BELOW: **This view gives a good idea of the substructure necessary to transfer the overhung weight of the island to the hull. A problem with the pair was underpowering, apparently caused by a mismatch between mercantile steam turbines and naval-pattern, destroyer-type boilers.**

TOP: **The massive hull of the *Junyo* betrays her passenger liner origins. As converted, this pair were the first Japanese carriers to incorporate funnel and island, although not without some idiosyncracy. Note the radar antennas, atop the bridge and on the light signal mast.** ABOVE: ***Junyo* was one of the few Japanese carriers to survive the war relatively intact. Despite the considerable weight of the funnel uptakes and island structure, it can be seen to be situated almost entirely outboard of the flight deck edge.**

Hiyo and *Junyo*

Class: *Hiyo*, Kawasaki, Kobe, commissioned July 31, 1942; *Junyo*, Mitsubishi, Nagasaki, commissioned May 5, 1942
Displacement: 24,600 tonnes/24,150 tons (standard); 28,300 tonnes/27,800 tons (full load)
Length: 206.1m/675ft 9in (bp); 219.5m/719ft 8in (overall)
Beam: 26.7m/87ft 7in
Draught: 8.1m/26ft 8in (full load)
Aircraft: 53
Flight deck: 210.5 x 27.3m/690 x 89ft 6in
Armament: 12 x 127mm/5in guns
Machinery: Geared steam turbines, 6 boilers, 2 shafts
Power: 41,800kW/56,000shp
Speed: 24 knots
Fuel: 2,950 tonnes/2,900 tons
Range: Not known
Armour: None
Complement: 1,200 men

Shokaku class

Having failed to gain agreement for equality of tonnage with the fleets of Great Britain and the United States, the Japanese delegation walked out of the Second London Naval Conference in January 1936. It was the end of naval limitation by mutual agreement, initiating new building programmes by the one-time signatories.

As with the US Navy, the early carrier conversions had demonstrated to the Japanese the advantages of larger vessels, and the *Akagi* design was in the process of being updated. During 1937–38, the two Shokakus were laid down to this design. No longer trammelled by limited displacement and indisputably the best of the Japanese carriers, they were so central to naval planning that the date for opening hostilities at Pearl Harbor was determined by their completion.

Slightly shorter than the *Akagi*, they were even finer-lined yet deployed an air group of comparable size. The double hangars that gave the *Akagi* a high profile were more fully incorporated into the Shokakus' main hull structure.

Outline statistics show that the design philosophy was closer to that of the Americans than to that of the British:

It will be noted that the British ship, more heavily protected, needed to be proportionately broader in the beam so that, although given greater propulsive power per ton, she was significantly slower and with a much smaller air group. The *Shokaku* compared more closely with an Essex, although the price of the latter's larger air group and superior protection was lower installed power.

Comparison of major carrier classes

	Length (wl)	Beam (wl)	L/B	Displacement	Power	SHP/ton	Speed	Aircraft
Shokaku	250m	26m	9.6	25,700 tons	160,000shp	6.2	34+ knots	84
Essex (US)	249.9m	28.4m	8.8	27,200 tons	150,000shp	5.5	32.5 knots	91
Implacable (UK)	222.7m	29.2m	7.6	23,450 tons	148,000shp	6.3	32 knots	54

TOP: **The *Zuikaku*, reputedly on her commissioning day in September 1941. A feature of Japanese carriers, visible here rigged right aft, was a collapsible mast and derrick for transferring aircraft.** ABOVE: **Not the sharpest of pictures, this photograph shows a ready A6M Type 0 "Zeke" ahead of several D3A Type 99 "Val" dive-bombers.**

The Shokakus' meagre weight allowance for protection needed to be devoted to covering machinery and magazine spaces, leaving the enclosed hangars and flight deck unprotected. Topwide weight-saving in all Japanese carriers was evident in the pronounced narrowing of the forward flight deck. In contrast, American and British flight decks were more nearly rectangular in plan.

Like the *Akagi*, the Shokakus had three elevators and two catapults, and featured starboard-side, horizontal funnel casings. Both Shokakus had starboard-side islands.

From the Japanese perspective, both ships had fine war records. Both formed part of the carrier force that devastated Pearl Harbor before going on to ravage the Indian Ocean. In May 1942, they were at the Coral Sea action, where the *Shokaku* survived three hits by dive-bombers. They participated in the Battle of the Eastern Solomons (August 1942) and at Santa Cruz (October 1942), during which the *Shokaku* took four more hits. The ship was finally sunk, not by aircraft but by submarine torpedoes, at the disastrous Battle of the Philippine Sea (June 1944). The *Zuikaku* was also severely damaged, and now the last survivor of the six Pearl Harbor raiders, she lasted a further four months, being expended as part of Ozawa's decoy force during the Leyte Gulf battles of October 1944, a Japanese ruse that nearly succeeded.

TOP: **The somewhat bland appearance of the class belies their true size, which can be gauged from the white-uniformed crew men visible against the shell plating.** ABOVE: **Loaded with thousands of tons of aviation fuel and ordnance, lightly built carriers are particularly vulnerable to the attentions of dive-bombers.** BELOW: **This particular incident is the bombing of the *Shokaku* at the battle of the Coral Sea in May 1942. A fierce blaze of aviation fuel has erupted right forward.**

Shokaku class

Class: *Shokaku*, Yokosuka Naval Yard, commissioned August 8, 1941; *Zuikaku*, Kawasaki, Kobe, commissioned September 25, 1941

Displacement: 26,150 tonnes/25,700 tons (standard); 32,700 tonnes/32,100 tons (full load)

Length: 236.2m/774ft 6in (bp); 257.7m/845ft (overall)

Beam: 26m/85ft 6in

Draught: 8.9m/29ft 3in (full load)

Aircraft: 84

Flight deck: 198.3 x 23m/650 x 75ft 6in

Armament: 16 x 127mm/5in guns

Machinery: Geared steam turbines, 8 boilers, 4 shafts

Power: 119,400kW/160,000shp

Speed: 34+ knots

Fuel: 5,350 tonnes/5,250 tons

Range: 17,590 km/9,500nm at 18 knots

Armour (over machinery and magazine spaces only): 165–210mm/6.5–8.3in (vertical belt); 100–130mm/3.9–5.1in (protective deck)

Complement: 1,650 men

Taiho

Japan's only purpose-built armoured carrier, the *Taiho* was laid down in July 1941. This pre-dates the navy's own battle experience, but the ship departed so drastically from domestic mainstream design that she was probably an experiment in response to well-publicized reports of the resilience of British carriers to German dive-bombing in the Mediterranean. Longer and finer-lined than a British Illustrious, she was of higher power, significantly faster and of far greater endurance. The fully plated bows, and the substantial island dominated by a massive funnel, gave her profile a passing resemblance to that of the British ship, but she boasted a far larger air wing. Although the armour was on a substantial scale, it did not run to protection of the hangar walls. This measure to reduce topweight was complemented by the elimination of a deck, compared with the Shokakus, resulting in a lower flight deck forward.

In the main battery, the earlier standard 127mm/5in gun was replaced by the new-pattern 100mm/3.9in, which possessed a higher rate of fire.

Up to seven follow-ons are believed to have been considered but, as none was ever commenced, it is likely that it was decided to build more, but smaller and simpler, vessels.

With an operational life of barely three months, the *Taiho* was never able to fully prove her utility. Neither her heavy horizontal nor vertical armour could protect her from the submarine torpedo that found her during the Philippine Sea battle of June 1944. Struck by this single weapon, she should have survived but, being in action, continued to be run hard. Ruptured aviation fuel lines resulted in the collection of vapour pockets and her destruction by catastrophic explosion was only a matter of time.

In order to operate at high tempo for maximum periods a carrier is a floating repository of fuel and explosives. Operational safety and survivability in action depend upon careful attention to design detail. Time contstraints meant that prolonging the design and construction process was not possible under war conditions, and the results were to prove fatal in the case of the *Taiho*.

ABOVE: **The enclosed bows and large, rectangular stack cause the *Taiho* to immediately be compared with a British Illustrious. She was also, however, the first Japanese carrier to have armour worked into flight and hangar decks. Ironically, she was sunk by submarine torpedo.** BELOW: **Previous Japanese carriers were armed with the standard destroyer-type 127mm/5in gun. Although dual-purpose, its rate of fire was insufficient to deal with air attack. The *Taiho* introduced a new and more effective 100mm/3.9in weapon.**

Taiho

Built: Kawasaki, Kobe
Commissioned: March 7, 1944
Displacement: 29,850 tonnes/29,300 tons (standard); 38,000 tonnes/37,300 tons (full load)
Length: 238.2m/781ft (bp); 260m/852ft 6in (overall)
Beam: 27.7m/90ft 9in
Draught: 9.6m/31ft 6in (full load)
Aircraft: Up to 75
Flight deck: 257.4 x 30m/844 x 98ft 6in
Armament: 12 x 100mm/3.9in guns
Machinery: Geared steam turbines, 8 boilers, 4 shafts
Power: 119,400kW/160,000shp
Speed: 33.5 knots
Fuel: 5,800 tonnes/5,700 tons
Range: 14,820km/8,000nm at 18 knots
Armour: 100mm/3.9in (flight deck); 125mm/4.9in (lower hangar deck); 150mm/5.9in (vertical belt)
Complement: 1,750 men

Chitose class

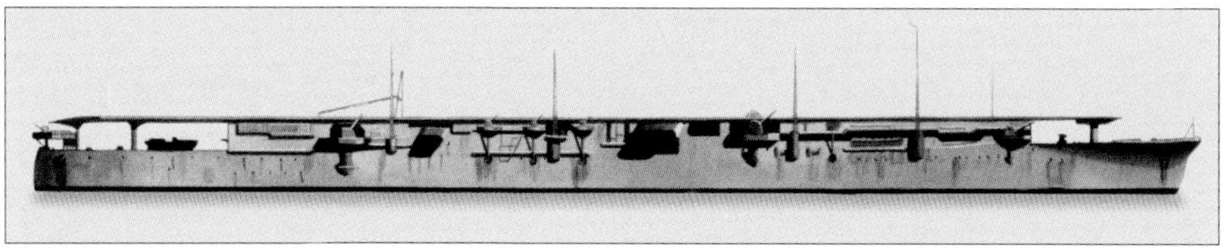

A further pair of ships designed for ready conversion were the seaplane carriers *Chitose* and *Chiyoda*. Extraordinarily lean in hull, they were laid down in 1934 and 1936 respectively as mother ships for up to 24 floatplanes. These were accommodated mainly below deck, and the after 60 per cent of the hull was dedicated largely to their handling and transfer by rail about the upper deck to any one of four catapults. A large, covered structure, supported on four pillars, dominated the centre section. Used for pre-flight preparation, it also supported several derricks and the diesel engine exhaust. The diesels were installed for economic cruise propulsion, a lower speed alternative to the main steam turbine installation.

Completed in 1938, both served in their original role in Chinese waters. During 1941, however, the below-deck seaplane accommodation was converted for the stowage and deployment (through the transom stern) of a dozen midget submarines, craft in which the Japanese Navy always showed great interest.

With the general shortage of carrier tonnage after Midway both ships were razed and rebuilt as single-hangar light carriers, re-entering service in 1943 (*Chiyoda*) and 1944 (*Chitose*). For this purpose, their hulls required to be bulged to restore an acceptable stability range.

Except for their unusual sterns, configured primarily for seaplane recovery, the pair appeared typical of Japanese carriers, totally flush-decked and conned from a difficult location beneath the forward overhang of the flight deck. The original machinery was retained, both groups exhausting through the customary starboard-side, horizontal funnel.

As carriers, the pair re-entered service as the Japanese Navy was in its twilight phase. They were called from training aircrew for the full mobilization that culminated in the Philippine Sea action. They survived this with no more than bomb damage to the *Chiyoda*, but both were expended in October 1944 in the successful decoy operation conducted during the Leyte Gulf battles.

TOP: **Reconnaissance floatplanes were an essential part of Japanese forward strategy in the Pacific. The navy's seaplane carriers were of unusual design and effective, but built for simple conversion into light aircraft carriers.**

ABOVE: **Although valuable in their original role, both were converted in 1942–43. Essential for aircrew training, they were then pressed into front-line service as carrier losses mounted.**

LEFT: **A detail from a Chitose, as built. The aircraft are Nakajima E8N Type 95 two-seat reconnaissance seaplanes. Used successfully in the Sino–Japanese War, production ended in 1940 when it gained the Allied codename "Dave".**

Chitose class

Data as carriers:

Class: *Chitose*, Kure Navy Yard, commissioned July 25, 1938; *Chiyoda*, Kure Navy Yard, commissioned December 15, 1938

Displacement: 11,400 tonnes/11,200 tons (standard); 14,800 tonnes/14,500 tons (full load)

Length: 174.1m/570ft 9in (bp); 192.6m/631ft 6in (overall)

Beam: 20.8m/68ft 3in

Draught: 7.4m/24ft 2in (full load)

Aircraft: 30

Flight deck: 180.4 x 23m/591ft 6in x 75ft 6in

Armament: 8 x 127mm/5in guns

Machinery: Geared steam turbines, 4 boilers, 2 shafts

Power: 32,800kW/44,000shp plus 9,550kW/12,800bhp

Speed: 28.5 knots

Fuel: 3,660 tonnes/3,600 tons

Range: 19,450km/10,500nm at 18 knots

Armour: None

Complement: 990 men

LEFT AND BELOW: ***Mizuho* and *Nisshin* were never converted to carriers as they might have been because they were both sunk. *Nisshin* lacked the two waist catapults of her sister and differed in having three centreline gun mountings forward. Being diesel-driven, both could increase useful deck area by dispensing with conventional funnels, exhaust ducts being built into the vertical pillars of the forward gantry.**

Mizuho and *Nisshin*

Chitose and *Chiyoda* represented a first solution to the Japanese Navy's requirement for high-endurance seaplane tenders but, even before their completion a third ship, *Mizuho*, was laid down. Where the lead pair were steam-propelled, with auxiliary diesel cruising engines, the *Mizuho* was all-diesel, with a direct-drive unit coupled to each shaft. As total developed power was barely one third that of the *Chitose*, while displacement and hull parameters were virtually identical, it has to be assumed that the resulting modest speed of 22 knots was intended. Puzzlingly then, it appears a contradiction that the fourth, and last, of these unusual ships should be fitted with diesel engines of comparable power to *Chitose*'s steam plant, resulting in a similar, 28-knot sustainable sea speed.

Although their deck arrangements for aircraft were identical, the ships differed in detail. The most obvious was that the second pair lacked the large funnel required by the steamers, their diesels exhausting via the forward pair of pillars that supported the aircraft handling gear. Neither did the second pair have this area roofed-in.

The *Chitose* pair had two twin 127mm/5in gun mountings forward, superimposed destroyer-fashion. *Mizuho* added a third but as two were now disposed flanking the bridge structure, could still use only two on targets other than straight ahead. The *Nisshin*, therefore, had her three all located on the centreline, with the aftermost superfiring the others.

All except *Nisshin* were modified with a type of stern chute for launching midget submarines. The *Nisshin*'s auxiliary function was, however, minelaying, with a reported capacity of 700. For this purpose, her stern was rounded, with minelaying doors on either quarter.

As the *Mizuho* was lost in May 1942 and the *Nisshin* in July 1943, neither was converted into a through-deck aircraft carrier, as were their predecessors.

Mizuho and *Nisshin*

Class: *Mizuho*, Kawasaki, Kobe, commissioned February 25, 1939; *Nisshin*, Kure Naval Yard, commissioned February 27, 1942
Displacement: 11,500 tonnes/11,300 tons (standard); 13,950 tonnes/13,700 tons (full load)
Length: 174.1m/570ft 9in (bp); 194.1m/636ft 6in (overall)
Beam: 19.7m/64ft 8in
Draught: 7.1m/23ft 2in (full load)
Aircraft: 25
Flight deck: None
Armament: 6 x 127mm/5in guns
Machinery: Two 6-cylinder, direct-drive diesel engines, 2 shafts
Power: 35,000kW/47,000bhp
Speed: 28 knots
Fuel: Not known
Range: 20,370km/11,000nm at 18 knots
Armour: None
Complement: Not known

LEFT: **With space both topside and below these ships could transport about two dozen aircraft to establish and maintain a forward reconnaissance base. An instance of this was at Tulagi in the Solomons in August 1942, an event that triggered the dour struggle for neighbouring Guadalcanal.**

Shinano

The shock of losing four fleet carriers at Midway stimulated the Japanese Navy to extraordinary measures for their replacement, none more so than the *Shinano*. Still under construction as the third *Yamato*-class battleship, the largest such ever built, she was converted to a carrier before her completion. Although relatively slow for her adopted role, she was robust and beamy, being able to retain much of her hull armour despite having a single, "open" hangar and armoured flight deck superimposed.

Despite her exceptional size, she was intended to deploy a relatively small air wing, the bulk of her great capacity being devoted to carrying spare aircraft, ordnance, etc for other carriers, thus extending their endurance. In retrospect, this would appear to be a very expensive and inefficient alternative to the Americans' highly-effective fleet train.

As completed, the *Shinano* bore more than a passing resemblance to the late *Taiho*, with a substantial island structure, offset well to the starboard edge of the flight deck and incorporating a large, rectangular funnel, again canted outboard. Unlike the *Taiho*, she lacked the plated-in bows, her forward flight deck being supported on the more usual open structure.

By the end of 1944, at the time of her completion, the threat of large-scale carrier-borne air strikes was such that every peripheral space was occupied by light automatic weapons. Standard issue was the small calibre 25mm/1in gun of obsolete Hotchkiss design. Where *Taiho* had carried over 70 of these, *Shinano* had twice as many.

The largest-ever carrier until the arrival of the American Forrestals, the *Shinano* never went operational. Moving between shipyards in order to complete fitting-out, she was hit by a full salvo of submarine torpedoes. Still riddled with openings, her bulkheads not yet watertight, she defeated all efforts at damage control, slowly foundering.

Shinano

Built: Yokosuka Navy Yard
Commissioned: October 8, 1944
Displacement: 66,000 tonnes/64,800 tons (standard); 73,200 tonnes/71,900 tons (full load)
Length: 244.1m/800ft 6in (bp); 266.1m/872ft 6in (overall)
Beam: 36.3m/119ft 2in
Draught: 10.3m/33ft 10in (full load)
Aircraft: About 50 (120 maximum)
Flight deck: 256.2 x 40.3m/840 x 132ft
Armament: 16 x 127mm/5in guns
Machinery: Geared steam turbines, 12 boilers, 4 shafts
Power: 112,000kW/150,000shp
Speed: 27 knots
Fuel: 9,060 tonnes/8,900 tons
Range: 18,520km/10,000nm at 18 knots
Armour: 80mm/3.15in (flight deck); 200mm/7.9in (hangar deck); 205–350mm/8.1–13.8in (vertical belt)
Complement: 2,400 men

ABOVE AND BELOW: **Constructed in great secrecy and destroyed before even being formally commissioned, the *Shinano* remains something of a mystery. The extent to which she was aircraft carrier, as opposed to aircraft transport and maintenance ship, is unclear. Her vast flight deck was fitted with arresters at either end, similar to American practice and on other large Japanese carriers, yet the disposition of catapults (if any) is unclear.**

LEFT: **US carrier aircraft hit Kure and Kobe on July 24 and 28, 1945 in an effort to account for the remaining heavy units of the Japanese Navy. Just three weeks before the end of the war, the attackers met little opposition.** ABOVE: **Hit by two carrier-based strikes and by US Army B-24s, the *Amagi* keeled over in shallow water. Note the many gun tubes and the pair of downswept funnel casings.**

Unryu class

The Pacific war was won by carrier strength, the Americans succeeding by adhering to a basic design and allowing no variation in specification. Despite holding the initiative, the Japanese had no such discipline, and the nearest to a standard class that they produced were the Unryus, for which the sorry record was of two variants and only three completed of a planned 17.

The class had little enough opportunity to prove itself but, if specifications can be believed, its designers had done a good job. Far smaller than an American fleet carrier, an Unryu equated approximately in dimensions and displacement to a British Centaur. There, however, the comparison finishes, for the Japanese vessel enjoyed nearly twice the installed power, 4 knots greater speed, heavier armament, and nearly 50 per cent larger air wing.

Superficially, there was a strong visual resemblance to the *Soryu*, but experience had improved the layout, allowing an Unryu to function with two elevators rather than three. Its similar main battery of six twin 127mm/5in gun mountings was also disposed more symmetrically.

Where the American war effort became ever more powerful, that of the Japanese soon began to falter, its resources simply inadequate to sustain a prolonged war. An example was the cruiser machinery that powered the Unryus. Unavailable for two units (*Aso* and *Katsuragi*) destroyer machinery had to be substituted. Such is the price of speed, however, that the loss of one-third designed power resulted in a reduction of only 2 knots.

Six of the initial design were laid down, but only three were completed. Three more were never laid down, nor a planned batch of eight with larger dimensions. Four major yards were involved in the programme but, subjected to changes in priority and specification, and short of materials, were unable to complete it. The carrier war was, however, already lost beyond redemption.

Unryu class

Class: *Amagi* (II), Mitsubishi, Nagasaki, commissioned August 10, 1944; *Aso*, Kure Naval Yard, launched November 1944, not completed; *Ikoma*, Kawasaki, Kobe, launched November 1944, not completed; *Kasagi*, Mitsubishi, Nagasaki, launched October 1944, not completed; *Katsuragi*, Kure Naval Yard, completed but not commissioned; *Unryu*, Yokosuka Naval Yard, commissioned August 6, 1944

Displacement: 17,450 tonnes/17,150 tons (standard); 22,900 tonnes/22,500 tons (full load)

Length: 207.2m/679ft 3in (bp); 227.5m/745ft 10in (overall)

Beam: 22m/72ft 2in

Draught: 7.6m/25ft 9in (full load)

Aircraft: 64

Flight deck: 217.2 x 27m/712ft x 88ft 6in

Armament: 12 x 127mm/5in guns

Machinery: Geared steam turbines, 8 boilers, 4 shafts

Power: 113,400kW/152,000shp

Speed: 34 knots

Fuel: 3,720 tonnes/3,650 tons

Range: 14,820km/8,000nm at 18 knots

Armour (over machinery and magazine spaces only): 45–150mm/1.8–5.9in (vertical belt); 25–55mm/1–2.2in (protective deck)

Complement: 1,590 men

LEFT: **The Unryus were the nearest that the Japanese came to constructing a standard series of carriers. Even these, however, differed between units, nullifying the benefits of strict standardization.**

Ibuki

The final pair of a long series of Japanese heavy cruisers, *Tone* and *Chikuma,* were unique in concentrating a four-turret main battery all forward, leaving the after one-third of the upper deck totally clear for the deployment of five floatplanes. These were permanently stowed topside, being transferred by rail to one or other of the sided catapults. Their function was to provide a reconnaissance service to extend a cruiser squadron's visual range.

Two more of the type were laid down in 1942 but as battle experience had questioned the earlier ships' utility, it was decided to complete the new ships as improved versions of the earlier Suzuya class, to be named *Kurama* and *Ibuki*.

Victim of yet another policy shift, one hull was dismantled, but the other was launched as the *Ibuki* in May 1943. Work then stopped on her as well, it being proposed to convert her into a fast fleet oiler before the decision was made to complete her as a light carrier. For four months, work progressed swiftly until, in March 1945, it halted for good with the ship complete to flight deck level. Never finished, she was broken up post-war.

If completed, the *Ibuki* would have been the only Japanese light carrier with an island superstructure. Otherwise, although the original line of the now heavily bulged cruiser hull remained obvious, her appearance was fairly standard, with a starboard-side horizontal funnel and with either end of the flight deck supported on an open structure, a measure to reduce weight and stress at the hull extremities.

With light anti-aircraft weapons proliferating, a feature of Japanese carriers was by now the ranks of deck-edge gun tubs with their deep, bracket supports. To the large number of standard 25mm/1in guns, of which the *Ibuki* had 48, were now being added multiple-barrelled rocket projectors, in a largely vain attempt to counter the menace of the mass air strike.

ABOVE: **Never completed, the *Ibuki* was surrendered at Sasebo in August 1945. Here, US personnel are seen aboard three small supply submarines, moored alongside. Note the carrier's pronounced bulge.**
TOP: **Soon afterward, the hull was transferred to the Sasebo Navy Yard's No. 7 Dock and was broken up.**

Ibuki

Built: Kure Naval Yard
Commissioned: Not commissioned
Displacement: 12,750 tonnes/12,500 tons (standard); 16,550 tonnes/16,250 tons (full load)
Length: 188m/616ft 4in (bp); 203m/665ft 6in (overall)
Beam: 21.2m/69ft 7in
Draught: 6.3m/20ft 7in (full load)
Aircraft: 27
Flight deck: 205.1 x 23m/672ft 4in x 75ft x 6in
Armament: 4 x 76mm/3in guns
Machinery: Geared steam turbines, 4 boilers, 2 shafts
Power: 53,700kW/72,000shp
Speed: 29 knots
Fuel: Not known
Range: Not known
Armour (may have been removed on conversion): 100–125mm/3.9–4.9in (vertical belt); 35–60mm/1.4–2.4in (protective deck)
Complement: 1,000 men

Taiyo class

Between May 1938 and January 1940 the Mitsubishi yard at Nagasaki laid down three 17,100-gross registered ton (grt) cargo-passenger liners to the account of Nippon Yusen Kaisha (NYK). They were launched 1939–40, but work then appears to have been halted. Not until May 1941 (still seven months before Japan entered the war) was construction resumed, the *Kasuga Maru* being transferred to the Sasebo Navy Yard and the other pair, *Yawata Maru* and *Nitta Maru*, going to Kure Navy Yard, all for conversion to escort carriers. When it is recalled that the pioneering British and American equivalents (HMS *Audacity* and *Long Island*) were first commissioned only in June 1941, it will be appreciated that the Japanese were well abreast of developments.

Even by escort carrier standards, however, the conversions were very basic. The hulls were larger and faster than Allied examples and could have made excellent carriers had they been fitted with the necessary catapult and arrester gear. As it was, their careers were limited largely to ferrying aircraft and training aircrew. For the former role, a large, port-side post and derrick were added.

The hulls possessed adequate stability without bulges and the original upper deck line remained clearly visible. There was no island and the somewhat truncated flight deck was served by two elevators. A respectable armament was shipped, but varied between vessels in both calibre and number of barrels, the ships obviously having to accept what was available.

Their occupation left them vulnerable to submarine attack. All three were thus sunk by submarine attack, only one of them in home waters.

BELOW: **At about 18,290 tonnes/18,000 tons, the three Taiyos should have made useful carriers but their speed was inadequate. Without either catapult or arrester gear, they were employed mainly for aircraft transport, the aircraft being loaded alongside but flown off.**

ABOVE: **The *Taiyo*'s original passenger liner hull is very obvious in this picture. Note the straight rake to the bows, the sheerline, the paired scuttles and lack of bulges. There is no island structure, the ship being navigated from a position beneath the forward overhang. By naval standards, commercial hulls are inadequately subdivided.**

Taiyo class

Class: *Taiyo* (ex-*Kasuga Maru*), Mitsubishi, Nagasaki, commissioned September 15, 1941; *Unyo* (ex-*Yawata Maru*), Mitsubishi, Nagasaki, commissioned May 31, 1942; *Chuyo* (ex-*Nitta Maru*), Mitsubishi, Nagasaki, commissioned November 25, 1942

Displacement: 18,290 tonnes/18,000 tons (standard); 22,200 tonnes/21,800 tons (full load)

Length: 168.1m/551ft 2in (bp); 180.4m/591ft 6in (overall)

Beam: 22.5m/73ft 10in

Draught: 6.3m/20ft 8in (standard); 7.8m/25ft 6in (full load)

Aircraft: 27

Flight deck: 172.2 x 23.6m/564ft 6in x 77ft 3in

Armament: 6 x 119mm/4.7in guns (*Taiyo*); 8 x 127mm/5in guns (all others)

Machinery: Geared steam turbines, 4 boilers, 2 shafts

Power: 18,650kW/25,000shp

Speed: 21 knots

Fuel: Not known

Range: 12,040km/6,500nm at 18 knots

Armour: None

Complement: 800 men

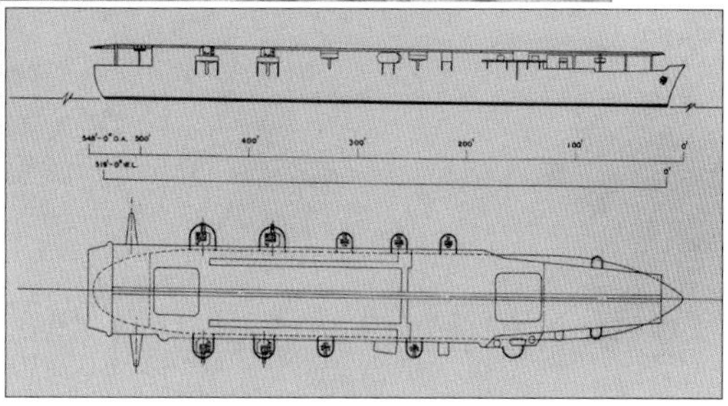

Shinyo and *Kaiyo*

Modern cargo-passenger liners were of great value to the Japanese for the movement of troops and supplies around their sprawling "co-prosperity sphere". It says much, therefore, for the urgency of the need for further flight decks that such ships were continually being withdrawn for conversion to escort carriers and aircraft transports.

Not to be confused with the regular warships of similar name, the *Scharnhorst* and *Gneisenau* were 18,200-gross registered ton (grt) liners built for Norddeutscher-Lloyd's Far East service.

Stranded in Japan by the outbreak of the European war, the former ship was purchased early in 1942 for the Japanese Navy. Early plans to use her as a transport were overtaken by the disaster at Midway, and she was put in hand for a carrier conversion in September 1942. The task was apparently complex, for it occupied 15 months. Renamed *Shinyo*, she emerged as a standard Japanese escort carrier, but recognizable immediately through her semi-Maierform bow profile and her prominent, angular bulges. A brief 11-month operational career was terminated by submarine torpedo.

Built in 1938–40 for Osaka Syosen Kabusiki Kaisha's (OSK) Japan–South America service were the appropriately named *Argentina Maru* and *Brazil Maru.* At 12,750grt, they were smaller than most taken for conversion, and they were diesel-powered for economy on their exceptionally long sea passages. The *Brazil Maru* being sunk by submarine early on in the war, her sister alone was taken in hand late in 1942. Her superstructure was razed and her diesel engines removed in favour of steam turbines. This considerable boost in propulsive power predictably increased her maximum speed by only 2 knots.

Another standard conversion, she was renamed *Kaiyo* and, lacking arresters and catapults, spent her career ferrying aircraft. She was scrapped, having been beached, badly damaged post-war.

TOP AND ABOVE: **This unusually fine image of the *Kaiyo* clearly betrays the passenger liner beneath the flight deck. Note the mercantile forecastle and complete original bridge front with prominent wings. She, too, was employed as an aircraft transport before being sunk in shallow water by carrier aircraft.**

Shinyo

Built: Bremer-Vulkan, Breman
Commissioned: May 28, 1936
Displacement: 19,100 tonnes/17,500 tons (standard); 23,250 tonnes/22,850 tons (full load)
Length: 185.1m/606ft 11in (bp); 195.8m/642ft 2in (overall)
Beam: 25.6m/84ft
Draught: 8.2m/26ft 10in (full load)
Aircraft: 33
Flight deck: 181 x 24.6m/590ft 6in x 80ft 6in
Armament: 8 x 127mm/5in guns
Machinery: Geared steam turbines, 4 boilers, 2 shafts
Power: 19,400kW/26,000shp
Speed: 22 knots
Fuel: Not known
Range: Not known
Armour: None
Complement: 950 men

LEFT: **The *Shinyo*'s forward sheerline, clearly visible, caused the hangar deck to be carried higher. This, in turn, required bulges to be fitted to restore the required stability range. Note the water disturbance around the leading edge of the bulge.**

LEFT AND ABOVE: **The lack of opposition to air strikes in the war's final days is demonstrated by the precision with which the *Shimane Maru* has been put out of action. A heavy bomb has destroyed her only elevator and the lightly constructed flight deck has been shot up. Her tanker origins are indicated by the funnel being located aft, on the starboard side.**

Yamashiro Maru and *Shimane Maru*

Despite needing her merchant fleet both to supply her many garrisons and to import basics and raw materials, Japan began by expending it heedlessly. No convoy strategy existed and there were few escorts. The strongly offensively minded Japanese Navy viewed such policy as "defensive", actively resisting it. Small wonder, therefore, that the highly focussed American submarine campaign caused a crisis before action was taken. Following the Allied lead, Japanese yards were directed at the series production of simple, standard designs. These particularly included tankers, which had been specifically targeted.

With a growing convoy network established, the Japanese adopted another Allied initiative in the adaptation of tankers at MAC ships. These retained their full liquid cargo capacity but had a flight deck built above.

Two conversions, the *Yamashiro Maru* and *Chigusa Maru*, were known to have been made to 2TL-type tankers of 10,000 gross registered tons (grt). At 15 knots, they were very slow for tropical conditions. They had no hangar, up to eight light Army aircraft being permanently ranged topside for the purpose of convoy air cover. The first-named was sunk in 1945 but it is doubtful if the other was ever completed as a carrier, trading as a tanker post-war.

From the slightly larger and fast 1TL type, four conversions were scheduled. Marginally more sophisticated, these featured a small hangar and single elevator. The *Shimane Maru* was thus converted by February 1945, only to be sunk by aircraft just five months later. Her sister, *Otakisan Maru* was never completed as a carrier and the final pair were never commenced.

Neither type had an island but their tanker origins were evident in that the familiar, starboard-side horizontal funnel was located well aft. Few tankers were fast enough to be considered as carriers.

BELOW: **Like the American Sangamon class, the *Yamashiro Maru* had a line of apertures in the shell plating amidships, marking the level of the upper deck of the original tanker hull.**

Shimane Maru

Built: Kawasaki, Kobe
Commissioned: February 28, 1945
Displacement: 12,000 tonnes/11,800 tons (standard)
Length: 150m/491ft 9in (bp); 160.6m/526ft 6in (overall)
Beam: 20m/65ft 8in
Draught: 9.1m/29ft 10in (mean)
Aircraft: 12
Flight deck: 155.1 x 23m/508ft 6in x 75ft 6in
Armament: 2 x 119mm/4.7in guns
Machinery: Geared steam turbines, 2 boilers, 1 shaft
Power: 6,400kW/8,600shp
Speed: 18 knots
Fuel: Not known
Range: 18,520km/10,000nm at 15 knots
Armour: None
Complement: Not known

TOP: **The simple nature of the *Akitsu Maru*'s conversion is evident in this view, the mercantile hull extending forward and aft. Note the lack of elevators and arrester gear.** ABOVE: **This early picture of *Kumano Maru* shows what appears to be a relocated original funnel.**

Akitsu Maru class and *Kumano Maru*

A wide variety of shipping, even cargo-carrying submarines, came under the control of the Japanese Army, but even the outstandingly successful campaign of early 1942 was undertaken by many with only ad hoc arrangements for amphibious warfare.

Exceptions to this were the *Akitsu Maru* (9,200 gross registered tons – grt) and *Nigitsu Maru* (9,550 grt), designed as small cargo-passenger liners but acquired and converted from the outset. Their uptakes were rerouted to the starboard side, but the amidships structure was retained as troop accommodation. To put the troops and light equipment ashore the ships carried a score of the ubiquitous Daihatsu landing craft on deck, which were effectively motorized sampans fitted with a bow ramp. These were handled by the ships' cargo gear.

Overall, a through flight deck extended from the bows to a point about 80 per cent aft. Up to 20 light Army aircraft were stored beneath and transferred by a simple after-end elevator. There was no provision for flying-on, it being presumed that a shoreside airstrip had been secured.

Akitsu Maru was completed as early as January 1942, her running mate some 14 months later. Both fell victim to submarine attack during 1944.

Of more workmanlike appearance, but not completed until March 1945, the *Kumano Maru* was converted from a standard dry-cargo vessel. Her through flight deck, which extended over the centre 80 per cent of her length, could accommodate about three dozen light Army aircraft. What appeared to be a partial hangar had no elevator, the flight deck being served by cargo derrick. Flanking the hangar was troop accommodation. The deck below gave storage for up to 25 Daihatsus of two varieties, which were discharged and recovered via stern doors.

Surviving the war, the ship was reconverted for commercial use.

BELOW: ***Kumano Maru* with her funnel angled downward. Army-controlled, with many boats and stern doors, the ship was among the earliest assault carriers.**

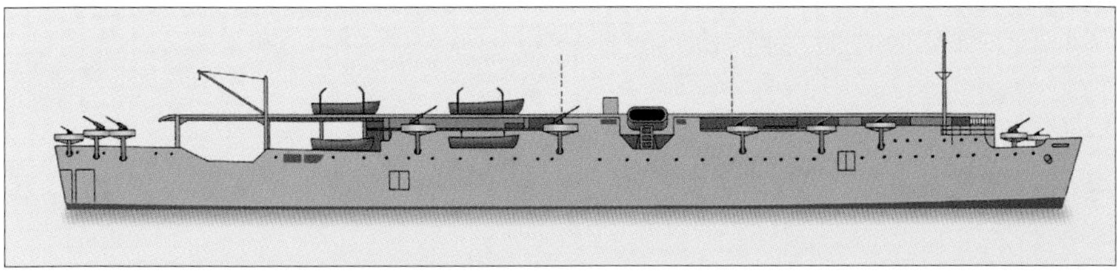

Akitsu Maru

Built: Harima Shipbuilding, Harima
Commissioned: January 30, 1942
Displacement: 12,000 tonnes/11,800 tons (standard)
Length: 143.8m/471ft 7in (bp); 159m/521ft 4in (overall, approximately)
Beam: 19.5m/64ft
Draught: 7.9m/26ft 3in (mean)
Aircraft: 20 light aircraft
Flight deck: 123 x 22.5m/403ft 2in x 73ft 8in
Armament: Up to 12 Army 76mm/3in guns
Machinery: Geared steam turbines, 4 boilers, 2 shafts
Power: 5,600kW/7,500shp
Speed: 20 knots
Fuel: Not known
Range: Not known
Armour: None
Complement: Not known

Akitsushima

The Seaplane Tender was a very specific type of aviation ship that, while it could vary considerably in size, was always identified through the outsize, trademark crane(s) at the after end. Many types of ship, mostly conversions, could deploy floatplanes but the seaplane tender was tailored to the heavy flying boat. In the context of a Pacific war, both the Japanese and United States navies were interested in the provision and maintenance of forward flying boat bases. These were required to be self-sufficient for considerable periods of time and, above all, mobile.

From 1940, American examples were configured around the Consolidated PBY Catalina and the 16.3-tonne/16-ton-plus Martin PBM Mariner, being able to lift them bodily from the water for repair or maintenance. The ships were mostly in the 8,128–9,144-tonne/8,000–9,000-ton bracket.

Newly introduced, Japan's large flying boat was the Kawanishi H8K2 Type 2. Known to the Allies as "Emily", it closely resembled the British Sunderland and conferred an increased medium-range potential in both reconnaissance and attack. Five specialist ships were ordered for its support but, like so many Japanese programmes, it was severely curtailed; only one ship, the *Akitsushima*, ever being completed.

Little more than half the displacement of her American equivalents, she resembled a large destroyer forward. Her second twin 127mm/5in mounting was poorly located, between the funnel and mast, commanding limited arcs. On a revolving base right aft was a long-jibbed crane with an "Eiffel-tower" profile. This served a heavy cradle which may (or may not) have been built to act as a trainable catapult for smaller floatplanes.

Japan's further territorial expansion after 1942 was obviously most unlikely, and the cancellation of the final four units probably resulted from a revised assessment of the future course of the war as much as by priorities in shipbuilding.

Akitsushima herself was sunk by air attack during 1944.

TOP: **Although published plans suggest a trainable catapult on the afterdeck of the *Akitsushima*, there seems little evidence of it in this profile. The disruptive camouflage includes false bow and stern waves of a magnitude hardly likely on a 19-knot ship.** ABOVE: **Well armed and protected, the Kawanishi H8K ("Emily") was considered the most difficult Japanese aircraft to shoot down.**

Akitsushima

Built: Kawasaki, Kobe
Commissioned: 1942
Displacement: 4,750 tonnes/4,650 tons (standard); 5,700 tonnes/5,600 tons (full load, approximately)
Length: 109.1m/357ft 7in (bp); 118m/386ft 10in (overall)
Beam: 15.8m/51ft 9in
Draught: 5.4m/17ft 9in (mean)
Aircraft: 1
Flight deck: None
Armament: 4 x 127mm/5in guns
Machinery: Four diesel engines, 2 shafts
Power: 5,970kW/8,000bhp
Speed: 19 knots
Fuel: Not known
Range: Not known
Armour: None
Complement: Not known

ABOVE: **The *Foudre* is seen here soon after her completion and still in her original configuration as mother-ship and carrier of torpedo craft. Her funnels were later raised and a temporary hangar erected aft.**

ABOVE: **Seen soon after conversion, the *Foudre* has acquired her garage-like hangar but retains her three short funnels. The take-off platform forward was later replaced by a square assembly platform.**

Foudre

Completed in the unrealistic role of cruiser-sized torpedo boat, carrier and mother ship, the *Foudre* had little use (although equipped with facilities for an observation balloon) and served as a multi-purpose auxiliary until, in 1911–12, she was converted for experimental naval aviation purposes. Much of the earlier top-hamper was removed and a large, permanent hangar erected. This could house about four of the eight floatplanes carried.

During 1914 a temporary platform was built over the forecastle and, on May 8, Réné Caudron used it to make the first-ever flight from a French ship. The aircraft was one of his own G.III amphibians.

The *Foudre*'s main contribution was in cooperation with similarly converted British seaplane carriers in the eastern Mediterranean. Naval aviation moved on quickly, however, and by 1917 the ship was again working as an auxiliary. She was scrapped in 1922.

Following British practice, the French requisitioned other ships for wartime aviation service. Largest of these was the 3,320-gross ton cargo-passenger ship *Campinas*, modified simply by protecting the forward and after well decks with canvas sides and roofing to accommodate about eight floatplanes. These were handled with the ship's cargo gear. She also worked in the eastern Mediterranean. Two cross-channel packets, *Nord* and *Pas de Calais*, were also pressed into service. Unusually, each was paddle-propelled and both worked in the English Channel as seaplane carriers.

All three latter ships alternatively deployed small, pusher-engined flying boats. These were the so-called FBAs, built on both sides of the Channel by the Franco-British Aviation Company.

Following hostilities, the mercantile naval sloop *Bapaume* was fitted with a launch platform extending from bridge to stem head. Although only experimental, it saw the first flight from a French ship of landplanes, fighters with wheeled undercarriages.

Foudre

Built: At. et Ch. de la Gironde, Bordeaux
Commissioned: September 17, 1896
Displacement: 6,080 tonnes/5,975 tons (standard); 6,210 tonnes/6,100 tons (full load)
Length: 118.9m/389ft 10in (overall)
Beam: 19.1m/62ft 6in
Draught: 7.2m/23ft 6in (full load)
Aircraft: Up to 8 floatplanes
Flight deck (launch platform): 34.5 x 8m/113ft 2in x 26ft 3in
Armament: 8 x 100mm/3.9in, 4 x 65mm/2.6in, and 4 x 47mm/1.85in guns
Machinery: Two sets triple expansion steam engines, 24 boilers, 2 shafts
Power: 8,650kW/11,600ihp
Speed: 19 knots
Fuel: 800 tonnes/786 tons (coal)
Range: Not known
Armour: 120mm/4.7in (protective deck), also protected casemates
Complement: 450 men

TOP LEFT AND ABOVE: **Too slow to be an efficient fleet carrier, the *Béarn* nonetheless possessed considerable "presence". The round-down to the forward end of the flight deck dates these pictures to the early 1930s. The massive island was completely outboard of the flight deck edge and, like those of Japanese carriers, was heavily buttressed beneath.** LEFT: **Biplanes such as these Morane-Saulniers were soon displaced by a succession of parasol-winged aircraft such as the Loire Gordou-Leseurre 32, the Morane-Saulnier MS225 and the Dewoitine D373.**

Béarn

Following the Washington Treaty of 1921–22, four of the incomplete hulls of the *Normandie*-class battleships were scrapped and the fifth, *Béarn*, was earmarked for conversion to a fleet carrier. However, she was not a good choice due to her low speed and her outer shafts being driven by vertical steam reciprocating engines, whose height resulted in the ship's high profile. This odd mix of machinery was for cruise economy, the steam turbine-driven inner shafts being coupled only for high speed boost.

Before reconstruction began, in August 1923, the hull was partially decked for static flying trials. As completed there was a near full-length flight deck which, in plan, narrowed significantly at either end. Here, it was supported on an open structure, the after end with a pronounced round-down and the forward end modified likewise following sea experience to improve airflow over the deck. There were three elevators, all on the centreline.

As with contemporary foreign carriers, the massive funnel casing dominated the island structure, all of which was located outboard of the flight deck's starboard edge. Abaft it was a prominent gooseneck crane.

Although her original armour plan was considerably reduced during her reconstruction, the *Béarn* remained well protected. Uniquely, her main battery of eight 155mm/6.1in guns was casemated.

During World War II, the ship was blockaded in the French Antilles until 1943 when the islands finally declared for the Allies. Refitted and rearmed in the United States she served as an aircraft transport, for which service her flight deck was truncated and a second prominent crane installed. Following post-war service in French Indochina she was withdrawn in 1948 but continued in static harbour service until 1966. Scrapping began in the following year.

ABOVE: **These sketches depict the *Béarn* in her original carrier configuration. Refitted in the United States, 1943–44, she lost either end of her flight deck in being reduced to aircraft transport status.**

Béarn

- **Built:** F. et Ch. de la Méditerranée, La Seyne
- **Commissioned:** May 28, 1927
- **Displacement:** 22,200 tonnes/21,800 tons (standard); 28,450 tonnes/27,950 tons (full load)
- **Length:** 170.6m/559ft 4in (bp); 182.6m/598ft 8in (overall)
- **Beam:** 27.1m/88ft 10in
- **Draught:** 8.4m/27ft 6in (standard); 9.3m/30ft 6in (full load)
- **Aircraft:** 35–40
- **Flight deck:** 177 x 21.3m/580ft 9in x 69ft 11in
- **Armament:** 8 x 155mm/6.1in, 6 x 75mm/2.9in, and 8 x 37mm/1.46in guns
- **Machinery:** Two sets steam reciprocating engines and two sets geared steam turbines, 12 boilers, 4 shafts
- **Power:** 29,850kW/40,000shp
- **Speed:** 21.5 knots
- **Fuel:** 2,250 tonnes/2,210 tons
- **Range:** 12,960km/7,000nm at 10 knots
- **Armour:** 83mm/3.25in (vertical belt); 25mm/1in (flight deck); 25–119mm/1–4.7in (protective deck)
- **Complement:** 880 men

Joffre class

Perhaps because of the disappointingly low speed of the *Béarn*, perhaps from a need to establish the ideal size of carrier for its requirements, the French Navy proposed during the early 1930s several designs based on hybrid cruiser technology. The ideas came to nought but the thinking influenced two new ships eventually authorized in 1936. France was permitted 60,963 tonnes/ 60,000 tons total carrier displacement by virtue of the Washington Treaty and, with an eye to an eventual third ship, the size was fixed at a target of 18,289 tonnes/ 18,000 tons each. Much of a size with a British Courageous but even finer-lined for greater speed, the ships, named provisionally *Joffre* and *Painlévé*, were of novel layout. The superstructure was long and narrow, and not cantilevered beyond the starboard side of the hull. Its considerable offset weight, however, allowed the flight deck to be built parallel and separate, extending beyond the port side of the hull. Two hangars, the lower of half length, would have been provided, accommodating up to 40 unspecified aircraft. Barely commenced, the ships were scrapped after France's occupation in 1940.

Joffre class

Built: At. Et Ch. de St. Nazaire
Laid down: November 1938, 1939
Displacement: 18,289 tonnes/18,000 tons (standard); 20,350 tonnes/20,000 tons (full load)
Length: 228m/747ft 6in (at waterline); 236m/ 773ft 9in (overall)
Beam: 25.5m/83ft 7in
Draught: 6.5m/21ft 3in (approximately)
Aircraft: 40
Flight deck: 200 x 28m/655ft 9in x 91ft 3in
Armament: 8 x 130mm/5.1in, and 8 x 37mm/1.46in
Machinery: Geared steam turbines, 8 boilers, 4 shafts
Power: 89,500kW/120,000shp
Speed: 32.5 knots
Fuel: Not known
Range: Not known
Armour: Not known
Complement: 1,200 men

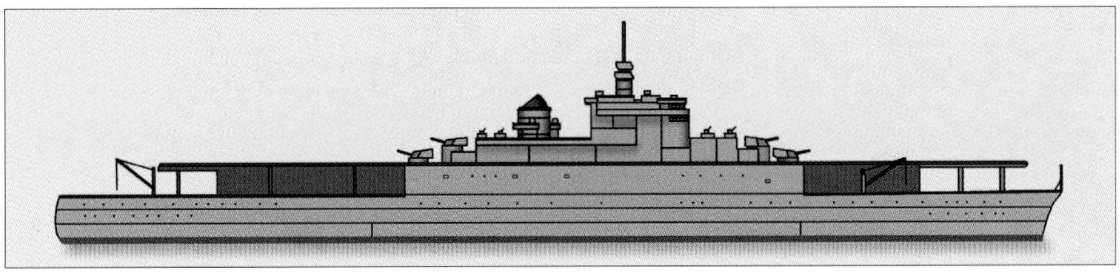

LEFT: **The Joffre design grouped its main armament similar to that of the later American Essex class. Aircraft appear to be taken aboard at upper hangar deck level and transferred within via roller doors at either end.**

Commandant Teste

Although described as a Seaplane Carrier, the *Commandant Teste* could accommodate both floatplanes and flying boats. Her generous freeboard enclosed a capacious hangar that was served either by a stern ramp or by any of four heavy cranes. Each crane also served an adjacent catapult, two ahead and two abaft the central funnel casing.

Her utility in a Far Eastern colonial context is obvious but nevertheless she spent her life mainly in the Mediterranean supporting flights from battleships and cruisers, and developing strike/reconnaissance roles. Scuttled at Toulon in 1942, she was salvaged and repaired, only to be broken up in 1950.

Commandant Teste

Built: F. Ch. de la Gironde, Bordeaux
Commissioned: November 17, 1932
Displacement: 10,200 tonnes/10,000 tons (standard); 11,900 tonnes/11,700 tons (full load)
Length: 156m/511ft 6in (bp); 167m/547ft 6in (overall)
Beam: 27m/88ft 6in
Draught: 6.9m/22ft 8in (full load)
Aircraft: Up to 26
Flight deck: None
Armament: 12 x 100mm/3.9in, and 8 x 37mm/1.46in guns
Machinery: Geared steam turbines, 4 boilers, 2 shafts
Power: 15,600kW/21,000shp
Speed: 20.5 knots
Fuel: 295 tonnes/290 tons (oil); 735 tonnes/ 720 tons (coal)
Range: 11,110km/6,000nm at 10 knots
Armour: 30mm/1.18in (partial protective deck)
Complement: 640 men

ABOVE: **The isolated single funnel, massive cranage and low freeboard aft combined to give the *Commandant Teste* a unique profile.**

ABOVE LEFT: **Depot and repair ships have impressive freeboards due to on-board workshops, and accommodation for both their own and visiting crews. Note the paravane chains rigged at the bows and the half-masted jack.**

LEFT: **Little altered post-war, the *Dixmude* performed useful service in what was then French Indochina. Note how the box-like island has the appearance of being supported by neither flight deck nor hull.**

Dixmude

One of the original *Avenger*-class escort carriers built in the United States for the Royal Navy, the *Biter* was returned in April 1945. She was immediately transferred on loan to the French Navy, being renamed *Dixmude*.

As the French were also acquiring more capable carriers on transfer, the *Dixmude*, herself an early type of CVE, was employed mainly in training. Then, disarmed, she assumed the role of aircraft transport, collecting machines from the United States, many for use in the Far East.

By 1960 she had been relegated to static harbour duties and, six years later, was returned to the Americans for scrapping. She was by then the last of the early escort carrier conversions still afloat. Where her two Royal Navy sisters had lives each of 9 months, hers had been of 24 years.

Dixmude

Built: Sun Shipbuilding, Philadelphia
Commissioned: May 4, 1942
Length: 141.8m/465ft (at waterline); 150m/492ft (overall)
Beam: 21.2m/69ft 6in
Draught: 7.7m/25ft 2in (full load)
Aircraft: 20+
Flight deck: 134.2 x 24.1m/440 x 79ft
Armament: 3 x 102mm/4in, and 12 x 20mm/0.79in guns
Machinery: Two 6-cylinder diesel engines driving 1 shaft
Power: 6,350kW/8,500bhp
Speed: 16.5 knots
Fuel: 3,260 tonnes/3,200 tons
Range: Not known
Armour: None
Complement: 850 men

LEFT: **With elevators lowered, probably to ventilate the hangar, the *La Fayette* transits the Suez Canal in the early 1960s, the date fixed by the additional lattice mast between the funnel pairs.**

La Fayette class

With little post-war potential, most American *Independence*-class CVLs were quickly discarded. Three, however, were transferred abroad, two of them to the French Navy. In January 1951, the *Langley* (CVL-27) hoisted her new colours as the *La Fayette* (R96) followed in September 1953, by the *Belleau Wood* (CVL-24), which became the *Bois Belleau* (R97). Transferred under the wide-ranging Mutual Defense Assistance Program, both ships assumed names redolent of Franco-American alliance.

Altered by the addition of a tall lattice mast amidships, both saw service in the Far East, the *La Fayette* at the Suez intervention. Both were returned for disposal in the early 1960s, leaving the Spanish *Dédalo* as the sole remaining CVL.

La Fayette class

Class: *La Fayette*, New York Shipbuilding, Camden, commissioned August 31, 1943; *Bois Belleau*, New York Shipbuilding, Camden, commissioned March 31, 1943
Displacement: 10,850 tonnes/10,650 tons (standard); 15,000 tonnes/14,750 tons (full load)
Length: 183m/600ft (at waterline); 189.9m/622ft 6in (overall)
Beam: 21.8m/71ft 6in
Draught: 6.4m/21ft (standard); 7.5m/24ft 6in (full load)
Aircraft: About 30
Flight deck: 165.9 x 22.3m/544 x 73ft
Armament: 28 x 40mm/1.57in guns
Machinery: Geared steam turbines, 4 boilers, 4 shafts
Power: 75,000kW/100,000shp
Speed: 32 knots
Fuel: 2,350 tonnes/2,300 tons
Range: 20,370km/11,000nm at 15 knots
Armour: 50mm/1.97in (vertical belt)
Complement: 1,200 men

FAR LEFT: **Toward the end of her life, the *Arromanches* worked as an ASW carrier deploying Breguet Alizé aircraft, of which one is seen here. Note the considerably altered masting and new funnel cap.** LEFT: **British carrier design always favoured the fully enclosed bow for its superior weatherliness.** BELOW: **Despite the alternative of compact whip aerials, British-built carriers still favoured the more efficient wire aerial strung between light lattice masts, here seen in the raised position.**

Arromanches

Designed and built for wartime exigencies, the British Light Fleet Carriers proved to be capacious and economical for peacetime use. They also lent themselves to a degree of modernization and proved to be surprisingly durable. These qualities were best seen in those examples which were acquired by foreign fleets, for they invariably served longer than those in the Royal Navy, which were superseded by later classes. Such was the *Colossus*, name ship of the original group, which was loaned to France in August 1946 and which was bought outright five years later.

Already impoverished by World War II, France was involved in a protracted struggle to regain authority over her former territory of Indochina. Initially, this benefited her armed forces by increased funding but, in the long term, it had the opposite effect with new equipment and, indeed, a planned new carrier, being cancelled due to the continued financial drain.

With the French aircraft industry still to re-establish itself, the ex-*Colossus*, renamed *Arromanches* (R95), deployed American-built aircraft of World War II vintage both in the Far East and at Suez in 1956. By this date, however, the first of two new carriers was, at last, on the stocks but, as these would be six years in build, it was worthwhile to modernize the *Arromanches* during 1957–58.

Remodelled, she gained a moderate angled deck of four degrees but no steam catapult. Not fully jet-capable, she could deploy the Breguet Alizé AS aircraft and, indeed, with the new carriers in service, she was further modified and redesignated a full anti-submarine carrier, with an air wing of two dozen helicopters.

Following final service as a training carrier, the *Arromanches* was laid up for four years prior to her scrapping in 1978.

Arromanches

Built: Vickers-Armstrong, Newcastle
Commissioned: December 16, 1944
Displacement: 13,600 tonnes/13,350 tons (standard); 18,550 tonnes/18,200 tons (full load)
Length: 192.2m/630ft (bp); 212m/695ft (overall)
Beam: 24.4m/80ft
Draught: 5.6m/18ft 6in (standard); 7.2m/23ft 6in (full load)
Aircraft: 35–40
Flight deck: 207.4 x 24.4m/680 x 80ft
Armament: 31 x 40mm/1.57in guns
Machinery: Geared steam turbines, 4 boilers, 2 shafts
Power: 29,850kW/40,000shp
Speed: 25 knots
Fuel: 3,300 tonnes/3,250 tons
Range: 22,220km/12,000nm at 14 knots
Armour: None
Complement: 1,450 men

ABOVE: **Cadet accommodation flanks the long, narrow hangar and is marked externally by the long "promenade" decks.** LEFT: **The *Jeanne d'Arc*'s light armament has been considerably strengthened in recent years through the addition of six Exocet MM38 canister launchers, located in two angled groups of three between the forward 100mm/3.9in guns.**

Jeanne d'Arc

Laid down in 1960 with the temporary name of *Résolue*, this ship commissioned as the *Jeanne d'Arc* (R97), assuming the name of a training cruiser that had just paid off. The primary function of both was the sea training of officer cadets but the new ship, to be cost-effective, was required to be capable of multiple roles. Of pleasing appearance she is, therefore, conventional warship forward and aviation vessel aft. This unusual combination bears comparison only with the Italian *Vittorio Veneto* and the Russian Moskvas.

Training (of nearly 200 cadets) is a peacetime activity, so that the accommodation that flanks the long, narrow hangar is allowed to encroach on its space. In an emergency, this could be removed to give accommodation for up to eight Supter-Frélon transport helicopters, or more WG-13 Lynx AS helicopters if the ship is required to lead an anti-submarine task group. Alternatively, the full accommodation could be retained for a 700-strong assault battalion, with its equipment.

The limitations of a multi-role ship are, however, evident. The American *Iwo Jima*-class LPHs were widely criticized for shipping no landing craft to move heavy equipment ashore. Only two are carried by the *Jeanne d'Arc*. With the superstructure as a barrier across the forward end of the flight deck, V/STOL aircraft can be operated only in the fuel-thirsty vertical mode. Forward, the ship's six Exocets are of use only against other ships, not as shore gun support, for which the ship's four 100mm/3.9in weapons are both lightweight and poorly located.

The already comprehensive range of electronics – radar, sonar, and control and command facilities – could well be supplemented to give the ship what would probably be her best combat role, as a Headquarters Ship. The "Jeanne" is scheduled to run until 2010.

ABOVE: **In company with four French destroyers, the *Jeanne d'Arc* lies alongside the Landungsbrücken for a port visit to Hamburg, probably in the early 1970s.**

Jeanne d'Arc

Built: Brest-Arsenal
Commissioned: June 30, 1964
Displacement: 10,180 tonnes/10,000 tons (standard); 12,570 tonnes/12,350 tons (full load)
Length: 172m/563ft 10in (at waterline); 182m/596ft 9in (overall)
Beam: 24m/78ft 8in
Draught: 6.9m/22ft 7in (full load)
Aircraft: 8+ helicopters
Flight deck: 62 x 21m/203ft 3in x 68ft 10in
Armament: 6 x MM38 Exocet SSM, and 4 x 100mm/3.9in guns
Machinery: Geared steam turbines, 4 boilers, 2 shafts
Power: 29,850kW/40,000shp
Speed: 26.5 knots
Fuel: 1,385 tonnes/1,360 tons
Range: 12,500km/6,800nm at 16 knots
Armour: None
Complement: 740 men (crew only)

LEFT: **This view shows well the short-range Crotale SAM launcher on the port quarter sponson, shipped in exchange for two 100mm/3.9in guns. The prominent dome abaft the funnel houses the antenna of the aircraft landing-air radar.** ABOVE: **A Super Etendard fighter on the *Clemenceau*'s port-side steam catapult.** BELOW: **This earlier picture of the *Clemenceau* shows the original armament of eight 100mm/3.9in guns in single mountings. Unusually the ship was deploying a mix of Lynx and Super-Frélon helicopters.**

Clemenceau class

After several false starts, the French Navy finally laid down its first two modern carriers, the *Clemenceau* (R98) in 1955 and *Foch* (R99) in 1957. They were late enough to incorporate an 8-degree angled deck and steam catapults from the outset. French ships tend to speed, the necessary power demanding space, a long hull and fine lines. Jet aircraft also require length but, being thirsty, also need considerable capacity for fuel storage. The usual design trade-offs still applied, however, for budget restraints required the smallest ship to meet the specification.

As designed, the pair therefore had a standard displacement comparable with that of a British Illustrious but with a length (between perpendiculars) greater by over 30.5m/100ft yet with less than 0.91m/3ft more on the beam. Even without the same degree of protection, and with armament reduced to save topweight, the first-of-class proved tender, and both needed to be bulged by nearly 1.82m/6ft. This measure increases freeboard, improves stability and increases fuel capacity, thought at the cost of a knot or so in speed.

Hangar design tends towards the fully enclosed, but one of the two elevators is a space-saving deck-edge unit, located immediately abaft the island. The carriers' strike component comprises 16 Dassault Super Etendards, trans-sonic aircraft capable of carrying tactical nuclear weapons or the air-launched AM 39 variant of the Exocet.

During their life under the French flag, both ships underwent two major upgrades of heavy equipment, structure and electronics. Four of the original eight 100mm/3.9in guns were landed in favour of two Crotale short-range SAM systems, although the sponson of the forward mounting looks vulnerable to heavy seas.

In 2000, the *Foch* was sold to Brazil, becoming the *Sao Paolo*, but the *Clemenceau* was scrapped in 2003. This left the French Navy with just one fleet carrier.

Clemenceau class

Built: Brest-Arsenal (Hull of *Foch* sub-contracted to Ch. de l'Atlantique, St. Nazaire)
Displacement: 22,400 tonnes/22,000 tons (standard); 33,300 tonnes/32,700 tons (full load)
Length: 238m/780ft 4in (bp); 265m/868ft 10in (overall)
Beam: 31.7m/103ft 11in
Draught: 7.5m/24ft 7in (standard); 8.6m/28ft 3in (full load)
Aircraft: 38–40
Flight deck: 257 x 28m/842ft 8in x 91ft 10in
Armament: 2 x octal Crotale SAM launchers, and 4 x 100mm/3.9in guns
Machinery: Geared steam turbines, 6 boilers, 2 shafts
Power: 94,000kW/126,000hp
Speed: 32 knots
Fuel: 3,800 tonnes/3,700 tons
Range: 13,800km/7,500nm at 18 knots
Armour: "Light protection"
Complement: 1,350 men

LEFT: **Seen running builder's trials the *Charles de Gaulle* is still devoid of topside clutter. Great efforts on the part of the French Navy to lower the radar signature of its ships has left them increasingly bland in appearance.** ABOVE: **Late acquisition of two Grumman E-2C Hawkeye airborne early warning (AEW) aircraft (see here forward of the island and right aft) caused last-minute modifications to the *de Gaulle*'s design.** BELOW: **Despite the prestige attached to the *de Gaulle*, her expensive new Rafale fighter-bombers are being procured very slowly. Four are seen here with two variants of Etendard beyond.**

Charles de Gaulle

The *Charles de Gaulle* is very much a prestige project and since the disposal of the two Clemenceaus, one in serious need of a running mate to guarantee the availability of at least one flight deck. However, a second ship is not planned before 2014 and may be constructed in the same programme and to the same basic design as the two British Queen Elizabeths. She will probably, therefore, be conventionally propelled and, despite the *de Gaulle* sharing much commonality with French nuclear submarine technology she will alone have to bear considerable infrastructure costs.

By modern standards, her layout is conventional but with a larger than usual island structure located well forward to allow space for two starboard-side, deck-edge elevators to be sited abaft it. There is no centreline elevator. To maximize flight deck area there is a very pronounced overhang to the angle deck. Two US-sourced catapults are fitted, one forward and one set obliquely across the angled deck. Some modification proved necessary to accommodate the late purchase of two E-2C Hawkeye airborne early warning (AEW) aircraft.

The customary composition of the air group-attack/bombers, fighters and AEW, reflects the downgrading of anti-submarine warfare (ASW) since the end of the Cold War. Only two helicopters are thus usually carried, and neither necessarily fitted for ASW.

The primary area defence SAM systems are located in deep, box-like sponsons that appear to be vulnerable to slamming in heavy seas.

Electronics are comprehensive, the suite including air and surface search radar, missile fire control, navigation and a laser-based deck landing system. The only guns are four multiple 20mm/0.79in Giat mountings for close-in defence.

The stern configuration is unusual, housing towed-array and variable-depth sonars as well as towed-decoy/anti-torpedo devices.

The much-delayed Rafale fighter programme will see final deliveries only in 2007, to finally replace the Etendards.

Charles de Gaulle

Built: DCN, Brest
Commissioned: May 18, 2001
Displacement: 37,250 tonnes/36,600 tons (standard); 42,750 tonnes/42,000 tons (full load)
Length: 238m/780ft 4in (at waterline); 261.5m/857ft 4in (overall)
Beam: 31.5m/103ft 3in
Draught: 8.7m/28ft 6in (mean)
Aircraft: 34 plus 2 helicopters (currently 20 x Super Etendard, 12 x Rafale F1, 2 x E-2C Hawkeye, and 2 x AS 322 or equivalent)
Flight deck: 261.5 x 64.4m/857ft 4in x 211ft 2in)
Armament: 4 octuple SAAM/F launchers, 2 sextuple Matra Sadral PDMS launchers
Machinery: 2 K15 reactors, 2 sets geared steam turbines, 2 shafts
Power: 61,200kW/82,000shp
Speed: 27 knots
Fuel: Nuclear
Range: Indefinite between recoring at 25-year intervals
Armour: Not known
Complement: 1,910 men, including aircrew

Balloon and seaplane carriers

Despite its nation's poor industrial base, the Imperial Russian Navy was always ready to embrace new technologies. Mine and torpedo warfare was thus followed by several, uncoordinated ventures involving the lofting and towing of balloons by warships (not to mention man-lifting kites). Stated objectives were the direction of gunfire, spotting for mines and to experiment in signalling.

The Russo-Japanese War of 1904–05 gave added impetus and, in May 1904, the armoured cruiser *Rossia* became the first warship to routinely use a kite balloon to extend her horizon while on an operational cruise.

Later that year the veteran passenger liner *Russ* was comprehensively modified for the deployment of nine balloons of three types. Dedicated and fully equipped for this function, she may lay claim to being the world's first true aviation ship. She was also a platform in the pioneering use of aerial photography.

On their arrival, heavier-than-air machines were greeted by the navy in equal fashion. Flying was conducted from 1910, with the first aircraft acquired soon after. Early reliance on small Curtiss-built flying boats was broken by the introduction of the domestically designed Grigorovich, which served aboard ship and from shore stations.

ABOVE: **M-5s were used in reconnaissance, spotting and bombing missions. They had an endurance approaching five hours maximum but, being poorly armed, needed to fly with escort, making single, ship-based aircraft vulnerable.**

ABOVE: **The M-5 was one of an evolving series of flying boats designed by Dmitri Pavlovich Grigorovich. Production runs of several hundred were made of the M-5, M-9 and M-15. Each type had a tail fin of distinctive shape.**

During World War I, a single but very active seaplane carrier served with the Baltic Fleet. She was the 3,800-gross registered ton *Orlitza*, a converted merchantman with steel-and-canvas hangars covering either well deck to give accommodation for half a dozen aircraft.

Based on Sevastopol, however, and part of the Black Sea Fleet, was a properly constituted aviation squadron of three Russian and, later, several Romanian vessels. Their aircraft were used offensively as well as in fleet and military cooperation. The best equipped was thought to have been the *Romania*.

Romania

Built: At. et Ch. de la Loire, St. Nazaire
Commissioned: 1904
Registered tonnage: 3,793grt; 1,340 net
Length: 108.9m/356ft 10in (overall)
Beam: 12.8m/41ft 10in
Draught: 4.4m/14ft 6in
Aircraft: Up to 4 flying boats
Flight deck: None
Armament: Possibly 4 x 152mm/6in, and 4 x 76mm/3in guns
Machinery: 2 sets vertical triple expansion, 5 boilers, 2 shafts
Power: 5,369kW/7,200ihp

Moskva class

Given the known range of the early Polaris missiles, it was apparent that to target the west Russian heartland, a western SSBN would need to operate either in the hostile and shallow White Sea (effectively a Soviet lake) or in the safer and more benign waters of the eastern Mediterranean. The *Moskva* design was therefore developed to operate primarily with the Soviet Black Sea Fleet, deploying a powerful force of anti-submarine (AS) helicopters to isolate and destroy an SSBN at the very earliest opportunity. As the landlocked Mediterranean would be dominated by hostile air power, a considerable anti-aircraft (AA) armament was shipped for the area defence of both ship and her support group. For defence against a surface threat, a Moskva would depend upon her escort.

These ingredients resulted in a unique design solution, comparable only with the more conventional French *Jeanne d'Arc* or the Italian *Vittorio Veneto*. Like them, however, the after end is dedicated to aviation, the forward end to multi-purpose armament.

To maximize the after-end capacity on limited dimensions, designers developed a hull which attained its maximum waterline width aft of amidships, maintaining this width to a point well aft. The resulting hangar was wide and spacious as, through moderate flaring, was the flight deck above. Although bold, the solution was not entirely satisfactory for the forward end, with its narrow waterplane, supported the considerable mass of armament, while the broad waterplane of the after end bore only the far lesser weight of hangar and aircraft. The result was a persistent trim by the bows, giving the pair, despite their prestigious names, a reputation as poor seakeepers in adverse sea states.

Their career, however, was most effectively circumscribed by the apparently unanticipated arrival of V/STOL. The introduction of the Harrier *doppelgänger*, the Yak-36 ("Forger"),

ABOVE: **The *Moskva*'s Kamor Ka-25 ("Hormone") helicopters were of three variants; Type A for ASW, Type B for mid-range targeting of long range ship-to-ship missiles (SSM) and Type C for general utility activities.**

ABOVE: **The duel functions of the *Moskva* design are sharply demarcated. Note how the plan attains its maximum width well aft in order to maximize flight deck area.** LEFT: **Known to the West as Top Sail, the enormous antenna of 3-D radar dominates the profile. The general impression is one of a huge fort-like superstructure.**

LEFT: **Forward and below the Top Sail antenna are a Head Net C air search radar and two Head Light director radars for the SA-N-3 launchers. Note one SA-N-3 ("Goblet") launcher in the elevated position. Pendant numbers were often changed.** ABOVE: **The wave formation around the bows does not indicate the presence of a large bulb. Any installation is, therefore, likely to be small, of medium frequency and of limited range.**

saw the *Moskva* acting as trials ship for its evaluation. The massive superstructure, a barrier across the forward end of the flight deck, totally precluded any fuel-saving rolling take-off, stamping the ships as "helicopter only".

Forward, the ships fairly bristled with both AA and AS weaponry. In the superfiring positions were two, twin-pedestal launchers for the SA-N-3 ("Goblet") area defence AA missile with a 30km/18.6-mile range. Further redundancy was provided through each launcher having its own director.

Further forward was the smaller, twin-pedestal launcher of the SUW-N-1 AS stand-off system, capable of targeting a submerged target with a conventional or nuclear charge at ranges of up to 24km/14.9 miles. This was backed by AS torpedo tubes amidships (later removed) and, right in the eyes of the ship, two of the venerable and well-trusted, 12-barrelled RBU-6000 AS rocket launchers (although, if the ship was close enough to use them she, herself, would be in dire danger from the submarine being hunted).

The dipping sonars deployed by the helicopters were backed by a medium/low-frequency unit mounted at the ship's forefoot and variable-depth sonars deployed from the stern gallery, below the flight deck.

Condemned by reduction in the Russian Fleet, the *Moskva* was discarded in 1995 and the *Leningrad* in 1992.

ABOVE: **Accommodation and maintenance facilities for helicopters are located in the superstructure and beneath the flight deck. Note the towed, variable-depth sonar (VDS) housed in the transom.**

Moskva class

Class: *Moskva*, Nikolaev South, commissioned 1967; *Leningrad*, Nikolaev South, commissioned 1968

Displacement: 15,200 tonnes/14,900 tons (standard); 18,950 tonnes/18,600 tons (full load)

Length: 179m/586ft 10in (at waterline); 190m/622ft 11in (overall)

Beam: 26m/85ft 3in

Draught: 7.6m/24ft 10in (standard); 8.5m/27ft 11in (full load)

Aircraft: 14 "Hormone" (Ka-25) helicopter equivalents

Flight deck: 86 x 34.1m/282ft x 111ft 9in

Armament: 2 x SA-N-3, 1 x SUW-N-1, 2 x RBU-6000, and 4 x 57mm/2.24in guns

Machinery: Geared steam turbines, 4 boilers, 2 shafts

Power: 74,600kW/100,000shp

Speed: 30 knots

Fuel: 2,800 tonnes/2,750 tons

Range: 25,930km/14,000nm at 12 knots

Armour: Not known

Complement: 830 men

LEFT AND BELOW: **A major development of the Moskva design, that of the Kievs includes a through flight deck to allow V/STOL operation and an armament more heavily oriented toward anti-surface ship warfare.**

Kiev class

Although an extrapolation of the Moskva, the leap in scale to the Kiev was very bold for a fleet that had never previously specified a through-deck carrier. Best appreciated by her Russian categorization as a Large Anti-submarine Cruiser she was designed to operate only helicopters and V/STOL aircraft. There were no catapults or arrester gear, precluding the deployment of conventional, higher-performance machines. As with the Moskvas the forward end was dedicated to armament and the after end to aviation.

To operate efficiently, V/STOL fighters require a rolling take-off. With the forward end fully populated, the preferred design solution was an angled flight deck and an island superstructure. Contrary to normal practice, the flight path was all on the port side so that, even with a moderate, 4.5-degree angle, the deck had a considerable overhang, thought to be simply counterbalanced by the island, which was massive by usual carrier standards. The layout left the starboard side and the centreline area abreast the island free for parking and marshalling. The outfit lacked some redundancy in that only one of the elevators was large enough for a V/STOL aircraft.

The ship's main weapon system was her AS helicopters, for which seven "spots" were provided on the flight path. They were, of course, only the sharp end of an AS suite that included also a large, bow-mounted, low-frequency sonar, variable-depth sonar (VDS) deployed from a stern gallery, and, on the foredeck, a SUW-N-1 stand-off system and two RBU-6000 rocket projectors.

Intended to hunt down SSBNs in the open ocean, a Kiev could expect to be opposed by American carriers. As her dozen or so V/STOL fighters would have availed her little, her major weapon was the SS-N-12 ("Sandbox") anti-ship missile, eight canister launchers for which were located forward. This

LEFT: **A Kiev bow wave is typical of that resulting from a large sonar bulb, housing a physically large, low-frequency, long-range unit. This is complemented by a higher-frequency VDS, deployed from the stern. In a submarine hunt, helicopters would deploy their "dunking sonars" and share data with the ship via a single data link.**

weapon's 500km/311-mile range required specialist helicopters to give mid-course correction to target. Two reload missiles were provided for each launcher.

As in the Moskvas, two SA-N-3 area defence anti-aircraft (AA) systems were provided. In the first two Kievs, these were complemented by the short-range SA-N-4 ("Gecko") AA missile, whose launcher retracted down into a small silo. As "last-ditch" defence against incoming anti-ship missiles, each quadrant of the ship was covered by a pair of 30mm/1.18in Gatling-style guns, each group working independently with its own adjacent-director.

Typical of Soviet designs, that of the *Kiev* gave the impression of being over-armed and overcrowded despite her not inconsiderable displacement. Certainly, the flight deck enjoyed limited freeboard and was probably wet by usual standards. Refits saw various baffles and windbreaks being provided to protect one weapon system from the effects of another. Redundancy in radar and director systems also allowed selection to avoid the effects of interaction.

Completed later, and to an improved specification, the *Admiral Gorshkov* (ex-*Baku*) currently awaits transfer to India. The remainder were discarded, the *Minsk* in 1992, *Novorossiysk* in 1993 and *Kiev* in 1994.

ABOVE: **Compared with the *Kiev* opposite, the *Minsk* has had the port sponsons extended and an improved leading edge fitted to the angled deck. The squared-off stem head houses a retractable radar associated with the guidance of the SS-N-12 ("Sandbox") anti-ship missiles.**

ABOVE: **With the superstructure mass to one side and the assorted large weaponry in front, the leading end of the angled deck has suffered problems with turbulence, evidenced by the addition of wind deflector plates and altered configurations. Note what appears to be an adjustable flow plate fitted transversely.**

Kiev class

Class: *Kiev*, Nikolaev South, commissioned May 1975; *Minsk*, Nikolaev South, commissioned February 1978; *Novorossiysk*, Nikolaev South, commissioned September 1982

Displacement: 36,650 tonnes/36,000 tons (standard); 43,250 tonnes/42,500 tons (full load)

Length: 249.5m/818ft (at waterline); 273.5m/896ft 9in (overall)

Beam: 32.7m/107ft 3in

Draught: 8.5m/27ft 10in (standard); 10m/32ft 9in (full load)

Aircraft: 14 or 17 "Hormone" (Ka-25) or "Helix" (Ka-27) helicopter equivalents and 12/13 "Forger" (Yak-38) V/STOL equivalents

Flight deck (irregular): 185 x 20m/606ft 6in x 65ft 7in (flight path)

Armament: 8 x SS-N-12, 2 x SA-N-3, 2 x SA-N-4, 1 x SUW-N-1, 2 x RBU-6000, and 4 x 76mm/3in and 8 x 30mm/1.18in guns

Machinery: Geared steam turbines, 8 boilers, 4 shafts

Power: 149,000kW/200,000shp

Speed: 32 knots

Fuel: 7,640 tonnes/7,500 tons

Range: 24,080km/13,000nm at 18 knots

Armour: Not known

Complement: Not known

Admiral Kuznetsov

Conceived during the Communist era, the *Admiral Kuznetsov* began life as the *Leonid Brezhnev*, then briefly becoming the *Tbilisi*. Although she was completed, her only sister, *Varyag*, was abandoned in 1993 when a reported 70 per cent complete, and acquired by Chinese interests.

Her design stems directly from that of the Kiev class, enlarged and with the major difference that the earlier anti-ship missile container/launchers that demanded the whole foredeck on the Kievs have been replaced by vertical launch silos. This improvement has permitted a through flush deck for the first time in Russian naval practice.

Despite her size and conventional layout, the ship is limited in the size and weight of aircraft embarked through the lack of a catapult. Nonetheless, she operates high-performance fighters; whole loaded take-off is assisted by a prominent forward "ski-jump". For their recovery, the angled deck is equipped with conventional arrester wires.

At a time when Western fleets are moving away from old, Cold War imperatives to equip for more flexible amphibious and littoral warfare, the Russian fleet has not assumed any discernable new role. The *Kuznetsov*, therefore, is still geared to leading a powerful ASW surface group, for which she provides reconnaissance, fighter cover, and long-range, anti-ship missile defence. Half of her aircraft accommodation is devoted to ASW helicopters.

Her current air wing comprises, typically, Su-27 ("Flanker") fleet air defence fighters and Su-25 ("Frogfoot") fighters in their hook-equipped UTG variant. These two-seaters are intended for ground attack. There are nine spots on deck for helicopter operations.

TOP: **Capable of operating in conventional take-off and land (CTOL) as well as V/STOL modes, the *Kuznetsov* was a fully-developed fleet carrier that had been evolved in a very short space of time from the Moskvas.** ABOVE: **Known to NATO as the "Flanker", the Sukhoi Su-27K is also known, somewhat confusingly, as the Su-33. It first operated from the ship in November 1989.**

The *Kuznetsov* has the usual layered armament encountered in Russian ships. The vertical launch silos for the SS-N-19s are beneath the forward flight deck and normally closed-off with flush-fitting covers. With its 483km/300-mile range, the missile requires aerial mid-course correction to position it for its terminal active radar homing phase.

The SA-N-9 missile ranges only to about 97km/60 miles, the ship being dependent for area defence on either her escorts or her aircraft. She has no less than eight point-defence systems, comprising short-range 7km/4.5-mile SAMs in a common mounting with a pair of 30mm/1.18in Gatling-type guns. These are backed by six sextuple 30mm/1.18in mountings, each with its own director.

FAR LEFT: **Besides attack fighters such as Su-27K (Su-33), seen here, and the Su-25 ("Frogfoot"), the *Kuznetsov* carried up to 18 Ka-27 ("Helix") helicopters, of which half a dozen appear here. Of two variants, those embarked were the Ka-27 PL ("Helix-A") ASW and Ka-27 PS ("Helix-D") planeguard/search and rescue.** ABOVE: **Su-27Ks (Su-33s) demonstrating non-catapult-assisted take-off from the *Kuznetsov*. Outer wings, horizontal tail surfaces and tail cone all fold to reduce aircraft size for stowage.**

RIGHT: **A philatelic miniature sheet commemorating 300 years of the Russian Navy, founded by Peter the Great, who had studied as a practical shipwright in Deptford and Zaandam.** BELOW: **Seen still wearing her completion name of *Tbilisi*, the *Kuznetsov* is fitted with a ski-jump bow of almost caricature proportions. She also carries a heavy anti-surface ship punch in the shape of the 12 vertical-launch SS-N-19 ("Shipwreck") missiles.**

The massive island is configured around the many electronics systems and follows closely the design of that of the *Baku*, the much-delayed fourth unit of the Kiev class. Much of its available area is devoted to the location, one per quadrant, of the four large, rectangular planar arrays of the ship's 3-D air search radar.

A full 7-degree angled flight deck is provided, with a pronounced overhang. There are no centreline elevators, both of those fitted being deck-edge units, one forward of, and one abaft, the island. The freeboard appears to be rather low although the ski jump would largely prevent loose water on the forward flight deck. The deep sponsons housing the four SA-N-9 groups look vulnerable to slamming.

In 1988, the Russians laid down the *Ulyanov*, the first of a new class of 75,000-tonne/73,815-ton vessels. She may have been nuclear powered but would certainly have had steam catapults, permitting her to deploy heavier aircraft. She was approaching launching stage when scrapped in about 1993.

Admiral Kuznetsov

Built: Nikolaev South
Commissioned: January 21, 1991
Displacement: 46,750 tonnes/45,900 tons (standard); 59,550 tonnes/58,500 tons (full load)
Length: 280m/918ft (at waterline); 304.5m/998ft 4in (overall)
Beam: 37m/121ft 4in
Draught: 10.5m/34ft 5in (mean)
Aircraft: 60 maximum; usually 18 x Su-27, 4 x Su-25, 15 x Ka-27, 2 x Ka-31
Flight deck: 304.5 x 70m/998ft 4in x 229ft 6in
Armament: 12 x SS-N-19 ("Shipwreck"), 4 x sextuple SA-N-9 ("Gauntlet"), 8 x CADS-N-1 PDMS, 6 x sextuple 30mm/1.18in CIWS, and 2 x RBU-12000 ASW mortars
Power: 150,000kW/200,000shp
Speed: 30 knots
Fuel: Not known
Range: 15,740km/8,500nm at 18 knots
Armour: Not known
Complement: 2,950 men, including aircrew

LEFT: **In her "colonial sloop" capacity, the *Albatross* deployed Supermarine Seagull amphibians. The paired cranes lifted these from below, the single crane locating them, if required, on the centreline catapult.**

Albatross

Built in Australia, the *Albatross* was an aviation ship forward and a colonial sloop aft. Vaguely modelled on the British *Ark Royal* (I) she was given a generous forward freeboard, the high forecastle containing a hangar for up to nine aircraft. These were accessed *Ark Royal* fashion via a hatch served by two cranes. A third crane transferred the aircraft to a centreline catapult.

Her ability to patrol and police large areas caused the Royal Navy to acquire her late in 1938. She spent much of World War II employed in this role in the relatively peaceful Indian Ocean. Post-war, she was sold for commercial use.

Albatross

Built: Cockatoo Docks & Eng. Pty, Ltd, Sydney
Commissioned: January 17, 1929
Displacement: 4,890 tonnes/4,800 tons (standard); 6,210 tonnes/6,100 tons (full load)
Length: 128.7m/422ft (bp); 135.3m/443ft 6in (overall)
Beam: 18.6m/61ft
Draught: 5m/16ft 6in (full load)
Aircraft: Up to 9 floatplanes or amphibians
Flight deck: None
Armament (as built): 4 x 119mm/4.7in (4 single), and 1 x quadruple 2pdr pom-pom guns
Machinery: Geared steam turbines, 4 boilers, 2 shafts
Power: 8,950kW/12,000shp
Speed: 22 knots
Fuel: 1,020 tonnes/1,000 tons
Armour: None
Complement: 370 men

LEFT: **HMS *Vengeance* before transfer to Australia on cold weather trials in the Arctic in 1949.**

Vengeance

Although the Royal Australian Navy had acquired both the *Sydney* (ex-*Terrible*) and *Melbourne* (ex-*Majestic*) from the British, the latter ship remained in European waters for the duration of the Korean War. Hard worked, the *Sydney* required a consort, so the Australians took the *Vengeance* on loan for two and a half years (1953–55). This allowed sea training for aircrew to continue pending the arrival of the *Melbourne*. As the *Vengeance* was never purchased, she received no change of name under Australian colours.

Worked-up again to operational status, she returned briefly to British service before being purchased by the Brazilian Navy as the *Minas Gerais*.

Vengeance

Built: Swan, Hunter, Wallsend
Commissioned: January 15, 1945
Displacement: 13,750 tonnes/13,500 tons (standard); 18,850 tonnes/18,500 tons (full load)
Length: 192.2m/630ft (bp); 211.4m/693ft 7in (overall)
Beam: 24.4m/80ft
Draught: 6.5m/21ft 4in (standard); 7.5/24ft 6in (full load)
Aircraft: 30+
Flight deck: 207.4 x 24.4m/680 x 80ft
Armament: 16 x 40mm/1.57in, and 24 x 2pdr pom-pom guns
Machinery: Geared steam turbines, 4 boilers, 2 shafts
Power: 29,850kW/40,000shp
Speed: 25 knots
Fuel: 3,260 tonnes/3,200 tons
Range: 22,220km/12,000nm at 14 knots
Armour: None
Complement: 1,320 men

ABOVE: **An early picture of *Sydney* at Portsmouth. She retained her tripod mast and plain bridge front but later acquired a light mast by the funnel, supporting the antenna of a homing beacon.**

FAR LEFT: ***La vie quotidienne.*** **Later-model, clipped-wing Fireflies await their turn for catapulting on what looks like a leisurely day's practice flying.**

LEFT: ***Sydney*** **wears her number as a Sea Fury, resplendent in Korean War stripes, awaits take-off. The piston-engined Sea Fury found itself fighting Soviet-built MiGs while supporting Fireflies in ground attack.**

Sydney

The Pacific war of 1942–45 was fought uncomfortably close to Australia, and its being decided principally by carrier-borne air power was not lost on the Royal Australian Navy (RAN), which therefore acquired the *Majestic*-class Light Fleet Carrier *Terrible* in December 1948. Renamed *Sydney*, she arrived in home waters during the following May, about a year before the outbreak of the war in Korea.

The greatest immediate contribution that the Western allies could make to stem the enemy onslaught was through air power and, lacking facilities ashore, this was necessarily carrier-based. Drastic post-World War II reductions in fleet strengths, however, had left few operational Allied warships in the Far East. For its part, the Royal Navy managed to maintain a single light carrier off the Korean west coast and, during 1951, invited the Australians to take a four-month shift.

In severe winter weather, *Sydney* operated her composite air group of two squadrons of Fireflies (two-seat, anti-submarine, reconnaissance and strike aircraft) and one of Hawker Sea Furies (single-seat, fighter-bomber). There was also aboard a lone US Navy helicopter and crew, the first helicopter to work from an Australian ship.

Of 64 days on station, 43 were flown, the *Sydney* chalking up 2,366 sorties for the loss of three pilots and 16 aircraft to enemy action.

In April 1955, shortly before the commissioning of the *Melbourne* into the RAN, the *Sydney* was reduced to training status. By 1962 she was in reserve, but was re-activated as a transport to assist the Australian army's involvement in Malaya. She repeated this service in Vietnam but, at the end of that war, she was sold out and scrapped in 1976, a further example of the longevity of what began as an emergency design.

Sydney

Built: HM Dockyard, Devonport
Commissioned: February 5, 1949
Displacement: 15,375 tonnes/15,100 tons (standard); 19,850 tonnes/19,500 tons (full load)
Length: 192.2m/630ft (bp); 212m/695ft (overall)
Beam: 24.4m/80ft
Draught: 6.6m/21ft 6in (standard); 7.6m/25ft (full load)
Aircraft: About 36
Flight deck: 207.4 x 24.4m/680 x 80ft
Armament: 30 x 40mm/1.57in guns
Machinery: Geared steam turbines, 4 boilers, 2 shafts
Power: 29,850kW/40,000shp
Speed: 25 knots
Fuel: 3,540 tonnes/3,480 tons
Range: Not known
Armour: None
Complement: 1,230 men

ABOVE: **The year of 1977, and *Melbourne*'s men are mustered for a special occasion. Note the American-style "21" identification on the flight deck, forward.** RIGHT: **As with other things naval, the Australians steadily moved away from British-sourced equipment. Following her major 1969 refit, the *Melbourne* emerged with uprated catapult, Philips electronics and an air wing comprising A-4 Skyhawks, S-2 Trackers and Sea King helicopters.**

Melbourne

Of the six incomplete *Majestic*-class Light Fleet Carriers, the name ship had to wait until 1949 before being taken in hand to remodel her as a "jet-capable" carrier. This being a period of significant innovation in carrier technology, the completion process took some six years and several changes of plan, eventually including the major advances of angled deck, steam catapult and mirror landing sight.

Early angled decks such as these were set at a shallow offset of only 5 degrees or so to the centreline, the flight path still involving much of the ship's length and, therefore, deck parking space. One advantage for a small carrier, however, was that it limited the size of the port-side overhand and consequent weight distribution problems.

Jet aircraft had poorer low-speed characteristics than earlier piston-engined machines, their higher landing speed requiring upgrading of the ship's arrester gear. Launch velocities also needed to be higher, demanding the steam catapult.

Rechristened *Melbourne*, the ship was completed in 1955 as the new flagship of the RAN. She was able to deploy the Sea Venom, the first British all-weather jet carrier fighter/strike aircraft. Most of her remaining aircraft were turbo-prop Gannets, reflecting the importance attached to AS operations during the Cold War.

Helicopters were now becoming widely accepted and, during the 1960s, replaced fixed-wing AS aircraft in the *Melbourne*'s air wing. With the increasing "Americanization" of the RAN, however, her flight deck was strengthened during the 1970s and catapult replaced in order to re-equip with A-4 Skyhawk fighters and the 12.2-tonne/27,000lb S-2 Tracker twin-engined AS aircraft. Sea King helicopters were also shipped in numbers proportional to mission.

At the end of the ship's operational life in 1983, the Australian government decided that she would be scrapped without replacement.

ABOVE: **Alterations and additions to the *Melbourne*'s island, particularly the acquisition of a lattice mast, did nothing for the previously classic "Light Fleet" profile.**

Melbourne

Built: Vickers-Armstrong, Barrow
Commissioned: November 8, 1955
Displacement: 16,400 tonnes/16,100 tons (standard); 20,620 tonnes/20,250 tons (full load)
Length: 192.2m/630ft (bp); 214m/701ft 6in (overall)
Beam: 24.4m/80ft
Draught: 8.0m/26ft 3in (full load)
Aircraft: About 24
Flight deck: 210.5 x 32m/690 x 105ft
Armament: 25 x 40mm/1.57in guns
Machinery: Geared steam turbines, 4 boilers, 2 shafts
Power: 29,850kW/40,000shp
Speed: 24 knots
Fuel: 3,050 tonnes/3,000 tons
Range: Not known
Armour: None
Complement: 1,250 men

Warrior

Starting almost from scratch, the Royal Canadian Navy (RCN) evolved, largely by its own magnificent effort, into one of the world's largest fleets between 1939 and 1945. Although remembered largely as a small-ship navy, inseparable from the North Atlantic convoy war, the RCN was already operating modern cruisers by 1945 and, with first-hand experience of the effect of naval air power on the conduct of the Atlantic war, was keen to acquire its own carrier. Its eventual choice, the Royal Navy's *Majestic*-class Light Fleet Carrier *Powerful*, had to be completed to Canadian requirements, and so in the interim the brand-new *Colossus*-class *Warrior* was loaned for training purposes. In this role, she served 1946–48.

TOP AND ABOVE: **Almost certainly taken at the same time, this pair of pictures is particularly interesting in accurately recording the *Warrior*'s unusual counter-shaded camouflage scheme, applied despite her completion early in 1946. Four shades appear to have been used, with near-white around the counter (and even below boats) ranging to darkest grey over normally illuminated surfaces. On this particular day, however, the light has defeated the planned effect.**

ABOVE: **A Fairey Firefly Mk.4 in Royal Canadian Navy (RCN) colours. It probably belongs to No.825 Squadron, which was on detachment to the RCN at this time.**

Warrior

See also *Independencia* (Argentina)
Built: Harland & Wolff, Belfast
Commissioned: January 24, 1946
Displacement: 14,250 tonnes/14,000 tons (standard); 19,950 tonnes/19,600 tons (full load)
Length: 192.2m/630ft (bp); 212m/695ft (overall)
Beam: 24.4m/80ft
Draught: 6.6m/21ft 6in (standard); 7.2m/23ft 6in (full load)
Aircraft: 35
Flight deck: 207.4 x 22.9m/680 x 75ft
Armament: 24 x 2pdr pom-pom guns, and 17 x 40mm/1.57in guns
Machinery: Geared steam turbines, 4 boilers, 2 shafts
Power: 29,850kW/40,000shp
Speed: 25 knots
Fuel: 3,250 tonnes/3,190 tons
Range: 15,740km/8,500nm at 20 knots
Armour: None
Complement: 1,100 men

LEFT: **Only ever serving under Canadian colours, here the *Magnificent* edges into an empty Grand Harbour in Malta. Note how the wings of the lone Sea Fury, right aft, fold upwards, while those of the line of Fireflies fold backwards.**

Magnificent

Loan of the *Warrior* to the Royal Canadian Navy had to terminate in 1948, before the Canadian government finalized the sale of the incomplete *Powerful*. For continuity in training and experience, therefore, a second Light Fleet Carrier, the *Majestic*-class *Magnificent*, was lent from 1948. Because the *Powerful*'s remodelling was to full current standards, it was subject to several changes of design. The process being protracted, it was necessary eventually to extend the loan of the *Magnificent* until 1957. Although the RCN was active during the Korean War, the carrier was not committed. The ship never served in the Royal Navy for, following her return, she remained in reserve until, lacking any foreign buyer, she was scrapped.

Magnificent

Built: Harland & Wolff, Belfast
Commissioned: March 21, 1948
Displacement: 14,760 tonnes/14,500 tons (standard); 19,950 tonnes/19,600 tons (full load)
Length: 192.2m/630ft (bp); 212.8m/698ft (overall)
Beam: 24.4m/80ft
Draught: 6.1m/20ft (standard); 7.2m/23ft 6in (full load)
Aircraft: About 36
Flight deck: 208.9 x 22.9m/685 x 75ft
Armament: 28 x 40mm/1.57in guns
Machinery: Geared steam turbines, 4 boilers, 2 shafts
Power: 29,850kW/40,000shp
Speed: 25 knots
Fuel: 3,510 tonnes/3,450 tons
Range: 17,320km/9,350nm at 12 knots
Armour: None
Complement: 1,170 men

LEFT: **The remodelled *Bonaventure* makes an interesting comparison with the *Magnificent* (above). She was unique in acquiring the faired sponsons, forward and aft on either side, to support her new twin 76mm/3in mountings.**

Bonaventure

Purchased outright by the Canadian government in 1952, the *Majestic*-class Light Fleet carrier *Powerful* then underwent a five-year transformation into the *Bonaventure.* She acquired a strengthened, 8-degree angled deck, upgraded arrester gear and steam catapult to operate American-sourced jet fighters and heavy anti-submarine aircraft. Her armament comprised American 76mm/3in 70s and her enlarged island supported two lattice masts carrying a full range of American radars. Stretched to her limits, she could not efficiently operate later carrier aircraft and, by the early 1960s, had downgraded to a pure anti-submarine carrier, operating only helicopters. With the continued drawdown of the navy due to changing political imperatives, she was discarded shortly after a major refit in 1970 and was not replaced.

Bonaventure

Built: Harland & Wolff, Belfast
Commissioned: January 17, 1957
Length: 192.2m/630ft (bp); 214.9m/704ft 6in (overall)
Beam: 24.4m/80ft
Draught: 7.6m/25ft (full load)
Aircraft: 30+
Flight deck: 208.9 x 34.3m/685 x 112ft 6in
Armament: 8 x 76mm/3in (4 double), later 4 x 76mm/3in guns
Machinery: Geared steam turbines, 4 boilers, 2 shafts
Power: 29,850kW/40,000shp
Speed: 24.5 knots
Fuel: 3,150 tonnes/3,100 tons
Range: Not known
Armour: None
Complement: 1,200 men

Giuseppe Miraglia

During 1924–27, the Spezia yard refashioned the incomplete coastal liner *Cittá di Messina* as the aviation ship *Giuseppe Miraglia*. The Italian Navy's first such, she was built up amidships with hangars before and abaft her superstructure. These were accessed by doors in the transverse screen bulkheads and were served by four folding cranes. Forward and aft were prominent catapults.

Besides undertaking experimental work, the *Miraglia* serviced the catapult flights found aboard all major Italian warships. She served spells as a fleet transport and, towards the end of her life, as a depot ship. The *Miraglia*'s period of greatest utility was in the mid-1930s, during the Italian conquest of Abyssinia (now Ethiopia). She is believed to have been scrapped following World War II.

Giuseppe Miraglia

Built: Not known
Commissioned: 1927
Displacement: 4,970 tonnes/4,880 tons (standard)
Length: 115m/377ft (unspecified)
Beam: 15m/49ft 2in
Draught: 5.2m/17ft (standard)
Aircraft: About 20
Flight deck: None
Armament: 4 x 102mm/4in guns
Machinery: Geared steam turbines, 8 boilers, 2 shafts
Power: 8,950kW/12,000shp
Speed: 21 knots
Fuel: Not known
Range: Not known
Armour: None
Complement: 180 men

LEFT: **Seen from a British battleship, the *Miraglia* is near the end of her career. Her catapults and aircraft derricks have been removed and she is carrying a deck cargo.**

Bolzano, proposed

Torpedoed and fire-damaged, the heavy cruiser *Bolzano* was stripped for conversion to a fast transport for carriage of supplies to North Africa. With all armament except light anti-aircraft weapons removed, her defence lay in a dozen Reggiane fighter aircraft. All top-hamper forward of the after funnel would be razed, the aircraft being parked along the centreline and moved forward sequentially for launch from two catapults set in the bows. There was no means of recovery, aircraft being expected to land ashore. Despite the loss of her forward boiler space, the *Bolzano* would still be capable of 25 knots. The ship was destroyed by "human torpedoes" before completion.

***Bolzano*, proposed**

Built: Ansaldo, Genoa
Commissioned: August 19, 1933
Displacement: 11,250 tonnes/11,050 tons (standard); 14,150 tonnes/13,900 tons (full load)
Length: 194.3m/637ft (bp); 197m/645ft 10in (overall)
Beam: 20.6m/67ft 6in
Draught: 6.1m/20ft (standard)
Aircraft: 12
Flight deck: None
Armament: 10 x 89mm/3.5in, and 20 x 37mm/1.46in guns
Machinery: Geared steam turbines, 8 boilers, 4 shafts
Power: 89,500kW/120,000shp
Speed: 25 knots
Fuel: Not known
Range: Not known
Armour: 70mm/2.7in (vertical belt); 25–50mm/1–2in (protective deck)
Complement: Not known

LEFT: **Stemmed in dry dock, the *Bolzano* is seen shortly before her near-fatal torpedoing. Note the extensions built along either side of the upper deck, probably for minelaying.**

TOP: **Structurally near-complete, but lacking vital equipment including catapults and compatible aircraft, the *Aquila* lies at Genoa in 1943.** ABOVE: **Although guarded by German soldiers following the Italian capitulation of September 1943, the *Aquila* was destroyed by a combination of Allied bombing and sabotage.**

Aquila and *Sparviero*

Allied with Germany, buoyed with confidence, Mussolini announced in 1938 a supplementary naval construction programme to protect Italy's "rights and interests in the Mediterranean". He emphasized the fleet's duties in "maintaining communications with Italy's immense overseas possessions" and winning access to the oceans beyond the "encircled" Mediterranean. Having thus effectively defined the need for a true blue-water navy, the Duce and his naval staff resolutely ignored their planners' advice by excluding aircraft carriers. Given its central geographical location, they repeatedly pointed out, "Italy *was* an aircraft carrier".

Following June 1940, naval action with the Royal Navy adequately demonstrated the folly of reliance on land-based naval air support, yet it still took a further year for the Duce to relent and to authorize conversion of a passenger liner.

During the 1930s wiser heads had tentatively identified the liners *Roma* (32,583 gross registered tons – grt) and *Augustus* (32,650grt) as suitable for this purpose and the former was taken in hand by her original builders during July 1941. The result, renamed *Aquila*, was a stylish vessel with full flight deck and cantilevered, starboard-side island that showed some influence from the designers of the *Graf Zeppelin.* Her appearance was marred somewhat by prominent bulges, added for both stability and protection. Incomplete at the Italian capitulation, the *Aquila* was sabotaged, scuttled, raised and scrapped by 1952.

Renamed *Sparviero*, the diesel-propelled *Augustus* would have received an austere, *Argus*-style conversion, flush-decked with no island. To avoid the necessity of remodelling her rather fine bow sections, the forward 25 per cent of the flight deck was narrowed to a mere take-off platform, supported on an open structure. Work commenced as late as September 1942, however, and never progressed beyond the razing of the original upper decks. Like the *Aquila*, she was scuttled and then scrapped by 1947.

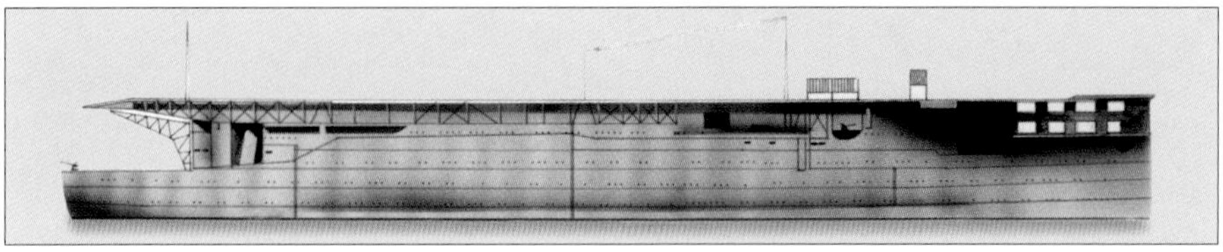

ABOVE: **Reminiscent of that on the *Argus* (I), the conversion of the *Sparviero* would have been in no way as thorough as that of the *Aquila*. The forward section was no more than a flying-off ramp.**

Aquila

Built: Ansaldo, Sestri Ponente
Commissioned: September 21, 1926
Displacement: 23,900 tonnes/23,500 tons (standard); 28,300 tonnes/27,800 tons (full load)
Length: 203.1m/666ft (bp); 231.2m/758ft (overall)
Beam: 29.5m/96ft 9in
Draught: 7.3m/24ft (standard)
Aircraft: About 36
Flight deck: 213.5 x 25m/700 x 82ft
Armament: 8 x 135mm/5.3in, and 12 x 65mm/2.6in guns
Machinery: Geared steam turbines, 8 boilers, 4 shafts
Power: 29,800kW/40,000shp
Speed: 20 knots
Fuel: 2,800 tonnes/2,750 tons
Range: 7,410km/4,000nm at 18 knots
Armour: 80mm/3.15in patches over magazines etc
Complement: About 1,500 men

LEFT: **Handsome ships, and useful in their day, the two Dorias were made obsolete by advances in helicopter and missile technology.**

Andrea Doria (I) class

Contemporary with the French *Jeanne d'Arc* and the Soviet Russian Moskvas, the Andrea Dorias reflected the powerful anti-submarine bias of Cold War warship design in the marriage of a cruiser-style forward end to an after end dedicated to helicopter aviation. The small helicopter of the day, the Agusta AB-212, was limited in capacity, and the fuel, data links, sonars and weaponry necessary to conduct a protracted submarine hunt were best shared between a flight of two aircraft with one stand-by. Accommodation for these and the bulky early guidance, storage and launch systems for the Standard SM-1 area defence SAM drove the ships' design parameters. Both ships were discarded in 1991–92 as their systems became obsolete.

Andrea Doria (I) class

Class: *Andrea Doria* (I), (C553), Tirreno, Riva Trigoso, commissioned February 23, 1964; *Caio Duilio* (C554), Navalmeccanica, Castellammare, commissioned November 30, 1964
Displacement: 6,620 tonnes/6,500 tons (standard); 7,430 tonnes/7,300 tons (full load)
Length: 144m/472ft 2in (bp); 149.3m/489ft 6in (overall)
Beam: 17.3m/56ft 9in
Draught: 5m/16ft 5in (standard); 7.5m/24ft 7in (full load)
Aircraft: 2/3 Augusta AB-212 ASW helicopters
Flight deck: 30 x 16m/98ft 4in x 52ft 6in
Armament: 1 x Standard SM-1 SAM system, 8 x 76mm/3in guns, 6 x ASW TT
Machinery: Geared steam turbine, 4 boilers, 2 shafts
Power: 44,750kW/60,000shp
Speed: 30 knots
Fuel: 1,120 tonnes/1,100 tons
Range: 11,110km/6,000nm at 15 knots
Armour: None
Complement: 480 men

LEFT: **With her odd mast/funnel combinations and unusual break in the sheerline the *Veneto* was something of an ugly duckling.**

Vittorio Veneto

Carrying twice the number of helicopters, the *Vittorio Veneto* (C550) derives directly from the preceding Andrea Dorias. Having under-deck (as opposed to superstructure) hangaring, her after end has its freeboard raised by one deck. Fitted to coordinate a major submarine hunt, the ship can participate with AS torpedoes deployed either by ASROC launcher, or directly by torpedo tube. The ASROC launcher also handles Standard SM-1 SAM missiles. In the waist are four canister-launchers for Otomat SSMs. Space has also been found for no less than 14 single gun mountings. Space is saved by combining funnels and masts. She is to be retired in 2007.

Vittorio Veneto

Built: Navalmeccanica, Castellammare
Commissioned: April 30, 1969
Displacement: 8,300 tonnes/8,150 tons (standard); 9,620 tonnes/9,450 tons (full load)
Length: 170m/557ft 4in (bp); 179,6m/588ft 10in (overall)
Beam: 19.4m/63ft 7in
Draught: 5.5m/18ft (standard); 7.8m/25ft 7in (full load)
Aircraft: 6 Augusta AB-212 ASW helicopters
Flight deck: 40 x 18.5m/131ft 2in x 60ft 9in
Armament: 1 x Standard SM-1/ASROC launcher, 4 x Otomat SSM launchers, 8 x 76mm/3in and 6 x 40mm/1.57in guns
Machinery: Geared steam turbines, 4 boilers, 2 shafts
Power: 54,450kW/73,000shp
Speed: 31 knots
Fuel: 1,270 tonnes/1,250 tons
Range: 11,110km/6,000nm at 20 knots
Armour: None
Complement: 550 men

LEFT: **In what is probably a trials picture, the *Garibaldi* still lacks her missiles and much of her electronics. The overall effect of her appearance is pleasingly "clean-cut".**

Giuseppe Garibaldi

Designed primarily as an anti-submarine helicopter carrier, this very neat vessel can equally well deploy V/STOL aircraft. She is Italy's first through-deck carrier. Her flight deck is served by two elevators and, forward, has pronounced sheer as opposed to a "ski-jump". For her AS role she mounts a large low/medium-frequency sonar in a bulbous bow, but also has four canister-launched Otomat SSMs located on the quarters. At either end of the monolithic superstructure are octal launchers for Aspide/Sea Sparrow SAM missiles. The *Garibaldi*'s funding was facilitated by giving her a disaster-relief capability.

Giuseppe Garibaldi

Built: Italcantieri, Monfalcone
Commissioned: September 30, 1985
Displacement: 9,570 tonnes/9,400 tons (standard); 13,440 tonnes/13,200 tons (full load)
Length: 162,8m/533ft 9in (bp); 180.2m/590ft 10in (overall)
Beam: 23.7m/77ft 9in
Draught: 6.7m/21ft 11in (full load)
Aircraft: Up to 12 (Sea King or Sea Harrier equivalents)
Flight deck: 173.8 x 30.4m/569ft 10in x 99ft 9in
Armament: 4 x Otomat SSM launchers, 2 x Octal Aspide SAM launchers, 6 x 40mm/1.57in guns, and 6 x ASW TT
Machinery: 4 gas turbines (LM 2500), 2 shafts
Power: 59,700kW/80,000shp
Speed: 30 knots
Fuel: Not known
Range: 12,960km/7,000nm at 20 knots
Armour: None
Complement: 575 men

Andrea Doria (II)

The new carrier *Andrea Doria* (II) is intended to replace the *Vittorio Veneto* in 2007. Designed only for V/STOL and helicopter operation, she has a non-angled flight deck, no catapult or arrester gear. Two elevators are provided, one of them a starboard-side, deck-edge unit. Port-side, forward there is a "ski-jump".

Fitted to act as a command ship, the *Doria* can also assist in amphibious assault. On-board equipment includes four landing craft, two cranes, three lifts, and two roll-on, roll-off ramps. In this mode, aircraft would be carried only in deck parks. Future air wings will comprise the JSF (after 2012) and EH-101 helicopters.

Andrea Doria (II)

Built: Fincantieri, Riva Trigoso
Commissioning: 2007
Displacement: 27,000 tonnes/26,500 tons (full load)
Length: 215.8m/707ft 3in (at waterline); 234.5m/769ft (overall)
Beam: 29.5m/96ft 10in
Draught: 7.5m/24ft 8in (full load)
Aircraft: 8 Sea Harrier/JSF and 12 Sea King/ EH-101 equivalents
Flight deck: 184 x 34m/603ft 3in x 111ft 6in
Armament: 4 x 8-cell vertical-launch systems for Aster 15 SAM, 2 x CIWS
Machinery: 4 x LM 2500 gas turbines, 2 shafts
Power: 88,000kW/118,000shp
Speed: 30 knots
Fuel: Not known
Range: 12,960km /7,000nm at 16 knots
Armour: Not known
Complement: 700 men as a private ship

LEFT: **Three times the displacement of the *Garibaldi*, the new *Doria* (which may yet be named *Conte di Cavour*) will be a fleet carrier of a size well suited to Mediterranean operation.**

Seaplane carriers, mercantile

During World War I, the German High Seas Fleet (HSF) observed an overall policy different to that of the British Grand Fleet. The anticipated decisive arena was the North Sea and as the HSF was numerically the inferior force, its intentions were to let the British take the offensive, while stimulating the occasional set-piece action where a British formation might be caught at a disadvantage. There was, however, a secondary theatre of operations in the Baltic, where the German Navy worked offensively against a somewhat passive Russian fleet.

Possessing only one Zeppelin airship in 1914 and recognizing that land-based aircraft could as yet patrol only a limited distance offshore, the navy chartered commercial tonnage for the deployment of seaplanes. This policy owed nothing to British initiatives, being undertaken completely in parallel and embracing an entirely different approach.

The British took up small, speedy vessels that, initially only primitively converted, worked directly with sections of the battle fleet. Only with time did the conversions become more sophisticated. In contrast, the Germans viewed aerial reconnaissance either as a routine measure or as a service to be undertaken ahead of a fleet operation. The choice of chartered ships reflected this. Not expected to cruise with the fleet, they were standard cargo carriers of anything between 2,500 and 7,500 gross registered tons (grt), and none with a speed exceeding 11 knots.

ABOVE: **Conversion of the *Santa Elena* involved the erection of steel-framed canvas hangars over No.2 and No.3 hatches, the relocation of cargo derricks for seaplane handling and the addition of powerful searchlights, sited on mast tables.**

Conversion of each was similar with large, canvas-covered, steel-framed hangars erected in way of existing hatch areas, usually in well decks. Cargo derricks were re-sited as required to handle up to six aircraft and large searchlights mounted on prominent mast platforms.

The Grand Fleet noted very little evidence of these ships but they were both active and aggressive in the Baltic.

ABOVE: **The *Answald* was a five-hatch ship with temporary hangars erected over Nos. 2 and 5. The sail effect of these considerable erections made her difficult to manage in a breeze.**

Santa Elena

Built: Blohm & Voss, Hamburg
Owner: Hamburg-Süd
Completed: 1907
Registered tonnage: 7,415grt; 4,732 net
Length: 131.4m/430ft 10in (overall)
Beam: 16.7m/54ft 9in
Draught: Not known
Aircraft: Hangar space for 6 floatplanes
Flight deck: None
Armament: 2 x 88mm/3.46in guns
Machinery: 1 set quadruple expansion steam engines, 3 boilers, 1 shaft
Power: 2,250kW/3,000ihp
Speed: 11 knots
Fuel: Not known
Range: Not known
Armour: None
Complement: 120 men

LEFT: **Considered obsolescent by the end of World War I, two surviving ships of the Stettin class were earmarked for conversion in 1918 to seaplane carriers. Only the *Stuttgart* was so converted, with temporary hangar and handling derrick. She could also double as a minelayer.**

Seaplane carriers, warship

German minelaying and minesweeping operations in the strategically important Heligoland Bight were constantly threatened by British incursions. To assist in giving advance warning, the German Navy decided to convert a pair of older light cruisers as seaplane carriers, specifically to accompany light forces in the Bight. In spring 1918, the *Stuttgart* had her mainmast moved further aft and the space between it and the aftermost funnel cleared for the installation of a steel-and-canvas hangar to accommodate two seaplanes. A third aircraft, with handling derrick, was located on the afterdeck. In compensation, armament was substantially reduced. The second ship, *Stettin*, was never modified.

Stuttgart

Built: Danzig Naval Dockyard
Commissioned: February 1, 1908
Displacement: 3,530 tonnes/3,470 tons (standard); 4,070 tonnes/4,000 tons (full load)
Length: 116.8m/383ft (at waterline); 117.4m/384ft 11in (overall)
Beam: 13.3m/43ft 8in
Draught: 5.4m/17ft 9in (full load)
Aircraft: 3
Flight deck: None
Armament: 4 x 105mm/4.13in, and 2 x 88mm/3.46in guns
Machinery: 2 sets vertical triple expansion steam engines, 11 boilers, 2 shafts
Power: 10,370kW/13,900ihp
Speed: 24 knots
Fuel: 410 tonnes/400 tons (coal)
Range: 7,590km/4,100nm at 12 knots
Armour: 50mm/2in (protective deck)
Complement: 350 men

Auxiliary carriers (World War I), proposed

Intelligence of British progress on the through-deck carrier *Argus* stimulated the German Navy to propose similar conversions. Hulls considered were those of Norddeutscher Lloyd's (NDL) *Bremen* (1897, 11,570 gross registered tons – grt), the *Konigin Luise* (1896, 10,711grt), and the *Ausonia* (11,300 grt) which, like the *Argus*, was still in build for an Italian company.

Sketch plans for the *Ausonia* indicated a starboard-side funnel and island and a landing deck occupying two-thirds the length of the ship. The hangar below opened directly on to a forecastle take-off platform. Below the hangar was indicated accommodation for seaplanes, handled aft by two derricks.

Had the *Ausonia* conversion ever been implemented, her long landing deck and funnel/bridge, starboard-side island layout would have worked well and pre-empted the island superstructure on the British *Hermes* and Japanese *Hosho.*

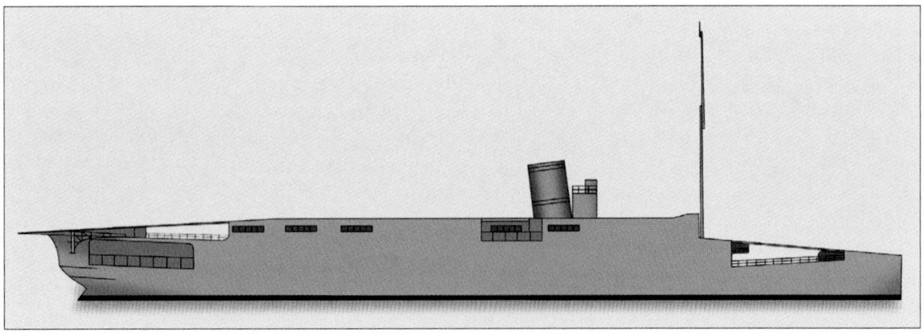

Ausonia, proposed

Built: Blohm & Voss, Hamburg
Launched: April 15, 1915
Displacement: 12,800 tonnes/12,580 tons (standard)
Length: 149.6m/490ft 6in (bp); 158m/518ft (overall)
Beam: 18.8m/61ft 8in
Draught: 7.4m/24ft 3in (standard)
Aircraft: 13+
Flight deck: 121 x 17.3m/396ft 9in x 56ft 9in (landing, approximately); 37 x 9.3m/121ft 3in x 30ft 6in (take-off, approximately)
Armament: Not indicated
Machinery: Geared steam turbines, 2 shafts
Power: 11,950kW/16,000shp
Speed: 20.5 knots
Fuel: 1,530 tonnes/1,500 tons (coal)
Range: Not known
Armour: None
Complement: Not known

LEFT: **With her minimal remaining superstructure the *Ausonia* as converted would have had a perfectly usable flying-on deck.**

ABOVE: **Following her launch in December 1938, Germany's first aircraft carrier, *Graf Zeppelin*, is ready for transfer to her fitting-out berth.**

BELOW: **To assist in achieving her relatively high maximum speed, the *Graf Zeppelin* was fitted with a bulbous bow. Note the overhang of the short flight deck and the carefully profiled embrasures for the casemates of two of the ship's 15cm/5.9in guns.**

Graf Zeppelin

Operating as part of a commerce-raiding group, a German carrier could have provided the means to both find and attack convoys, while being able to defend her own force against enemy air attack. Under the terms of the 1935 Anglo-German Naval agreement, the German Navy was allowed about 42,672 tonnes/42,000 tons carrier tonnage, and two ships, each of a nominal 20,320 tonnes/20,000 tons, were authorized.

German lack of experience in carrier design was now evident, as requirement for high speed, good protection *and* a heavy armament progressively escalated design parameters to levels comparable with those of an American Essex.

High speed and good sea keeping demanded a long hull with generous freeboard. An air group of reasonable size required double hangars, resulting in a high flight deck. The flight deck was heavy, being lightly armoured and serving as the strength deck, resulting in the hull needing to be compensated with bulges to ensure adequate stability.

Horizontal protection comprised an armoured flight deck and protective deck, while a vertical belt was proof against cruiser gunfire. Three major calibres of defensive armament were provided. Fitted with three elevators and two catapults, the flight deck terminated a little short of the bows, for, at one stage, aircraft were to have been able to take off directly from the upper hangar and over the forecastle.

The lead ship, *Graf Zeppelin*, was launched in 1938; however, the project was bedevilled by design problems, particularly with catapults and aircraft, the latter not assisted by a Luftwaffe high command antagonistic attitude toward aircraft being operated under naval control.

Further problems arose through constant changes in naval construction priorities. Progress on the carriers was thus spasmodic. The second hull was never launched while the *Graf Zeppelin* was shunted between ports. Incomplete still in 1945, she was captured by the Russians. Also unable to complete her, they scrapped her in about 1949.

ABOVE: **A probably unofficial shoulder patch for a ship that never even came within a year of completion.** BELOW: **The design displacement of the *Graf Zeppelin* conformed initially to international agreement but, in the course of construction, increased by a factor of nearly 50 per cent.**

Graf Zeppelin

Built: Deutsche Werke, Kiel
Launched: December 8, 1938
Displacement: 23,620 tonnes/23,200 tons (standard); 28,600 tonnes/28,100 tons (full load)
Length: 250m/819ft 9in (at waterline); 262.5m/860ft 8in (overall)
Beam: 31.5m/103ft 3in
Draught: 6.4m/21ft (standard); 7.4m/24ft 3in (full load)
Aircraft: 42 (12/30 dive-bombers and 30/12 fighters)
Flight deck: 240 x 27m/786ft 10in x 88ft 6in
Armament: 8 x 15cm/5.9in, 10 x 10.5cm/4.13in, and 22 x 8.8cm/3.46in guns
Machinery: Geared steam turbines, 16 boilers, 4 shafts
Power: 149,200kW/200,000shp
Speed: 33.5 knots
Fuel: 6,860 tonnes/6,740 tons
Range: 14,750km/8,000nm at 19 knots
Armour: 20–45mm/0.8–1.8in (flight deck); 60mm/2.4 in (protective deck); 100mm/3.9in (vertical belt)
Complement: About 1,750 men plus aircrew

LEFT: **On paper, the reconstruction of the express liner *Europa* should have resulted in a formidable carrier. In practice, however, the structural, engineering and stability problems combined to make the project non-viable.**
BELOW LEFT: **Code-named "Elbe" (not her final planned name), the NDL liner *Potsdam*'s conversion was possible only by building on to both sides of the hull over 60 per cent of its length.**

Auxiliary carriers (World War II), proposed

Having failed to produce a useful auxiliary aircraft carrier during World War I, the Germany Navy did no better the second time around. As progress on the fleet's first regular carrier was only intermittent, with technical difficulties besetting both ship and her intended aircraft, it is difficult to provide a rationale for the later (1942) proposals to convert a number of passenger liners and warships to auxiliary carriers, which presumably would have encountered the same problems.

Three Norddeutscher Lloyd passenger liners were selected, the late Blue Riband holder *Europa* (49,746 gross registered tons – grt), the *Gneisenau* (18,160grt) and the *Potsdam* (17,528grt). In addition was the German heavy cruiser *Seydlitz* and the captured French cruiser *de Grasse*. Conversion of the latter ships should have resulted in carriers equivalent to American *Independence*-class CVLs.

The *Gneisenau* and *Potsdam* as auxiliary carriers would have been larger than any beyond a few Japanese conversions but would, themselves, have been dwarfed by the rebuilt *Europa*. Razed to her upper deck, she would have received a near full-length flight deck, overhanging at its after end. The comparatively large island superstructure proved impossible to balance within the narrow-gutted hull of the express liner, a problem not fully resolved by comprehensive bulging. To fashion a hangar also meant cutting deeply through the passenger decks, including the strength deck, necessitating complex structural compensation. Beyond the stripping of passenger fittings, none of the liners were rebuilt.

Very nearly complete, the cruiser *Seydlitz* had, in contrast, most of her superstructure removed before the project was abandoned in 1943. The *de Grasse* lay at Lorient, where priority for labour and materials was always directed at the U-boat facility. The hull of the *Seydlitz* was eventually scuttled, whereas the *de Grasse* survived to be completed for the post-war French Navy.

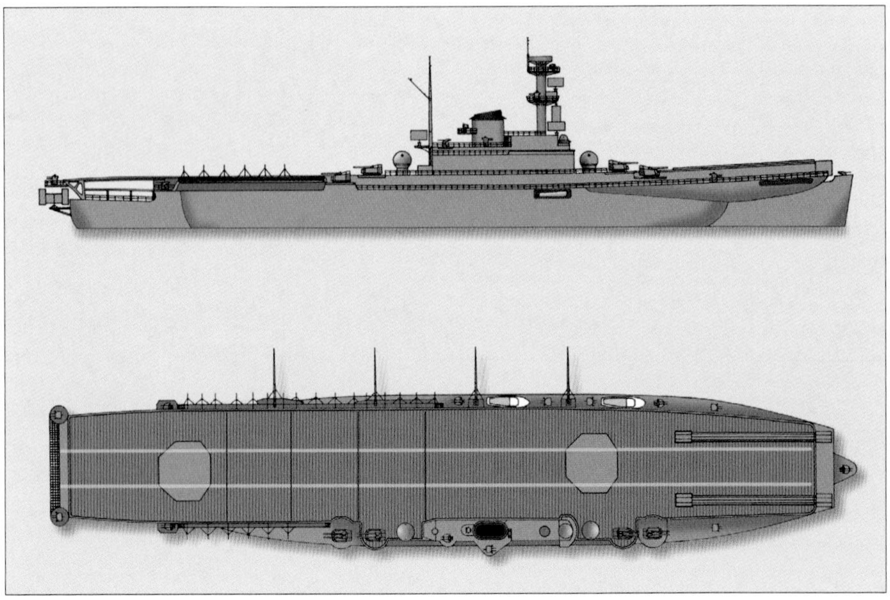

Europa, proposed

Built: Blohm & Voss, Hamburg
Completed: March 19, 1930
Displacement: 44,800 tonnes/44,000 tons (standard); 57,520 tonnes/56,500 tons (full load)
Length: 280m/918ft (at waterline); 291.5m/955ft 9in (overall)
Beam: 37m/121ft 4in
Draught: 8.5m/27ft 10in (standard); 10.3m/33ft 9in (full load)
Aircraft: About 42 (18–20 dive-bombers, 20–24 fighters)
Flight deck: 276 x 30m/904ft 10in x 98ft 4in
Armament: 12 x 10.5cm/4.13in, and 20 x 37mm/1.46in guns
Machinery: Geared steam turbines, 24 boilers, 4 shafts
Power: 74,600kW/100,000shp
Speed: 26.5 knots
Fuel: 8,650 tonnes/8,500 tons
Range: 18,520km/10,000nm at 19 knots
Armour: None
Complement: Not known

LEFT: **Having served the British and Canadian navies for some 12 years already, the *Independencia* was well up to date when acquired by Argentina in 1958. Her disposal in 1971 terminated a life short by the standards of the *25 de Mayo* (below).**

Independencia

Built as the British Light Fleet Carrier HMS *Warrior*, the *Independencia* served in the Royal Canadian Navy during 1946–48. Following her return to the Royal Navy she was twice upgraded receiving, besides new electronics and bridgework, an interim angled deck, improved arrester gear, a more powerful catapult and a flight deck strengthened for 9.1-tonne/20,000lb aircraft.

Before this, the *Warrior* had been used in unsuccessful experiments to operate jet aircraft on skids rather than conventional wheeled undercarriages. For these, the forward end of the flight deck was covered in rubber sheeting supported by airbags.

Sold to Argentina, she operated piston-engined aircraft until her disposal in 1971.

Independencia

Built: Harland & Wolff, Belfast
Commissioned: January 14, 1946
Displacement: 14,250 tonnes/14,000 tons (standard); 19,950 tonnes/19,600 tons (full load)
Length: 192.2m/630ft(bp); 212m/695ft (overall)
Beam: 24.4m/80ft
Draught: 6.6m/21ft 6in (standard); 7.2m/23ft 6in (full load)
Aircraft: 20–30, depending upon type
Flight deck: 207.4 x 22.9m/680 x 75ft
Armament: 24 x 40mm/1.57in (1 quadruple, 10 double) guns
Machinery: Geared steam turbines, 4 boilers, 2 shafts
Power: 29,850kW/40,000shp
Speed: 25 knots
Fuel: 3,250 tonnes/3,190 tons
Range: 15,650km/8,500nm at 20 knots
Armour: None
Complement: 1,075 men

Veinticinco de Mayo (25 de Mayo)

Like the *Independencia*, the *25 de Mayo* is an ex-British *Colossus*-class Light Fleet Carrier. Completed as the *Venerable,* she was sold to the Netherlands in 1948. Modernized during 1955–58, she gained an angled deck and a distinctive new superstructure with extensive electronics suite. Badly damaged by fire in 1968, she was rebuilt with components cannibalized from British reserve carriers and sold on to Argentina. Considerable sums were then devoted to updating her data and information systems and in increasing her flight deck area. The intention was to operate French-built Super Etendards but this proving impracticable, A-4Q Skyhawks were substituted. Mechanically worn out, she was not fully operational after 1985, but was not deleted until 1997.

ABOVE: **The existence of the *25 de Mayo* was prolonged beyond her useful life. The Argentinian Navy was greatly disappointed that the ship's limitations did not permit the effective operation of its Super Etendard fighter-bombers.**

Veinticinco de Mayo

Built: Cammell Laird, Birkenhead
Commissioned: January 17, 1945
Displacement: 14,250 tonnes/14,000 tons (standard); 19,950 tonnes/19,600 tons (full load)
Length: 192.2m/630ft (bp); 211.4m/693ft 2in (overall)
Beam: 24.4m/80ft
Draught: 6.5m/21ft 4in (standard); 7.5m/24ft 6in (full load)
Aircraft: 22–34, depending upon type
Flight deck: 208.9 x 32m/685 x 105ft
Armament: 12 x 40mm/1.57in (12 single) guns
Machinery: Geared steam turbines, 4 boilers, 2 shafts
Power: 29,850kW/40,000shp
Speed: 25 knots
Fuel: 3,260 tonnes/3,200 tons
Range: 22,220km/12,000nm at 14 knots
Armour: None
Complement: 1,400 men

Vikrant

Launched in1945 as HMS *Hercules*, the *Vikrant* was a *Majestic*-class Light Fleet Carrier.

Incomplete, she was purchased by the Indian government in 1957 and finished with angled deck, steam catapult, and air conditioning. Her original air wing comprised Sea Hawk ground-attack jet fighters and Breguet Alize ASW aircraft, used to effect in the short war against Pakistan.

ABOVE: **With a career of 35 years, the *Vikrant* demonstrated the extraordinary longevity of the ex-British Light Fleet carrier. For the Indian Navy charged with oceanic operations, she proved the necessity of naval aviation, her Seahawks being invaluable during the dispute with Pakistan.**

During the 1980s, she was updated in electronics and armament, and her facilities were reorganized for the Sea Harrier V/STOL. These operated alongside an ASW component of Sea King helicopters, whose overall height prevented their being struck below.

Vikrant

Built: Vickers-Armstrong, Newcastle
Commissioned: March 4, 1961
Displacement: 16,000 tonnes/15,700 tons (standard); 19,850 tonnes/19,500 tons (full load)
Beam: 24.4m/80ft
Draught: 7.2m/23ft 7in (full load)
Aircraft: About 20
Flight deck: 207 4 x 32m/680 x 105ft
Armament: 15 x 40mm/1.57in guns
Machinery: Geared steam turbines, 4 boilers, 2 shafts
Power: 29,850kW/40,000shp
Speed: 24 knots
Fuel: 3,200 tonnes/3,150 tons
Range: 22,220km/12,000nm at 14 knots
Armour: None
Complement: 1,300 men

She finished her career as an all-V/STOL attack carrier, being discarded in 1996, having been fitted with a "ski-jump".

Viraat

As fourth and much–delayed unit of the British Centaur class, the *Hermes* (III) was greatly modified in the course of her career. First completed in 1959 she was converted from 1971 to a commando carrier, operating helicopters and stowing four assault landing craft under davits (a facility that she retains). Five years later she was modified to an ASW carrier, deploying mainly Sea Kings. In 1980–81, in a further role change, she received a ski-jump forward and new facilities to operate V/STOL aircraft. These modifications were timely, permitting the ship to play a prominent role in the recovery of the Falklands in 1982.

Paid off in 1984, she was purchased by India in 1986 and, little changed beyond updated major electronics, continued to operate Sea Harrier and Sea King squadrons.

Viraat

Built: Vickers-Armstrong, Barrow
Commissioned: November 18, 1959
Displacement: 24,282 tonnes/23,900 tons (standard); 29,220 tonnes/28,700 tons (full load)
Length: 198.1m/650ft 3in (bp); 226.9m/744ft 7in (overall)
Beam: 27.4m/90ft
Draught: 8.80m/28ft 10in
Aircraft: Up to 30; usually 6 V/STOL and 9 helicopters
Flight deck: 226.9 x 48.8m/744ft 7in x 160ft 2in
Armament: 2 Sea Cat quadruple short range SAM launchers
Machinery: Geared steam turbines, 4 boilers, 2 shafts
Power: 56,700kW/76,000shp
Speed: 28 knots
Fuel: 4,275 tonnes/4,200 tons
Range: 10,400km/5,610nm at 14 knots
Armour: None
Complement: 1,170 men

LEFT: **Wearing the dark grey of the Indian Navy, the *Viraat* gives the impression of being larger than her 24,282 tonnes/23,900 tons. She was the only Royal Navy carrier to retain a deck-edge elevator, here seen in the raised position. Note the completely revised range of electronics. As the Royal Navy's last operational fixed-wing carrier, she was heavily used, not least during the Falklands War. Her hull and machinery are now over 60 years old and must have only limited remaining life.**

LEFT: **As built, the *Gorshkov* shipped an advanced and very comprehensive electronics suite. If retained by the Indians its maintenance will prove expensive.** BELOW: **Although revised in its layout, the armament of the *Gorshkov* still occupied the complete foredeck. As the Indian Navy's objectives are very different from the Russian Navy's it will probably be removed in its entirety.**

Ex-*Admiral Gorshkov*

Currently due to be transferred to India by 2008 is the Russian carrier *Admiral Gorshkov*. Damaged by fire, the ship requires a four-year refit.

The only survivor of four *Kiev*-class ships, the *Gorshkov* commissioned late in order to incorporate the then new Sky Watch planar radar, whose fixed arrays dictate the size and configuration of a large island superstructure. Whether this and the remainder of the comprehensive "command ship" electronics suite will be transferred with the ship, is, as yet, unknown.

Apparently evolved from the early *Moskva*-class ships in order to utilize the new concept of V/STOL, the Kievs had a through-angled deck that suggested that they could operate conventional fixed-wing aircraft, although they were never fitted with arrester gear or catapults.

The Indian Navy requires carriers, and the 17-year-old *Gorshkov* is young compared with the *Vikrant*, which has seen 45 years of use. To maximize her carrier potential, the service will have little interest in the massive offensive armament of canister-launched SSN-12 SSMs, silo-launched SA-N-9 SAMs and AS rocket launchers that crowd the foredeck. Cleared, they will vacate useful flight deck parking space, space that could be increased by widening the forward flight deck by giving the bow sections greater above-water flare.

Effectiveness of the earlier large force of Helix-A (Ka-27) ASW helicopters was greatly enhanced by a massive low/medium-frequency sonar housed in the ship's bulbous forefoot, and variable-depth sonar deployed aft.

It is reported that the ship's future armament will comprise only six combination gun/close-range missile CIWS mountings.

The Indian Navy has long harboured a desire to build indigenous carriers and has been commissioning foreign design studies. It is likely that orders for one or more of 38,608 tonnes/38,000 tons from home yards will be confirmed in the near future to underline India's status as a major regional power.

ABOVE: **Stripped of its foredeck clutter, the ex-*Gorshkov* could emerge as a very capable carrier, as seen in this impression. The implication here is that the electronics will be retained to allow her to act as a command ship. Compatibility with other units could be a problem.**

Ex-*Admiral Gorshkov*

Built: Nikolaev South
Commissioned: January 11, 1987
Displacement: 38,900 tonnes/38,200 tons (standard); 46,200 tonnes/45,400 tons (full load)
Length: 249.5m/818ft (at waterline); 283.2m/928ft 6in (overall)
Beam: 32.7m/107ft 4in
Draught: 8.5m/27ft 10in (standard); 9.9m/32ft 6in (full load)
Aircraft: About 30 (Sea Harrier equivalents and Sea King equivalents)
Flight deck: 283.2 x 51m/928ft 6in x 167ft 2in
Armament (revised): 6 Kortik/Kashtan CIWS mounts
Machinery: Geared steam turbines, 8 boilers, 4 shafts
Power: 130,500kW/175,000shp
Speed: 32 knots
Fuel: 7,130 tonnes/7,000 tons
Range: 24,080km/13,000nm at 18 knots
Armour: Not known
Complement: About 1,500 men

LEFT: **Postwar operation of an escort carrier was a logical extension of the Royal Netherlands Navy's wartime activities, extending its expertise to the point where a "Light Fleet" could be acquired and competently operated.**

Karel Doorman (I)

Following wartime experience with MAC tankers and the consequent formation of the Fleet Air Arm's 860 (Royal Netherlands) Squadron the Netherlands acquired the British-built escort carrier *Nairana* (II) in 1946. She was renamed after Rear Admiral Karel W.F.M. Doorman who, as Allied Flag Officer at the Battle of the Java Sea (February 1942), went down with his ship. Being of riveted construction, the *Nairana* had been preferred for Arctic service and differed further from American CVEs by having the flight deck as main strength deck. She served the Netherlands Navy until 1948, when she was returned and converted for commercial service.

Karel Doorman (I)

Built: John Brown, Clydebank
Commissioned: September 27, 1943
Displacement: 14,050 tonnes /13,800 tons (standard); 17,400 tonnes/17,100 tons (full load)
Length: 152m/498ft 3in (bp); 161.2m/528ft 6in (overall)
Beam: 20.7m/68ft
Draught: 7.8m/25ft 8in (mean)
Aircraft: 21
Flight deck: 153.1 x 20.1m/502 x 66ft
Machinery: Two 5-cylinder diesel engines, 2 shafts
Power: 8,000kW/10,700bhp
Speed: 16 knots
Fuel: 1,685 tonnes/1,655tons
Range: 24,080km/13,000nm at 15 knots
Armament: 2 x 102mm/4in (1 double), and 16 x 2pdr pom-pom (4 quadruple) guns
Armour: None
Complement: 640 men

Karel Doorman (II)

LEFT: **Acquired from the Royal Navy in 1948, the *Karel Doorman* (II) gave the Dutch 20 years' useful service before suffering serious fire damage. Already obsolescent, she was repaired and sold on to the Argentinian Navy as the *25 de Mayo*.**

As they gained experience with the ex-*Nairana*, the Dutch negotiated the sale of the larger *Venerable* from the Royal Navy. On transfer in 1948 she assumed the same name of *Karel Doorman*. Until 1955 she operated British-sourced, piston-engined aircraft but was then given an extensive three-year modernization. She emerged with an 8-degree angled deck, steam catapults, improved elevators and a mirror landing sight. Her island structure had been completely re-modelled, with a lofty lattice mast, the better to locate a revised electronics outfit, all of domestic origin.

The upgrade permitted the operation of the jet-propelled Hawker Sea Hawk, a ground-attack fighter which remained in Royal Navy front-line service until 1958. These were partnered by the anti-submarine AS.4 variant of the Grumman Avenger. In addition, there was a flight of Sikorsky HSS-1N helicopters, configured for nocturnal ASW operations.

By 1965, with the Cold War emphasizing ASW, the *Doorman* lost her strike and air defence role, carrying only helicopters and the heavy Grumman S-2 Tracker. A single, obsolete carrier, her future was already doubtful when, in 1968, she suffered a serious fire. Still worth refitting, however, she was purchased by Argentina, beginning a new career as the *25 de Mayo*.

Karel Doorman (II)

Built: Cammell Laird, Birkenhead
Commissioned: January 17, 1945
Displacement: 14,250 tonnes/14,000 tons (standard); 19,950 tonnes/19,600 tons (full load)
Length: 192.2m/630ft (bp); 211.4m/693ft 2in (overall)
Beam: 24.4m/80ft
Draught: 6.5m/21ft 4in (standard); 7.5m/24ft 6in (full load)
Aircraft: 24
Flight deck: 208.9 x 32m/685 x 105ft
Armament: 34 x 40mm/1.58in guns
Machinery: Geared steam turbines, 4 boilers, 2 shafts
Power: 29,850kW/40,000shp
Speed: 25 knots
Fuel: 3,260 tonnes/3,200 tons
Range: 22,220km/12,000nm at 14 knots
Armour: None
Complement: 1,320 men

Minas Gerais

Named after one of the 20 Brazilian states, the *Minas Gerais* began life as HMS *Vengeance*, a *Colossus*-class Light Fleet Carrier. Purchased in 1956, she went to Rotterdam for a comprehensive modernization. Upgraded to operate 9,072kg/20,000lb aircraft, she received new elevators, arrester gear and steam catapult. A relatively large, 8.5-degree angled deck was counter-balanced by an access track outside the new island. Replacing the austere good looks of the original structure, this arrangement was topped by a raked funnel casing and a substantial lattice mast. The ship was deleted in 2001, having been replaced by the French carrier *Foch* which was purchased and renamed *Sao Paolo*. At the time of writing, it has been announced that plans are afoot to acquire this last working example of a "Light Fleet" for exhibition in the UK.

TOP: **A huge nation of enormous potential wealth, Brazil needs carriers, or "air-capable" ships, to police her extensive offshore waters.** ABOVE: **Reduced effectively to an ASW carrier, the *Minas Gerais* operated several types of helicopter in a variety of roles. These are two naval SH-3 Sea Kings.**

BELOW: **Plans to acquire A-4 Skyhawk fighter-bombers from the United States came to nought and the ship's usual fixed-wing component was limited to Grumman S-2 Trackers.**

Minas Gerais

Built: Swan Hunter, Wallsend
Commissioned: January 15, 1945
Displacement: 16,200 tonnes/15,900 tons (standard); 20,250 tonnes/19,900 tons (full load)
Length: 192.2m/630ft (bp); 212m/695ft 3in (overall)
Beam: 24.4m/80ft
Draught: 6.6m/21ft 6in (standard); 7.4m/24ft 3in (full load)
Aircraft: 20–30
Flight deck: 207.4 x 32m/680 x 105ft
Armament: 10 x 40mm/1.57in (4 double, 2 single) guns
Machinery: Geared steam turbines, 4 boilers, 2 shafts
Power: 29,850kW/40,000shp
Speed: 24 knots
Fuel: 3,260 tonnes/3,200 tons
Range: 22,220km/12,000nm at 14 knots
Armour: None
Complement: 1,300 men

Dédalo (I)

Converted during 1921–22 from an ex-German merchantman, Spain's first aviation ship, *Dédalo*, was officially classified as an Aviation Transport. She was more than that, however. From centre island aft, she was decked over, creating space for four Italian-built flying boats. These were handled by derricks stepped to a goalpost structure. Below, the previous hold space, now accessed by elevator, housed and supported two kite balloons. Right forward, a single, tall mast acted as a mooring point for either of two especially built, 40m/131ft 2in dirigibles. These could also alight on the cleared forward end. The ship was scrapped in 1940.

BELOW: **Reconstructed from a 20-year-old cargo ship the *Dédalo* was equipped with an afterdeck large enough for four to six flying boats, handled by derricks, and a forward well to accommodate a large kite balloon, which could be moored to the foremast.**

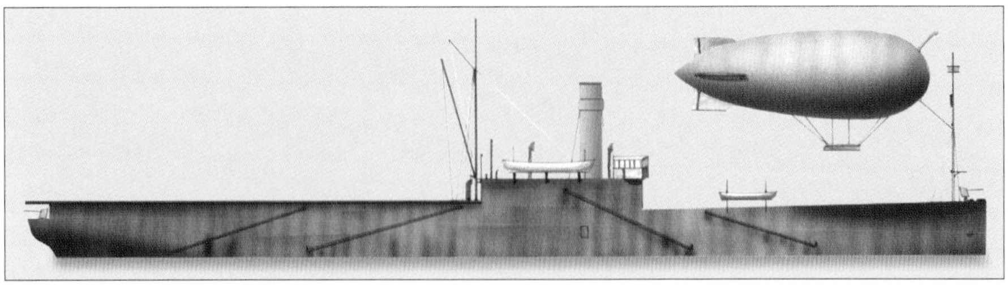

Dédalo (I)

Built: Wigham Richardson, Newcastle
Completed: May 1901
Displacement: 11,000 tonnes/10,800 tons (standard)
Registered tonnage: 5,510grt
Length: 128.1m/420ft (overall)
Beam: 16.8m/55ft 2in
Draught: 6.3m/20ft 6in (mean)
Aircraft: Up to 25 floatplanes, or 7 flying boats plus 1 airship
Flight deck: None
Armament: 2 x 100mm/3.9in, and 2 x 57mm/2.24in guns
Machinery: 1 set quadruple expansion steam, 3 boilers, 1 shaft
Power: 2,390kW/3,200ihp
Speed: 10 knots
Fuel: 920 tonnes/900 tons (coal)
Range: 5,560km/3,000nm at 10 knots
Armour: None
Complement: 400 men

Dédalo (II)

Following a long period in reserve, the *Independence*-class light carrier *Cabot* (CVL-28) was reactivated by the Americans for a five-year loan to the Spanish Navy. Transferred in 1967, and assuming the name *Dédalo*, she was purchased outright in 1973. Reconstruction had left her with only two of her earlier four funnels and, although now with strengthened flight deck, up-rated catapult and classed as an aircraft carrier with a nominal capacity of 20 aircraft, she appears to have operated from the outset as an anti-submarine (ASW) carrier, deploying only helicopters. In preparation for the entry into service of the new *Principe de Asturias,* the *Dédalo* acted as a V/STOL training ship.

She was sold out in 1989, the last example of an effective emergency class.

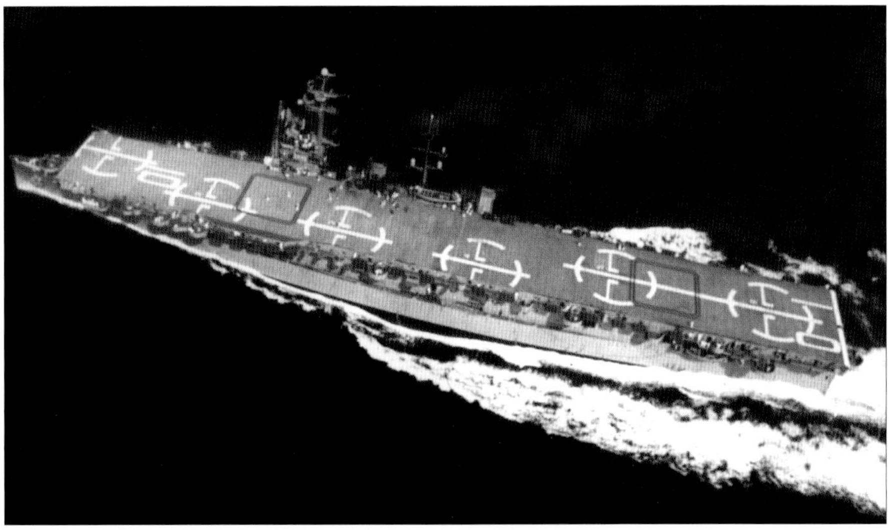

Dédalo (II)

Built: New York Shipbuilding, Camden, N.J.
Commissioned: July 24, 1943
Displacement: 14,750 tonnes/14,500 tons (standard); 16,750 tonnes/16,450 tons (full load)
Length: 183m/600ft (at waterline); 190m/623ft (overall)
Beam: 21.8m/71ft 6in
Draught: 7.9m/26ft (mean)
Aircraft: 7 Harrier V/STOL equivalents plus 16 Sea King helicopter equivalents, or 22 Sea Kings
Flight deck: 166.2 x 32.9m/545 x 108ft
Armament: 26 x 40mm/1.57in guns
Machinery: Geared steam turbines, 4 boilers, 4 shafts
Power: 74,600kW/100,000shp
Speed: 30+ knots
Fuel: 1,830 tonnes/1,800 tons
Range: 13,330km/7,200nm at 15 knots
Armour: 83–127mm/3.25–5in (vertical belt); 50mm/2in (protective deck)
Complement: 1,100 men plus aircrew

LEFT: **Although the US Navy had little use for its *Independence*-class CVLs after 1945, the reactivated *Cabot* (CVL-28), renamed *Dédalo*, gave the Spanish Navy over 20 years' service.**

ABOVE LEFT: **The *Principe de Asturias*' three gas turbines are located in the superstructure, driving electrical generators which power the propulsion motor, connected to a single shaft.** ABOVE: **No angled deck is fitted, but the flight path, as is evident here, is angled from port quarter to centreline. The ship is usually very lightly armed.**

Principe de Asturias

During the early 1970s, the US Navy developed the Sea Control Ship (SCS) as a replacement for escort carriers (CVE). Heading an escort group in the defence of a convoy, the SCS's helicopters would follow up contacts made by the towed sonar arrays of frigates. Her V/STOL fighters would deal with aerial threats, both direct and from horizon-distance "snoopers" charged with the mid-course correction of incoming surface-to-surface missiles (SSM) launched by submarines or by surface ships. For these duties, the air wing comprised 11 anti-submarine (ASW) helicopters, 3 airborne early warning (AEW) helicopters, and 3 V/STOL fighters. In US Navy circles, the SCS's deliberately austere design attracted powerful opposition, which also emphasized its supposed vulnerability to battle damage. It was thus never adopted but the design was purchased by the Spanish Navy as an affordable replacement for the ageing *Dédalo*, somewhat similar in size.

An angled deck is not fitted, but the marked flight path is angled to starboard, extending from the port quarter and culminating in a 12-degree "ski-jump" right forward. A low quarterdeck is linked to the flight deck by elevator and to the hangar via doors. A second elevator is fitted forward of the island. Armament is limited to four 12-barrelled 20mm/0.79in "Meroka" guns, forming the close-in weapon systems (CIWS) for use against anti-ship missiles.

A pair of repair-by-replacement gas turbines generate the power to drive a single shaft, the perceived vulnerability of which is offset by two retractable, self-contained "get-you-home" propulsion units.

The Spanish Navy's remit for the *Principe de Asturias* is far wider than any envisaged for an SCS. Her air group of approximately 20 aircraft will therefore vary considerably in its constitution, dependent upon the ship's current role.

ABOVE: **Known as Matadors in Spanish service, the Harrier IIs were built in the United States by McDonnell Douglas as the EAV-8B. Deliveries began in 1976.**

Principe de Asturias

Built: Bazán, et Ferrol
Commissioned: February 17, 1989
Displacement: 11,700 tonnes/11,500 tons (standard); 16,500 tonnes/16,200 tons (full load)
Length: 187.5m/614ft 9in (bp); 195.1m/639ft 8in (overall)
Beam: 24.4m/80ft
Draught: 6.7m/22ft (full load)
Aircraft: About 20, usually 12/14 ASW/attack helicopters and 6/8 V/STOL fighters
Flight deck: 175.3 x 29m/574ft 9in x 95ft 1in
Armament: 4 x 12-barrelled 20mm/0.79in "Meroka" CIWS guns
Machinery: 2 LM 2500 gas turbines, 1 shaft, plus 2 retractable Pleuger directional thrusters
Power: 34,300kW/46,000hp or, 2 x 600kW/800hp
Speed: 26 knots
Fuel: Not known
Range: 12,000km/6,500nm at 20 knots
Armour: None
Complement: 775 men

Balloon ship

Not noted, in modern times at least, for the size or bellicosity of her navy, Sweden can nonetheless claim to have constructed the first-ever craft redesigned purely for aviation purposes. Inasmuch as it was not self-propelled, it was termed a "barge", although a sophisticated barge. The shallow hull boasted ship-shaped fore-and-after-end, and conventional ground tackle. A long, rectangular central well was surrounded by a very deep (about 4m/ 9ft 10in high) coaming, creating a sheltered box for the inflation of a German-supplied kite balloon.

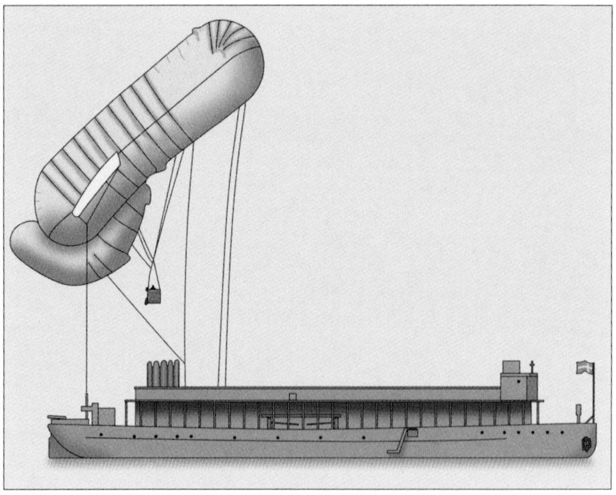

LEFT: **It is not clear why the Swedish Navy chose to design its first balloon vessel without means of propulsion for this limited the utility of an otherwise useful asset.**

Balloon ship

Built: Lindholmens Mek. Verkstad, Göteborg
Commissioned: 1904
Displacement: 224 tonnes/220 tons
Length: 47m/154ft (overall)
Beam: 10m/33ft
Draught: 1.8m/6ft
Aircraft: 1 kite balloon
Flight deck: None
Armament: None
Machinery: Non-propelled
Armour: None
Complement: 25

Accommodation/workshops occupied the hull's wing spaces flanking the central well. Hydrogen generation and compression equipment was powered by petrol-driven generators, as were the lofting winches. Although the craft operated until 1924, its utility must have been very limited by its lack of any means of self-propulsion.

Gotland

Light cruiser forward and aviation ship aft, the Gotland's concept pre-dated those such as the Japanese Ise and Tone classes, and more modern hybrids such as the Moskvas, *Jeanne d'Arc* and *Vittorio Veneto*.

Her six 152mm/6in guns were disposed in twin turrets forward and aft (the latter with restricted arcs) and two singles flanking the bridge structure in the last known use of casemates.

A light spar deck aft was laid with three tracks, bearing eight self-propelled trollies, each of which could support a float plane with wings folded. Three more aircraft could be stowed below. Forward of the tracks was a turntable-mounted, compressed-air catapult which could be aligned with any of the tracks.

Following the transfer of an aircraft, the catapult was trained on the beam for launching. The system was designed around the Hawker Osprey, which aircraft were recovered from the water by a crane located right aft. With the aircraft landed, the tracks could be used to load up to 100 mines, released over the stern.

By 1943, the ship was obsolete and the Swedes (neutral during World War II) removed all aviation-related equipment, converting the Gotland Into an anti-aircraft/training cruiser. Ten years later she received an up-grade, acquiring new secondary and automatic weapons, together with up-to-date control equipment. She finally went for scrap in 1962.

Gotland

Built: AB Götaverken, Göteborg
Commissioned: December 16, 1934
Displacement: 4,850 tonnes/4,750 tons (standard); 5,650 tonnes/5,550 tons (full load)
Length: 130.1m/426ft 6in (at waterline); 133.4m/437ft 6in (overall)
Beam: 15.4m/50ft 7in
Draught: 5.0m/16ft 6in (standard); 5.5m/18ft (full load)
Aircraft: 11 floatplanes
Flight deck: None
Armament: 6 x 152mm/6in, and 4 x 75mm/2.95in guns
Machinery: Geared steam turbines, 4 boilers, 2 shafts
Power: 24,600kW/33,000shp
Speed: 27.5 knots
Fuel: 855 tonnes/840 tons
Range: 7,410km/4,000nm at 12 knots
Armour: 28–50mm/1.1–2in (protective deck); 28–50mm/1.1–2in (turrets)
Complement: 450 men

LEFT: **In pre-helicopter days, a floatplane-carrying light cruiser made sense for the policing of Sweden's long and complex coastline. Observation of strict neutrality during World War II was never an easy task for the Swedish Navy, and the *Gotland*'s aircraft helped cover large areas.**

Chakri Naruebet

Having built the Spanish *Principe de Asturias* to the basic American Sea Control Ship (SCS) design, the Bazán yard went on to produce a diminutive for the Thai Navy. The *Chakri Naruebet* bears a strong family resemblance but is far more simply equipped, mainly on a "for but not with" basis.

As her main task is the patrol of Thailand's considerable coastline, she is fitted with an economical CODOG installation, cruising usually on diesel engines but with the ability to change to gas turbines for high speed.

Six ex-Spanish-built Matador AV-8S V/STOL aircraft have been acquired but the ship usually works only with helicopters.

Her armament is defensive, an America-sourced Mk.41 eight-cell vertical launch system not yet fitted. There are a reported three French Matra Sadral point-defence systems (PDMS) and four Vulcan/Phalanx 20mm/0.79in CIWS. Very much a figurehead for an extensive but small-ship fleet, she still lacks a medium-range surface search radar and proper fire control. Electronic warfare support systems and countermeasures are also lacking, as is a planned hull-mounted sonar. Thailand plans to acquire submarines.

ABOVE: **A smaller version of Spain's *Principe de Asturias*, the *Chakri Naruebet* makes an interesting comparison. Compact and economical, the design would provide a good basis for a conventional trade-protection carrier.**

ABOVE: **Beyond acting as prestige flagship for the Thai Navy and also as royal yacht, it is difficult to envisage any role for the *Chakri Naruebet* that could not better be undertaken by smaller, helicopter-equipped warships. The key probably lay in growing rivalry with other regional fleets, such as those of Malaysia and Indonesia.**

Chakri Naruebet

Built: Bazán, Ferrol
Commissioned: March 27, 1997
Displacement: 11,700 tonnes/11,485 tons (full load)
Length: 164.1m/538ft (at waterline); 182.6m/598ft 8in (overall)
Beam: 22.5m/73ft 9in
Draught: 6.2m/20ft 4in (mean)
Aircraft: Up to 6 x AV-8S Matador V/STOL, 6 x S-70B-7 Seahawk helicopters
Flight deck: 174.6 x 27.5m/572ft 6in x 90ft 2in
Armament: 3 x Matra Sadral PDMS, or 4 x Vulcan/Phalanx CIWS, and 2 x 30mm/1.18in guns
Machinery: 2 x LM 2500 gas turbines or 2 x MTU 16-cylinder diesels, 2 shafts
Power: 33,000kW/44,250hp or 8,800kW/11,800bhp
Speed: 26/16 knots
Fuel: Not known
Range: 18,520km/10,000nm at 12 knots
Armour: None
Complement: 600 men, including aircrew

Glossary

AAM Air-to-Air Missile.

AEW Airborne Early Warning.

AS Anti-Submarine.

ASM Air-to-Surface Missile or Anti-Ship Missile.

ASW Anti-Submarine Warfare.

Accelerator Catapult which accelerates a trolley-mounted aircraft.

Aerostat Tethered, non-navigable lighter-than-air craft, e.g. kite balloon.

Anglo-German Naval Agreement (1935) Agreement for German fleet to be built up to fixed proportion of Royal Navy strength. *Inter alia*, this approved two 22,353-tonne/22,000-ton aircraft carriers for the German Navy.

"Arapaho" Proposed means of deploying V/STOL aircraft from large merchantmen by containerization of all associated services.

Arrester (system) A series of (now) retractable transverse wires, engaged by an aircraft's tailhook to bring it to a halt. Historically also fore-and-aft wires in combination with ramps.

Avgas Aviation fuel.

bhp Brake horsepower. Power actually developed by an engine.

Ballast Additional weight put aboard to improve stability, to correct trim or to modify ship movement.

Barrier Flexible entanglement to make emergency arrest of aircraft that has jumped the arrester wires, with minimum damage to aircraft or pilot.

"Batman" *See* Deck Landing Officer.

Beam Width of hull at the waterline at Standard Displacement.

Belt Heavy vertical side armour designed to defeat low-trajectory gunfire.

"Blimp" Non-rigid dirigible. Small airship primarily for coastal duty.

Blister *See* Bulge.

Bulge Watertight compartment(s) added and faired to mainly underwater section of hull to increase buoyancy or to improve stability.

Bunkers Compartments for stowage of fuel.

C3 (C-3) US Maritime Commission designation for a cargo ship of between 137–152m/450–500ft waterline length and carrying less than 100 passengers.

C-in-C Commander-in-Chief.

CAP Combat Air Patrol. A ship or squadron's organic air cover.

CIWS Close-In Weapon System, e.g. Goalkeeper.

CMB Coastal Motor Boat. The Motor Torpedo Boat (MTB) was a derivative.

CTG Carrier Task Group.

CTOL Conventional Take-Off and Land.

CV Aircraft Carrier.

CVA Attack Aircraft Carrier.

CVE Escort Carrier.

CVL Light Aircraft Carrier.

CVN Nuclear-Propelled Aircraft Carrier.

CVS Anti-Submarine Aircraft Carrier.

Calibre Bore diameter of gun barrel. Also measure of barrel length, e.g. a 3in 70 will be 3 x 70 = 210in in length.

Camber Athwartships curve or rise of a ship's deck.

Cantilever Overhung structure supported at only one side or end.

Casing (funnel) Outer plating surrounding exhaust end of uptake.

Catapult Device to accelerate an aircraft directly.

Deadweight (tonnage) Actual carrying capacity of a cargo ship, expressed in tons of 2,240lb. Abbreviated to dwt.

Deck Landing Officer (or "Batman") Crew man who guides landing aircraft with visual signals. Largely superseded by Mirror Landing Sight.

Derrick Pivoted spar, rigged with winches, for lifting loads.

Dirigible Powered, navigable airship. May be framed (rigid) or unframed (non-rigid).

Displacement, full load or "deep" Weight of ship (in tons of 2,240lb) when fully equipped, stored and fuelled.

Displacement, standard Weight of ship less fuel and other deductions allowed by treaty.

Draught (or Draft) Mean depth of water in which a ship may float freely.

ECM Electronic Countermeasures.

ESM Electronic Support Measures.

Fleet Air Arm (FAA) Air Wing of the Royal Navy.

Fighter Catapult Ship Naval-manned equivalent of Catapult Armed Merchantman (CAM).

Flare Outward curvature of hull plating.

Fleet Train World War II term for Afloat Support. The assembly of auxiliary vessels which keep a fleet supplied and operational.

Floatplane Same as Seaplane. Aircraft supported on water by external floats.

Flying boat Aircraft supported on water by its own hull, and steadied by wingtip floats.

Freeboard For aircraft carriers, the vertical distance from waterline (at standard displacement) to the flight deck.

Gross registered tons (grt) Measure of volumetric capacity of a merchant ship. One gross ton equals 100cu ft (2.83m^3) of reckonable space.

Grand Fleet Title carried by the British battle fleet during World War I.

HAPAG Acronym for Hamburg-America Line.

Heavier-than-air Applied to aircraft supported by lift generated by airflow over horizontal surfaces.

High Sea(s) Fleet Title carried by German battle fleet during World War I.

Horsepower Unit of power equal to 746 watts.

ICBM Intercontinental Ballistic Missile.

ihp Indicated horsepower. Specifically the power delivered by the pistons of a reciprocating steam engine.

JSF Joint Strike Fighter.

Kite balloon Aerostat deployed by ships for observation purposes.

LCA Landing Craft, Assault. 12.5m/41.1ft, 35 troops. Carried under davits.

LCAC Landing Craft, Air Cushion. 26.8m/87.9ft, 61 tonnes/60 tons capacity. Carried in well.

LCT Landing Craft, Tank. 58.5m/192ft, 203 tonnes/200 tons capacity. Sea-going.

LCU Landing Craft, Utility. 41m/134.7ft, 145 tonnes/143 tons capacity. Carried in well.

LCVP Landing Craft, Vehicle, Personnel. 10.9m/35.8ft, 35 troops. Carried under davits.

LHA Amphibious Assault Ship.

LHD Helicopter/Dock Landing Ship.

LPD Amphibious Transport, Dock.

LPH Amphibious Assault Helicopter Carrier.

LSD Dock Landing Ship.

Landplane Aircraft with wheeled undercarriage, as opposed to Seaplane with floats.

Length (bp) Length between perpendiculars. Customarily the distance between forward extremity of waterline at standard displacement and the forward side of rudder post. For American warships, lengths on designed waterline and between perpendiculars are synonymous.

Length (oa) Length overall.

Length (wl) Length, waterline. Waterline length at standard displacement.

Lighter-than-air Applied to aircraft whose lift depends upon the buoyancy of gas.

London Treaty (First of 1929–30 and Second of 1935–36) Treaties seeking to reaffirm but to modify the terms of the Washington Treaty (1921–22).

NATO North Atlantic Treaty Organization.

NDL Norddeutscher Lloyd, Bremen.

PDMS Point Defence Missile System. Short-range missile system, often on common mount with a rapid-fire gun, for "last-ditch" defence.

Pallisade Windbreak erected to screen launch area on early carriers.

Plan "Orange" American war plan for use against Japan.

Protective deck Either flat, or incorporating slopes or pronounced curvature, the protective deck protects spaces beneath from bombs, plunging fire or splinters.

Royal Air Force (RAF) Unified force created in April 1918 through the amalgamation of the RFC and the RNAS.

RFA Royal Fleet Auxiliary. Afloat support ships of the Royal Navy.

RFC Royal Flying Corps. The army's air wing prior to 1918.

RNAS Royal Naval Air Service. The navy's air wing prior to 1918.

SAM Surface-to-Air Missile.

SCS Sea Control Ship.

shp Shaft horsepower. Power at point in shaft ahead of stern gland. Does not include frictional losses in stern gland and A-bracket, if fitted.

SSBN Nuclear-Propelled, Ballistic Missile Submarine.

SSM Surface-to-Surface Missile.

SSN Nuclear-Powered Fleet Submarine.

STOVL Short Take-Off, Vertical Land.

STUFT Ships Taken Up From Trade. Merchant ships chartered for the support of naval requirements.

Seaplane *See* Floatplane.

Sheer Curvature of deckline in fore-and-aft direction, usually upward at either end.

Sided Situated toward sides of ship, usually as opposed to centreline location.

Ski-jump A pronounced upward curvature of forward end of flight deck of a V/STOL carrier. Enhances the effect of short take-off run.

Stability range Total angle through which, from a position of equilibrium, a ship is statically stable.

TF Task Force, e.g. TF38. A group of warships assembled for a specific purpose.

TG Task Group, e.g. TG38.1, TG38.2 etc. The major components of a Task Force.

TU Task Unit, e.g. TU38.1.1, TU38.1.2. The major components of a Task Group.

TSR Torpedo/Spotter/Reconnaissance. Roles for which aircraft such as the Fairey Swordfish were designed.

Trim Amount by which a ship deviates, in the fore-and-aft axis, from her designed draught.

Turbo-electric Propulsion system in which a steam turbine drives an electrical generator. This supplies energy via cable to a propulsion motor coupled to the propeller shaft.

UN United Nations.

Uptake Conduit conducting products of combustion to the funnel.

V/STOL Vertical or Short Take-Off and Land.

Volume critical A ship whose design is driven by needs of space rather than weight, e.g. aircraft carrier.

Warsaw Pact Eastern military bloc, essentially a counter to NATO.

Washington Treaty (c1921–22) Arms limitation agreement that had a profound effect on the development of the aircraft carrier.

Weight critical A ship whose design is driven by considerations of weight rather than space, e.g. a heavily armoured battleship.

Index

Abraham Lincoln CVN-72, 135
Activity, 169
Admiral Gorshkov, 225, 243
Admiral Kuznetsov, 226–7
Admiralty Islands CVE-99, 113
Aerospatiale UH-13 Ecureuils, 75
Africa, 176
Agusta AB-212 helicopter, 235
Aichi
  D1A1 (Type 94), 45
  D1A2 (Type 96) "Susie", 45, 192
  D3A1 (Type 90) "Val", 45, 63, 200
  D4Y3 "Judy", 194
  M6A1 Seiren, 43
Akagi, 59, 190–1, 192–3, 200–1
Akitsu Maru, 211
Akitsu Maru class, 211
Akitsushima, 212
Akron ZRS.4 (airship), 30–1
Albatross, 228
Albion, 76, 178–9
Albion (L14) commando carrier, 90–1, 181, 186
Almirante Cochrane, 154
Almirante Latorre, 154
Alva Bay CVE-103 (AVB-103 Roi), 112, 113
Amagi, 190, 206
Amagi class, 190
Ameer, 171
Ameer class, 171
America CVA-66, 125, 130
Andrea Doria (I) class, 235
Andrea Doria (II), 236
Answald, 237
Antietam CV-36, 71, 73, 117
Anzio CVE-57, 113
Aquila, 199, 234
Arbiter, 171
Archer, 108, 170
Archer class, 170
Argentina Maru, 209
Argus
  (I), 6, 21, 36, 40, 97, 150–1, 152–3, 156–7, 183, 234, 238
  (II), 50, 183
Ark Royal
  (I), 14, 15, 16, 140–1, 228
  (II), 46–7, 51, 158–9, 160–1, 164, 174
  (III), 7, 47, 70, 81, 86–7, 174–5
  (IV), 185
armoured carriers, 160, 178, 202
Armstrong Whitworth (Hawker) Sea Hawk, 76–7, 81, 178,` 242, 244
Arromanches, 74, 76, 217
Aso, 206
Aspide SAM, 236
Atheling, 171
Atlantic Conveyor, 93
Attacker, 170
Attacker class, 109, 170–1
Attamaha CVE-18, 109
Attu CVE-102, 113
Audacious, 175
Audacity, 107, 167, 168, 170, 208
Augustus, 234
Ausonia, 238
Auxillary carriers, 60–1, 167, 168, 238, 240
Avenger, 170
Avenger class, 216
Avro 504, 27

Badoeng Strait CVE-116, 115
Bairoka CVE-115, 115
Baku, 225, 227
Balloon ship, 138, 221, 248
Bapaume, 213
Barnes CVE-20, 109
Basaan Bay CVE-69, 113
Bataan
  CVL-29, 119
  LHD-5, 137
Battler, 170
Bay class, 91
Béarn, 214, 215
Begum, 171
Bell
  AH-1 Sea Cobra, 136
  HTL/HUL, 78
Bellau Wood
  CVL-24, 69, 75, 119, 216
  LHA-3, 87
Ben-my-Chree, 16, 17, 21, 142
Bennington CV-20, 117
Besson MB.411 seaplane, 43
Bismarck Sea CVE-95, 113
Bismarck, sinking of, 36, 44, 50–1
Biter, 170, 216
Blackburn
  Buccaneer, 81, 174, 180
  Firebrand, 62
  Roc, 62
  Shark, 157
  Skua, 44
Block Island
  CVE-106, 115
  CVE-21, 109
Boeing
  Apache, 79, 186
  Chinook, 92–3, 186
  F2B, 44, 97, 99
  F3B, 44
  F4B, 44, 97
  FB-2, 44
  FB-5, 44
Bogue CVE-9, 108–9
Bogue class, 108–9, 110, 112, 170
Bois Belleau (R97), 75, 216
Bolzano, 233
Bon Homme Richard
  CV-31, 117
  LHD-6, 137
Bonaventure, 75, 173, 232
Bougainville CVE-100, 113
Boxer
  CV-21, 72, 85, 90, 117
  LHD-4, 137
Breguet Alizé, 217, 242
Breton CVE-23, 109
Bristol Scout, 18, 142
British airships 30–1
Brocklesby, 143
Bulwark, 76, 178–9
Bulwark (L15) commando carrier, 78, 86, 90, 181, 186
Bunker Hill CV-17, 67, 78, 116–17

Cabot CVL-28, 75, 119, 246
CAM ships, 95, 141, 165
Campania
  (I), 18, 19, 24, 144–5, 146, 150
  (II), 168–9
Canada, 154
Cape Engano, Battle of, 69
Cape Esperance CVE-88, 113
Cape Gloucester CVE-109, 115
Caradoc, 138
Card CVE-11, 109
Carl Vinson CVN-70, 133
Casablanca CVE-55, 60, 113
Casablanca class, 112–13, 114, 171
Caspar-Heinkel U-1 floatplane, 42
Caudron G.III, 15, 23, 213
Cavendish, 148
Centaur, 178–9
Centaur class, 178–9, 181, 206, 242
CH-46 Sea Knight, 90, 132, 136
CH-53 Sea Stallion, 83, 136
Chakri Naruebet, 249
Chambers, Captain Washington Irving, 10, 96
Chance-Vought F4U Corsair, 60, 62, 73, 76, 103, 115, 160, 162
Charger, 108
Charles de Gaulle, 81, 220
Chaser, 60, 170
Chenango CVE, 111
Chitose class, 203, 204
Chitose CVL, 69
Chiyoda, 203, 204
Churchill, Winston, 10, 20, 21, 23, 26–7
Chuyo, 208
City of Oxford, 138
Clemenceau class, 219
Colossus, 74, 217
Colossus class, 74, 172–3, 177, 181, 231, 241, 245
Commandant Teste, 215
Commando Carriers, 77, 90–1, 181, 242
Commencement Bay class, 114–15
Consolidated
  B-24 Liberator, 61, 206
  P2Y, 97

PBY Catalina, 51, 55, 64, 212
Constellation CVA-64, 6, 82, 125, 130
Copahee CVE-12, 109
Coral Sea CVB-43, 47, 121
Coral Sea, Battle of, 56–7, 58, 99, 197, 201
Core CVE-13, 109
Corregidor CVE-58, 113
Courageous, 36, 41, 156–7
Courageous class, 100, 146, 158, 191, 215
Cowpens CVL-25, 119
Croatan CVE-25, 109
Cunningham, Admiral Andrew, 49, 52–3
Curtiss
AB-3, 40
CS, 44
F9C/O9C Sparrowhawk, 31
Falcon F8C Helldiver, 45
flying boat, 96
F-Type, 15
Model 24 (CT-1), 21
N-9H floatplane, 96
R-6L, 21
SB2C Helldiver, 62–3, 68, 116
Triad A-1 hydroplane, 10
Curtiss, Glen, 10, 11, 14, 15
CVA-01 (unnamed), 86, 182, 184
CVN-21 class – modified, 135
CVN-78 (unnamed), 135
CVN-79 (unnamed), 135

Dardanelles campaign, 16, 17, 21, 141
Dasher, 170
Dassault
Etendard, 81, 220
Mirage, 92
Rafale, 81, 220
Super Etendard, 93, 219, 241
de Havilland
(Hawker) Sea Venom, 76, 230
F.20 Sea Vampire, 80–1
Sea Hornet, 163
Sea Vixen, 180
Vampire I, 81
Dédalo
(I), 75, 216, 246
(II), 246, 247
Dewoitine D373, 214
Dixmude, 216
Doolittle Raid, 56–7, 103
Douglas
A3D Skywarrior (A-3), 70–1, 80, 120, 123, 130
AD-1 Skyraider (Spad), 62, 73, 82–3, 126, 179
F6D Missileer air defence fighter, 131
SBD Dauntless, 44, 57, 58, 62–3, 101, 111
TBD Devastator, 44, 58
Dwight D. Eisenhower CVN-69, 133

Eagle
(I), 48, 151, 152, 154–5
(II), 76, 174–5
Eastern Solomons, Battle of the, 195, 201
EH-101 helicopter, 236
Ely, Eugene, 10, 11, 14, 40, 96
Emperor, 171
Empress, 40, 171
Empress (seaplane carrier), 18, 26, 138–9
Engadine, 18, 24–5, 26, 139, 146
Enterprise
CV-6, 56, 58–9, 64–5, 66, 102–3, 104
CVAN-65, 83, 124–5, 128–9, 130–1, 132–3
Escort carriers (CVE), 60–1, 73, 90, 107, 108–9, 112–13, 114–15, 118, 137, 166, 167, 168–9, 177, 216, 244, 247
Essex
CV-9, 116–17, 127
LHD-2, 137
Essex class, 9, 47, 66, 68, 70, 72–3, 79, 80, 85, 90, 107, 111–12, 116–17, 118, 120, 126–7, 132, 136, 175, 200, 215, 239
Europa, 240

Fairey
Albacore, 62
Barracuda, 62, 161, 174
F.17 Campania, 29, 143, 145
Firefly, 62, 72, 172, 229, 231, 232
Flycatcher, 44, 155
Fulmar, 44, 62, 165
Gannet, 175, 230
III F, 36–7, 44–5, 140, 152, 155
Swordfish, 44, 48, 50–1, 52–3, 60–1, 62, 157, 166, 167, 170
Falklands War, 83, 87, 92–3, 181, 183, 184, 242
Fanshaw Bay CVE-70, 113
Fencer, 170
Fisher, Admiral Sir John ("Jackie"), 6, 7, 146
Fletcher, Rear Admiral Jack, 56–7
Foch (R99), 219, 245
Focke-Wulf Fw200 Condor, 60–1, 165, 167
Formidable, 52–3, 120, 161, 174
Forrestal class, 80, 121, 123, 124–5, 133, 134, 205
Forrestal class, Improved, 124–5, 129
Forrestal CVA-59, 123, 134, 179
Foudre, 15, 213
Franklin CV-13, 116–17
Franklin D. Roosevelt CVB-42 (CVA-41), 80, 121
Friedrichshafen, 26–7
Friedrichshafen FF-29a, 42
Furious
(I), 19, 27, 29, 40, 146–7, 148, 150, 152–3
(II), 146–7
(III), 156–7

Gallipoli Peninsula, 16, 17, 138
Gambier Bay CVE-73, 113
General Dynamics F-111, 182
George H. W. Bush CVN-77, 134–5
George Washington CVN-73, 130, 134–5
Gibraltar, 176
Gilbert Island CVE-107, 115
Giuseppe Garibaldi, 236
Giuseppe Miraglia, 233
Glorious, 41, 156–7
Glory, 173
Gotland, 248
Graf Zeppelin, 234, 239
Great Lakes
BG-1, 44
TG.2, 44
Grigorovich, Dmitri Pavlovich, 221
Grumman
A-6 Intruder, 80–1, 130–1
E-2 Hawkeye (AEW), 71, 130, 220
EA-6B Prowler, 123
F-14 Tomcat, 81, 88
F2F, 44–5, 99
F3F, 44–5
F4F Wildcat (Martlet), 44, 58, 61, 62–3, 64, 167, 170, 171
F6F Hellcat, 61, 62–3, 67, 69, 78, 116–17
F7F Tigercat, 62
F9F Panther, 72, 80, 126
S-2 Tracker, 75, 173, 230, 244, 245
TBF/TBM Avenger, 40, 61, 62, 69, 76, 101, 103, 109, 110–11, 112, 116–17, 160, 170, 171, 178, 244
Guadalcanal, 56, 64–5, 204
Guadalcanal
CVE-60, 113
LPH-7, 136
Guam LPH-9, 136

Halsey, Admiral William F., 68–9
Hancock CV-19, 71, 116–17
Harry S Truman CVN-75, 135
Hawker
GR.1 Harrier, 86, 181, 184–5
Hurricane, 165
Osprey, 44, 248
P.1127 "Kestrel", 86, 184
Sea Fury, 72, 163, 172, 178, 229, 232
Sea Harrier, 86, 91, 92–3, 137, 184–5, 242, 247
Sea Huricane, 62
Hector, 17
Heinkel He 66, 45
Heligoland Bight, 26–7, 238
Hercules, 75, 173, 242
Hermes
(I), 15, 28, 138–9, 140, 144, 148, 238
(II), 86–7, 91, 92, 151, 152–3, 154
(III), 179, 181, 242
Hiryu, 59, 196
Hiyo, 67, 199
Hoggatt Bay CVE-75, 113
Hollandia CVE-97, 113
Hornet
CV-12, 116–17
CV-8, 56–7, 58, 64–5, 102–3, 116

Hosho, 33, 189, 238
Hunter, 170
Hyuga, 194

I-400 class (submarine), 43
Iachino, Admiral, 52–3
Ibuki, 207
Ichon LPH-12, 83, 136
Illustrious, 47, 48, 53, 120, 161, 174
Illustrious (II), 185
Illustrious class, 160–1, 202, 219
Illustrious-class derivatives, 162
Implacable, 162–3, 174, 200
Indefatigable, 162–3
Independence
  CVA-62, 80, 85, 123
  CVL-22, 119
Independence class, 66, 118–19, 216, 240, 246
Independencia, 241
Indomitable, 162–3
Intrepid CV-11, 9, 70, 116–17
Invincible, 84, 86–7, 92, 95, 184–5
Invincible class, 184–5
Ise, 194, 248
Israel Aircraft Industries Dagger, 92
Iwo Jima
  LHD-7, 137
  LPH-2, 90, 136
Iwo Jima class (LPH), 91, 136, 137, 218

Java Sea, Battle of, 244
Jeanne d'Arc (R97), 218, 222, 235, 248
Jellicoe, Admiral John, 13, 18, 24–5, 146, 150
Joffre, 215
Joffre class, 215
John C. Stennis CVN-74, 85, 135
John F. Kennedy CVA-67, 125, 130–1
Junyo, 65, 199
Jutland, Battle of, 24–5, 33, 139, 144, 146, 150

Ka-27 "Helix", 227, 243
Kadashan Bay CVE-76, 113
Kaga, 190, 192–3
Kaiser, Henry, 112–13, 114
Kaiyo, 209
Kalinin Bay CVE-68, 113
kamikaze, 69, 85, 111, 163, 176
Kamoi, 188
Karel Doorman (I), 244
  (II), 75, 244
Kasaan Bay (CVE-69), 113
Kashiwara Maru, 199
Katsuragi, 206
Kawanishi
  E7K (Type 94), "Alf", 37
  H8K2 (Type 2) "Emily", 212
Kearsarge
  CV-33, 117, 126
  LHD-3, 137
Khedive, 171
Kiev, 224–5
Kiev class, 224–5, 226–7, 243
Killingholme, 143
kite balloon, 138, 144, 221, 246, 248
Kitkun Bay CVE-71 (AVG-71), 112–13
Kitty Hawk CVA-63, 84, 125, 130
Königsberg, 22, 23
Korean War, 72–3, 78–9, 80–1, 115, 117, 123, 126, 133, 164, 173, 228, 229, 232
Kula Gulf CVE-108, 115
Kurama, 207
Kure, 32, 194, 198, 206, 208
Kurita, Admiral, 68–9
Kwajalein CVE-98, 60, 113

La Fayette (R96), 75, 76, 216
La Fayette class, 216
Lake Champlain CV-39, 117
Langley
  CV-1, 40, 97, 98, 100, 107, 121
  CVL-27, 119, 216
Lee, Vice Admiral Willis A., 66
Leningrad, 223
Leonid Brezhnev, 226
Leviathan, 173
Lexington
  CV-16, 71, 116–17, 127
  CV-2, 35, 36, 56–7, 98–9, 105
Lexington (CV-2) class, 37, 98–9, 100, 102, 116
Leyte CV-32, 80, 117
Leyte Gulf, Battle of, 68–9, 112, 194, 197, 201, 203
LHD-8 (unnamed), 137
Light Fleet Carriers (CVL), 72–3, 74–5, 76, 90, 118–19, 162–3, 164, 173, 177, 197, 203, 207, 216, 217, 229, 230, 231, 232, 241, 242, 244, 245, 246
Liscombe Bay CVE-56, 113
Lockheed
  Merlin F-35 (JSF), 81, 87, 187, 236
  S-3 Viking, 128
Long Island AVG-1, 107, 108, 208
Los Angeles ZR.3 (airship), 31
Louis Gordon-Leseurre 32, 214
Lunga Point CVE-94, 113

M2 (submarine), 42
MAC ships, 95, 166, 210, 244
Macon ZRS.5 (airship), 31
Magnificent, 74, 173, 232
Majestic, 74, 173, 228
Majestic class, 74, 173, 229, 230, 231, 232, 242
Makassar Strait CVE-91, 113
Makin Island CVE-93, 113
Malta, 105, 155, 161
Malta, 46, 176
Malta class, 176
Mancia (merchantman), 138
Manila Bay CVE-61, 113
Manxman, 142
Marcus Island CVE-77, 113
Martin
  MS-1, 43
  PBM Mariner, 212
  T3M, 44
  T4M, 44
Matador (Sea Harrier), 247, 249
Matanikau CVE-101, 113
Matapan, Battle of, 36, 44, 50, 52–3
Matra Sadral PDMS, 249
McDonnell
  F2H Banshee, 79, 80, 121, 122, 173
  F3H Demon, 80
  FH-1 Phantom I, 80
McDonnell Douglas
  A-4 Skyhawks, 71, 80, 83, 92–3, 130, 173, 230, 241, 245
  F/A-18 Hornet, 81, 123, 135
  F4H Phantom II (F-4), 6, 80–1, 130, 174
McDonnell Douglas/BAE Systems AV-8A/B Harrier II, 86, 91, 92–3, 137, 184–5, 242, 247
Melbourne, 74, 173, 228, 229, 230
Merchant Aircraft Carriers (MAC), 75
Merlin helicopter, 79, 186, 187
Midway, Battle of, 58–9, 103, 191, 193, 194, 196, 199, 203, 205, 209
Midway class, 62, 80, 120–1, 124, 133, 176
Midway CVB-41, 47, 71, 120–1
Mikoyan-Gurevich MiG-15, 76
Minas Gerais, 75, 245
Mindoro CVE-120, 115
Minsk, 225
Mission Bay CVE-59, 113
Mitchell, Brigadier General William "Billy", 38–9
Mitscher, Vice Admiral Marc A., 57, 66–7, 68–9, 84
Mitsubishi
  A5M4 (Type 96) "Claude", 45
  A6M (Type O) "Zeke" or "Zero", 45, 63, 69, 200
  B1M1 (Type 13), 33
  B1M1 (Type 13), 45
  B2M1 (Type 89), 45
  J2M Raiden, 63
Mizuho, 204
Monterey CVL-26, 119
Morane-Saulnier MS225, 214
Moskva, 222–3, 224
Moskva class, 218, 222–3, 224–5, 235, 243, 248
Munda CVE-104, 113
MV-22 Osprey tilt-rotor aircraft, 79, 137

Nabob, 171
Nagato class, 35
Nagumo Chuichi, Admiral, 54–5, 58–9, 64–5
Nairana, 143
Nairana (II), 169, 244
Nakajima
  A1N1 (Type 3), 44
  A2N1 (Type 90), 44, 192
  A2N2, 33
  A4N1 (Type 95), 45
  B5N1, 63

B5N2 (Type 97) "Kate", 45, 54, 59, 63, 65
B6N Tenzen, 63
E8N (Type 95) "Dave", 203
Nassau
CVE-16, 109
LHA-4, 90, 91
Natoma Bay CVE-62, 113
Nehenta Bay CVE-74, 113
New Orleans LPH-11, 136
New Zealand, 176
Nieuport Two-seater, 17
Nimitz, Admiral Chester, 58
Nimitz class, 132–3
Nimitz (CVN-71) class, Improved, 134–5
Nishimura, Admiral, 68
Nisshin, 204
North American
A.J. Savage, 70, 126–7
A-5 Vigilante, 6, 130
B-25 Mitchell, 56–7
Northrop BT, 44
Novorossiysk, 225

Ocean, 72, 76–7, 80–1, 173, 181
Ocean (L12), 91, 186
Okinawa LPH-3, 136
Ommancy Bay CVE-79, 113
Oriskany CV-34, 117, 126–7
Orlitza, 221
Otakisan Maru, 210
Ozawa Jisaburo, Admiral, 66–7, 68, 201

Painleve, 215
Palau CVE-122 (ACV-122), 114–15
Parnall Peto floatplane, 42
Patroller, 171
Pearl Harbor, attack on, 37, 54–5, 56, 191, 200–1
Pegasus, 19, 140–1, 143
Perseus, 71, 177
Petrof Bay CVE-80, 113
Pfalz Otto biplane, 23
Philippine Sea, Battle of, 66–7, 68, 84, 199, 202, 203
Philippine Sea CV-47, 85
Piasecki HRP, 114
Pioneer, 177
Plasecki Vertol HUP-2, 79
Point Cruz CVE-119, 115
Powerful, 75, 173, 231, 232
Premier, 171
Pretoria Castle, 168–9
Prince of Wales, 187
Prince William CVE-31, 109
Princetown
CV-37, 117
CVL-23, 119
Principe de Asturias, 246-7, 249
Puget Sound CVE-113, 115
Puncher, 171
Pursuer, 170

Queen, 61
Queen Elizabeth class, 187, 220
Queen Rajah, 171

Rabaut CVE-121, 115
Randolph CV-15, 116–17
Ranee, 171
Ranger
CV-4, 46–7, 56, 100–1, 102, 104–5
CVA-61, 123
Ravager, 170
Reaper, 171
Reggiane fighter, 233
Rendova CVE-114, 115
Renown, 51
Resolue, 218
Riviera, 18, 26, 139
Roi (CVE-103), 113
Romania, 221
Ronald Reagan CVN-76, 135
Rudyerd Bay CVE-81, 113
Ruler, 171
Rutland, Squadron Commander Frederick J. ("of Jutland"), 18, 24–5, 33
Ryuho, 198
Ryujo, 195, 196

S-1 (submarine), 42
Sable IX-81, 107
Saginaw Bay CVE-82, 113
Saipan, 66–7, 198
Saipan LHA-2, 91
Salamaua CVE-96, 113
Saldor CVE-117, 115
Salerno Bay CVE-110, 115
Samar, Battle of, 68–9, 113
Samson, Wing Commander Charles Rummney, 10, 11, 17
San Antonio class (LPD), 137
San Jacinto CVL-30, 119
Sandy Bay CVE-118 (AVC-118 Sicily), 115
Sangamon class, 110–11, 112, 114, 210
Sangamon CVE, 111
Santa Cruz, Battle of, 64–5, 103, 201
Santa Elena, 237
Santee CVE, 111
Sao Paolo, 219, 245
Saratoga
CV-3, 35, 36–7, 65, 98–9
CVA-60, 123
Sargent Bay CVE-83, 113
Savo Island CVE-78, 113
Scheer, Admiral, 24–5
Sea King, 75, 86, 92, 173, 181, 184, 186, 230, 242, 245
Seaplane carriers, 138, 188, 212, 221, 237, 238
Searcher, 61, 170
Sempill Mission, 32–3
Seuter, Captain Murray, 138, 150–1
Shah, 171
Shamrock Bay CVE-84, 113
Shangri-la CV-38, 117, 127
Shenandoah ZR.1 (airship), 31
Shimane Maru, 210
Shinano, 205
Shinyo, 209
Shipley Bay CVE-85, 113
Shoho, 56–7, 197
Shokaku, 7, 54, 56–7, 64–5, 67, 200–1
Shokaku class, 200–1, 202
Short
166, 14, 16
184, 16, 17, 24–5, 29, 146
827/830, 23
Brothers, 28
Folder, 20
S.27, 10
S.38, 11
S.64, 15
Seaplane, 23, 141
Sunderland, 212
Siboney CVE-112, 115
Sikorsky
H03S-1, 78
HNS-1 (R-48), 79
HR25, 90
HSS-1N, 244
HUS Seahorse, 91
R-4 Hoverfly I, 78
S-51, 73, 78
S-55, 73, 79, 115
S-58, 79
VS-300, 78
VS-316 (R-4), 78
Sitkoh Bay CVE-86, 113
Slinger, 14, 40
Slinger (II), 171
Smiter, 171
Solomons CVE-67, 61, 113
Somerville, Admiral, 51
Sopwith
1½-Strutter, 18, 29, 144, 150
2F.1 Camel, 12, 19, 27, 29
2F.2 Camel, 18, 44
Baby, 28–9, 144
Pup, 18, 19, 27, 28–9, 33, 40–1, 142, 144, 146–7, 188
Schneider, 17, 28–9, 141
T.1 Cuckoo, 20, 21, 29, 33, 151
Tabloid, 28
Type "C", 20
Sopwith, Thomas, 20, 21
Soryu, 196, 206
Sparviero, 234
Speaker, 171
Spruance, Admiral Raymond A., 58–9, 66–7
St Lo CVE-63, 113
Stalker, 170
Steamer Bay CVE-87, 113
Stettin class, 238
Striker, 170
Stuttgart, 238
Sueter, Captain Murray, 20, 21
Suez, 76–7, 181, 216, 217
Sukhoi
Su-25 "Frogfoot", 226–7
Su-27 "Flanker", 226–7
Su-33, 226–7
Super-Frélon Transport, 218, 219
Supermarine
Attacker, 81
Scimitar, 81
Sea Otter, 177
Seafire, 62, 72–3
Seagull, 228
Spiteful, 81
Spitfire, 104–5
Surcouf (submarine), 42–3

Surigao Strait, 68
Suwannee CVE, 111
Suzuya class, 207
Sydney, 18, 72–3, 74, 228, 229

Taiho, 67, 202, 205
Taiyo class, 208
Takagi Takao, Vice Admiral, 56–7
Takanis Bay CVE-89, 113
Takasaki, 197
Taranto, raid on, 44, 48–9
Tarawa class, 87, 91, 137
Tarawa LHA-1, 91
Tbilisi, 226
Terrible, 74, 173, 228, 229
Thane, 171
Theodore Roosevelt CVN-71, 135
Theseus, 73, 76–7, 173, 181
Thetis Bay CVE-90 (CVHA-1), 90, 113
Tinian CVE-123, 115
Ticonderoga CV-14, 117, 126
Tondern Zeppelin base, 19, 27
Tracker, 170
Tracker class, 170
Tripoli CVE-64 (AVG-64), 113
  LPH-10, 136
Triumph, 71, 72, 173
Trouncer, 171
Trumpeter, 61, 171
Tsurugisaki, 197, 198
Tsurumi, 188
Tsushima, Battle of, 32
Tulagi CVE-72, 113
Tyrwhitt, Commodore, 19, 26

UH-1 Iroquois utility helicopter, 136
UH-46 Sea Knight, 132
Ulyanov, 227
Unicorn, 164, 177
United States CVA-58, 80, 122, 123
Unryu class, 206
Unyo, 208

Valiant, 49
Valley Forge CV-45, 72
Varyag, 226
Veinticinco de Mayo (25 de Mayo), 93, 241, 244
Venerable, 75, 173, 241, 244
Vengeance, 75, 173, 228, 245
Vetta Gulf CVE-111, 115
Victorious, 50, 160–1, 163, 180
Vietnam War, 82–3, 117, 133, 229
Vikrant, 75, 242, 243
Vindex, 18, 142
Vindex (II), 169
Vindictive, 148–9, 152
Viraat, 242
Vittorio Veneto (battleship), 52–3
Vought F8U Crusader (F8), 6, 71, 80, 82, 130

Wakamiya, 15, 33, 188
Wake Island CVE-65, 113
Warrior, 24, 75, 172–3, 231, 232, 241
Washington Treaty (1921–22), 34–5, 46, 98, 100, 102–3, 104, 156, 158, 162, 164, 168, 190, 195, 214, 215
Wasp
  CV-18, 116–17
  CV-7, 104–5
  LHD-1, 137
Wasp class (LHD), 137
Watanabe
  E14Y1 ("Glen"), 43
  E9W1 ("Slim"), 43
West Virginia, 55
Westland
  Dragonfly, 78
  Sycamore, 77
  Wasp HAS.1, 79
  Wessex, 78, 79, 181
  Whirlwind, 77, 79, 181
  Wyvern, 70, 76
WG-13 Lynx, 218, 219
White Plains CVE-66, 113
Williamson, Flight Commander Hugh, 150–1
Windham Bay CVE-92, 113
Wolverine IX-64, 107
Wright, Orville, 6

Yak-36 "Forger", 222
Yak-141, 87
Yalu, Battle of the, 32
Yamamoto Isoroku, Admiral, 55, 58–9
Yamashiro Maru, 210
Yokosuka
  B3Y1 (Type 92), 45
  B4Y1 (Type 96) "Jean", 45
  D4Y1 Suisei, 63
  E6Y1, 43
Yorktown
  CV-10, 116–17
  CV-5, 56–7, 58–9, 67, 102–3, 104–5, 106
Yorktown class (CV-5), 102, 104–5, 116

Zeppelin, 9, 12–13, 18–19, 24–5, 26–7, 28, 30–1, 60, 139, 142, 143, 144, 165, 237
Zeppelin, Graf Ferdinand von, 12, 13
ZR.2 (airship), 31
Zuiho, 64–5, 197
Zuiho class, 197, 198
Zuikaku, 7, 56, 64–5, 67, 69, 200–1

Acknowledgements

Research for the pictures used to illustrate this book was carried out by Ted Nevill of TRH Pictures. Ted Nevill would like to thank all those who contributed to the research and supply of these images, in particular the staff at the Photographic Section of the Naval Historical Center, Washington, DC, and at Still Pictures at the National Archives at College Park, Maryland, USA.

The artworks used in this book were drawn by Jan Suermondt for Cody Images or supplied by ArtTech. Photographs and other illustrations were supplied by Cody Images with help from ArtTech, Chrysalis Image Library, Leo Marriott, Robert Hunt Picture Library and the following (l=left, r=right, t=top, b=bottom, m=middle). Every effort has been made to acknowledge the pictures properly; however, we apologize if there are any unintentional omissions, which will be corrected in future editions.

AgustaWestland: 79.
BAE Systems: 7br; 88t; 187t; 187m.
The Defence Picture Library: 94; 184t.
Fincantieri: 236.
Monthly Maru: 188tr; 188tl; 195t; 198t; 199t; 202t; 207tr; 208t; 210b; 211t; 211m; 212t.
Simon Watson: 242.
Jim Winchester: 186.

Key to flags

The nationality of each aircraft carrier or carrier class is identified in the relevant specification box by the national flag that was in use at the time of the vessel's commissioning and service.